Dirt for Art's Sake

Dirt for Art's Sake

Books on Trial from
Madame Bovary to *Lolita*

ELISABETH

LADENSON

CORNELL UNIVERSITY PRESS
Ithaca & London

First published 2007 by Cornell University Press

Printed in the United States of America

Library of Congress Cataloging-in-Publication Data

Ladenson, Elisabeth.
  Dirt for art's sake : books on trial from Madame Bovary to Lolita / Elisabeth Ladenson.
    p. cm.
  Includes bibliographical references and index.
  ISBN-13: 978-0-8014-4168-4 (cloth : alk. paper)
  ISBN-10: 0-8014-4168-4 (cloth : alk. paper)
  1. French literature—19th century—Censorship. 2. English fiction—20th century—Censorship. 3. American fiction—20th century.—Censorship. 4. Trials (Obscenity)—France—History—19th century. 5. Trials (Obscenity)—Great Britain—History—20th century 6. Trials (Obscenity)—United States—History—20th century.   I. Title.
PQ295.C47L33 2007
840.9'007—dc22

2006023313

Cornell University Press strives to use environmentally responsible suppliers and materials to the fullest extent possible in the publishing of its books. Such materials include vegetable-based, low-VOC inks and acid-free papers that are recycled, totally chlorine-free, or partly composed of nonwood fibers. For further information, visit our website at www.cornellpress.cornell.edu.

Cloth printing   10 9 8 7 6 5 4 3 2 1

In loving memory
of my parents

IRENE AKHIMOFF LADENSON
January 22, 1931–January 15, 2005

SAM LADENSON
April 5, 1927–March 2, 2004

L'art sans règle n'est plus l'art;
c'est comme une femme qui
quitterait tout vêtement.

—ERNEST PINARD

Oh! it is absurd to have a hard-and-fast rule about what one should read
and what one shouldn't. More than half of modern culture depends on
what one shouldn't read.

—OSCAR WILDE, *The Importance of Being Earnest*, Act I

I have never felt inclined to condemn people who look for dirt in
literature: looking for dirt, they may find something else.

—ANTHONY BURGESS, *ReJoyce*

Contents

Preface: Red Hot Chili Peppers   xi

Acknowledgments   xxiii

Prologue: History Repeats Itself   1

CHAPTER ONE *Gustave Flaubert: Emma Bovary Goes to Hollywood   17*

CHAPTER TWO *Charles Baudelaire: Florist of Evil   47*

CHAPTER THREE *James Joyce: Leopold Bloom's Trip to the Outhouse   78*

CHAPTER FOUR *Radclyffe Hall: The Well of Prussic Acid   107*

CHAPTER FIVE *D. H. Lawrence: Sexual Intercourse Begins   131*

CHAPTER SIX *Henry Miller: A Gob of Spit in the Face of Art   157*

CHAPTER SEVEN *Vladimir Nabokov: Lolitigation   187*

Epilogue: The Return of the Repressed   221

Notes   237

Bibliography   257

Index   263

Preface

Red Hot Chili Peppers

In the spring of 2001, as I was beginning work on this book, a strange thing happened. I was at Berkeley, on leave from the University of Virginia on a visiting appointment, and I had seemingly endless problems getting my e-mail account to function properly. When I finally resolved the difficulty, I wrote a message to a friend and colleague describing my electronic travails. In my frustration I used a number of what used to be called "Anglo-Saxon" four-letter terms in my description, and when I hit "send" a message popped up on the screen, accompanied by a sinister computer-generated voice emanating from the machine's speaker. Both of these informed me that my message contained language which might be considered offensive by the average reader, and that I should reconsider sending it, lest my keyboard, the warning continued with ponderous virtual jocularity, be washed out with soap. Stunned by this interpellation I set out to find what was behind it, and discovered that the version of Eudora I had been furnished with included a default option called "Moodwatch," designed to protect unwary e-mailers from their own linguistic impetuosity. Moodwatch operates through a series of offensiveness ratings iconically represented by little cartoon chili peppers. According to the degree of offensiveness, one's message is assigned one, two, or three chili-pepper icons, and when one uses language that Moodwatch judges to be beyond the pale, as was the case for my message complaining about the inconveniences of e-mail itself, the warning message inviting one to change one's ways is delivered in simultaneous visual and auditory form.

I had, in fact, already noticed occasional chili-pepper icons attached to my missives, and had vaguely wondered why condiments were popping up seemingly at random in my e-mail, but my computer illiteracy and general technophobia had prompted me to conclude that this was merely one of the infinite number of computer-related phenomena I would never understand and had best ignore. The experience of being vocally berated by my e-mail program, however, shook me out of my luddite torpor and caused me to do two things: first, I spent hours typing various terms into Eudora in an effort to discern the contours of its sensitivity to linguistic offense. I discovered at length that Eudora (which means, after all, "beautiful gift," a name its originators apparently intend to be taken seriously) is sensitive indeed, but selectively so. It is, for one thing, sexist: a number of both slang and technical references to male genitalia and related sex practices (e.g., fellatio) are deemed unacceptable by its vigilant software, while equivalent terms referring to female anatomy and sexuality (e.g., cunnilingus) pass without comment. This represents a suggestive reversal of tradition, since for centuries representations of female rather than male sexuality were viewed as dangerous and therefore to be suppressed.

But the historical implications of Moodwatch were not my immediate concern. In the midst of my prurient research into the parameters of Eudora's offendability, it occurred to me that since I had been seeing inexplicable chili peppers for weeks, I should investigate their causes. This was the second action I took, and what I found was perplexing. Chili peppers were affixed here and there to outgoing messages containing "strong" language. "You should be ashamed of yourself!" was one pepper-festooned message I had for instance written to a friend in a spirit of irony, but irony-detection is not Eudora's strong point. I then tried out "I should be ashamed of myself," a sentiment of which, in my case at least, Moodwatch presumably approved; at any rate it remained silent. What horrified me, though, was the discovery of two chilli peppers appended to a message I had written to an undergraduate student in one of my classes who was in the hospital. As it happened, the course in question was on censorship in nineteenth-century French literature, and the message I had sent her, to tell her that week's assignment, consisted in the main of a list of the thirteen poems the imperial prosecutor had named as obscene or blasphemous in the prosecution of Baudelaire's *Fleurs du mal* in 1857.

With increasing consternation I scanned the message: Had I somehow, in an unprecedented and unnoticed fit of typographical Tourette's syndrome, included some obscenity or blasphemy in the salutation or expressions of hope that the student's condition would soon improve? No; I could find nothing but the expected formulas. With the hallucinatory feeling that Eudora was somehow channeling the spirit of the imperial prosecutor himself, I turned to the list of poem titles. There, after an embarrassingly long period of contemplation, I found the offending article. There was no other possibility; what had alerted Eudora to my nefarious designs was the poem title "Lesbos."

At first, although I realized this was the only possible culprit, I could not figure out why. I typed various related terms into the computer: "lesbian," "lesbianism": nothing. At length I realized what the perspicacious reader will already have grasped. Eudora (despite the Greek heritage of its name) had taken Baudelaire's reference to the birthplace of Sappho for its homonym, the insulting epithet, as in "I hate fags and lesbos." In other words, Eudora and the French government in 1857 had both been offended by the same title, but for approximately opposite reasons. Whereas the imperial prosecutor had objected to Baudelaire's depicting female homosexuality in the first place (as discussed in chapter 2, the two "lesbian" poems in *Les Fleurs du mal* were, alone among the inculpated poems, cited not on the basis of specific lines or passages but in their entirety, because of their subject matter), Eudora, while tacitly approving the depiction of lesbianism itself, vigorously objected to its denigration.

Times, clearly, have changed. But it is remarkable that the title of Baudelaire's poem, which offended public sentiment in Second Empire France, still—or again—manages, although for wildly different reasons, to elicit stern disapproval in our own notoriously permissive age. I bring up this incident in introducing this book because it seems to me to provide a neat example of some of the more absurd and unexpected vagaries of the history of "indecency." Notably, the Eudora Moodwatch censure of "Lesbos" exemplifies some of the strange paradoxes in the history of modern disapproval. It is at once astonishing and predictable that a politically correct software option in 2001 should have censured the same word, albeit for different reasons, as the French imperial prosecutor in 1857, in the context of the trial of what has long been considered one of the foundational works of modern literature. The history of modern literary censorship is rife with irony, paradox, and absurdity: this is the subject of this book. Specifically, the question I have set out to examine here is: How is it that so many of the works once designated as obscene have ended up on required reading lists? Or, to take up the question from the other end, how is it that so many of the works on today's required reading lists were once prosecuted as obscene? In short: *How does an obscene work become a classic?* As the Moodwatch example suggests, this already thorny question is further complicated by the related issue of what is considered indecent in our own culture.

The pages that follow offer nine examples of works that were banned or prosecuted, or both, when they first appeared and have since achieved, in one way or another, "classic" status. The prologue establishes the historical background up to 1857, after which individual chapters are devoted to *Madame Bovary, Les Fleurs du mal, Ulysses, The Well of Loneliness, Lady Chatterley's Lover, Tropic of Cancer,* and *Lolita.* The epilogue offers briefer examinations of *Fanny Hill* and the works of the Marquis de Sade, books dating from the eighteenth century that formed the basis of the last great literary obscenity trials in the United States and France in the 1950s and 1960s. A question that inevitably arises in a book of this sort, predicated on the idea of "classic literature," is: What is classic status? How does one arrive at this sort of distinction? Given the amount of conflict over the past decades around just such issues, it may seem surprising that in most of these cases it was remarkably easy. *Madame Bovary, Les Fleurs du mal, Ulysses,* and *Lolita* are all obvious cornerstones of the modern canon; *Lady Chatterley's Lover,* which has fallen out of favor in recent decades, is still not far behind. *Fanny Hill* and the works of Sade are consecrated by the mere fact of having survived so long only to provoke fresh controversy, along with obscenity proceedings, in the mid twentieth century. These choices would seem clear, even if their availability in various "classic" editions (except for *Ulysses* and *Lolita,* which are still under copyright) did not make the case for them. I will therefore not belabor these selections; the reputations of the books themselves—as well, I hope, as the chapters I have devoted to them—are self-evident in this regard. As it is customary to say of famous speakers, they need no introduction. *The Well of Loneliness* and *Tropic of Cancer,* however, are perhaps less obvious choices, and therefore a bit of explanation is in order.

Anthony Burgess, who wrote books on both Joyce and Lawrence, observes at one point that *Ulysses* and *Lady Chatterley's Lover* form, along with *The Well of Loneliness,* the great "trilogy of literary dirt" that was so notorious during his youth. Radclyffe Hall's novel has no claim to literary greatness along the lines of Joyce's modernist classic or even Lawrence's polemic last novel. Nonetheless it merits inclusion here for two reasons: first, because of its tremendous fame in its own day, a direct result of the obscenity trials to which it gave rise in England and the United States in 1928; and second, because the very controversy generated by those trials earned Hall's work a special place not only in the history of literary obscenity in general but also in terms of the specific censorship history of representations of homosexuality. *The Well of Loneliness* is now regularly taught and argued over as a classic of gay literature—even though it might well be said that the novel is ultimately "gay" in neither sense of the word. The fourth chapter of this book discusses its place in that history, with particular attention to the very different roles played not only by Hall but also by Oscar Wilde and E. M. Forster, among others, in the story of queer literature in our time.

As for *Tropic of Cancer,* one does not hear much about it or about Henry Miller these days. Along with most of his other works, it is still in print, although a short-lived Signet Classics edition from the mid 1990s is no longer available. Miller's work imposes itself in this context because of the Supreme Court trial that brought *Tropic of Cancer* to an American readership a full thirty years after its initial publication in Paris in 1934. In addition, I felt it important to recognize the fact that if Miller's star has faded, it is in large part because the innovations he brought to twentieth-century literature have long since been absorbed into literary norms, and thus no longer seem innovative. Miller is also offensive in ways which offend in our own day more than they did in 1934. We may no longer mind four-letter words or explicit descriptions of sexual activity, but we mind very much the sort of misogyny and ethnic stereotyping to which he is given. He was only incarnating his era in this regard, but since he insisted on recounting his story frankly, his narrative is now appalling for different reasons. What is more, the author himself lived long enough to embody a parodic version of his own legend long after his artistic high jinks had ceased to be refreshingly transgressive and instead had come to seem embarrassingly retrograde. Fashion passed Miller by, but *Tropic of Cancer*, it seems to me, endures, in its exuberant rejection of all extant values, including—especially—that of art itself. His emphatic repudiation of art for art's sake, the very doctrine the slow acceptance of which eventually led to the unhindered publication of his work in the United States, is both an extraordinary milestone in modern literature's extended commentary on itself, and a telling example of the more extravagantly self-contradictory turns taken by the history of literary censorship in modern times.

If the main question this book tries to answer is, how does an "obscene" book become a "classic"? its main attempt at an answer goes something like this: over the course of roughly a century, from the mid nineteenth century to the 1960s, two ideas which had already been circulating for some time in the form of avant-garde heresy, gradually became accepted clichés, and then grounds for legal defense. The first is most conveniently encapsulated in the formula "art for art's sake," the notion that a work of art functions on its own terms, exists in a realm independent of conventional morality, and should therefore be exempt from the strictures of moral judgment. The second is that of "realism," the idea that the function of the work of art may legitimately include, and perhaps should even obligatorily take on, the representation of all aspects of life, including the more unpleasant and sordid. Both these ideas now seem obvious, but they were unmentionable for a very long time. What follows is among other things the story of their legal acceptance, as traced through the most highly visible literary obscenity trials in modern history in the West.

The central argument of this book (as opposed to its general observations) concerns not so much canonical literature as the vagaries of moralistic disapproval. In considering the history of such matters as literary censorship, it is extremely tempting to build a narrative according to which works that are now appreciated as timeless classics, such as *Madame Bovary*, *Les Fleurs du mal*, *Ulysses* and *Lolita*, as well as others that figure as minor yet important, were once considered obscene, but now we live in more enlightened times and therefore are in a position to judge these works on their own merits. Those merits, seen in this light, are often proportionate to the amount of opprobrium originally heaped on the works.

Thus it is that Ernest Pinard, for instance, the Second Empire imperial prosecutor in France in 1857, reviled by Flaubert and many others for decades as the moralistic philistine responsible for persecuting two of the greatest figures in nineteenth-century literature, found himself enjoying posthumous rehabilitation in the late twentieth century as a remarkably perspicacious reader. Where once opinion had divided only on the question of whether Pinard was simply a sanctimonious imbecile or whether he was also a hypocrite (the discovery that he had later in life produced a volume of salacious verse suggested the latter, at least to Flaubert), he was now lauded for his fine literary sense. As should be clear from the most cursory perusal of the transcript of Flaubert's trial, though, Pinard is no literary critic. Instead he is a public prosecutor, and as a result the reading he gives of *Madame Bovary*, often highly inaccurate, is not designed to highlight the nuances of Flaubert's novel. To the contrary, his aim is to show it in the most damning possible light.

Despite the fact that Pinard greatly distorts the text, he has nonetheless been heralded in recent years as a subtle literary analyst for the simple reason that the *Madame Bovary* he describes in his prosecution speech is necessarily a dangerous one, one that if allowed free dissemination will corrupt its readers, especially young women. In 1857 this was grounds for throwing its author, publisher, and printer in jail. Now, however, it is precisely what we want to hear about Flaubert's novel. In our day *Madame Bovary* no longer resembles anything that might corrupt youth; instead it features prominently on required reading lists and as such represents what we wish to impose on young people more interested in the corrupting influences of television, film, video games, and the Internet. Ernest Pinard has become a good reader because he gives us back a sense of what has been irrevocably lost. We are titillated by the idea of dangerous literature—especially the idea of a classic like *Madame Bovary* as dangerous—precisely because literature no longer poses any danger. It has become anodyne, if not entirely irrelevant, at least in terms of ambient threats to the status quo.

The main problem, then, in dealing with a subject such as the one treated here is the temptation of cultural self-congratulation: chronological chauvinism, as I term it in the first chapter. I have tried to deal with this temptation by examining its importance in the history dealt with in this book. While decrying what are generally agreed on as real dangers in matters of representation (such as, notably, child pornography), our culture tends to hold up transgression as something like an absolute value. This is why a book like *Madame Bovary*, which would no doubt be regarded as a great classic anyway, has much to gain from its censorship history. Flaubert's story is rendered all the more piquant by the knowledge that he was dragged into court for having written it, and we as readers are that much more appreciative in the knowledge that we are in a position to assess it on what we take to be its true merits when we know that our benighted nineteenth-century predecessors viewed it as subversive.

The story told here is in some ways a familiar one. Because the subject is "obscene" literature that becomes "classic," I necessarily deal with books that have been the focus of much scholarly and popular attention. Viewed from this angle, however, their profile changes. Most of the critical writing on these works addresses their censorship history only peripherally. Several books deal directly with the history of literary censorship, most of them from the point of view of legal history. The most comprehensive of these is Edward de Grazia's *Girls Lean Back Everywhere: The Law of Obscenity and the Assault on Genius*. Charles Rembar's *End of Obscenity*, an account of the American trials of *Lady Chatterley's Lover*, *Tropic of Cancer*, and *Fanny Hill* by the attorney who defended their publishers, is also extremely useful as well as entertaining; and Marjorie Heins's *Not in Front of the Children* is an invaluable study of the role played by the protection of youth in the history of censorship proceedings, concentrating on modern America. A number of other works deal with censorship history in England, especially John Sutherland's *Offensive Literature* and Alan Travis's *Bound and Gagged*. In terms of the French tradition, Yvan Leclerc's *Crimes écrits* is especially rich in its overview of all the literary censorship trials in France during the nineteenth century and gives a thorough account of the cases of Flaubert, Baudelaire, and Barbey d'Aurevilly. Other treatments of specific works and areas are referred to in the notes and bibliography.

In the main such studies tend to confine themselves to a single national tradition, whereas it seemed to me that the major literary obscenity trials of the nineteenth and twentieth centuries, which occurred in France, England, and the United States—I searched in vain for comparably well-known examples from other countries—should be looked at together, since common themes and cross-references emerge, as well as an overall coherent history. Another salient way in which my approach differs from most of the above is that I do not address the subject from the point of view of a narrative recounting successive stages in a continuing march toward complete freedom of artistic expression. To the extent that his *History of Sexuality: An Introduction* first pointed out the prevalence and obfuscating character of such progress-narratives, Michel Foucault has laid important groundwork to which this book owes a fundamental debt. My aim is not, however, theoretical or philosophical, and while it situates itself at the crossroads of judicial and cultural history, this book is primarily literary in its ambitions.

Along the way I also deal not only with questions of law but film history as well. *Madame Bovary*, *Lady Chatterley's Lover*, and *Lolita* all encountered censorship problems in cinematic as well as literary form, and the history of film censorship informs that of literature in a variety of ways. In some instances the censorship problems encountered by filmmakers taking on previously suspect novels call to mind Karl Marx's dictum about history repeating itself first as tragedy and then as farce. One particularly rich example is offered by the effects of the Hays Code in shaping Vincente Minnelli's 1949 Hollywood version of *Madame Bovary*. The first chapter accordingly concerns itself at length with Minnelli's film in its strange repetitions of the trial of Flaubert's novel. Similarly, the epilogue makes a final point through an examination of recent films about the Marquis de Sade. For the most part, though, this is a work of literary history, concentrating on the paradoxes that have animated the debates around literary works deemed obscene. My focus is on the sometimes odd and unexpected ways in which history insists on repeating itself in the face of all claims to the contrary and efforts to align its movements forward.

The arguments around censorship go back to Plato and Aristotle, and all debates on this subject, whether about *Lady Chatterley's Lover*, rap lyrics, Robert Mapplethorpe's homoerotic photographs, or internet pornography, take their cue from the basic lines set up in Plato's *Republic* and Aristotle's *Poetics*. Plato regards artistic representation with great suspicion—he banishes poets from his ideal republic—for a number of reasons, the most pertinent one in this context being that people tend to imitate what they see, and it is therefore not a good idea to give free reign to works of the imagination, as the public cannot be trusted to discern the good from the bad. It follows that only good examples should be permitted, and since good examples do not generally tend to make compelling stories, storytelling itself is a slippery slope. Aristotle, on the other hand, despite having been Plato's student, views matters in an entirely different light. His famous theory of catharsis is based on the idea that the audience of a tragedy like *Medea* or *Oedipus Rex*, for instance, will be moved by pity and terror to be purged, essentially, of their own darker tendencies, rather than being moved to imitate the characters and follow the examples of Medea's infanticide or Oedipus's inadvertent misdeeds. Unlike Plato, Aristotle himself is much more interested in the aesthetic rather than the ethical dimensions of literature, but his followers have often insisted on the moral implications of his analysis of classical tragedy.

If these arguments sound familiar, it is because variations on them are trotted out anew each time the subject comes up. For Plato and Aristotle and for centuries afterward, such debates centered on the morality of theater, since theater was the main mode of representation to which large sections of the populace had access. (This is also, of course, why film, television, and then the internet became the central battlegrounds of censorship debates over the course of the twentieth century, and as I discuss in the prologue, the increasing anxiety over literature in the nineteenth century was largely due to increased literacy rates and cheap print-ing techniques.) The Fathers of the Church also weighed in with similar arguments, Saint Augustine translating the Platonic line into Christian terms while Thomas Aquinas took a more tolerant Aristotelian approach. These divergences then went on to fuel vigorous conflict over the morality of theater in France, for instance, starting in the seventeenth century and continuing through the nineteenth. In England John Milton's pamphlet against censorship, his *Areopagitica* (1644), takes its main cue from the Aristotelian heritage in arguing that a knowledge of vice is important to the pursuit of virtue. This line of thought was to be repeated many times, among legions of others by the Marquis de Sade in an essay published in 1800.

Plato's followers in the ongoing censorship debates also include the im-probable late-twentieth-century American alliance between the religious right and antipornography feminists such as Catharine MacKinnon and Andrea Dworkin. The latter's chief line of attack, like most such argu-ments, is based on the idea that representation causes action. In 1857 Ernest Pinard maintained that the story of Emma Bovary should be sup-pressed because its example would incite immoral behavior in young women. MacKinnon and Dworkin, concentrating on the effect of pornog-raphy on men's behavior, operate on the assumption that "pornography is the theory, rape is the practice." The terms of the debate change with the cultural context, but the basic ideas remain the same. Women are still to be protected, for instance, but in a different way, indirectly (by controlling what men read and see) rather than directly (by shielding women them-selves from corrupting influences). One of the main differences, then, is that the central focus of concern seems to have shifted from female to male comportment. Another is that such conflicts now tend to arise around either hard-core visual pornography or films like *Child's Play III*, rather than Euripides or Sophocles, or for that matter *Madame Bovary* or *Ulysses*. Larry Flynt and Chucky may have replaced Medea and Molly Bloom, but in most other respects the debate remains essentially the same.

One thing, however, has changed greatly, not only since the fourth cen-tury BC but over the period dealt with in this book. Starting in the notori-ously bourgeois nineteenth century and picking up steam with dadaism, surrealism, and existentialism, to name only a few of the major -isms pred-icated on destruction of the status quo, artistic trends have progressively emphasized an aesthetics and ideology founded on convention-baiting and most neatly expressed in the formula *épater le bourgeois*. By the end of the twentieth century, countercultural aesthetics had thoroughly filtered into such mainstream media as advertising, and it went without saying that one of the major functions of art is to challenge commonly accepted views

and ideas. In other words, subversion and transgression had become positive values in themselves. Or at least the ideas of subversion and transgression. One of the points I have tried to make in this book is that while our
culture—especially in the academy—pays constant and emphatic lip service to these concepts, they tend not to be examined per se but most often
function as empty signifiers, paradoxical guarantors of the contemporary
equivalent of moral seriousness.

As evidenced in late-twentieth-century celebrations of Ernest Pinard's
critical acumen, we tend to read books like *Madame Bovary* and *Lolita* for
their "subversive" qualities, but what gets lost in the shuffle is that the subversion in question always concerns values that diverge from our own. Subversion and transgression are necessarily relative. They are relative to what
is being subverted and transgressed: witness the software program that objected to Baudelaire's "Lesbos." Obviously, Moodwatch does not share the
values of the Second Empire government, but it is not a coincidence that
the offending word was also the title of a poem deemed objectionable in
1857. We are still very touchy about representations of sexuality, but we
are differently touchy. It is not only absurd but probably in any case impossible truly to adopt subversion as an absolute value. As I have tried to
demonstrate in the epilogue through an examination of the fate of the
Marquis de Sade in recent times, when the literature of the past retains a
real capacity to disturb, it tends to be celebrated in a form that circum-
vents its actual content and appears instead in the guise of an abstract
ideal of transgression.

The title of this book refers to the terms of the debate around literary
censorship as they have been shaped over the course of the past 150 years.
In 1933, when pronouncing *Ulysses* fit to be read by the American public,
Judge John M. Woolsey of the New York Federal District Court, played on
the phrase "art for art's sake": he wrote that his decision was based on his
finding that Joyce's novel was not "dirt for dirt's sake." From that moment
on legal as well as popular discussions on the subject have been haunted
by this formula. "Smut for smut's sake," sex for sex's sake," "pleasure for
pleasure's sake," and—perhaps most tellingly—"dirt for money's sake" are
some of the variations on the theme that have found their way into public
debates on literary censorship. In this way, at least in the United States
since then, the notion of art for art's sake retained a central role in these
debates throughout, even if in mostly negative form. I have chosen to title
this book *Dirt for Art's Sake* because it seems to me that the vagaries of the
conflict are neatly encapsulated in this phrase: where the celebratory concept of "art for art's sake" assumes that morality is beside the point, the
censorious formula "dirt for dirt's sake" implies that immorality is precisely the point. "Dirt for art's sake" is meant to conjure up an image of the
author of writings viewed as obscene as a child playing with his own ex-

crement and calling it art, a figure that haunted these discussions over the course of the period in question. This theme has in recent years spurred renewed controversy in less metaphorical form around public funding of artworks such as the infamous Andres Serrano "Piss Christ" (1987) and Chris Ofili's religious iconography executed with elephant dung.

As for literature itself, "dirty books" are still with us, but this phrase no longer designates the likes of *Ulysses*. We hear less these days about art for art's sake and by the same token dirt for dirt's sake, mostly because cultural and legal acceptance of the former has rendered the latter essentially a moot point. These historical debates, however, are all the more important to remember in a cultural climate which seems amenable to abridging freedom of speech while at the same time purporting to value above all transgression for transgression's sake.

ELISABETH LADENSON

Avignon, France

Acknowledgments

Embarking on a project of this scope I needed help, and I am pleased to report that a number of intelligent and qualified people have been generous enough to read and comment on parts of this book and thereby reduce my chances of making a fool of myself in public. Sherry Sable, Suzanne Nash, Inès Weikel, Laure Murat, Mary McKinley, Julian Barnes, Priscilla Ferguson, Lenard Berlanstein, Sophia Rosenfeld, Joseph Valente, John Lyons, Julian Connolly, Isabelle Chagnon, Joanna Stalnaker, and Pierre Force read and commented on parts of the manuscript and thus have my enduring gratitude. Antoine Compagnon, Françoise Meltzer, and David Halperin have been invaluable interlocutors, and the book is richer for their comments. Kirsten Cather provided information about the Japanese trials of *Lady Chatterley*. Lucienne Frappier-Mazur read a preliminary version of the epilogue and helped prevent me from making embarrassing errors about Sade. Bernhard Kendler, who earned my enmity by retiring, nonetheless merits great thanks not only by having encouraged me on this project from the outset but also by reading the prologue and first four chapters and advising me on readability. Luckily, Cornell University Press provided Roger Haydon, Teresa Jesionowski, and Jack Rummel, who have done an excellent job of textual midwifery.

Gordon Braden has been a source of morale as well as advice from the first, and he also took me out to lunch more than a few times. Gerald Prince provided useful comments as well as delightful companionship. Elena Russo has served as my chief consultant on matters eighteenth century, and therefore any remaining errors in that area may safely be attributed to her. Marjorie Heins has been generous enough to read through the entire thing and tactfully point out some of the ways in which I am not a legal scholar. Cheryl Krueger has been a true friend and interlocutor throughout, as have Élisabeth Lebovici and Catherine Facerias. Edmund White has provided encouragement and advice in addition to stimulating conversation about the many forms indecency takes. Delphine Dufour's capable and intelligent assistance allowed me to complete the final stages of editing without going insane. As for Jean-Yves Pouilloux, who has among other impressive feats read the manuscript more than once, my intellectual debt to him can never adequately be repaid, but I have not stopped trying.

I am grateful to the University of Virginia for providing the Sesquicentennial Research Grant that allowed me to get going on this project in 2001–2, as well as several Summer Research Grants and also University Seminar Grants, which provided me with a forum for trying out my ideas on innocent first-year students. The latter too deserve thanks, for gamely bearing with me through the reading, watching, and discussion of works, some of which they found alarming. I thank the University of California–Berkeley, Columbia University, Vassar College, Johns Hopkins University, Emory University, the École des Hautes Études en Sciences Sociales, the Sorbonne, and Royal Holloway University of London, as well as the University of Virginia Queer Scholarship Series, for giving me the chance to pontificate about my ideas on indecency in front of captive audiences.

Emma Cobb remains Emma Cobb, for which I will always be grateful; tautology alone conveys the measure of my affection. And finally, words can never express my loving gratitude to Brigitte Mahuzier, for reading everything, being willing to listen to innumerable monologues about literature and censorship, and for sticking with me through all of this.

E.L.

Dirt for Art's Sake

Prologue

History Repeats Itself

Art can be morally good, lifting men to higher levels. This has been done through good music, great painting, authentic fiction, poetry, drama.

Art can be morally evil in its effects. This is the case clearly enough with unclean art, indecent books, suggestive drama. The effects on the lives of men and women are obvious.

The Motion Picture Production Code, 1930

1857 was a landmark year in the history of literary obscenity. In England 1857 saw passage of the Obscene Publications Act, which was to set the tone for more than a century of legal conflict and seizure of allegedly obscene material, much of it coming from France. In France during the course of that same year the authors, publishers, and printers of three literary works were brought up on charges of offending public morals, along with various accessory charges of religious and political offenses. The defense won the first trial, although the verdict included a stern reprimand; the second book was found to be in partial violation of the law and stripped of a portion of its contents; the third was suppressed in its entirety. The first two books went on to achieve international fame and are now regarded as cornerstones of the modern canon: they are Gustave Flaubert's *Madame Bovary* and Charles Baudelaire's *Fleurs du mal*. The third is a novel that even specialists in nineteenth-century French literature have seldom read.

The work that was found unacceptable in toto in 1857 was *Les Mystères du peuple* by Eugène Sue. Sue was one of the most prominent writers in France at the time: in 1850, just after the death of Balzac, Charles Augustin Sainte-Beuve, the most influential critic of the era, noted that Balzac's most famous contemporaries were George Sand, Eugène Sue, and Alexandre Dumas (in that order).[1] A century and a half later, Balzac,

1

Sand, and Dumas are all familiar names, almost all of their works still, or again, in print, even if they now occupy very different positions on the scale of literary greatness. Eugène Sue, however, whom Sainte-Beuve judged in 1850 "perhaps the equal of M. de Balzac in invention, in fecundity and in composition [peut-être l'égal de M. de Balzac en invention, en fécondité et en composition]" (327), has been largely forgotten as a literary figure. He had made his reputation with the hugely successful *Les Mystères de Paris* (1842–43), whose populist themes and melodramatic approach anticipated Victor Hugo's *Les Misérables* (1862). *Les Mystères du peuple*, the title of which clearly indicates that he was trying to reproduce the formula of his magnum opus, was a sixteen-volume novel sold directly by subscription (a popular format in that pretelevision era) starting in 1849. In it Sue had attempted nothing less than a history of France from Roman times to the revolution of 1848, as seen through the story of one proletarian family. The novel was a precursor of the sort of multigeneration saga continued by the likes of Emile Zola, among many others, and a remote ancestor of the television miniseries.[2] On completion of serial publication of what turned out to be Sue's last work, the French government brought remarkably comprehensive charges against its author, publisher, and printer, accusing them of:

> Offenses against public morals and decency. Offenses against the Catholic religion. Incitement to hatred and contempt among citizens. Incitement to hatred and contempt of the government. Defense of acts defined as crimes or misdemeanors by penal law. Attack against the principle of authority.

> [Outrage à la morale publique et aux bonnes moeurs. Outrage à la religion catholique. Excitation à la haine et au mépris des citoyens les uns contre les autres. Excitation à la haine et au mépris du gouvernement. Apologie des faits qualifiés crimes ou délits par la loi pénale. Attaque contre le principe de l'autorité.][3]

It is rare, even in nineteenth-century literary trials, to find such a panoply of accusations against a single work. Nonetheless, the court found that *Les Mystères du peuple*, written "in an evident intent to demoralize," contained, "in each volume, on every page, the negation or subversion of all the principles on which religion, morality and society are based."[4] Eugène Sue died, aged fifty-three, in August 1857 during the course of court proceedings against his novel. As a result, the decision handed down in September affected only the publisher and printer, condemned respectively to a two-month prison sentence and 2,000F fine and one month and 1,000F fine; Sue's posthumous sentence was a year in prison and a fine of 6,000F. The book itself was to be destroyed, although since it had already been sold by subscription it is difficult to see how this could have been carried out.

The work was for a long time all but forgotten, its author remembered chiefly for *Les Mystères de Paris*.[5] If *Les Mystères du peuple* remains of interest beyond the murkier bywaters of the history of popular literature it is because of the accident of chronology that brought it to trial the same year as two of the foundational works of modern fiction and poetry. Sue's formulaic and long-forgotten novel might serve as a reminder, if one were needed, that it is not only great works, or even innovative ones, that have been seen as subversive enough to attempt to suppress. The list of objections to *Les Mystères de Paris* is far more encyclopedic than the charges against either *Madame Bovary* or *Les Fleurs du mal*, or for that matter almost any other book during that period. By the same token, Sue's example clearly demonstrates that subversive elements alone are not enough to propel a work into posterity.

Over the course of the nineteenth century, from 1821 to 1892, twenty-six literary works were prosecuted by the French government—or rather the various French governments, since the history of literary trials in France changes to some extent with changing political regimes. The Second Empire of Napoléon III (1851–70) was particularly zealous in pursuing literary works for moral offenses, which accounts in part for the prosecutions of Flaubert and Baudelaire. Despite the varying approaches of successive political regimes, though, for most of the century, artistic works were prosecuted according to a law passed May 17, 1819, which decreed that "any offense against public and religious morals, or against decency, by one of the means referred to in article 1, will be punished by imprisonment of one month to one year, and by a fine of 16F to 500F [tout outrage à la morale publique et religieuse, ou aux bonnes moeurs, par l'un des moyens énoncés en l'article Ier, sera puni d'un emprisonnement d'un mois à un an, et d'une amende de 16F à 500F]."[6] In 1822 this law was revised in the direction of greater severity, but for the most part, and through all the political upheavals of the century, its terms remained constant until 1881, when a new law declared that "the press and the book trade are free [L'imprimerie et la librairie sont libres]." What this meant in practice was that the categories of "offenses against public and religious morals [outrage à la morale publique et religieuse]" disappeared, leaving in place "offenses against decency [outrage aux bonnes moeurs]." This phrase had a more restricted meaning corresponding approximately, and with analogous elasticity, to the English notion of "obscenity": in question were "offenses against modesty, manifestations of the spirit of debauchery [les outrages qui blessent la pudeur, les manifestations de l'esprit de débauche]."[7] In declaring the press and the publishing industry free of censorship despite the fact that a major category of punishability remained, the Third Republic government was not making a trivial claim. The disappearance from French law in 1881 of the crimes of "offenses against public and religious morality [outrage à la morale publique et religieuse]" did not shield literary works from legal reprisal, but it did herald the advent of a movement that would eventually, over the course of the following century, do away with such trials entirely. It is not a coincidence that the following year, in *The Gay Science* (1882), Nietzsche was to announce that God was dead. The category of "offenses against public and religious morality [outrage à la morale publique et religieuse]" rests on a collectively accepted morality grounded in Christian religion, a moral basis that was steadily eroding, as witnessed in France during the Third Republic by the development of the *écoles laïques* (state-sponsored secular education) spurred on by Jules Ferry's educational reforms in the 1880s, and especially by the official separation of church and state in 1905. In 1857, though, such measures were unthinkable, even if it was already clear that much had changed in the preceding decades.

One of the many ironies of the legal events of 1857 was that in July, some six months after Flaubert's trial but just as Baudelaire's was about to get underway, Pierre-Jean de Béranger died and was accorded a state funeral by the Second Empire government. Béranger, the author of popular song lyrics with political overtones criticizing the Restauration regime, had been the first writer prosecuted under the law of 1819. In fact Béranger was brought to trial—largely for political reasons—three times during the Restauration, initially in 1821 (the year in which Napoleon I died and both Flaubert and Baudelaire were born). He was found guilty of "offenses against decency; offenses against religious morality; offenses against the person of the king [outrage aux bonnes moeurs; outrage à la morale religieuse; offenses envers la personne du roi]," and finally, the strange charge of "provocation, not followed by effects, to display publicly an exterior sign of political intent not authorized by the king [provocation, non suivie d'effets, à porter publiquement un signe extérieur de ralliement non autorisé par le roi]" (Leclerc, 360); he was fined 500F and sentenced to three months in prison. Two factors make Béranger's case particularly memorable in the history of these matters in nineteenth-century France. One is that the following year, in 1822, he ran into fresh trouble due to a rather remarkable wrinkle in the law. Because the newspapers of the era only printed the speech for the prosecution in reporting on the first trial, Béranger had a brochure printed up including the speech for the defense and the final judgment. Since the pamphlet contained some of the lyrics that had been inculpated—mostly quoted in the speech for the prosecution—he was again prosecuted, on the grounds that article 27 of the law of May 26, 1819, prohibited publication of a text that had been suppressed: these charges, therefore, were based on his having cited the very argument of the prosecution against him (Leclerc, 362). He was acquitted this time, his defense having successfully cited the legal contradiction between article 27 and the right to publish judicial proceedings. Ten days later a new law went into effect, prohibiting dissemination of legislative or judicial debates (362). In 1828 he was again prosecuted on political charges for new song lyrics, and again found guilty; this new fine was paid by popular subscription.

The second noteworthy aspect of this case is the way it was alluded to in 1857. Despite his three trials and two convictions, by the time of his death, Béranger, who had never had pretensions to high art or subversive social commentary, and moreover had long been an object of mockery by the likes of Flaubert and his circle, had reacquired bourgeois respectability. This was largely because his criticisms of the Restauration government and nostalgia for Napoleonic glory made him an official hero for the Second Empire. These same traits had led him to figure as a martyr in the writings of Stendhal, especially *The Red and the Black* (*Le Rouge et le noir*, 1830), with its cult of Napoléon I and indictment of Restauration culture. In 1857, however, Flaubert and Baudelaire, fans of neither Bonaparte, responded with indignation to the fact that "this dirty bourgeois who sang of facile loves and tattered clothes [ce sale bourgeois qui a chanté les amours faciles et les habits râpés]," as Flaubert put it in a letter to Baudelaire (August 23, 1857), was being posthumously lauded by the government, given the mediocrity of his lyrics. To add injury to insult, this now officially celebrated writer had been prosecuted under the same law that was being invoked in their own cases. Not only Flaubert but also Sainte-Beuve, whose advice and political support the poet had sought (the critic gave only the former), suggested that the example of Béranger be referred to in Baudelaire's defense. In his notes to his attorney, he duly brings up the matter (referring to himself in the third person, as his lawyer would):

> Should M. Charles Baudelaire not have the same rights as Béranger? Baudelaire has been reproached for subjects treated by Béranger. Which do you prefer? The sad poet or the gay and audacious poet, the horror of evil or folly, remorse or impudence?

> [M. Charles Baudelaire n'aurait-il pas le droit d'arguer des licenses permises à Béranger? Tel sujet reproché à Ch. Baudelaire a été traité par Béranger. Lequel préférez-vous? Le poète triste ou le poète gai et effronté, l'horreur dans le mal ou la folâtrerie, le remords ou l'impudence?][8]

Aware of the dangers of such an approach, his defense attorney did end up—respectfully—citing Béranger toward the end of his speech. But Baudelaire's rhetorical question received a clear answer, furnished by the verdict in his case: the public, or at least the judicial system, preferred eroticism to be treated with a light touch, and refused to tolerate the dark approach of *Les Fleurs du mal*. Béranger's example illustrates, among other things, the extent to which tone and genre participate in the making of "offenses against decency [outrages aux bonnes moeurs]," as well as what the history of such trials would demonstrate repeatedly over the course of the following century: that one era's cultural detritus is another's cele-brated classic, and also vice versa.

Aside from theatrical performances, which provided an important forum for censorship during this era, the works prosecuted in France over the course of the nineteenth century include plays, song lyrics, essays, po-etry collections, and novels (eleven: far more than any other literary genre). Aside from *Madame Bovary* and *Les Fleurs du mal*, only two of the books that got into trouble with the French government during the nine-teenth century have retained, or reacquired, any degree of eminence. The first is Jules Barbey d'Aurevilly's *Les Diaboliques* (1874), a collection of still quite risqué stories that has fully entered the French canon (by which I mean that, even if it has never become well known outside France, the book has long been required reading for literature students in France). Barbey d'Aurevilly, who was already an old man and a well-known writer by the time he ran into problems with the law over *Les Diaboliques* during the Third Republic, managed to escape full prosecution after a court hearing by promising not to attempt further publication of the collection of short stories. (He almost immediately broke this promise, but was not subject to renewed prosecution.) The other work prosecuted by the gov-ernment in France in this era that retains some currency is *Monsieur Vénus*. As its title suggests, *Monsieur Vénus* is a gender-bending novel. It was pub-lished in 1884, written by the twenty-four-year-old Marguerite Eymery under the pseudonym Rachilde. The novel, which was found guilty as charged ("offenses against decency [outrage aux bonnes moeurs]"), re-mains interesting in terms of its representations of gender and sexuality; as in Rachilde's other works (e.g., *La Marquise de Sade*, to give an example of her other equally provocative titles), the men in *Monsieur Vénus* are con-sistently feminine and the women masculine. For this reason, more than for the quality of Rachilde's prose, *Monsieur Vénus* has been reprinted in French and has found an audience, especially in the American academy, in the context of studies in the history of gender and sexuality.

The list of works pursued for moral offenses by the French government in nineteenth-century France also includes a number of writers whose names have been preserved by posterity on the basis of works other than those that interested the judicial system. In 1853 the Goncourt brothers of *Journal* fame were brought to trial on the seemingly nugatory basis of an essay in which they quoted five lines from an erotic poem by the obscure sixteenth-century poet Jacques Tahureau; they had in fact taken the lines from an anthology of sixteenth-century verse published in 1828 by Sainte-Beuve. They received a judgment of "acquittal with blame [acquittement avec blâme]": that is, they were found not guilty, but reprimanded for having presented readers with "clearly licentious and therefore blameworthy images [des images évidemment licencieuses et dès lors blâmables]."[9] Post-1857, two other authors who are now squarely canonical were pursued on the basis of minor, relatively unknown works: Paul Verlaine and Guy de Maupassant. In 1868 Verlaine saw a twenty-page volume of erotic verse, published in Brussels under a pseudonym, seized and destroyed when copies of the Belgian publication were imported into France. It is perhaps not a coincidence that the collection, entitled *Girlfriends* [*Les Amies*], contained six poems, as this was the number of poems that had been removed from *Les Fleurs du mal* following Baudelaire's trial eleven years earlier (and had subsequently also been reprinted in Belgium, where many such works in French were published). *Les Amies* consists of pale imitations of Baudelaire's "lesbian" poems, two of which had been among those found to be in violation of French law.

In 1876 Maupassant, whose career as a writer would not take off for several years, published a mildly erotic poem entitled "At the Water's Edge [Au bord de l'eau]" in a literary journal, under the pseudonym Guy de Valmont (an allusion to the libertine Vicomte de Valmont from Laclos's *Liaisons dangereuses*). Three years later the poem was reprinted, apparently without Maupassant's knowledge, in another journal, under the less poetic title "A Girl [Une fille]."[10] The journal that reprinted the poem was already under warning by the Third Republic government, which then brought charges against everyone concerned. Maupassant's prosecution on charges of "offenses against decency and public morals [outrage aux bonnes moeurs et à la morale publique]" is memorable not so much on aesthetic grounds—the author made his reputation as a prose stylist, and the poem in question is not especially remarkable in itself—but because of the intervention of Gustave Flaubert, the author's literary mentor.[11] Flaubert was instrumental in helping to bring about the judgment of *non-lieu* in the case (the same judgment as had been pronounced in the case of Barbey's *Diaboliques*, meaning that there were deemed to be insufficient grounds to pursue full judicial proceedings) by publishing an open letter to Maupassant in the newspaper *Le Gaulois* (February 21, 1880). Written twenty-three years after the trial of *Madame Bovary*, Flaubert's letter in support of his young protégé (Maupassant was thirty at the time) reads as a manifesto against literary censorship. It remains, in effect, his only public statement on the subject, and it is explicitly framed as a commentary on his own trial, which had launched his career and left an indelible mark on his literary output. In the letter he anticipates, by retrospective identification with his protégé, what will happen to the latter and to his prosecutors if the government continues with its case: it will look ridiculous, and he will win notoriety.

The open letter to Maupassant serves as a clear warning to those in power regarding the dangers of such proceedings: "the trial created enormous publicity for me, and I attribute to it three fourths of my success."[12] This was a persuasive argument indeed, suggesting that if the government persisted in its charges against Maupassant it could look forward to defeat, ridicule, and the knowledge that it had in the end served the best interests of its adversary. Flaubert goes on to repeat Baudelaire's credo of aesthetic morality: "What is Beautiful is moral, that is all, and nothing more [Ce qui est Beau est moral, voilà tout, et rien de plus]" (Leclerc, 389). The history of legal proceedings against literary and artistic works in the nineteenth and twentieth centuries, not only in France but in England and the United States as well, would always come back to this central question of the relation between aesthetics and morality. All the major trends in aesthetic ideology during the nineteenth century, from the doctrine of art for art's sake to the credo of faithful representation of the seamiest realities in the service of scientific objectivity and social change, became caught up in the ongoing public argument over what the reading public had a right to have access to, and what it should expect to be shielded from.

One of the reasons for the explosion of literary indecency trials in France during the nineteenth century was a fundamental shift, starting with the revolution, in the way unacceptable material was dealt with by successive governments. During the Middle Ages censorship had been exercised by the Catholic church. The invention of the printing press and development of publishing techniques led the government to intervene; a 1566 ordinance required printers to seek official permission to publish. The church responded by creating its notorious *Index librorum prohibitorum* in the sixteenth century, a list of prohibited works that exhibited remarkable staying power, on which for example the complete works of André Gide could still be found in the 1950s (despite his 1947 Nobel Prize); the index continued to list works offensive to the church until 1966. In 1617 the office of Royal Censor was created in France, so that all material had to be vetted, before publication, by governmental and ecclesiastical bodies, which in compensation granted printers what amounts to copyright: the exclusive rights to works once they had been approved. This system led in turn to the development of a vigorous clandestine publishing industry, operating for the most part in neighboring countries, with the further result of increased surveillance at the borders and punitive measures taken against the growing illegal book trade.

By the mid eighteenth century, a remarkably large percentage of what are now considered to be the masterpieces of French literature from that period circulated only in clandestine form. Most of the great figures of the Enlightenment, including Voltaire, many of whose works were banned; Diderot, who spent five months in jail in 1749 for his *Letter on the Blind* [*Lettre sur les aveugles*]; and Rousseau, a number of whose most famous works, including the *Confessions*, never saw publication at all during his lifetime, routinely had to publish in this manner. The *Encyclopédie* itself, the first modern encyclopedia, was eventually censored, despite the vigorous self-censorship efforts of Diderot, d'Alembert, and company. Clandestine books were referred to indiscriminately as *philosophie*, whether political, philosophical, or sexual in content. Some of these works combined elements of both political philosophy and what would later be called pornography, leading to now-strange hybrids such as Sade's *Philosophie dans le boudoir* and Boyer d'Argens's *Thérèse philosophe*. In light of this tradition it is not difficult to see how certain depictions of sexual desire, as in *Madame Bovary*, were instantly seen as posing a direct sociopolitical threat to the established order. Of course, sexuality, and especially female sexuality, have always held a power to disturb, but the link between subversive political thought and explicit representation of sex has perhaps never been so evident as in the clandestine literature of eighteenth-century France.

The French Revolution set about immediately to announce an unprecedented freedom of the press, but as in most if not all such cases, freedom of the press is always relative, and always more or less means freedom to publish anything at all, as long as it does not violate prevailing mores. This is why there have long been obscenity laws in the United States, for instance, a country that prides itself on the ostensibly complete freedom of the press inscribed in the First Amendment to the Constitution.[13] On August 26, 1789, by article 11 of the *Declaration of the Rights of Man and of the Citizen* [*Déclaration des droits de l'homme et du citoyen*], the National Assembly abolished censorship in the following terms:

> The free communication of thoughts and opinions is one of the most precious rights of man; every citizen may therefore speak, write, and publish freely, *except in cases of abuse of this freedom as determined by law.*

> [La libre communication des pensées et des opinions est un des droits les plus précieux de l'homme; tout citoyen peut donc parler, écrire, imprimer librement, *sauf à répondre de l'abus de cette liberté dans les cas déterminés par la loi.*] [emphasis added]

This relative freedom of the press became a tradition, to be carried on by a number of successive governments. Napoléon Bonaparte was a particularly avid opponent of censorship, writing for instance to his stepson Eugène, viceroy of Italy: "I want you to suppress censorship of books entirely. This country is already narrow-minded, without narrowing it further. [Je désire que vous supprimiez entièrement la censure des livres. Ce pays a déjà l'esprit étroit, sans l'étrécir davantage]." The letter continues: "Of course the publication of any work hostile to the government should be stopped [Bien entendu que la publication de tout ouvrage qui serait contraire au gouvernement serait arrêtée]." And, later, writing to Montalivet, the French minister of the interior, Napoléon notes: "My intention is to allow complete freedom of the press, that it be entirely unhindered, that only obscene works or those tending to foment political trouble be stopped [Mon intention est qu'on laisse une liberté entière à la presse (à l'imprimerie), qu'on n'y mette aucune gêne, qu'on se contente d'arrêter les ouvrages obscènes ou tendant à semer des troubles dans l'intérieur]."[14] In 1806 he was thus able to declare, "There is no Censorship in France [Il n'existe point de Censure en France],"[15] despite having had the Marquis de Sade thrown in jail for writing *Justine*, and despite his energetic repression of writings by, among others, Mme de Staël and Chateaubriand.

The seeming contradiction between theory and practice during this period is due in part to a certain ambiguity inscribed in the word "censorship" (*censure*) itself. For centuries *censure* had meant preventive censorship (*censure préalable*), the formal prepublication vetting by the government in tandem with the church of works slated for publication; since this was no longer the case, there was no more censorship in France. (In 1810 Napoleon modified his position, reverting to the sort of direct governmental regulation and prepublication censorship of the book trade that the revolution had abolished.) What had changed between the Ancien Régime and most of the nineteenth-century regimes was essentially that one could now attempt to publish anything, although always with the risk of seeing one's work brought to trial and suppressed after publication, along with fines and prison sentences for everyone involved.

Another major reason for the large number of literary indecency trials in France in the nineteenth century is that exponentially increasing literacy rates, combined with innovations in cheap printing techniques, produced a greatly expanded reading public. In particular, two intersecting groups that promised, once tainted by inappropriate literary influence, to pose inestimable dangers to the status quo began to read novels in vast quantities: women and the working classes. This was why *Les Mystères du peuple* was seen as so dangerous: because it afforded the working classes a narrative in which to inscribe themselves as central to French history and able to influence its course at will, at a time when popular political uprisings occurred with increasing frequency. Sue's novel began serial publication just after the Revolution of 1848, which had been imputed in large part to the spread of literacy and resulting corruption of the working classes by reading, especially of socialist and populist works such as Sue's.[16] Women and the working classes were both viewed as inherently infantile, with all the potential dangers of childhood unleashed. As a result the rise of cheap novels and especially of novels serialized in daily newspapers (*feuilletons*), a phenomenon inaugurated in France by Balzac's scandalous *The Old Maid* [*La Vieille fille*] in 1836 and in England the same year by Dickens's *Pickwick Papers*, was increasingly seen as a social and political problem.[17] In other Western countries a similar phenomenon occurred, with publishers of fiction even likened to drug dealers. By the 1870s, for instance, a majority of novels published in the United States were written, and presumably read, by women, and an American magazine issued the following warning in 1880: "Millions of young girls and thousands of young men are *novelized* into absolute idiocy. Novel-readers are like opium-smokers." The editorial continued: "the more they have of it the more they want of it, and the publishers, delighted at this state of affairs, go on corrupting public taste and understanding and making fortunes out of this corruption."[18]

By the time *Madame Bovary* came to trial following its serial publication in *La Revue de Paris* in 1856, the terms of this debate were already firmly established in France. Ernest Pinard, the government prosecutor who presented the case against Flaubert's novel, as well as the other two cases that came to trial later in 1857, puts the point succinctly in his speech for the prosecution:

> Who are the readers of M. Flaubert's novel? Are they men interested in political and social economy? No! The light pages of *Madame Bovary* fall into even lighter hands, into the hands of girls, and sometimes married women.
>
> [Qui est-ce qui lit le roman de M. Flaubert? *Sont-ce* des hommes qui s'occupent d'économie politique et sociale? Non! Les pages légères de *Madame Bovary* tombent en des mains plus légères, dans les mains de jeunes filles, quelquefois des femmes mariées.] (*Madame Bovary* [Pléiade], 631–32)

Women, it is clear, posed the major problem in terms of the readership of novels, because of the idea that women in general, like the newly literate working classes, were unable to distinguish between fiction and reality. This is also precisely Emma Bovary's problem, which is why the trial of *Madame Bovary* provides such an exemplary case in terms of the dangers of literature. Pinard continues:

> And so! When the imagination has been seduced, when that seduction has descended to the heart, when the heart has spoken to the senses, do you

think cold reasoning will prevail against this seduction of the senses and
emotions?

[Eh bien! Lorsque l'imagination aura été séduite, lorsque cette séduction
sera descendue jusqu'au coeur, lorsque le coeur aura parlé aux sens, est-ce
que vous croyez qu'un raisonnement bien froid sera bien fort contre cette
séduction des sens et du sentiment?] (632)

The answer, it seems, is no, and the imagination in question is just as evidently a female imagination, unburdened by the weight of extensive education and discernment.

Just as novels and theatrical performances had fueled public debate
around censorship in France in the nineteenth century, a similar conflict
would break out in the early twentieth century, this time around the bur-
geoning film industry. As with plays and novels in the mid nineteenth century, film, especially when it became clear that technological innovations
were making possible the relatively inexpensive diffusion of talking pictures, began to look increasingly like a dangerous medium, because it was
accessible to all. Like popular theater and mass-produced serialized novels—and more so, more even than silent pictures with their intertitles, because unlike the latter they required not even the most rudimentary literacy—talking films were available not merely to a male elite who were
expected to handle whatever they encountered with intellectual
sangfroid, but also to those most likely to be immediately affected by what
they saw or read: that is to say, women and the lower classes. In France, as
in other countries, controversies around indecency in the cinema would
lead to various forms of local and national government censorship. The
United States was the only major film-producing country to avoid direct
federal government intervention in the motion picture industry. The solution hit on in Hollywood in the early 1930s was approximately the opposite of what had led Napoleon to proclaim France free of censorship in
1806. Censorship was viewed as un-American, just as it had been viewed as
un-French from 1789 on, but the concept of censorship was construed differently in America, as a result of its different history. The nineteenth-
century French system of noncensorship, that is, the relatively free diffusion of works, contingent on postpublication governmental review and
censure, was deemed unacceptable in Hollywood in the late 1920s and
early 1930s when these matters were being negotiated with the advent of
talking pictures.

A political and an economic factor prevented the establishment of an
American government censorship office charged with vetting films postproduction. First, no one wanted a visible federal censorship office vetting
films before release, because this would have been viewed as obvious cen-

sorship and therefore un-American. Second, unlike books, films cost enormous amounts of money to produce, and no one was willing to make whole films only to have them subject to postproduction suppression. Protracted negotiations among the League of Decency, Hollywood producers, and the Hoover administration resulted in what became known as the Motion Picture Production Code, or Hays Code, after Will Hays, former postmaster general, one of its authors and its zealous initial administrator. The Production Code in effect represented a cinematic throwback to the Ancien Régime system of prepublication vetting by a designated office. Despite the fact that censorship in the purest sense of the term was evidently the point, since the code provided a clear yet interpretable set of guidelines as to what could and could not be shown on screen, the compromise solution nevertheless managed to avoid the appearance of censorship. Instead there was a highly organized system of enforced self-censorship, the office in question operating not through the government but rather in Hollywood, specifically to preclude government intervention. Through the Hays Office, it was the motion picture industry itself that screened, as it were, its own products.

The Motion Picture Production Code held sway in increasingly attenuated form through the mid 1960s, the same period that saw the last literary obscenity trials in the United States. It was finally abolished in 1968 and replaced by the Ratings Code that continues, in principle, to protect American youth from cinematic turpitude. The difference between the Motion Picture Production Code and the Ratings Code is an important one in terms of the history of censorship, and not just because of the historical irony offered by an apparent innovation that, in the name of social progress, brought back something very like the Ancien Régime system of literary censorship to make sure film did not corrupt the public in twentieth-century America. The Ratings Code divides the public among age groups, deciding which films may be seen according to age. In contrast, the Production Code had functioned under the assumption that the public as a whole was at risk in regard to every film: the entire public was viewed as infantile, to be protected from the representation of sexuality, among other subjects.[19] At no time in the history of publishing has a similarly calibrated age-based system been in effect, even if some works have been, formally or informally, labeled "not for sale to minors."

Instead, various other methods of protecting the younger or more vulnerable members of the reading public have been applied at different times and in different countries. The most common approach has been expurgation: passages deemed shocking or offensive are simply removed, or in some cases rewritten with potentially harmful terms or phrases replaced by innocuous "equivalents." Although this practice may sound quaintly Victorian, variations on it survived well into the twentieth century in terms of books and continue to thrive in the print and visual media.[20] In England and America this approach was for some time called bowdlerization, after the Reverend Thomas Bowdler (d. 1825). Bowdler was the editor of a version of the works of Shakespeare, from which, as he announces in his preface, he had set out to exclude "whatever is unfit to be read aloud by a gentleman to a company of ladies."[21] During the Ancien Régime in France edulcorated editions of classic works were produced *ad usum delphini* (for the use of the dauphin). In some instances, though, language has been viewed as its own best censor, decipherable according to the reader's age and level of education. Since Latin and Greek were the cornerstones of a classical education, works of an explicitly sexual nature were often published entirely in Latin for consumption by an educated—that is, necessarily, male and elite—audience, or with dicey passages translated into Latin or even Greek on the same principle. This is the public equivalent of adults spelling out words they do not wish young children to understand, or having recourse to another language; and just as the latter practice sometimes has the unintended side-effect of precocious language skills, the existence of sexually explicit works and passages in Greek and Latin may well have inspired generations of young scholars to apply themselves to the study of classical languages. Along the same lines, Anthony Burgess, recalling his autodidactic literary adventures in the 1930s, writes that books were "the way into a forbidden world," and recounts his experiences reading Shakespeare for erotic content, as well as Boccaccio's *Decameron,* "which, in the edition then available, either left out the story about putting the devil in hell or presented it in the original Tuscan. The impulse to get hold of an Italian primer was great. Thus are we led to learning," he concludes.[22]

In 1857, in a letter to Baudelaire just prior to the latter's trial, Sainte-Beuve expressed particular admiration for one of the most explicitly and violently sexual poems in *Les Fleurs du mal,* "À celle qui est trop gaie." Calling the poem "exquisite," he went on to wonder why Baudelaire had not written it "in Latin, or preferably in Greek," the latter being the language least accessible to any but the most highly cultivated reader, and therefore the best internal safeguard against corruption of women, children, and anyone else who had not had the benefit of a classical education.[23]

No one, to my knowledge, ever proposed making films or providing silent film intertitles in Latin, ancient Greek, or Tuscan dialect as a way of protecting the more morally vulnerable members of the filmgoing public.[24] If the rise of general literacy and the wide diffusion of serialized novels led to alarm about the effects of novel-reading among the general public during the nineteenth century, movies, and especially talking pictures, engendered a similar fear, on an even greater scale. Because films were more widely accessible than books and had a much more immediate sensory impact, and because the financial stakes were so much greater and there was no equivalent potential for internal de facto censorship, they produced a resurrection of the debate over how to control the stories to which the general public has access. The Hays Code itself alludes to this problem. In an explanatory section designed to elaborate and justify its strictures, the 1930 text notes the following, under the heading "The motion picture, because of its importance as entertainment and because of the trust placed in it by the peoples of the world, has special moral obligations":

> Most arts appeal to the mature. This art appeals at once to every class, mature, immature, developed, undeveloped, law abiding, criminal. Music has its grades for different classes; so have literature and drama. The art of the motion picture, combining as it does the two fundamental appeals of looking at a picture and listening to a story, at once reaches every class of society.

Written in apparent ignorance of its many precedents, the Hays Code gives the impression of having been created in a historical vacuum, as though such measures had never been taken, or needed, before the development of talking pictures. It presents the need for such controls purely on the basis of the dangers posed by this new art form. The text continues:

> it is difficult to produce films intended only for certain classes of people. The exhibitors' theatres are built for the masses, for the cultivated and the rude, the mature and the immature, the self-respecting and the criminal. Films, unlike books and music, can with difficulty be confined to certain selected groups.[25]

The grounds of the debate had shifted, so that books were once again seen, along with music, as the anodyne entertainment of the privileged classes, the danger zone being displaced onto film. This trend has continued until, by the late twentieth century, it had become a commonplace that the reading of books was always to be encouraged, whereas film (along with other visual media such as television and video games), was seen as the evident major problem.[26]

I have taken this detour into film history because it is relevant to the general story of the history of censorship of narrative forms in the nineteenth and twentieth centuries that is the subject of this book as a whole. What happened in Hollywood in the early 1930s also has an indirect bearing on what happened to Gustave Flaubert in 1857. In 1948, almost a century after the initial publication and trial of *Madame Bovary,* Vincente Minnelli directed a Hollywood film based on Flaubert's novel (one of many film versions made in various countries at different times). Given that the Motion Picture Production Code was still in full effect at the time, this was, to say the least, a problematic undertaking from the outset, since one of the major interdictions of the Production Code was a prohibition of unnecessary or positive depictions of adultery. *Madame Bovary*, of course, is nothing if not a story of adultery; this is what had gotten it into trouble in the first place. Adultery may not be positively depicted in the novel—this is a matter of interpretation, as became clear during the trial—but it is certainly necessary in terms of the plot. In fact, it *is* the plot, and this was explicitly discouraged by the Hays Code. Minnelli and company had a very hard time getting the picture made because of this fundamental problem. Eventually they hit on what turned out to be an extremely effective device for getting their script past the censors: they decided to frame the story Flaubert had written with a mise-en-scène of his trial. The film owes its existence to this inventive device designed to shame the Hollywood censors into compliance. Nonetheless, because its script still had to adhere to the strictures of the Production Code, the final product grossly distorts the novel's plot and main characters. Minnelli's *Madame Bovary*, featuring James Mason as a highly sanctimonious Flaubert defending his work at his trial, does not merely represent history repeating itself. In this film version of Flaubert's novel we find history reeling around, grabbing us drunkenly by the collar and repeating itself in such loud and insistent tones that we can only sit back and listen to its incoherent tale.

CHAPTER ONE

Gustave Flaubert

Emma Bovary Goes to Hollywood

> The book is concerned with adultery and contains situations and
> allusions that shocked the prudish philistine government of Napoleon
> III. Indeed, the novel was actually tried in a court of justice for obscenity.
> Just imagine that. As if the work of an artist could ever be obscene. I am
> glad to say that Flaubert won his case. That was exactly a hundred years
> ago. In our days, our times . . . But let me keep to my subject.
>
> VLADIMIR NABOKOV, *Lectures on Literature*

Few books are as closely associated with their legal histories as is *Madame Bovary*. Most editions of *Ulysses* include in a preface Judge John M. Woolsey's 1933 decision allowing Joyce's novel into the United States, and the trial of *Lady Chatterley's Lover* was not only published as a book in its own right but also famously commemorated by Philip Larkin in his poem "Annus mirabilis" as an epoch-making milestone:

> Sexual intercourse began
> In nineteen sixty-three
> (Which was rather late for me)—
> Between the end of the *Chatterley* ban
> And the Beatles' first LP.[1]

Neither sexual intercourse per se nor even adultery began in 1857, but it might be fair to say that modern literature did. And along with modern literature, efforts to stamp it out: as we have seen, 1857 was something of an *annus horribilis*, producing a bumper crop of literary trials in France, as well as unprecedented obscenity legislation in England. As Flaubert put it shortly after his trial, grandiosely but with a certain amount of justification, "my cause was that of contemporary literature itself [ma cause était celle de la littérature contemporaine tout entière]."[2] The trial, in any case, remains part of *Madame Bovary*, even more than is true for *Ulysses* and *Lady Chatterley's Lover*, for a number of reasons. For one thing, the novel carries a dedication to Jules Senard, Flaubert's defense attorney, in which the author notes that it was through Senard's efforts that the book was able to appear at all in book form. It had been prosecuted on the basis of publication in six installments in the *Revue de Paris* in October through December 1856, and if Senard had not won the case it would not have been able to see the light as a volume. Flaubert might just as well, though, have dedicated the novel to Ernest Pinard, the hated imperial prosecutor, since the prosecution launched his career as an author. *Madame Bovary* was his first published book, and while it had attracted a certain amount of attention on first publication, it was the trial that made Flaubert famous, as he himself recognized. "My Bovary continues to be a hit [La *Bovary* continue son succès]," he wrote to his brother just prior to the start of judicial proceedings. ''It has become spicy. Everyone has read it, is reading it, or wants to read it [Il devient *corsé*. Tout le monde l'a lue, la lit ou veut la lire]." The letter continues, in a spirit of coy cynicism: "My persecution has won me endless sympathy. If my book is bad, the trial will serve to make it seem better; if on the contrary it is to last, this will be its pedestal [Ma persécution m'a ouvert mille sympathies. Si mon livre est mauvais, elle servira à le faire paraître meilleur; s'il doit au contraire demeurer, c'est un piédestal pour lui]."[3]

Even so, the trial might have remained a salty detail in Flaubert's career, since he went on to publish five more books and establish himself as an eminent author in general and not just the focus of a judicial scandal. But *Madame Bovary* is still his most famous work, and the trial remains literally part of the novel. Most editions of the novel available in French, from the prestigious Bibliotheque de la Pléiade volumes of Flaubert's complete works to the cheapest paperbacks designed for casual readers and students, contain the transcript of the trial proceedings.[4] The first edition of *Madame Bovary* to feature the trial dates from the author's lifetime and was published with his consent.[5] Not only was the trial included in the 1873 "definitive" edition of the novel with the author's imprimatur, it was also at Flaubert's behest that the judicial proceedings had been retained in full in the first place. When Flaubert came to trial in 1857, transcription of such cases was not automatic, and the author hired a stenographer to record the trial at his own expense. This gesture, coupled with that of agreeing to include the transcript in the definitive text of the novel in 1873, ensured that the trial proceedings would continue to figure as part of the text of *Madame Bovary*, which was already well on its way to becoming an established classic by the time of the author's death in 1880.

Among the many unforeseen consequences of these decisions on Flaubert's part, perhaps the most spectacular is Vincente Minnelli's 1949

Hollywood film version, which frames the plot of the novel itself with the 1857 trial. Minnelli's film begins and ends with the trial, the intervening scenes from the novel itself—that is, most of the movie—subsumed in the story of the trial and presented as the author's defense. This decision to frame the gist of the novel as evidence for the defense is to some extent quite in keeping with what happened during the actual trial. As in most such proceedings, the prosecution cited specific passages out of context as evidence of indecency (*outrage à la morale publique et religieuse et aux bonnes moeurs*), whereupon the defense expressed indignation that passages were being cited out of context, lamenting—as had the prosecution, for that matter—that for obvious reasons the novel could not be read aloud in its entirety during the trial. The defense attorney then proceeded to take up the passages cited by the prosecution and place them back into context, always, of course, in a way carefully chosen to highlight what he depicted as the extremely moral message of the work as a whole. Minnelli's film begins in medias res, at the moment when the prosecution rests and Flaubert (or rather James Mason, since Flaubert did not in fact speak during his trial) is allowed to begin his rebuttal. The unfolding of the novel's plot is therefore a perfectly logical device to follow and support his opening argument: you have mischaracterized my novel by selective quotation; I shall now demonstrate, by showing you the story as a whole, that your account is a distortion; here is what really occurs in my work.

The terms of the defense as represented in the 1949 version and the defense in Flaubert's actual trial in 1857 differ greatly, though, and not just because Flaubert did not speak on his own behalf. The cinematic spectacle of Flaubert delivering his own defense speech is symptomatic of the most important overarching difference between the trial as it happened in 1857 and the trial as represented in Minnelli's film. The speech delivered by James Mason as Flaubert presents the Romantic picture of the artist defending his art, and doing so according to two basic principles: the integrity and independence of art, and the idea that art is based on truth and has a special relation to it. The central element of his defense, which he repeats several times and which closes the film, is that his art represents the truth, and the truth will always triumph. Although all this is delivered in overblown, melodramatic Hollywood style, it says little that cannot be found in Flaubert's letters. In this sense, Minnelli's version of the speech for the defense is quite true to its subject. Where it diverges from the original is that, while Flaubert may have made similar statements in his correspondence, very little of this sort of rhetoric found its way into his attorney's speech for the defense, which was conducted on quite different grounds.

The central points of the defense speech in the film—again, that art delivers truth and truth will always triumph—represent an amalgam of Romantic and realist aesthetic dogma. If they sound like clichés it is because the basic tenets of both romanticism and realism have, in the past 150 years or so, filtered into common discourse and become what Flaubert liked to call *idées reçues*: "received ideas."[6] The speech made by James Mason in the film contains many pronouncements that echo Flaubert's correspondence not because the authors of the screenplay had researched the author's letters, but because the concepts Flaubert deploys in his correspondence to defend his work, although iconoclastic at the time, have since entered common parlance. After all, the 1949 *Madame Bovary* was a Metro Goldwyn Mayer production, and therefore opens with the familiar roaring lion, surrounded by MGM's motto: *ars gratia artis*, art for art's sake: the once-revolutionary slogan popularized in France by Flaubert's mentor Théophile Gautier.

Art for art's sake—"l'art pour l'art"—a phrase borrowed from German romanticism, first used in French by the novelist Benjamin Constant in 1804, was made into a credo by Gautier in the polemical preface to his somewhat raunchy novel *Mademoiselle de Maupin* in 1834. (This work was itself to enter the annals of literary obscenity proceedings in the United States when an English translation of Gautier's novel was unsuccessfully prosecuted by the New York Society for the Suppression of Vice in 1922; the preface is an argument against censorship in general and in the theater in particular.) In the mid nineteenth century in France, "l'art pour l'art" became the motto of the Parnassian movement, an offshoot of romanticism that reacted against some aspects of the French Romantic movement as represented for instance by Victor Hugo, himself a proponent of "l'art pour le progrès" (whereas writers such as Flaubert and Baudelaire were resolutely antiprogress). In any case, art for art's sake, as slogan and ideology, took root in the avant-garde imagination starting in the 1830s, even as it remained anathema for a very long time in the context of official notions of the role art was meant to serve. By the time Minnelli, producer Pandro Berman, and screenwriter Robert Ardrey concocted the courtroom scenes for their Hollywood version, the ideas put forth in them must have seemed like the obvious self-justifications of any writer accused of obscenity. As Minnelli somewhat incoherently puts it in his autobiography, *I Remember It Well*, "We devised the historically accurate courtroom proceedings" (203). As mentioned earlier, they were not historically accurate, nor were they the arguments his attorney used. More to the point, these were not arguments that could conceivably have been advanced in the courtroom in 1857.

One of the most striking aspects of Flaubert's trial, and of such trials in general, to the modern—or rather postmodern—reader is the extent to which the defense and the prosecution appear to be arguing from the same viewpoint. As cultural historian Dominick LaCapra puts it, "discus-

sion and decision turn on a simple binary choice of a positive or a negative answer to a set of shared questions."[7] Historians and critics discussing
literary obscenity trials often focus on this aspect, which now seems remarkable because of the extent to which such arguments have shifted
ground in recent decades: specifically, since "the end of obscenity," as attorney Charles Rembar, who defended *Lady Chatterley's Lover, Tropic of Cancer*, and *Fanny Hill* in the United States in the 1950s and 1960s refers to the
cessation of such proceedings. The British critic Rachel Bowlby makes the
same point as LaCapra in terms of the 1960 trial of *Lady Chatterley's Lover*
in England:

> The prosecution rests its case on the idea that this is a dirty book, likely to
> "deprave and corrupt" the minds of those who read it. The defense does not
> say that that is an inappropriate way of putting the matter, that it might be
> difficult or futile to determine the difference between a dirty book and a
> non-dirty book. Instead, it claims that *Lady Chatterley's Lover* is an exception-
> ally clean or wholesome book. . . . In other words, the defense too adopts
> the categories of clean and dirty, wholesome and unwholesome, moral and
> immoral.[8]

"Dirt" per se (that is, the explicit representation of sex or use of obscene
terms), which was to preoccupy twentieth-century censors and would-be
censors, is not at issue in the *Bovary* trial, but the now-peculiar phenomenon of defense and prosecution arguing according to the same standards,
and disagreeing only as to whether the work met those standards, held true
for more than a century. In 1857 both Ernest Pinard, the imperial prosecutor, and Jules Senard, Flaubert's attorney, ground their arguments in the
assumption that the status quo (which, as Pinard emphasizes, is based on
Christian morality) is to be upheld. Literature, they agree, should serve a
morally uplifting purpose. The main point of divergence between the arguments for the prosecution and the defense during the actual trial is
whether *Madame Bovary* serves such a purpose: this is the "simple binary
choice" referred to by LaCapra. They disagree only as to whether the desired, and achieved, effect of the novel was to uphold or rather to subvert a
moral framework that itself remains unquestioned by both sides.

Some weeks before his novel came to trial, Flaubert wrote the following
in a letter: "The morality of Art consists in its beauty, and I value above all
style, and, after that, Truth [La morale de l'Art consiste dans sa beauté
même, et j'estime par-dessus tout d'abord le style, et ensuite le Vrai]."[9]
This sentence, which resembles many such pronouncements in Flaubert's
correspondence, would not be entirely out of place in James Mason's
speeches in Minnelli's film (at least the part about Truth with a capital T,
style having little part in "Flaubert"'s perorations in the film). However,

nothing like it can be found in Senard's speech in Flaubert's defense during his actual trial. In 1857 this was a heretical position, one that would have been unthinkable in the courtroom. If, as LaCapra puts it, Senard's "interpretation is in one sense more narrowly conservative than that of the prosecutor, for—despite his apparently 'liberal' conclusion—he construes the novel as a simple, clear, and distinct confirmation of existing morality and society" (34), this was out of necessity. Whether or not Senard's personal convictions coincided with his speech for the defense, the shape that defense was to take was essentially preordained along the lines LaCapra describes. Even if Senard had, against all probability, wanted to make an argument similar to the one "devised" for the 1949 film, he could not have done so, since the arguments put forth in the film represent to a great extent the very bases on which Flaubert was being charged.

One of the key concepts involved in the 1857 trial, and which also explains in part the immense difference between that context and that of the 1949 film, is "realism." In principle this means the idea that what is being represented in Flaubert's novel is no more than the truth: that is to say, in the context of the novel's defense, the real social conditions described in *Madame Bovary*. Flaubert himself, although he ended up being labeled as one of the founding fathers of realism, was no fan of the latter, as is clear from a letter written shortly before his trial: "People think I am infatuated with the real, whereas I can't stand it. I wrote this novel out of hatred for realism [On me croit épris du réel, tandis que je l'exècre. Car c'est en haine du réalisme que j'ai entrepris ce roman]." He then adds: "But I also detest the false idealism that's shoved down our throats these days [Mais je n'en déteste pas moins la fausse idéalité, dont nous sommes bernés par le temps qui court]."[10] Flaubert was nothing if not an equal-opportunity iconoclast. Still, his rejection of both realism and the idealism it was reacting against is not just his characteristic curmudgeonly stance. (In politics, for instance, he systematically inveighed against all extant parties and insisted that the only workable form of government would be a coalition of *mandarins*: what might be termed a philosophocracy.) The idea of art for art's sake as espoused by Flaubert and Baudelaire represented an alternative to the binary choice offered by idealism on the one hand and realism on the other, one that was crucial to the development of modern notions of the function of art.[11] For this very reason, the concept harped on by the prosecution was realism, which with its obvious anti-idealist agenda was demonstrably antagonistic to the aesthetic and (therefore) moral status quo. Senard himself is led to invoke the idea of realism in the course of defending the novel, but in a way that illustrates the extent to which it was a reviled term at the time: "He belongs to the realist school only in the sense that he is attached to the reality of things [Mon Dieu! Il appartient à l'école réaliste, en ce sens qu'il s'attache à la réalité des choses]" (*Madame Bovary* [Pléiade], 636). It is clear from this mention of realism by Flaubert's defense attorney that his client was not to be understood as a realist in any sense other than that of wishing to be true to his subject. The categorization as "realist" was to be avoided, especially in terms of the defense of a novel accused of violating prevailing mores.

In the interim, "realism" has become mostly a term of approbation in literary criticism, and it has long been a cliché to praise a novel for its "gritty realism." The faithful representation of life's seamiest aspects has been a sanctioned goal of literature for many decades, so much so that it can be difficult to recall the extent to which the proper function of literature was for centuries to be the repository of ideal representation. In fact the term *realism* has a variety of different meanings in different contexts. As used in Flaubert's and Baudelaire's trials in 1857, "realism" functions as an incriminating category, a cornerstone of the prosecution, alluded to by the defense only defensively: to offset the very accusation of "realism." In this context the word refers to the general phenomenon of literary or artistic representation of reality including, or rather harping on, its baser aspects, in contrast to the traditional function of art as representing an ideal view of things. It also, as Senard's defensive assertion indicates, refers to the "realist" school of representation that was getting a lot of press at the time; by insisting that his client belonged to the realist school only in that he was attached to the reality of things, Flaubert's attorney clearly wishes to suggest that he can be considered a realist in no other sense.

Controversy raged over the idea of "realism" during the 1850s, a debate sparked at the beginning of the decade by Gustave Courbet's painting "A Burial at Ornans [Un enterrement à Ornans]," an object of scandal for its grand-scale representation of a provincial working-class burial. Courbet himself was hardly less reluctant than Flaubert to take on the mantle of realism: "The label of realist was imposed on me as the label of Romantic was imposed on the generation of 1830," he complained in 1855.[12] The "realist" school of literature was spearheaded by the novelist and critic Champfleury (pseudonym of Jules Husson), who published a collection of essays under the title *Le Réalisme* in 1857, and his protégé Louis Edmond Duranty, also a novelist and in 1856 founder of a short-lived but influential journal also entitled *Le Réalisme*. The Goncourt brothers are the only adherents of the self-proclaimed realist movement in France whose works are still well known. Both they and Champfleury had friendly relations with Flaubert, but for the most part literary *réalistes* tended, perhaps unsurprisingly, to be as ill-inclined toward Flaubert as the latter was toward the category of realism.

Later in the century the cause of "realist" representation of the grimier aspects of life was taken up by the *naturalistes*, headed by Émile Zola, a

great admirer and friend of Flaubert. The latter was regarded as a pathbreaking hero by Zola and his disciples in the naturalist school, a literary
movement based on the principles of scientific naturalism (e.g. entomology) applied to human society. Its proponents included not only such
young writers as Maupassant and Joris-Karl Huysmans, but also the formerly realist Goncourt brothers. In an essay first published in 1875, Zola
lauded *Madame Bovary* as the exemplary naturalist novel, a category which
had not, of course, existed in 1857: "The first characteristic of the naturalist novel, of which *Madame Bovary* is the prototype, is the exact reproduction of life, the absence of all novelistic elements [Le premier caractère
du roman naturaliste, dont *Madame Bovary* est le type, est la reproduction
exacte de la vie, l'absence de tout élément romanesque]."[13] The naturalist
novel was therefore, according to this definition, one that excluded all
novelistic touches. Zola goes on to name a number of other characteristics
of "the naturalist formula" (*la formule naturaliste*), as he likes to call it in his
theoretical works, apparently unafraid of the formulaic overtones of the
phrase, as anticipated by Flaubert's first work. Almost all of these were the
same "realist" elements of the 1857 novel that attracted critical opprobrium and featured centrally in its prosecution: notably, its lack of heroic
characters, banality of subject, and absence of identifiable moral viewpoint.[14] Flaubert seems to have enjoyed his new status as hero of a major
literary trend in the 1870s, while retaining a certain mocking distance
toward the dogmatic fervor of Zola and some of his cohorts.

Twenty years after its trial and acquittal, *Madame Bovary* was no longer
seen as scabrously realistic, whereas Zola was routinely caricatured in the
press as writing his naturalist novels while seated on a chamber pot. Although Zola himself was never prosecuted on literary grounds in France,
several of his minor disciples faced obscenity charges in the 1880s, perhaps
the most memorable example being Paul Bonnetain, acquitted in 1884 for
Charlot s'amuse ("*Charlot's Diversions*"), his naturalist novel about masturbation. The consequences were much more dire for Zola's British publisher
Henry Vizetelly. The latter was hauled into court by the National Vigilance
Association and convicted twice: once for translations of *La Terre*, *Nana*,
and *Pot-Bouille*, in 1888, and sent to jail the following year for having published thirteen French "realist" works, including a translation of *Madame
Bovary* by Karl Marx's daughter Eleanor.[15] He died not long afterward. His
son, Ernest Vizetelly, was one of the translators of Zola's novels.

If the qualifier "realist" has long since lost its pejorative connotations in
common parlance, the nuances among realism as a once-maligned approach, realism as a self-defined movement, and various other fine distinctions, such as the one between the realists of the mid nineteenth century and the naturalists toward the end of the century, have also in the
interim lost their punch. Today Flaubert is generally considered to be one
"realist" among others who established the ground—the depiction of

everyday life including its less picturesque aspects—for the modernists to come: Joyce, Proust, Woolf, Kafka, with their emphasis on a solipsistic description of the experience of the alienated subject trapped in the dailiness of daily life in the twentieth century. Flaubert's name is associated with those of others: especially, Balzac, Zola, Daudet, and Maupassant. In his 1881 collection of essays *Naturalist Novelists* [*Les Romanciers naturalistes*], Zola marshals not only Flaubert but also Balzac and Stendhal, as well as the Goncourts, Daudet, and others under the rubric of naturalist writers. For some time the umbrella category for such writers was "naturalist," but by the late twentieth century "realism" had become the operative term, designating not a self-defined ideological adherence but a more general aesthetic trend.[16]

Finally, in addition to this use as a capacious category in literary taxonomy referring to an influential tendency in premodernist French writing, "realism" has at length come to be employed as an all-purpose critical term of praise used for works representing the violence of working-class life (which is what "gritty" usually means). If the word did not acquire an automatically positive resonance until well into the twentieth century, this is because the concept itself—that art should represent all aspects of life, even or especially those that tend to shock middle-class sensibilities—took some time to gain acceptance. The process had begun in France not with Courbet's 1850 painting, but in the wake of the French Revolution, when writers such as Balzac began to foreground a subject never before seriously treated in literature: money problems. In this sense Flaubert's "realism" is a direct descendent of Balzac's, as Emma Bovary's problems may stem from her Romantic aspirations, but it is the financial difficulties to which they give rise, the sordid entailments of her lofty illusions, that lead her to suicide.

The official position on the function of literature in France in 1857 is stated explicitly in the judgment of *Madame Bovary*. Although the novel was exculpated, the pronouncement issued by the judges makes plain the extent to which the verdict had not been based on anything resembling a notion that art could function independently of the moral strictures governing the rest of society. Instead, the judgment, even while finding Flaubert innocent of the charges leveled against him, takes pains to explain why he is nonetheless to be blamed for his novel:

> The work in question merits severe blame, since the mission of literature should be to beautify and enhance the spirit by elevating the intelligence and purifying morals rather than to inspire disgust for vice by offering a portrait of the disorder that may exist in society.

> [L'ouvrage déféré au tribunal mérite un blâme sévère, car la mission de la littérature doit être d'orner et de recréer l'esprit en élevant l'intelligence et

> en épurant les moeurs plus encore que d'imprimer le dégoût du vice en of-
> frant le tableau des désordres qui peuvent exister dans la société.] (*Madame
> Bovary* [Pléiade], 682)

As was also to be the case for almost all the authors brought to trial for offending public morals during the course of the nineteenth and twentieth
centuries, Flaubert's defense was essentially the one implied by the text of
the verdict: to the extent that his novel depicted vice, it was only in order
to promote virtue. But since the officially designated function of literature was to uplift the spirit by good example, this defense only went so far.
In Flaubert's case it was enough to bring about an acquittal, despite the
blameworthy aspects noted in the eventual verdict.[17]

The notion that the novel, in particular, was to depict life in its most
rosy aspects had a venerable history. In France in the seventeenth century,
as the novel was becoming accepted as a genre—already a largely feminine
genre—a division of roles was assumed: the role of the novel was to depict
an ideal version of things, reality being confined to historical narrative.
This was why, for example, *La Princesse de Clèves* (1678), often considered
the first modern—in the sense of psychological—novel, with its less than
ideal portrait of goings-on at the court of Henri II, had to be framed as a
historical narrative, its plot set a full century prior to its publication during the reign of Louis XIV. By the mid nineteenth century, the era of the
serialized novel or *feuilleton,* this division still obtained, and it was by now
visible within newspapers. Novelists whose works appeared in daily papers
could be prosecuted for alluding to the same sorts of events that could be
described in the same pages, in detail and with impunity, as news. As history in the making—reality on the hoof, as it were—the reporting of news
was considered to be exempt from the rules of *bienséance* or literary decorum that continued to apply to fiction. The contrast between books and
newspapers was repeatedly alluded to in connection with Baudelaire's
prosecution some six months after Flaubert's. In an article written in support of the poet just before his trial Charles Asselineau writes:

> I do not blame our newspapers for having moralized their serials in the in-
> terest of their subscribers and the daughters of same. But, frankly, must we
> make a commercial consideration into a literary matter? Is a book the same
> as a newspaper? No: a newspaper looks for its readers, a book waits for them.

> [Je n'en veux donc pas à nos journaux d'avoir moralisé leur feuilleton dans
> l'intérêt de leurs abonnés et des filles d'iceux. Mais, franchement, d'une né-
> cessité commerciale, d'une condition d'abonnement, doit-on faire une
> question littéraire? Le livre est-il le journal? Mais non: le journal va chercher
> ses lecteurs, le livre attend les siens.][18]

Pinard in his prosecution speech in Baudelaire's trial makes the same comparison, to opposite ends: "I would add that the book is not some light pages that get lost and forgotten like the newspaper [J'ajoute que le livre n'est pas une feuille légère qui se perd et s'oublie comme le journal]."[19] Instead of emphasizing the ubiquity of access offered by newspapers, as Asselineau does, Pinard focuses on their ephemeral nature, destined to be discarded and forgotten. Obviously, he could draw no such contrast between literature and the popular press in Flaubert's case, not only because fiction lacked the gravity of verse (see chapter 2), but because *Madame Bovary* was being prosecuted in periodical form. In 1880, shortly before Flaubert's death, Zola published an article entitled "On Morality [De la moralité]" in which he complained about the radically different criteria applied to news and to fiction:

> The public that tolerates the bloody sewer of the courts expects novels to provide little birds and daisies as consolation. It's a contract, what scandalizes in one context becomes inoffensive in the other.

> [Le public qui tolère l'égout sanglant des tribunaux, demande aux romans des petits oiseaux et des paquerettes pour se consoler. C'est un contrat, ce qui scandalise à une place devient inoffensif à l'autre.][20]

This division in genre had everything to do with gender, since women were the target audience of daily *feuilletons* as of most novels in general, whereas the news section of the newspaper, like history and most nonfiction, was taken to be a masculine realm: hence Asselineau's reference to newspaper subscribers and their daughters.

The fate of *Madame Bovary*, like that of its heroine, was inextricably bound up with the question of fiction's failure to perform its assigned role of providing consolation and moral uplift, of serving as an antidote to reality rather than a reflection of it. Flaubert's novel itself provides a sort of running commentary on this theme: as has been pointed out by LaCapra among others, *Madame Bovary* seems to anticipate and even in some sense to incorporate its own trial. One of the most obvious instances of this takes place when the first Mme Bovary, Charles's mother, accurately observes that her daughter-in-law's problems stem from her reading of novels:

> It was therefore decided that Emma should be prevented from reading novels. The enterprise did not seem simple. The good lady offered to take care of it: when she went to Rouen, she would go in person to the booklender and tell him that Emma was canceling her subscription. Would they not then be able to call the police, if the booklender persisted nonetheless in his profession of poisoner?

[Donc, il fut résolu que l'on empêcherait Emma de lire des romans. L'entreprise ne semblait point facile. La bonne dame s'en chargea: elle devait, quand elle passait par Rouen, aller en personne chez le loueur de livres et lui représenter qu'Emma cessait ses abonnements. N'aurait-on pas le droit d'avertir la police, si le libraire persistait quand même dans son métier d'empoisonneur?] (*Madame Bovary* [Pléiade], 406)

In this and other passages of *Madame Bovary*, Flaubert foregrounds the commonly accepted idea that excessive novel-reading is poisonous, and should be prevented, if necessary by official intervention. The reference to poisoning in this passage anticipates the heroine's death. She takes arsenic, imagining a painless demise of the sort featured in fiction, and especially in plays. From the classicism of Racine's *Phèdre* (1677) through the extravagant romanticism of Hugo's *Ruy Blas* (1838), the rules of *bienséance* forbid violent death on stage, but protagonists regularly take poison in the final act, delivering moving speeches as they expire, before collapsing picturesquely, to the extended lamentations of the other characters. The fate Emma meets is differently literary: dying in sordid agony, she is plagued by a persistent taste of ink, a nauseous reminder of the books that had intoxicated her.[21]

This sort of ironic inclusion within the work of the very ideas that were to serve the arguments of both defense and prosecution during the trial is also present in slightly less explicit form in the scene in which Emma and Charles first arrive in Yonville and dine among the locals. In that passage she meets Léon Dupuis, soon to be her first adulterous temptation and later her second lover. While Charles talks shop with the pharmacist Homais, Emma and Léon seduce one another, in a vertiginous exchange of Romantic clichés. Having exhausted sunsets, seascapes, and the relative merits of German and Italian music, they arrive at the inevitable subject of novels. The ensuing discussion is an index of received ideas about the role of literature, and also an accurate prediction of the terms according to which the tribunal would assign Flaubert blame for his novel even while exculpating it. "I detest common heroes and tepid sentiments as are found in nature [Je déteste les héros communs et les sentiments tempérés, comme il y en a dans la nature]," opines Emma, in an implicit critique of realism with which Léon hastily agrees:

> Indeed, observed the clerk, such works, because they do not touch the emotions, are estranged, it seems to me, from the true aim of Art. It is so nice, amid the disappointments of life, to be able to fall back in spirit on noble characters, pure affections and visions of happiness!

> [En effet, observa le clerc, ces ouvrages, ne touchant pas le coeur, s'écartent, il me semble, du vrai but de l'Art. Il est si doux, parmi les désen-

chantements de la vie, de pouvoir se reporter en idée sur de nobles carac-
tères, des affections pures et des tableaux de bonheur!] (*Madame Bovary*
[Pléiade], 367)

Here we have a pronouncement which neatly combines Romantic cliché
and official dogma. Flaubert mockingly anticipates the terms under which
his novel would be prosecuted, revealing them to be the very sort of *idées
reçues* cherished by the heroine whose representation violated their sanctity. In this way *Madame Bovary* does indeed, as LaCapra asserts, uncannily
appear to "read" the trial that would judge it.

If an antirealist view of the role of literature is propounded by Emma
and Léon, however, the doctrine of art for art's sake, that is, the conception of art as independent from prevailing societal mores and divorced
from the notion of moral utility that underlies them, is as absent from the
novel as it is from Senard's speech for the defense. The idea propounded
by both Flaubert and Baudelaire, that art has its own set of morals as distinct from those that obtain elsewhere, finds its pale equivalent in the
novel only in the mouth of Rodolphe Boulanger, the local rake and
Emma's first adulterous lover. During their initial seduction scene, set in
counterpoint to the agricultural fair going on around them, Rodolphe attempts to disarm Emma's fairly weak resistance. When she objects to his
ostensibly iconoclastic statements, saying, "we must surely . . . follow public opinion and obey its morality [il faut bien . . . suivre l'opinion du
monde et obéir à sa morale]," Rodolphe retorts:

> —Ah! But there are two. . . . The petty, commonly accepted morality, that of
> men, the one that changes all the time and makes so much noise, so much
> agitation down here among the common people, like this assembly of fools
> you see here. But the other morality, the eternal one, is all around and
> above, like the landscape that surrounds us and the blue sky shining down
> on us.

> [Ah! C'est qu'il y en a deux, répliqua-t-il. La petite, la convenue, celle des
> hommes, celle qui varie sans cesse et qui braille si fort, s'agite en bas, terre à
> terre, comme ce rassemblement d'imbéciles que vous voyez. Mais l'autre,
> l'éternelle, elle est tout autour et au-dessus, comme le paysage qui nous en-
> vironne et le ciel bleu qui nous éclaire.] (*Madame Bovary* [Pléiade], 423)

In other words, there are at least two moral orders: that of the common
herd, and the one that transcends the realm of petty bourgeois society.
Here, the transcendent morality is that of the seducer. The basic structure
of Rodolphe's statement closely resembles the concept advanced at various points by Flaubert in his correspondence, and perhaps most succinctly

expressed by Baudelaire in his "Notes for My Attorney [Notes pour mon avocat]," written in anticipation of his trial:

> There are several moralities. There is the positive and practical morality that everyone must obey. But then there is the morality of the arts. This one is entirely different, and since the beginning of the world the Arts have proved it.

> [Il y a plusieurs morales. Il y a la morale positive et pratique à laquelle tout le monde doit obéir. Mais il y a la morale des arts. Celle-ci est tout autre, et depuis le commencement du monde, les Arts l'ont bien prouvé.] (Baudelaire, *Œuvres complètes*, 1:139)

The fact that this important and revolutionary idea should be put forth in *Madame Bovary* in the grotesque form of a speech made by Rodolphe as a strategic move in his campaign to win Emma's favors is, among other things, testimony to the degree to which nothing was safe from providing grist for Flaubert's satirical mill. It also reveals that the idea of alternative morality had evidently filtered into common parlance to the extent that Rodolphe's assertion registers as at once seemingly subversive and easily digestible: a cliché along the lines of Léon's pronouncements about literature, even if more effective for the task at hand. What is most remarkable, though, is that Rodolphe's version, when juxtaposed with the Romantic dictum it parodies, implies the equivalence between the artist and the banal seducer that lies at the heart of indictments of the novel as a genre whose inevitable and even desired effect is to lead virtuous women astray. It is in part for this very reason that nowhere in the speech for the defense do we find any whiff of the idea that is here put forth in parodic form. The concept of a morality specific to art is no more present in Senard's speech for the defense than it is in the tribunal's judgment.

The verdict in Flaubert's trial, with its pronouncement about the function of literature being to elevate the spirit rather than debase it by the depiction of unseemly realities must, of course, be taken as the governmental party line that it necessarily represented. To place that judgment in perspective and gauge the extent to which the function of literature as expressed by the tribunal deciding on Flaubert's case was representative of the general climate of opinion in France in 1857, it is instructive to look at other contemporary readings of *Madame Bovary*. With a single exception, responses to Flaubert's novel, whether positive or negative, whether in published reviews or private letters, all start from the same assumption as suggested by the verdict delivered by the tribunal: that the proper function of literature is moral. Unsurprisingly, therefore, almost all accounts of the novel, whatever their judgments of its literary merits, and regardless of whether they are expressed before or after Flaubert's trial, arrange themselves along the same binary divide noted by LaCapra in the trial itself.

Sainte-Beuve's article on *Madame Bovary* is exemplary in this regard. Written in the wake of the trial, the essay by this most influential of contemporary critics is overall a laudatory review of the novel. After praising various aspects of the novel, including its objectivity, though, Sainte-Beuve goes on to regret that its realism was not tempered by a bit of idealism: "It would not take much, at certain moments of these situations, for the ideal to be added to reality [Il faudrait peu de chose, à certains moments de ces situations, pour que l'idéal s'ajoutât à la réalité]" (346). Finally, after lamenting the lack of any morally sound characters with whom the author—and therefore the reader—might identify, he notes the following as to the moral profile of the work:

> The book, certainly, has a moral: the author has not spelled it out, but it is there for the reader to infer, and it is in fact a terrifying one. However, is the function of art to refuse to console, not to admit any element of clemency and sweetness, on the pretext of being the more true to reality? Truth, for that matter, even aside from anything else, is not altogether and necessarily on the side of evil, on the side of stupidity and human perversity.

> [Le livre, certes, a une moralité: l'auteur ne l'a pas cherchée, mais il ne tient qu'au lecteur de la tirer, et même terrible. Cependant, l'office de l'art est-il de ne pas vouloir consoler, de ne vouloir admettre aucun élément de clémence et de douceur, sous couleur d'être plus vrai? La vérité d'ailleurs, à ne chercher qu'elle, elle n'est pas tout entière et nécessairement du côté du mal, du côté de la sottise et de la perversité humaine.] (347)

He goes on to provide a real-life counterexample of a bored provincial lady in a situation similar to that of Emma Bovary who managed to devote her life to good works. Clearly, Sainte-Beuve wants to have it both ways. He is able to praise the novel for its uncompromising realism and at the same time to lament its lack of idealism because, in citing his unnamed virtuous provincial lady, he manages anecdotally to conflate the two categories, incorporating the ideal into the real. Because of Sainte-Beuve's prominence as a critic, and also because of the way in which he takes up the terms of the governmental verdict, this essay is particularly important in understanding the stakes of the realism debate around *Madame Bovary*. The latter had been published in the *Gazette des tribunaux* on February 9, 1857; Sainte-Beuve's article appeared in *Le Moniteur universel* on May 4. Where the tribunal's verdict had intoned the normative admonishment "the mission of literature should be to beautify and enhance the spirit [la mission de la littérature doit être d'orner]," Sainte-Beuve phrases a similar edict negatively, in the form of a rhetorical question: "Is the function of art to refuse to console, not to admit any element of clemency and sweetness? [l'office de l'art est-il de ne vouloir pas consoler?]" He thus appears to reject the bases on which the judgment had been based even as he repeats almost identical objections. Sainte-Beuve's review stands as evidence of the extent to which the criteria that came into play during the trial were also, despite apparent ideological divergences, the terms of public debate in general.

Le Moniteur universel, in which Sainte-Beuve's article was published, was in fact the official organ of the Second Empire government, and so it is hardly surprising that his review did not completely contradict the tribunal's verdict.[22] But almost all early readings of *Madame Bovary* foreground the same sorts of issues. Duranty, for instance, rejected the novel on the rather remarkable basis that it contained too much description, calling it "a masterpiece of obstinate description, but without emotion, or feeling, or life [le chef-d'oeuvre de la description obstinée, mais sans émotion, ni sentiment, ni vie]." In his attack on Flaubert this major spokesman for the realist school thus managed ironically to resume one of the main general objections to realism itself, as well as the naturalism that succeeded it.[23] Duranty's mentor Champfleury, who had friendly relations with Flaubert, wrote the author a letter expressing admiration and support, but he too felt that some details were best left unmentioned: "Three or four details shocked me, and you would be well advised to remove them from the book in a future edition: I especially recommend your beggar's pustules, and perhaps a bit too much surgery in the clubfoot operation [Trois ou quatre details m'ont choqué, que vous ferez bien d'enlever dans une prochaine édition: je vous recommande surtout les *gales* de votre mendiant, et peut-être un peu trop de chirurgie dans la jambe coupée]."[24] Flaubert thus evidently proved too realistic even for the realists themselves. Other reviews, including the positive ones, made similar points. Two assessments of the novel, both written in correspondence with Flaubert and neither intended for publication, are particularly pertinent in that they exemplify the extent to which moral issues were always at the forefront in these sorts of debates. The first correspondent was an Englishwoman named Gertrude Collier who Flaubert had met in 1842 at Trouville, when they were both young. They remained in contact after she became Mrs. Tennant, and he sent her an affectionately dedicated copy of *Madame Bovary* once it was published in book form. In response Mrs. Tennant sent him a letter in which she announces that she has only read part of the novel, as that was all she could bear:

> I will tell you quite simply that I am astonished that you, with your imagination, with your admiration for all that is beautiful, that you have written,

that you could have taken pleasure in writing something as hideous as this book! I find it all so awful! And the talent that you put into this book doubly detestable!!

[Je vous dirai tout bonnement que je suis émerveillée, que vous, avec votre imagination, avec votre admiration pour tout ce qui est beau, que vous ayez écrit, que vous ayez pu prendre plaisir à écrire quelque chose de si *hideux* que ce livre! Je trouve tout cela si mauvais! Et le *talent* que vous y avez mis dans ce livre [*sic*] doublement détestable!!]

This last sentiment sounds a theme that was to be a constant in literary trials for decades to come, and which had already been emphasized by Pinard's prosecution: the idea that the more talented a writer is, the more pernicious his representation of immorality. Pinard repeatedly lauds Flaubert's talent as an artist, the better to indict him on moral grounds. He depicts the novel as "an admirable depiction in terms of talent, but an execrable depiction from the standpoint of morality [une peinture admirable sous le rapport du talent, mais une peinture exécrable au point de vue de la morale]" (627). Mrs. Tennant goes on, similarly, to wonder "why on earth reveal all that is petty and miserable: no one can have read this book without feeling more unhappy, and more nasty [à quoi bon faire des révélations de tout ce qui est mesquin, et misérable: personne n'a pu lire ce livre sans se sentir plus *malheureux*, et plus *mauvais*]." She nonetheless concludes her letter amicably, with the hope that Flaubert's career "will be employed toward something *good* [sera employée à quelque chose de *bon*]."[25]

Several months earlier, before the trial, in December 1856, one Mlle Leroyer de Chantepie wrote Flaubert a fan letter just after the completion of *Madame Bovary* in serialized form in *La Revue de Paris*. This letter, which ended up inaugurating a long and somewhat improbable correspondence between the two, expresses essentially the opposite of Gertrude Tennant's assessment of the novel. Mlle Leroyer de Chantepie, another bored provincial woman, although in her case never married (twenty years older than Flaubert, she was herself a novelist, and an established old maid), at once identifies fully with Emma Bovary and finds in the novel an excellent moral lesson. Her letter anticipates with remarkable exactitude many of the terms of Sainte-Beuve's essay, published some six months later; the similarities between the two readings, which reach different conclusions, point once again to the extent of cultural consensus on the function of literature. Sainte-Beuve concludes his essay with an analogy that became a commonplace, the pen as scalpel: "Son and brother of distinguished physicians, M. Gustave Flaubert wields his pen as others wield the scalpel [Fils et frère de médecins distingués, M. Gustave Flaubert tient la plume

comme d'autres le scalpel]" (349). Mlle Leroyer de Chantepie had used
the same metaphor in her first letter to Flaubert:

> Ah! sir, where have you learned this perfect knowledge of human nature, it
> is a scalpel applied to the heart, to the soul, it is, alas! the world in all its
> hideousness. The characters are real, too real, since none of them uplifts the
> soul, nothing is consoling in this drama that leaves us with an immense de-
> spair, but also a severe warning. Here is the moral that emerges from it:
> women should stick to their duty, no matter what the cost.

> [Ah! monsieur, où donc avez-vous pris cette parfaite connaissance de la na-
> ture humaine, c'est le scalpel appliqué au coeur, à l'âme, c'est, hélas! le
> monde dans toute sa hideur. Les caractères sont vrais, trop vrais, car aucun
> d'eux ne relève l'âme, rien ne console dans ce drame qui ne laisse qu'un
> immense désespoir, mais aussi un sévère avertissement. Voici la morale qui
> ressort de ceci: les femmes doivent rester attachées à leurs devoirs quoi qu'il
> leur en coûte.] (Flaubert, *Correspondance* 2:655)

Senard's defense speech, of course, heavily emphasizes the reading put
forth in this last sentence. From the scalpel to the idea of total realism in
which no character offers a consoling view of humanity or human existence, though, this letter points out the same qualities later cited by
Sainte-Beuve, except that where the critic, like the tribunal, sees moral
flaws, Mlle Leroyer de Chantepie finds both realist accuracy and morally
positive value in this negative depiction. Her evaluation of the novel is di-
ametrically opposed to the reading (or partial reading) of Gertrude Tennant, but this is because—like the defense and the prosecution in
Flaubert's trial and in later trials—both apply essentially the same criteria
to their ultimate judgment. These were, what is more, the criteria applied
as well by all other contemporary readers, with a single exception.

The one reader whose assessment diverges radically from the rest during this period is Charles Baudelaire. Baudelaire's article on *Madame Bovary* did not appear until October 1857, in the journal *L'Artiste* (the editor
of which was Théophile Gautier, dedicatee of *Les Fleurs du mal* and for
some time the most vocal proponent of art for art's sake in France); its
publication had been delayed by his own trial. This essay is the only contemporary account written in accordance with Flaubert's own view of the
function of criticism, as he had expressed it in a letter to Louise Colet:
"Criticism must be like natural history, *with absence of moralism* [Il faut faire
de la critique comme on fait de l'histoire naturelle, *avec absence d'idée
morale*]" (October 12, 1853; *Correspondance* 2:450). (Of course, the impera-
tive of leaving aside moral concerns is itself a moral stance, but in this context it is impossible to exit the realm of morality even in paradox.) After

fulsomely congratulating the judicial system on its excellent taste in exculpating Flaubert, and praising Flaubert for having taken on the mantle
of Balzac and created a work of art out of the most banal, unlyrical of subjects, Baudelaire responds to the major criticisms that had been leveled at
the book. He takes on the most common accusation against *Madame Bovary*, that is, the complaint voiced repeatedly, among others by Pinard in
his prosecution speech and Sainte-Beuve in his review, that the novel lacks
a moral center of gravity:

> Where is he, the proverbial and legendary character meant to explain the
> fable and direct the understanding of the reader? In other words, where is
> the prosecution speech?

> [Où est-il, le personnage proverbial et légendaire, chargé d'expliquer la
> fable et diriger l'intelligence du lecteur? En d'autres termes, où est le
> réquisitoire?]

He dispatches this objection by terming it an absurdity, an "eternal and incorrigible confusion of functions and genres [éternelle et incorrigible
confusion des fonctions et des genres]." That is, the novel was prosecuted
because it lacked an internal prosecution; this was to confuse literature
with other forms of public discourse. Baudelaire goes on to explain:

> A true work of art has no need for a prosecution speech. The logic of the
> work suffices for all postulations of morality, and it is left up to the reader to
> draw conclusions from the conclusion.

> [Une véritable oeuvre d'art n'a pas besoin de réquisitoire. La logique de
> l'oeuvre suffit à toutes les postulations de la morale, et c'est au lecteur de
> tirer les conclusions de la conclusion.] (*Œuvres complètes*, 2:81–82)

Baudelaire does not, however, simply defend the novel in his article. He
also offers a reading of *Madame Bovary* according to which the great
strength of the work lies in the fact that in Emma Bovary, Flaubert has
created a great heroine whose greatness lies in her sexual ambiguity. She
represents, in Baudelaire's view, an idealized version of Flaubert himself.[26]
"Like Athena emerging fully armed from Zeus's head, this bizarre androgyne retains all the seductions of a virile soul in a charming feminine body
[Comme la Pallas armée, sorti du cerveau de Zeus, ce bizarre androgyne a
gardé toutes les séductions d'une âme virile dans un charmant corps
féminin]" (ibid., 81). As we shall see in the next chapter, Baudelaire's taste
for masculine women in literature was a major factor in his own prosecution and conviction. In terms of Emma Bovary, his reading of her as mas-

culine, a female dandy, was a first. Numerous critics, along with Ernest Pinard, had complained that she was licentious, libidinous, and given free range to do as she liked, unconstrained by either her dimwitted, indulgent husband or her malicious author. No one before Baudelaire had characterized her as masculine; instead, she had been taken to represent femininity unleashed. In his reading of Emma Bovary's androgyny Baudelaire identifies one of the crucial elements in his own trial, and indeed in his own work: his characterization of Flaubert's heroine is in the end a more accurate depiction of the lesbians that he celebrates in two of the suppressed *Fleurs* than Emma Bovary herself. Baudelaire's portrayal of the latter also, though, anticipates a factor that would play an important role in almost all the literary trials to come during the next hundred years. Repeatedly during the course of the following decades literary works were brought to court in part because the men and women depicted in them refused to know their sexual place.

Perhaps predictably, therefore, the androgyny that Baudelaire sees in Emma Bovary was one of the many aspects of the novel that posed problems when Vincente Minnelli was trying to bring the story to the screen in Hollywood in 1949. What makes this film such a remarkable example of history's capacity for eccentric self-repetition is that, even as the filmmakers were able to bring their project to fruition only after coming up with the idea of framing it with the story of the trial, and even as their version of the trial was itself a testimony to the fact that many of the factors at issue in 1857 had since mutated into cliché, Minnelli and company were still only able to get their *Madame Bovary* past the censors by greatly changing the plot and characters. The strictures of the Hays Code in operation in 1949 were very similar to the criteria applied to Flaubert's novel in 1857. Consequently, the film that was the result of prolonged negotiations between the filmmakers and the Production Code office looks as though it were the product of some strange cinematic collaboration between Pinard and Senard. Since the aspects of the novel deemed objectionable by the imperial prosecutor are also, for the most part, those that had to be changed before the film could be passed by the Production Office, Minnelli's *Madame Bovary* bears more than a passing resemblance to the defense attorney's characterization of the novel during the trial. In this respect, therefore, although it was not Flaubert himself who delivered the speech, and although many of James Mason's arguments were not advanced in 1857, the story as it appears in the film under the guise of evidence for the defense is remarkably accurate.

One of the most salient differences between the trial as recorded by Flaubert's stenographer in 1857 and the trial as represented in the 1949 film is that the central issue in the former is adultery, whereas the latter emphasizes artistic integrity. The arguments between Pinard and Senard in 1857 are grounded, as we have seen, in a disagreement not over whether Flaubert has the right to depict objectionable truths in the service of art, but over whether or not the depiction of Emma Bovary's adulterous liaisons serves a morally positive purpose, moreover one sufficiently uplifting to justify the novel's lingering over her sins. The prosecution maintains that the novel provides a glorification of adultery and a debasement of marriage. Pinard is so intent on proving this that he performs an obvious misreading of a line from the book. In his argument for the prosecution he quotes from a passage describing the boredom that sets in for both parties once Emma's liaison with Léon has run its course:

> They knew each other too well to experience those surprises that multiply the enchantments of possession. She was as disgusted by him as he was tired of her. Emma rediscovered in adultery all the tedium of marriage.

> [Ils se connaissaient trop pour avoir ces ébahissements de possession qui en centuplent la joie. Elle était aussi dégoûtée de lui qu'il était fatigué d'elle. Emma retrouvait dans l'adultère toutes les platitudes du mariage.] (*Madame Bovary* [Pléiade], 556, cited by Pinard, 628)

Pinard cites this last sentence and then draws the following conclusion from it: "Tedium of marriage, poetry of adultery! Sometimes it's the defilements of marriage, sometimes its tedium, but always we find the poetry of adultery! [Platitudes du mariage, poésie de l'adultère! Tantôt c'est la souillure du mariage, tantôt ce sont ses platitudes, mais c'est toujours la poésie de l'adultère]" (628). His precedent for this evident mischaracterization is a previously cited passage, which includes the phrase "the defilements of marriage and the disillusions of adultery [les souillures du mariage et les désillusions de l'adultère]" (497).

Here we see the crux of the prosecution's case: what made Flaubert's novel objectionable lies somewhere between these two pronouncements cited by Pinard. On the one hand we have the reversal implicit in the phrase "the defilements of marriage and the disillusions of adultery [les souillures du mariage et les désillusions de l'adultère]," which suggests that between marriage and adultery, the former is more sullying than the latter, which leads to mere disillusion. Pinard points out the reversal offered by this phrase, noting that "there are those who might have said: the disillusions of marriage and the defilements of adultery [il y en a qui auraient dit: les désillusions du mariage et les souillures de l'adultère]" (625). He adds: "you have just heard about the defilements of marriage; you are about to be shown adultery in all its poetry, in its ineffable seductions [on vous a parlé tout à l'heure des souillures du mariage; on va vous montrer encore l'adultère dans toute sa poésie, dans ses ineffables séductions]" (497). On the other hand, though, we have the sentence that he then goes on to quote: "Emma rediscovered in adultery all the tedium of marriage [Emma retrouvait dans l'adultère toutes les platitudes du mariage]," which establishes an equivalence between adultery and marriage on the grounds that they are equally unsatisfying. Here Pinard draws his conclusion, as though he had found both phrases in the novel: "Tedium of marriage, poetry of adultery! [Platitudes du mariage, poésie de l'adultère!]." It is not in fact Flaubert—or even Emma Bovary—who talks of the "poetry of adultery [poésie de l'adultère]," but Pinard himself, who has by this time repeated the expression often enough to make it sound as though it came from the book. Instead of exalting the poetic aspects of adultery in contrast to the flatness of marriage, the passages cited refer to the "defilements" of marriage, and the "tedium" of both marriage and adultery. Pinard attributes to the novel a poetics of adultery that is notably absent from it. Why does he present this mischaracterization of the lines he cites? The only plausible answer is that the prosecution was more likely to succeed if all ambiguity could be removed from the novel. More to the point, since the sentence "Emma rediscovered in adultery all the tedium of marriage [Emma retrouvait dans l'adultère toutes les platitudes du mariage]" is anything but ambiguous, his case could be won only if all possibility of latitude could be removed from the interpretation of Flaubert's intent.

According to the binary moral system that we have seen operating in all contemporary accounts of the novel except Baudelaire's, and which was to continue to dominate for more than a century (cf., e.g., the *Chatterley* trials in the late 1950s), a work that depreciates marriage, as this one obviously does, must necessarily, by the same token, glorify adultery. There is no room in this black-and-white scheme of things for a novel depreciating both marriage and adultery, and for that matter glorifying nothing at all, beyond its own austere style. Pinard, the tribunal, Sainte-Beuve, and the rest were all quick to notice that the novel contained no characters embodying moral virtue or any positive view at all. Adultery is no more exalted in the novel than is marriage. When push came to shove, though, the prosecution was unable, even as it cited passages clearly demonstrating this central aspect of the novel, to acknowledge that while marriage is represented as essentially empty, so is adultery. Pinard took an essentially amoral work, upholding no particular moral system, denigrating at once marriage and adultery, and depicted it as immoral, rejecting the prevailing system in favor of an alternative order, denigrating marriage in order to promote adultery, in accordance with the binary criteria in operation at the time. It is as though Pinard were trying to turn Flaubert into Sade, a writer the author of *Madame Bovary* greatly admired, but whom he was hardly imitating in this work.[27]

Minnelli and company ran up against the same set of problems when they set out to make their film. The Hays Office was no more alive to the nuances of Flaubert's story than the imperial prosecutor had been, and the criteria they employed in deciding what to let pass were familiar ones. In order to avoid a repetition of Pinard's charges, the story had to be refashioned into one that clearly denigrates adultery and, as far as possible, exalts marriage. The "General Principles" section of the Motion Picture Production Code of 1930 reads as follows:

1. No picture shall be produced that will lower the moral standards of those who see it. Hence the sympathy of the audience should never be thrown to the side of crime, wrongdoing, evil or sin.

2. Correct standards of life, subject only to the requirements of drama and entertainment, shall be presented.

3. Law, natural or human, shall not be ridiculed, nor shall sympathy be created for its violation.

This last principle explains why Minnelli's film begins at the very end of the prosecutor's speech. Since Pinard represented the government, if the case for the prosecution had been shown, it would have had to be either plausible, which would have compromised the point of the framing narrative, or else ridiculous, in which case the opening scene itself would have violated the code. But the first and second principles most clearly illustrate the extent to which the producers of *Madame Bovary* were up against similar objections to those leveled against Flaubert. In 1949 as in 1857, the moral standards of the audience were to be watched over, with particular reference to whether they would be lowered by being put into the position of sympathizing with "crime, wrongdoing, evil or sin," and toward this aim "correct standards of life" were to be presented. Under the rubric "Sex," in the section "Particular Applications," moreover, the code explicitly states that "the sanctity and the institution of marriage and home shall be upheld. Pictures shall not infer [*sic*] that low forms of sex relationships are the accepted or common thing." More precisely still, "Adultery, sometimes necessary plot material, must not be explicitly treated, or justified, or presented attractively."

Under these conditions it is surprising that the Hollywood version of *Madame Bovary* was made at all.[28] In order to make sure that adultery would not appear to be presented attractively, Minnelli and company were forced to renounce their original choice of the actress to play Emma Bovary, Lana Turner, because she was viewed by the Production Code office as too sexy. They settled on Jennifer Jones, who they felt would bring to the role "a strange and uncertain quality which would work well in the neu-

rotic part."[29] The filmmakers prided themselves on the "neurosis" and
"narcissism" they made into the crux of their portrayal of the heroine. The
film was filled with mirror imagery to underscore this theme, and the
scene for which it remains most famous, the ballroom scene, not only features spectacular mirror effects but also had "neurotic waltz" music written to order.[30] Nonetheless, and perhaps relatedly, the "masculine" qualities Baudelaire identified in the character shine through, and to a great
extent Minnelli's Emma Bovary resembles nothing so much as Scarlett
O'Hara. The resemblance between the two characters is, of course, accen-
tuated by the hoop skirts both wear: the costume designer was in fact the
same for both films (*Gone with the Wind* [1939] was also an MGM product).
Jennifer Jones's Emma schemes and plots her way through *Madame Bovary*
much like her predecessor, although one major difference between the
two heroines is that, however Machiavellian Scarlett O'Hara may be, *Gone
with the Wind* is not a story of adultery.[31] The examples of Emma Bovary
and Scarlett O'Hara, in any case, similarly illustrate the peculiar way in
which hyperbolic femininity and masculinity in female characters can be
conflated. In both cases attributes traditionally viewed as feminine (e.g.,
manipulativeness, seductiveness, and vanity), when pushed to a certain
point become figured as a masculine will to dominate. Baudelaire's list of
Emma's "virile qualities [qualités viriles]" amply demonstrates this, as his
final proof of her masculinity is her "immoderate taste for seduction, for
domination [goût immodéré de la séduction, de la domination]" (Baudelaire, *Oeuvres complètes*, 2:82).[32]

In trying to bring *Madame Bovary* to the screen, the filmmakers had to
contend with the obvious problems of how not to treat adultery explicitly—and even the few conjugal love scenes had to be toned down in accordance with the code's guidelines on "Scenes of Passion"[33]—or to present it attractively. Perhaps even more difficult was the obstacle of
"justification." The main reason the story of Emma Bovary had been seen
as dangerous in the hands of girls and married women in 1857, after all, is
that she is a sympathetic figure, and her adulterous forays are understand-
able in the context of her marriage. If the imperial prosecutor managed
to miss the fact that adultery is shown to be no more satisfying than marriage in the novel, then so presumably would most readers. Pinard had
complained about the characterization of Charles, noting that the absence of husbandly rigor contributes to the novel's moral anarchy ("I ask
you, can you stigmatize this woman in the name of conjugal honor, when
there is not a single word in which the husband does not acquiesce before
adultery? [Je vous le demande, est-ce au nom de l'honneur conjugal que
vous pouvez stigmatiser cette femme, quand il n'y pas dans le livre un seul
mot où le mari ne s'incline devant l'adultère]" [*Madame Bovary* (Pléiade),
632]).

Minnelli and company encountered the same problem, in the form of the Hays Code edict that adultery must not be justified. In the novel, Charles is in many ways an ideal husband: he is a dutiful breadwinner and deeply in love with his wife, to the point of being oblivious to her faults and misdeeds. Of course this greatly contributes to the book's subversive edge, since he is the very sort of husband a girl is supposed to pine for, and yet his wife remains dissatisfied to the point of suicide. Senard would have us believe that she is unhappy only because she has received an inappropriate education, read too many novels, and consequently become incapable of contentment in the real world. But Flaubert makes it clear that she has, in addition to her romantic fantasies, real reasons for her discontent, chief among them her husband's personality: "Charles's conversation was as flat as a sidewalk, and ordinary ideas trotted forth on it, in everyday clothes, without inspiring emotion, laughter or reverie [La conversation de Charles était plate comme un trottoir de rue, et les idées de tout le monde y défilaient, dans leur costume ordinaire, sans exciter d'émotion, de rire ou de rêverie]" (*Madame Bovary* [Pléiade], 328). In other words, he is irremediably boring, and therefore his blind devotion serves only to irritate. A faithful representation of Flaubert's novel was impossible in Hollywood in 1949, for this reason alone: Flaubert's characterization of Charles can easily be seen as justifying Emma's adultery.

The film's most striking departure from the book is that both major characters undergo radical transformation. It was not enough that Emma be made more neurotic than sexy. In order to make sure the film would not appear to justify adultery, Charles had to become an attractive figure. This was accomplished on every level. He is played by Van Heflin, a handsome actor who served as romantic lead in many pictures during the same era: two years earlier, in *Possessed* (1947), he played a rake whose seduction and abandonment of Joan Crawford had been enough to drive the latter mad. What is more, the plot itself is greatly modified so as to make Emma's adultery clearly unjustified as well as unattractive. In the film, when he asks Emma to marry him, Charles explicitly warns her of his flaws. "Emma, listen to me before you say anything," he tells her. "I'm easy to get along with and I'll be a good husband, but I'm . . . I'm . . . not very exciting." This speech does not just serve the evident purpose of spelling things out for the more feeble-minded members of the viewing public. It also demonstrates a degree of candid self-awareness on the part of Charles, which means both that Emma knows full well what she is getting, and furthermore that what she is getting is not in fact the genuinely boring, completely unself-aware Charles depicted in the novel. She replies, not altogether implausibly: "Charles, Charles, you're the handsomest, most distinguished man in all this world." The scene departs from the book in a number of ways, among them that Flaubert depicts Charles asking her father, and not Emma herself, for her hand, nor does he show us her immediate reaction.

But this much can be put down to cinematic expediency. What the changes more significantly indicate is that in the film Emma can have no subsequent cause for complaint, and therefore her adultery appears as entirely unjustified, and even unjustifiable. No matter how charming, beautiful (and French: Frenchness serving for the American viewer as a reinforcement of the urbanity Emma sees in Rodolphe) Louis Jourdan may be, the discrepancy between him and Van Heflin is a mere nuance compared to the unbridgeable chasm between the dull, devoted Charles and the raffish Rodolphe of the novel.[34] (James Mason's Flaubert lies somewhere between Heflin and Jourdan in charm; and he too is foreign, as is the actor playing Leon). In fact, it is not clear from the book what Charles looks like. He is physically described only as an awkward adolescent in the opening scene, and even so only peripherally: we learn about his famous hat, his clothes, and his shoes, but almost nothing of his actual person. And, since his initial meetings with Emma are depicted from his point of view, we are only privy to her later ruminations on his shortcomings, never to the physical impression he makes. This is very different from Flaubert's early notes, in which he specifies that Charles is attractive: "At first she loves her husband who is handsome enough—well built and not bad looking [Aime d'abord son mari qui est un assez beau garçon—bien fait & bellâtre]."[35] Once this and almost all other physical descriptions of the character were removed from the text, Charles could only be visualized in accordance with his character. In Claude Chabrol's very literal 1991 film version, played by Jean-François Balmer, Charles is heavily built and lacking in physical charm.

The Minnelli *Madame Bovary* presents a Charles who is good looking and solidly self-aware. He is not without flaws, certainly, but they are not the same ones depicted in the novel. The Vaubyessard ball scene, for instance, is in both book and film the one occasion on which Emma manages briefly to taste the sort of life she has imagined herself living. In this scene in the film Charles gets drunk and makes a fool of himself, loudly claiming his right to dance with his wife, who is busy blending in with the aristocratic crowd. In the same scene in the novel, Emma forbids him to dance, specifically to preclude his embarrassing her: it is as though she had seen Minnelli's film and were trying to avoid the mistakes her cinematic counterpart makes ("But you've lost your mind! People would make fun of you, don't make a spectacle of yourself [Mais tu as perdu la tête! On se moquerait de toi, reste à ta place]," she tells him when he mentions dancing [*Madame Bovary* [Pléiade], 336]). While she dances away, perhaps to some fictional equivalent of the "neurotic waltz," and enjoys her beatific glimpse of the good life, he spends five hours looking on at the whist tables, understanding nothing of what he sees (340). Charles's drunken humiliation in the film certainly makes better cinema than what Flaubert describes, but this added aspect of the scene also emphasizes Emma's perfidious neglect of her husband, along with the latter's active, albeit inelegant, devotion to her, whereas in the book he remains inertly passive. The spectator's sympathy is necessarily thrown toward the awkward Charles rather than the ambitious, fickle Emma.

Similarly motivated changes are to be found in almost every frame of the film. One notable omission is the notorious *fiacre* scene, in which Emma and Léon have their first assignation in a hired carriage that roves around Rouen as they (presumably) disport themselves inside. This passage had been deemed too suggestive for the *Revue de Paris*: the editors removed it—among many other, less obviously significant passages—enraging Flaubert and prompting him to insert a note in the journal saying that the work had been cut and was to be considered as fragments rather than a whole. The scene's absence from the work as published in 1856 did not prevent Pinard, even as he lauded the discretion of the editors, from citing the censored passage during the trial, despite the fact that it had not appeared in print. Senard responded by quoting similar, more explicit passages from well-regarded works. One of the ironies of the *fiacre* scene was that its omission from the *Revue de Paris* seems to have been what attracted the government's notice in the first place. Another is that the passage contains almost nothing but a description of a carriage wandering the streets. In this case it is abundantly clear that, as Charles Rembar memorably put it, "pornography is in the groin of the beholder."[36]

The changes made in the plot of *Madame Bovary* for the 1949 film are far too many to catalogue here in full; I will confine myself to mentioning a few of the more salient omissions. The 1857 charge of offenses against religious morality (*outrage à la morale religieuse*) found its equivalent in the Hays Code's strictures on religion, with the notable result that the episode in which Emma tries vainly to seek spiritual guidance from the village priest, who is too blindly materialist even to understand what she wants, was simply removed from the story. Two other major elements from the book that were dropped from the film involve the same details cited by the realist Champfleury as being offensively realistic: the pustulant beggar and the clubfoot operation. Both involve medical descriptions. As the son and brother of prominent physicians, and having played as child next to the autopsy room of the Hôtel-Dieu in Rouen, Flaubert was much given to detailed accounts of unpleasant physical phenomena. The blind beggar makes his first appearance shortly after the *fiacre* scene, reappears at intervals during the third section, and is heard singing his mocking song about love as Emma lies dying. This character has been interpreted in various ways, but whatever ultimate meaning one may assign to him, it is clear that he accompanies and in some sense comments on Emma's downfall. What doubtless prompted the filmmakers to leave him out of the 1949 version was not his symbolic value but the same aspect that led Champfleury to suggest that Flaubert omit the character, or at least the detailed account of his condition, from future editions.

Even though the filmmakers would not have had to reproduce the truly revolting aspects of Flaubert's description, under the rubric "Vulgarity" in the Hays Code we find the following: "The treatment of low, disgusting, unpleasant, though not necessarily evil, subjects should always be subject to the dictates of good taste and a regard for the sensibilities of the audience." The blind beggar is unavoidably low, disgusting, and unpleasant. His role in the novel is precisely to violate the dictates of good taste and offend the sensibilities of the audience, and he continues to do so long after Emma's death. In the last chapter the pharmacist Homais, having tried in vain to treat his condition, expends a great deal of energy attempting to get rid of the vagrant. He conducts an increasingly sensationalistic newspaper campaign against the beggar, has him jailed, and finally packs him off to a hospice. In this sense the blind beggar incarnates the return of the repressed. The endless irruption of reality in its most incurably unpleasant aspects is what he represents in the book, which is why even the foremost champion of realism had objected to his depiction in 1857, and it is also why he does not appear in the 1949 film.

Champfleury had objected to the excessively detailed description of surgery in the club foot operation scene on the same grounds; in the words of the Hays Code, it is disgusting and unpleasant (although surely not "low"—which qualifier carries a suggestion of socioeconomic disapprobation—as the beggar is). The passage runs as follows: Homais convinces Charles to try his hand at fixing the club foot of Hippolyte, the servant at the inn. Emma too encourages Charles to attempt the operation, reasoning that if her husband becomes a professional success she will at least be able to feel proud of him: "She longed to lean on something more solid than love [Elle ne demandait qu'à s'appuyer sur quelque chose de plus solide que l'amour]" (*Madame Bovary* [Pléiade], 450). In the novel Charles performs the operation, fails miserably, and there follow several pages of detailed description of the gangrenous consequences. A surgeon eventually has to be called in to amputate the leg. It was clear that this could not be shown, or even suggested, in the film. Even aside from the interdiction of disgusting and unpleasant material, the "Repellant Subjects" section of the Hays Code includes a ban on surgical operations.[37]

The filmmakers accordingly modified the scene. Instead of performing the operation, Charles at the last moment declines to go through with it, announcing that he knows the operation will not accomplish its promised miracles and that he therefore refuses to attempt what is beyond his capacities. Only those who have read the book, of course, can measure the full force of this change, since only in the context of the novel is it clear from what dire consequences Hippolyte, as well as Charles himself, have been spared. In his autobiography Minnelli mentions this decision, noting that "we thought this sequence would be too gory to be shown," but maintains that the result was psychologically true to the novel, since Emma is as disgusted by Charles's refusal to perform the operation as she had been in the book by its failure (*I Remember It Well*, 206). This somewhat disingenuous explanation fails to take into account, however, the fact that Charles emerges from the scene in the film looking like a hero, with a courageous awareness of his own limitations that is entirely absent from the book and serves to bolster the representation of Emma's adultery as unattractive and unjustifiable. Indeed, this aspect of his character places Minnelli's Charles Bovary in the peculiarly American lineage that would find its apotheosis in the heroically simpleminded Forrest Gump.

As all these changes made in the plot of *Madame Bovary* in 1949 demonstrate, the Motion Picture Production Code performed a similar function from the 1930s into the 1960s in American film to that of the judicial prosecution of novels in France a century earlier, except that it was much more efficient, in part because it was much less public. What is so exceptional about Minnelli's *Madame Bovary* is that it takes a story already filled with historical ironies and adds its own peculiar twentieth-century twist. Flaubert had been reluctant to publish at all; his first novel got him dragged into court and made him famous, for what he considered to be the wrong reasons. The editors of the *Revue de Paris* insisted on censoring *Madame Bovary* because they were afraid of getting into trouble with the government; the cuts they made attracted official attention and brought about the prosecution. The most notorious literary trial of the nineteenth century involved a novel whose central theme is the dangerous consequences of reading too much.

Minnelli's film opens with one of those ornate text-panels often used in historical films, sporting the legend: "In 1857 there was a scandal in Paris, and a trial before the law. A book had been published." The factual inaccuracies begin here, of course, since a book had not actually been published, only a less photogenic *feuilleton* (nor did the book once published resemble the huge leather-bound tome brandished in the opening sequence), but that is not the point. The point is that by the time the film was made *Madame Bovary* had become a great classic, which was why the film had been proposed in the first place. Therefore, the idea that the novel had created a scandal and prompted a lawsuit had come to seem ludicrous, even as the reasons for the trial retained full currency. The 1949 film partakes of what might be termed chronological chauvinism, a view of history in which the strangeness of the past is at once demonized and trivialized, and we of the present are ultimately invited to congratulate ourselves for living in such repression-free times. The history of censorship lends itself with particular ease to this sort of approach, and Minnelli's *Madame Bovary* represents an especially salient example of its absurdity. Despite MGM's motto *Ars gratia artis,* and despite James Mason's florid speeches about the ultimate triumph of Art and Truth, the film could be made only once Flaubert's art had been transformed in a way that Ernest Pinard would fully have approved.

CHAPTER TWO

Charles Baudelaire

Florist of Evil

All those bourgeois imbeciles who are constantly saying "immoral, immorality, morality in art" and other nonsense make me think of Louise Villedieu, a two-bit whore who once came with me to the Louvre, where she'd never been, started blushing, covering her face, and pulling me by the sleeve, asked me, in front of the immortal statues and paintings, how such indecency could be on public display.

BAUDELAIRE, *My Heart Laid Bare* [*Mon coeur mis à nu*]

In 1949, the year Minnelli's *Madame Bovary* came out in the United States, the six poems that had been removed from Baudelaire's *Fleurs du mal* by court order in 1857 were rehabilitated by the French judicial system. A law passed in 1946, specifically geared to Baudelaire's case, allowed such previous decisions to be overturned, and the poet and his six poems, along with the publisher and printer, were duly exonerated (posthumous restitution of their fines was not, however, included in the new ruling). The rehabilitation does not exactly state that the original verdict had been wrong, but implicitly places matters in historical perspective, decreeing that the condemned poems could no longer be held to pose the public danger they had seemed to represent a century earlier.

This ruling is remarkable in a number of ways: laws are not usually written with particular cases in mind, nor are verdicts often overturned long after the fact on the basis that aesthetics and mores have changed in the interim. (Indeed, if this last became standard practice the courts would soon be busy rehabilitating witches and heretics, not to mention Socrates, Joan of Arc, Sacco and Vanzetti.) Even so, the most notable aspect of the rehabilitation in this context may well be that its text suggests the original judges had erred because they had mistakenly applied a form of "realism":

while due to their originality, certain depictions may have alarmed some sensibilities at the time of first publication of *Les Fleurs du mal* and appeared to the judges to offend decency, this reading, which depends exclusively on a *realistic interpretation* of the poems and neglects their symbolic meaning, has been shown to be arbitrary.

[si certaines peintures ont pu, par leur originalité, alarmer quelques esprits à l'époque de la première publication des *Fleurs du mal* et apparaître aux premiers juges comme offensant les bonnes moeurs, une telle appréciation, ne s'attachant qu'à *l'interprétation réaliste* de ces poèmes et négligeant leur sens symbolique, s'est révélée de caractère arbitraire.] [Emphasis added.][1]

Here, it seems, a "realist" interpretation is a literal one, which goes to show, if further evidence were needed, just how elastic the term *realist* can be. The original judgment which this new finding annuls, and which it quotes in the course of overturning it, cites "a vulgar realism offensive to decency [un réalisme grossier offensant pour la pudeur]" in Baudelaire's poems as the decisive factor in the verdict. The judges in 1949 were accusing the original tribunal of finding an inappropriate realism in *Les Fleurs du mal* only because it was interpreting too realistically. They were also suggesting that their predecessors were bad readers of Baudelaire because at the time of his trial "Baudelaire" as a literary touchstone did not yet exist, nor did the Symbolist movement he inspired. To read Baudelaire properly, and therefore to find him innocent of the charges leveled against him, it seems, it was necessary to have been educated in a post-Baudelairean cultural climate.

The formal rehabilitation was at any rate somewhat moot, since despite the fact that in principle the 1857 judgment had made it illegal to publish or circulate the six inculpated poems in France, editions of *Les Fleurs du mal* including those poems had proliferated following the passage of Baudelaire's magnum opus into the public domain in 1917. During Baudelaire's lifetime (he died in 1867) the suppressed poems were published along with new poems in a volume entitled *Les Épaves* in 1866 in Belgium. A shipment of *Épaves* was seized in Lille in 1868, subject to a new trial in that city, and destroyed. The second (1861) and third (1868) editions of *Les Fleurs du mal* omitted the six condemned poems, but the volumes grew successively larger as the author kept adding new poems to take their place. The first critical edition of the collection, including the condemned poems as well as a commentary on the trial, was published in France by the *Nouvelle Revue française* in 1917. By the time of its official rehabilitation in 1949 *Les Fleurs du mal* had become a centrally established classic, France's most venerable poetic monument. Baudelaire's collected poems, for instance—including those that had been suppressed—inaugurated Gallimard's Pléiade collection, the closest approximation of a published canon in France, in 1931; his prose formed a second volume the following year.[2] Georges Pompidou's 1961 *Anthologie de la poésie française,* an official inventory if ever there was one given that its editor became president of France in 1969, features far more poems by Baudelaire than by any other author. What is more, among the forty-three poems under his name there figure two of the suppressed poems, "Les Bijoux" and "À celle qui est trop gaie." Pompidou's anthology is still in print, and still a standard reference.

Baudelaire's case is in many ways analogous to Flaubert's, not only because of the accident of history that caused them both to be brought up on identical charges in the course of the same year and prosecuted by the same man, albeit with somewhat different results. Both writers were born in 1821, and it may be said without much exaggeration that *Madame Bovary* and *Les Fleurs du mal,* both prosecuted by the French government in the person of Ernest Pinard in 1857, ended up bringing about a revolution that would change the face of literature definitively. Nor do the similarities, both aesthetic and biographical, end there. Julian Barnes presents a page-long biographical passage, beginning "Born 1821, into a professional family," and ending with "He described himself as an Old Romantic, considered he was old at forty, and greatly disliked steel-nibbed pens." He defies the reader to discern whether this description characterizes Flaubert or Baudelaire; in fact, despite its odd specificity, it does service for both. "At times the parallels are eerie," Barnes notes, adding, "at times, you almost feel sorry for Ernest Pinard, now remembered only for shooting himself in the foot twice in the same year."[3] In terms of their place in literary history the similarities are striking as well, since both authors are generally credited with having inaugurated modern, and also modernist, literature. There are, however, major biographical divergences, and these are echoed in their literary differences. Flaubert led a very comfortable, if reclusive, existence in his family home in Normandy, with occasional excursions to Parisian salon society, whereas Baudelaire was extravagantly bohemian, constantly hard-up for cash, and at the behest of his family remained a legal minor for his entire short life. Despite their common preoccupations and despite the fact that both were dragged into court on the same charges and prosecuted by the same man in the same year, there is also an immense difference between a novel and a collection of poems, and in the context of France in the mid nineteenth century it is a different difference, so to speak, than what we might imagine today.

On August 17, 1857, having just discovered that Baudelaire was being prosecuted, Flaubert wrote the poet a letter in which he notes the following: "This is a new one: prosecuting a book of verse! Up until now the legal system left poetry alone [Ceci est du nouveau: poursuivre un livre de vers! Jusqu'à présent la magistrature laissait la poésie fort tranquille]." He adds: "I am thoroughly outraged [Je suis grandement indigné]."[4] Baudelaire's was in fact the first volume of serious poetry to be brought up on obscenity charges in France. (Béranger's repeated problems in the 1820s did not count, because he wrote light verse or song lyrics, an entirely different genre.) Subsequently (as also discussed in the first chapter), Maupassant and Verlaine came up on similar charges on the basis of poems, but *Les Fleurs du mal* was the first collection of lyric poetry to run into trouble with the French government in the nineteenth century.

The volume first appeared for sale on June 25, 1857. Baudelaire sent Flaubert a copy, for which the novelist thanked him in a letter dated July 13, in which he notes that "the first thing I did was devour your book from cover to cover, like a scullery maid with a serial novel [J'ai d'abord dévoré votre volume d'un bout à l'autre, comme une cuisinière fait d'un feuilleton]." Now, having had the time to reread the collection less frenetically, Flaubert delivers his appreciation: "You have found the way to rejuvenate romanticism. You resemble no one (which is the best of all traits) [Vous avez trouvé le moyen de rajeunir le romantisme. Vous ne ressemblez à personne (ce qui est la première de toutes les qualités)]." He adds a list of favorite poems, none of them, as it happened, among those that would shortly be inculpated, then concludes by remarking: "In sum, what especially pleases me in your book is that art predominates [En résumé, ce qui me plaît avant tout dans votre livre, c'est que l'art y prédomine]."[5] This was, clearly, the highest of compliments for both these writers, for whom Art was the supreme value. Flaubert, who had explicitly set out to make Art out of banality, insisted that beauty resided not in subject but in style, and famously dreamed of writing "a book about nothing [un livre sur rien]," sustained by its style alone: "The most beautiful works are those that have the least subject matter [Les oeuvres les plus belles sont celles où il y a le moins de matière]," he writes to Louise Colet, adding: "That's why there are neither beautiful nor nasty subjects and one could almost take as an axiom, from the viewpoint of pure Art, that there aren't any at all, style being all by itself an absolute manner of seeing things [C'est pour cela qu'il n'y a ni beaux ni vilains sujets et qu'on pourrait presque établir comme axiome, en se posant au point de vue de l'Art pur, qu'il n'y en a aucun, le style étant à lui tout seul une manière absolue de voir les choses]."[6] *Madame Bovary* is not the fantasized book about nothing. In the context of his letter "nothing" is a positive attribute, a liberation of Art, pure style, from the shackles of reference, in something like an anticipation of Mallarmé's ethereal poetics, but doubly impossible because applied to the most prosaic of media. His first published novel is, however, among other things, a book about nothingness: the boredom of provincial bourgeois life. While writing the story of Emma Bovary, Flaubert repeatedly complains to his correspondents about how hard it is to make art out of vulgarity and platitude, and for this reason he is especially well placed to appreciate the work of a poet, one of whose chief obsessions was a peculiarly modern form of "alchemy," which consisted in making gold out of mud: "I have kneaded mud and made it into gold [J'ai pétri de la boue et j'en ai fait de l'or]," as Baudelaire puts it in one of a number of variations on this theme.[7] Between the muddy boredom of bourgeois provincial life that animates Emma Bovary's dreams of romantic escape, and Baudelaire's "mud," certainly, the difference is one of tone as well as genre and subject. Flaubert is at heart an ironist, whereas Baudelaire sets out to shock. In some essential sense, though, the project of both *Madame Bovary* and *Les Fleurs du mal*—and it is perhaps this above all that makes them the founding texts of modern literature—was to take "mud" and turn it into art. For Flaubert, whose ultimate fantasy was to make gold out of nothing at all, "mud" would mean the metaphorically viscous mediocrity of contemporary existence; for Baudelaire the viscosity is, as we shall see, more disturbingly literal.

Later in the century, Zola, whom one of Proust's characters refers to as "The Homer of sewage [l'Homère de la vidange]" (recalling Barbey d'Aurevilly's similar epithet "The Michelangelo of crap [le Michel-Ange de la crotte])," was repeatedly caricatured as writing on a chamber pot.[8] One of his indignant contemporaries called him, with admirable concision, a "monomaniacal coprographer [monomane coprographe]," adding hopefully that "this will be the last word and final judgment on the man and on his work [tel sera le dernier mot et le jugement final sur l'homme et sur l'oeuvre]."[9] This prophesy may not have proved entirely accurate, but the writing-as-defecation metaphor had staying power, even appearing in a 1992 biography of the novelist: "The desire to write grabbed him in the belly like diarrhea [L'envie d'écrire le saisit au ventre comme une colique]."[10] In his review of *The Belly of Paris* [*Le Ventre de Paris*], Zola's 1873 novel about les Halles, the fabled food market, Barbey d'Aurevilly laments that despite the vulgarity and "materialism" of Zola's latest effort, the worst is surely yet to come. "There is lower than the belly [Il y a plus bas que le ventre]," Barbey writes. "There is what goes into it and what comes out. Today we're given cold-cuts. Tomorrow, it will be sewage [Il y a ce qu'on y met et ce qui en sort. Aujourd'hui on nous donne de la charcuterie. Demain, ce sera de la vidange]."[11] Barbey situates the beginning of this "materialist" descent in the arts in Hugo's *Notre-Dame de Paris* (1831), and includes on his list of offenders Courbet and Manet in painting, and Baudelaire's "Une Charogne" in poetry (about which more in a moment), despite having been one of the poet's defenders in 1857.

In order to understand the complexity of relative unacceptabilities in this context, Barbey's indignation at Zola and other "materialists" should be read in the context of *Les Diaboliques*, the collection of stories for which he was brought up on obscenity charges in 1875. The book includes such scenarios as: an impassive young woman of good family who becomes so frenetically lascivious upon losing her virginity that she dies from excessive sexual exertions; a man who seals up his unfaithful mistress's sex with sealing wax; a woman who becomes a prostitute and deliberately contracts syphilis to exact revenge on her husband for having killed her lover and fed his heart to dogs; and a couple who fight over the preserved heart of their dead infant. Barbey was not merely, as we might assume, being hypocritical in throwing stones from such an obviously glass house. His criticism of Zola focuses on the sordid banality of the latter's subjects. Barbey also heartily disliked Flaubert, for the same reason: the grimy problems of the bourgeoisie, much less the working class, were not appropriate fodder for Art.

In contrast, Barbey appreciated Baudelaire, despite and even because of such excesses as "Une Charogne," because of the dandyism they shared. He recognized a kindred spirit in the poet in that their transgressions were similarly animated by a taste that Baudelaire spelled out in "Fusées": "What is intoxicating in bad taste is the aristocratic pleasure of displeasing [Ce qu'il y a d'enivrant dans le mauvais goût, c'est le plaisir aristocratique de déplaire]" (*Œuvres complètes*, 1:661). Flaubert and Zola were offensive in an entirely different way, one that was anything but aristocratic. They were accused of being democratic, an accurate charge in the case of Zola, but one that must have enraged the emphatically antidemocratic Flaubert.[12] The influential but now forgotten critic Armand de Pontmartin, who in the 1880s wrote that "the triumphs of democracy have dethroned the ideal in favor of realism [les triomphes de la démocratie ont détrôné l'idéal au profit du réalisme]," had warned in 1857: "M. Flaubert represents democracy in the novel. . . . *Madame Bovary* represents the unhealthy excitation of the senses and the imagination in discontented democracy [M. Flaubert, c'est la démocratie dans le roman. . . . *Madame Bovary*, c'est l'exaltation maladive des sens et de l'imagination dans la démocratie mécontente]."[13]

As opposed to Baudelaire's grandiose poeticization of the horrible or the over-the-top behavior inspired by sexual passion in *Les Diaboliques*, the "realist" trend in fiction concentrated on daily life and lingered over such unmentionable banalities as ordinary food. The very first cut the *Revue de Paris* editors asked Flaubert to make in *Madame Bovary* was a sentence in which Charles's mother sends her son a weekly care package of roast veal while he is a student; this was felt to be more than the reader needed to know.[14] Barbey's glib dismissal of Zola on the grounds that if cold cuts are discussed in literature sewage cannot be far behind is part of a widespread and long-lasting assumption that once art begins to break the boundaries of traditional *bienséance*, all hell will necessarily break loose, "hell" often taking on the contours of the lower digestive tract.

Attempts to escape an idealist conception of the function of literature, whatever the subject matter and whether they end up labeled "realism" or "naturalism," inevitably culminate in notions of writing as the very opposite of idealism, that is, of writing as taking on the subject most horrifyingly democratic and offensively foreign to an ideal vision of human life: shit. This is the version (albeit in general more delicately phrased) advanced by detractors of "realism" in its various guises, and as we shall see in the following chapters it was to become a leitmotif in literary obscenity trials in the twentieth century, for the very good reason that writers such as Joyce, Lawrence, and Miller took the idea and made it their own. Defecation had been a theme in overtly comedic (e.g., Rabelais) or otherwise transgressive (e.g., Sade) literature for centuries, but in the early twentieth century shit was consecrated, as it were, in the "serious" literature that took transgression as its byword and as a result paved the way for later "realism" and courted censorship.[15] This tradition began, in more subtle form, with the two now-classic works prosecuted by the French government in 1857. Flaubert discusses not only the nothingness of bourgeois life in the provinces but also in passing describes both banal foodstuffs and disgusting medical anomalies, which perturbed even Champfleury, the leading proponent of realism. Baudelaire, though, goes so far as to take putrefaction as a central theme, what is more in a genre traditionally devoted only to the loftiest of concerns. As one critic complained in 1869, "the reader holds his nose; the page stinks [le lecteur se bouche le nez; la page pue]."[16] Contrary to his stated design of turning mud into gold—or perhaps it would be more accurate to say because of it—Baudelaire was ultimately convicted of taking gold and turning it into mud, or worse.

In fact, as we have seen, he was convicted of realism. Like Flaubert, he rejected both the term and the idea: in the mid 1850s he writes notes for an essay to be entitled "Since Realism Exists [Puisque réalisme il y a]," opening with the observation "Champfleury wanted to play a joke on the human race [Champfleury a voulu faire une farce au genre humain]," and going on to take issue with what he identifies as Champfleury's nefarious brain-child, Courbet's application of it in painting, and the misleading vagueness of the term itself. He also mentions with ironic perplexity having been told that the term had been applied to him, "despite the fact that I have always tried not to deserve it [bien que je me sois toujours appliqué à le démériter]."[17] It is a much more surprising charge here than in Flaubert's case, because the genre in which the poet was writing might have seemed proof enough against such an accusation. By the same token, though, the fact that his work consisted of lyric poetry made his transgressions all the more transgressive. The imperial prosecutor himself never names the category of realism per se in his prosecution of Baudelaire, doubtless because literary realism was associated with novels. He opens his case by noting that "Charles Baudelaire does not belong to a school [Charles Baudelaire n'appartient pas à une école]," but he identifies his "principle, his theory [principe, sa théorie]," as being "to depict everything, to lay everything bare [de tout peindre, de tout mettre à nu]," and to this extent Pinard's characterization of Baudelaire is in accordance with the poet's own.[18] Toward the end of his speech, though, he exhorts the judges to react "against these growing tendencies, against this unhealthy fever of wanting to depict everything, to say everything, as though the law against offending public morality had been suspended, and as though that morality did not exist [contre ces tendances croissantes, mais certaines, contre cette fièvre malsaine qui porte à tout peindre, à tout décrire, à tout dire, comme si le délit d'offense à la morale publique était abrogé, et comme si cette morale n'existait pas]." Especially since he goes on to point out that a verdict of acquittal with blame is a gesture only, since "the public sees only the final result [que le public ne voit que le résultat final]," it is clear that he is inviting the tribunal to rectify the precedent set by Flaubert's verdict, which he suggests has paved the way for an unbridled literary attack on public morality (*Œuvres complètes*, 1:1209). The judges accordingly rose to the challenge, moreover putting the explicit label of realism on the tendency Pinard had described:

> The poet's error in terms of the goal he wished to attain and the course he pursued, however much stylistic effort he may have expended, however much blame precedes or follows his depictions, cannot obviate the unfortunate effect of the pictures he presents to the reader, which, in the relevant poems, lead necessarily to an excitation of the senses through a vulgar realism that offends decency.

> [Attendu que l'erreur du poète, dans le but qu'il voulait atteindre et dans la route qu'il a suivie, quelque effort de style qu'il ait pu faire, quel que soit le blâme qui précède ou qui suit ses peintures, ne saurait détruire l'effet funeste des tableaux qu'il présente au lecteur, et qui, dans les pièces incriminées, conduisent nécessairement à l'excitation des sens par un réalisme grossier et offensant pour la pudeur.] (*Œuvres complètes*, 1:1181–82)

As in the case of Flaubert and almost all the defense arguments in subsequent literary censorship trials, the cornerstone of Baudelaire's defense was the idea that although his work represented immorality, it was only in order better to warn against it. Nonetheless the tribunal found that his "realistic" depictions were bound to excite the senses—the verdict also cites the presence of "obscene and immoral passages or expressions [des passages ou expressions obscènes et immorales]" (1182)—and thus had to be suppressed. (As will be discussed in the next chapter, an echo of this sort of judgment can be heard in Judge Woolsey's decision allowing *Ulysses* into the United States in 1933: although his verdict sets a precedent by exculpating Joyce's novel partly on grounds of artistic merit, Woolsey also feels compelled to note that his friends who read the book found its depictions of sexuality to be "somewhat emetic" rather than "aphrodisiac.") While Flaubert had been assigned blame for his novel even as he was acquitted, it was not on quite the same grounds as those according to which the poet was convicted: the verdict in Flaubert's case does mention "a vulgar and often shocking realism [un réalisme vulgaire et souvent choquant]," a category very similar to that evoked in Baudelaire's judgment, but it goes on to assert that "there are limits that literature, *even the most frivolous*, must not cross, and which Gustave Flaubert and his codefendents do not seem to have taken sufficiently into account [il y a des limites que la littérature, *même la plus légère*, ne doit dépasser, et dont Gustave Flaubert et co-inculpés paraissent ne s'être pas suffisamment rendu compte]" (emphasis added).[19] In other words, Flaubert's "realism" was blameworthy despite the frivolity of the medium he was working in. Baudelaire, in contrast, had no excuse for introducing base reality into his work, which by virtue of its genre had no business trafficking in unpleasantness.

Given their common "realist" design, in any case—"realism" to be taken here as the literary representation of unseemly realities—it is not surprising that both ran into problems with the law, since the law at the time was intimately and overtly bound up with prevailing aesthetic guidelines (e.g., *Le Moniteur universel*'s status as at once most influential literary arbiter and official government organ). But again, because they were working in different genres, they ran into different problems, and this is one of the major reasons Baudelaire was convicted while Flaubert was acquitted. The novel was in the mid nineteenth century still viewed with a certain amount of suspicion, and Flaubert's jocular comparison of his first reading of *Les Fleurs du mal* with a scullery maid's feverish reading of a *feuilleton* in his first letter to Baudelaire gives some indication of the degree to which much of contemporary fiction was generally regarded as both lower-class and feminine. As Édouard Thierry puts it in an article in *Le Moniteur universel*, "The serial novel speaks for everyone. A book like *Les Fleurs du mal* is not meant for those who read serial novels [Le feuilleton parle pour tout le monde. Un livre comme *Les Fleurs du mal* ne s'adresse pas à tous ceux qui lisent le feuilleton]."[20] One of the provocative aspects of Flaubert's *cuisinière* reading a *feuilleton* analogy is that *Madame Bovary* itself had first appeared in serial form. Because the *Revue de Paris* was a weekly literary journal rather than a daily newspaper, read mostly by educated men rather than working-class women, though, Flaubert's own novel

was not classified as a *feuilleton* and therefore was in principle not implicated in the vividly inappropriate comparison of his first reading of
Baudelaire's volume to a cook's devouring of a newspaper serial. Nonetheless, novels in general were in 1857 still somewhat suspect, not entirely removed from the realm of the *feuilleton,* as the phrase "literature, even the
most frivolous [la littérature, même la plus légère]" in Flaubert's verdict
indicates. His correspondence too reflects this presumed guilt by association: shortly before his trial, sure that he would be convicted if only because of the government's dislike of *La Revue de Paris,* Flaubert wrote to
Émile Augier that "I especially need people in influential positions who
can attest that I am not in the business of writing books for hysterical
scullery maids [j'ai besoin surtout d'avoir des gens considérables par leur
fonction qui affirment que je n'ai pas pour industrie de faire des livres à
l'usage des cuisinières hystériques]."[21]

It was the fact that women, perhaps not hysterical servants but bourgeois girls and women, were the likely audience of *Madame Bovary* that
had gotten the book into trouble in the first place. Flaubert's work had not
been prosecuted because of its subject matter. The amorous and financial
problems of the provincial bourgeoisie, and the relations between the two
sets of problems, had already been amply treated by Balzac among others,
although with the important difference that most of Balzac's characters
spend their time attempting to marry for financial or social gain, whereas
Emma Bovary's problems start with her marriage. A scene in *Madame Bovary* itself highlights the novel's divergence from the standard theme of
marriage being the solution to women's problems rather than their cause.
Félicité the servant, faced with the spectacle of Emma's despair, tells her
the story of a woman whose similar symptoms, which had proved impervious to the ministrations of doctors and clergy alike, disappeared once she
was married. "But in my case, said Emma, I started feeling like this after I
got married [Mais, moi, reprenait Emma, c'est après le mariage que ça
m'est venu]" (*Madame Bovary* [Pléiade], 1:390–91). Flaubert's novel was
seen as dangerous for this reason: not so much because of its treatment of
adultery but because of its treatment of marriage; because of its relentlessly pessimistic approach to Emma's problems and its lack of any morally
redeeming viewpoint, character, or outcome.

Baudelaire, working in the much more traditionally exalted medium of
lyric poetry, faced a very different set of expectations. Lyric poetry was
still in the mid nineteenth century a major genre. By the early twentieth
century, the same period in which the novel was shaking off the remains
of its dubious, and dubiously feminine, reputation, poetry was becoming
increasingly marginal: as Walter Benjamin observes, "*Les Fleurs du mal* was
the last lyric work that had a European repercussion."[22] As we saw in previous chapters, the centerpiece of Pinard's prosecution of Flaubert was the

idea that the target audience, or at least the actual audience, of novels such as his was bound to be primarily female. The novel was therefore at once trivial as literature and, by the same token, important as a social phenomenon that had to be controlled, at the risk of dire consequences:

> Who are the readers of M. Flaubert's novel? Are they men interested in political and social economy? No! The light pages of *Madame Bovary* fall into even lighter hands, into the hands of girls, and sometimes married women.

> [Qui est-ce qui lit le roman de M. Flaubert? Sont-ce des hommes qui s'occupent d'économie politique et sociale? Non! Les pages légères de *Madame Bovary* tombent en des mains plus légères, dans les mains de jeunes filles, quelquefois des femmes mariées.] (*Madame Bovary* [Pléiade], 631–32)

No such argument was available to the imperial prosecutor in the case of Baudelaire. Lyric poetry was at the time a heavily masculine genre, read almost exclusively, at least in principle, by educated men: the very audience least in need of governmental protection, according to the traditional view of such matters. The "young person," that is, young girl or woman, was the exemplary figure to be protected from pernicious literary influences. Dickens summed up the idea under the label "Podsnappery" in the mid 1860s in *Our Mutual Friend*: "The question about everything was, would it bring a blush into the cheek of the young person?"[23] Baudelaire himself repeatedly makes ironic reference to this tradition, for instance in his various "Projets de préface" for the second (1861) edition of *Les Fleurs du mal*:

> This book was not written for my wives, my daughters, or sisters; nor for my neighbor's wives, daughters or sisters. I leave that task to those interested in confusing virtuous acts with beautiful language.

> [Ce n'est pas pour mes femmes, mes filles ou mes sœurs que ce livre a été écrit; non plus pour les femmes, les filles ou les sœurs de mon voisin. Je laisse cette fonction à ceux qui ont intérêt à confondre les bonnes actions avec le beau langage.][24]

The second attempt at a preface takes up the same theme: "The aim of poetry. This book is not made for my wives, my daughters or my sisters [Le but de la poésie. Ce livre n'est pas fait pour mes femmes, mes filles ou mes sœurs]" (182). Baudelaire's insistence on the plurality of his hypothetical wives, daughters, and sisters in these remarks (in fact he had no wives at all, nor any daughters or sisters) makes it clear that his stance toward such concerns was somewhat mocking, although he seems also to have been se-

rious in maintaining that the readership of his book was not intended to
be a feminine one. Many of the poems are actually addressed to women—
even, in the case of "L'invitation au voyage," a woman he calls "my child,
my sister [mon enfant, ma sœur],"—but of course the women for whom
these poems were written were already necessarily corrupt. His repeated
objection that the book was not meant to be read by women suggests that
Baudelaire subscribed to the idea that female readers might well be corrupted by a book such as his, which in this context means that reading his
volume might turn innocent girls into the very sort of women described in
its pages. In a letter he wrote to his mother following publication of the
book, he says that he will send her a copy, although he had originally decided not to do so: while he insists with some irony on the categories of
wives, daughters, and sisters, both his correspondence and the poems
themselves demonstrate that his relation to the readership represented by
his mother was far from a humorous subject for the poet. (The opening
stanzas of the first poem in the volume, "Bénédiction," describe the horror inspired in a mother by having given birth to a poet.) Since she will
not have been able to escape hearing rumors of its scandal, he continues—this letter was written during the brief period between publication
and the announcement of judicial proceedings—he is sending her a copy
so that she may judge his innocence for herself. The letter goes on to out-
line Baudelaire's aesthetic approach ("You know that I have always considered literature and the arts as pursuing an aim that has nothing to do with
morality, and that beauty of conception and style are enough for me [Vous
savez que je n'ai jamais considéré la littérature et les arts que comme
poursuivant un but étranger à la morale, et que la beauté de conception
et de style me suffit]") and to justify the work on the basis of its title. What
is most striking, though, is that he includes an injunction not to let the
work be seen by the young daughter of the family with whom his mother
was living at the time: "Just one suggestion: since you are living with the
Émon family, don't leave the volume where Mlle Émon can get her hands
on it [Une seule recommandation: puisque vous vivez avec la famille
Émon, ne laissez pas le volume traîner dans les mains de Mlle Émon]."[25]
At the same time, he invites her to show it to the local priest. The latter, he
predicts, will assume the poet is going straight to hell, but will not dare say
this to his mother.

It thus seems likely that Baudelaire took seriously, despite all his ponderously ironic comments about wives, daughters, and sisters, the idea that
his book could only be a corrupting influence on young girls—and, despite his intense dislike of the senior members of the Émon family, worried that his work might fall into the hands of its young daughter. In one
of the four *articles justificatifs* which the poet marshaled in his defense,
Charles Asselineau takes up this same theme, quoting Théophile Gau-

tier's *Albertus* on the subject (the quotation is taken up in the defense speech as well):

> Et d'abord, j'en préviens les mères de famille,
> Ce que j'écris n'est pas pour les petites filles
> Dont on coupe le pain en tartines.

[And first, let mothers be warned / What I write is not for little girls / Whose toast is cut up for them at breakfast.]

Asselineau then comments:

> Little girls! Little girls! My God, aren't there books for little girls? Aren't there writers dedicated, by vocation or necessity, to composing nice little stories? Aren't there authors for children and even for ladies? Ignorance is a virtue for girls, therefore art is not for them.

> [Les petites filles! les petites filles! Mon Dieu! N'y a-t-il pas une littérature pour les petites filles? n'y a-t-il pas des écrivains qui se dévouent par vocation ou par nécessité à composer de petites historiettes sans dard et sans venin? Est-ce qu'il n'y a pas des auteurs pour enfants et même des auteurs pour dames? L'ignorance est une vertu pour les filles, l'art n'est donc pas fait pour elles.][26]

Both Baudelaire and his defenders seem to take for granted that literature can be a corrupting influence, that the prime target of corruption is girls, and that this potential audience should therefore be shielded from such works as his. We are far from Flaubert defending the morality of his work, as in the following letter:

> People think I am too real. That's the basis of their outrage. I myself find I am very moral and deserve the Montyon Prize, since this novel offers a clear lesson, and even if "mothers cannot permit their daughters to read it," I do think a lot of husbands might do well to permit their wives to read it.

> [On trouve que je suis trop vrai. Voilà le fond de l'indignation. Je trouve, moi, que je suis très moral et que je mérite le prix Montyon, car il découle de ce roman un enseignement clair, et si "la mère ne peut en permettre la lecture à sa fille," je crois bien que des maris ne feraient pas mal d'en permettre la lecture à leur épouse.][27]

(Flaubert's proclamation that husbands would be well advised to have their wives read his novel finds an echo a century later in the debates around *Lady Chatterley's Lover,* in which one wag, when asked if he would permit his wife to read Lawrence's novel, replied that it was not his wife he was worried about so much as his gamekeeper.) In his speech in defense of *Madame Bovary,* Senard had in fact suggested that the novel would make edifying reading for girls and women. The paraphrased citation in Flaubert's letter refers to a comic play by the eighteenth-century dramatist Alexis Piron, *La Métromanie* (1738):

> Je veux que la vertu plus que l'esprit y brille.
> La mère en prescrira la lecture à sa fille.

[I want virtue more than wit to be on display. / Mothers will prescribe it to their daughters to read.][28]

This idea continued to have great currency for centuries, including—and neither Flaubert nor Baudelaire could have failed to know this, as both were admirers of Sade—the Marquis de Sade's ironic quotation of the second line of this dictum which he placed as an epigraph on the title page of his *Philosophie dans le boudoir.* "Mothers will prescribe [i.e., recommend] it to their daughters [La mère en prescrira la lecture à sa fille]" can also be read as a distortion of the phrase, almost identical but opposite in meaning, "mothers will proscribe [i.e., forbid] it to their daughters [la mère en proscrira la lecture à sa fille]," which is closer to what Baudelaire seems to have had in mind with his exhortation to his mother not to let Mlle Émon get her hands on *Les Fleurs du mal.* At any rate, it seems clear that the stakes are both similar and different in Flaubert's case and in Baudelaire's: both defended the morality of their works, but the former insisted that women in particular might benefit from the reading of his novel, whereas the latter fully acknowledged that his book was not meant for female eyes.

Again, though, by virtue of its medium, *Les Fleurs du mal* was already, in contrast to *Madame Bovary,* not destined for a female audience. Because it belonged to a lofty genre, Baudelaire's work was more or less exempted from the charge of corrupting women. However, even if he is unable to cite the possible corruption of female readers, Pinard takes another tack along the same lines, maintaining—in contradiction, it seems, of the evidence—that because of its low price the collection is available to a wide readership ("since you have printed several thousand copies which you are selling at a low price [car vous tirez à plusieurs milliers d'exemplaires et vous vendez à bas prix]").[29] Baudelaire himself insists that the volume's relatively elevated price attests to the extent to which it is neither intended nor available for popular consumption: "The book is, relative to the usual low prices in bookstores, expensive. This is in itself an important guarantee. It shows I am not addressing the masses. [Le volume est, relativement à l'abaissement général des prix en librairie, d'un prix élevé. C'est déjà une garantie importante. Je ne m'adresse donc pas à la foule.] "[30] The phenomenon we have seen in the trial of *Madame Bovary* is thus clearly visible in the conflict over *Les Fleurs du mal* as well: both sides argue from the same premises, agreeing that the potential for corruption is there, and to be avoided, disagreeing only as to whether it has in fact been avoided in the work in question.

Because of its genre, and paradoxically, since as Flaubert points out, poetry had thus far been left alone by the judicial system because of its generically limited readership, Baudelaire's work was especially subject to the charge of obscenity. Despite the officially designated function of literature in general as defined, for instance, by the tribunal pronouncing Flaubert's verdict, novels had for some time taken on mundane subjects, whereas lyric poetry was still the repository of the ideal. If daily life was the very substance of fictional narrative, the banal details of the "real" had little place in lyric poetry, which was given over in the Romantic tradition to meditations on nature, the heritage of the past, and the meaning of life in the face of death. In fact, Victor Hugo, to whom Baudelaire dedicated three of his poems, had been one of the first to tackle daily life in poetry. In a poem written in 1846 but first published ten years later in *Les Contemplations*, a year before *Les Fleurs du mal* came out, for instance, Hugo radically broke with tradition by referring to breakfast: "On déjeune en lisant le journal [We have breakfast while reading the newspaper]." This highly unpoetic observation was shocking, poetry existing in principle in a realm beyond such profane functions as daily meals and reading the paper. Hugo's poem, of course, mentions both breakfast and the newspaper purely as counterpoint, in order to highlight the life-and-death concerns which form the main subject of the poem, the final line of which reads: "Puis, le vaste et profond silence de la mort! [Then, the vast and deep silence of death!]"[31]

In *Les Fleurs du mal* the treatment of inappropriate subjects for lyric poetry is both similar and different. It is similar in that, like Hugo, Baudelaire introduces profane subjects only in the service of a consecrated theme, as when in "Une Charogne" he describes in some detail the rotting corpse of an animal. The poem tackles the very classic theme of "memento mori," the reminder of death in life sometimes treated in the lighter form of the "carpe diem" motif that had been a standard subject of poetry for centuries and a favorite theme during the Renaissance in particular, as in Ronsard's "Ode à Cassandre" ("Mignonne, allons voir si la rose"). "Une Charogne," which figures on Flaubert's list of his favorite poems from the volume, is one of the most notorious of *Les Fleurs du mal*, and while it was not among those cited by Pinard in his prosecution, the piece greatly contributed to Baudelaire's reputation as an iconoclast in general and played a major role in bringing the volume to the attention of the government. One of the factors leading to the trial was an article in *Le Figaro* on July 5, 1857, in which the author, Gustave Bourdin, specifically indicts four poems, not including "Une Charogne." He also calls them "four masterpieces of passion, art and poetry [quatre chefs-d'oeuvre de passion, d'art et de poésie]," a qualification which only serves to exacerbate their dangers. Bourdin then adds that the poet "curiously analyzes the process of bodily decomposition, he links vices to impure or ferocious animals! Why display all these hideous wounds of the spirit, of the heart and of matter? [analyse curieusement les progrès de la décomposition cadavérique, il assimile les vices aux animaux impurs ou féroces! Pourquoi donc étaler toutes ces plaies hideuses de l'esprit, du coeur et de la matière?]."[32] It was also doubtless this poem that inspired Sainte-Beuve's accusation that Baudelaire had "petrarchized on the horrible [pétrarquisé sur l'horrible]."[33] The critic's famous formula, with its reference to the Italian Renaissance poet Petrarch, neatly encapsulates the potent blend of formal classicism—gold—and thematic provocation—mud—that characterizes the volume and led to its prosecution.

"Une Charogne" consists of a monologue directed at the poet's beloved on the occasion of a walk during which they come across the rotting carcass of an animal: it might well be translated as "Ode on Roadkill." After a remarkably detailed description of various effects of putrefaction, starting off with a comparison of the decomposing animal to a sexually voracious woman ("Les jambes en l'air, comme une femme lubrique [Legs spread wide, like a lubricious woman]"), the poem's concluding stanzas offer a lyrical analogy between the rotting carcass and the poet's beloved:

> —Et pourtant vous serez semblable à cette ordure,
>   À cette horrible infection,
> Étoile de mes yeux, soleil de ma nature,
>   Vous, mon ange et ma passion![34]

[—And yet you will resemble this refuse, / This horrible infection, / Star of my eyes, sun of my nature, / You, my angel and my passion!]

The final stanza evokes another familiar theme, also present in the works of Renaissance poets such as Ronsard, that of the eternal endurance of the work of art as contrasted with bodily decline and death, but Baudelaire's specific terms present themselves in violent contrast to his classical theme and form:

> Alors, ô ma beauté! dites à la vermine
>   Qui vous mangera de baisers,

Que j'ai gardé la forme et l'essence divine
De mes amours décomposés!

[And so, o my beauty! tell the vermin / As they devour you with kisses, /
That I've kept the form and divine essence / Of my decomposed loves!]

Again, the device is precisely the same in structure as that used by many
poets during the Renaissance to treat the same theme, and yet we are
clearly in a different realm from Ronsard's pointing out to his object of
desire that her beauty will fade just as the petals wither on the rose.[35] We
are also far from the poetic realism of Hugo's breakfast. With the image of
the beloved's body not only being devoured by vermin but *amorously* so
("qui vous mangera de baisers"), the poem collapses the elements of decomposition and sexuality into a single arresting metaphor that seems to
provide an unsavory corrective to Marvell's famous lines from "To His Coy
Mistress": "The grave's a fine and private place, / But none, I think, do
there embrace." It is true that Marvell's poem also includes the somewhat
Baudelairean prediction that "then worms shall try / That long preserv'd
virginity: / And your quaint Honour turned to dust." Still, in Baudelaire's
poem the macabre vision of eroticism continuing into the grave is less abstract than Marvell's. In neither is it an aphrodisiac prospective, but
Baudelaire's version is especially emetic, because it retains the language of
eroticism. The worms in "Une Charogne" are not assaulting the woman's
dusty virginity but devouring her with kisses. Furthermore, here the mistress does not seem to be especially coy, nor can the poet's evocation of
her less than rosy future as a decomposing corpse be construed, by any
stretch of the imagination, as a seduction device, which is the point, or at
least the pretext, in "carpe diem" poems. This lingering on bodily putrefaction means that despite the theme it takes from Ronsard, "Une
Charogne" has as much in common with the ascetic tradition of contrast-
ing women's outer beauty with the anatomical reality of their inner organs
in order to ward off carnal temptation as it does with Renaissance poets'
insistent floral analogies.[36] Baudelaire too is centrally concerned with
flowers, but as the title of his volume clearly indicates, they are flowers of a
different sort.

In 1859 the artist and photographer Nadar published a caricature of the
poet walking among sinister-looking vegetation labeled "fleurs du mal"
and coming across what appears to be a dead dog with its legs in the air.
Baudelaire wrote Nadar, who was a good friend of his, a letter in which he
complains about the cartoon: "I find it painful to be known as the Prince of
Putrefaction. You have doubtless not read that many of my poems, which
are nothing but musk and roses [Il m'est pénible de passer pour le Prince
des Charognes. Tu n'as sans doute pas lu une foule de choses de moi, qui

ne sont que musc et que roses]."[37] This is one of the many instances in Baudelaire's correspondence in which he expresses ambivalence about the sulfurous reputation poems such as this one could hardly fail to promote. The use of the phrase "musk and roses" to characterize his work in defense against the idea of being "Prince of Putrefaction [Prince des Charognes]" suggests that the poet wanted to be read primarily in the context of the classical poetic tradition already alluded to (roses), with a heavy admixture of more overt sensuality (musk). The olfactory emphasis in this characterization is entirely representative of Baudelaire's work, which relies on odor, in the form of both alluring scents and revolting stenches, to an extent unequaled by that of any other poet before or since. Life itself reeks in *Les Fleurs du mal*, starting with "To the Reader [Au lecteur]," the verse preface, nor is any amorous or nostalgic image unaccompanied by its signal aroma.[38] ("Au lecteur" also features references to vermin in general and intestinal parasites in particular, although the latter sound more like flowers, disguised under the Greek term "helminthes.") Roses, however, the canonical flowers of love poetry, are underrepresented, the dominant notes coming from various exotic aromas such as ambergris and *benjoin*. The scent that predominates is musk, an animal-based perfume the mere mention of which was—and in fact still is—enough to suggest carnal lust. Musk and perfume in general tend to figure as *odor di femina*, an association made especially clear in "Lethe [Le Léthé]," one of the poems suppressed in the 1857 court decision.

"Le Léthé," the title of which refers to the underworld river of forgetfulness in Greek mythology, is one of many poems in the collection in which sensuality is inextricably mixed with melancholy images of death and sadomasochistic aggression. Author of a poem entitled "L'Héautontimoroumenos," the self-torturer, Baudelaire is obsessed with analogies between love and torture, as well as the idea that "It might be nice to be alternately victim and torturer [Il serait peut-être doux d'être alternativement victime et bourreau]" (*Œuvres complètes*, 1:676). "Le Léthé" was deemed unacceptable mostly because of its final stanza, in which the poet declares his intention of sucking hemlock from a woman's nipples:

> Je sucerai, pour noyer ma rancoeur,
> Le népenthès et la bonne ciguë
> Aux bouts charmants de cette gorge aiguë,
> Qui n'a jamais emprisonné de coeur.

[I shall suck, to drown my rancor, / Nepenthes and good hemlock / From the charming points of that sharp breast, / That has never imprisoned a heart.]

This anatomical reference to nipples predictably attracted Pinard's attention. He cites "the sharp breast with charming points [la gorge aiguë aux bouts charmants]" in his prosecution speech, after having already cited the stanza as a whole, but the unmistakably sexual overtones of a reference to perfume in the second stanza are also mentioned by the imperial prosecutor:

> Dans tes jupons remplis de ton parfum
> Ensevelir ma tête endolorie
> Et respirer, comme une fleur flétrie,
> Le doux relent de mon amour défunt.[39]

[In your slips filled with your scent / I'll shroud my pain-wracked head / And breathe in like a withered flower / The sweet stench of my dead love.]

As these lines demonstrate, however much he may have protested, to Nadar and in general, that his poetry was all musk and roses, Baudelaire's work conflates three thematic registers, here neatly resumed in olfactory form. The fact that the perfume is coming from the woman's undergarments indicates that it is not Chanel Number Five but rather the scent of her sex; the withered flower might have come straight from Ronsard except for its proximity to the former; and the word *relent* (stench) could not shed its note of decomposition even if the rest of the poem were not filled with images of death. The scent of roses is in the air, but it tends to be overwhelmed by musk and putrefaction, and, as is especially clear from "Le Léthé," Baudelaire's volume caused a public disturbance in part because in it they are inseparable: they are in the end all the same odor. Sex and death had been linked in poetry for centuries, but Baudelaire's scandalous innovation was to bring death into his poems not as an abstraction but as a purulent actuality, and to link it as such to eroticism. As much as his anatomical references, it is surely this which accounts for the charge of "vulgar realism offensive to decency [Réalisme grossier et offensant pour la pudeur]." The decomposing roadkill in "Une Charogne" seems to have lent some of its stench to the volume as a whole. Nonetheless, only the most obviously sexual references were deemed worthy of suppression.

As we saw in the chapter 1, the tribunal judging Flaubert's case had officially declared that "the mission of literature should be to beautify and enhance the spirit by elevating the intelligence and purifying morals rather than to inspire disgust for vice [la mission de la littérature doit être d'orner et de recréer l'esprit en élevant l'intelligence et en épurant les moeurs plus encore que d'imprimer le dégoût du vice]." Since aesthetic value alone was unavailable as a line of defense, Baudelaire's only substantive argument for the moral probity of his work was precisely what is suggested in this last phrase. His defense attorney, Gustave Chaix d'Est-Ange, maintained that Baudelaire's poems set out "to depict vice, but to depict it in violent colors . . . in order to display its odious and repulsive qualities [peindre le vice, mais le peindre sous des couleurs violentes, . . . pour mieux faire ressortir ce qu'il renferme d'odieux et de repoussant]" (*Œuvres complètes*, 1:1211). This had also been Senard's central argument ("an incitement to virtue through the horror of vice [une excitation à la vertu, par l'horreur du vice]" [664]), and it worked to the extent that Flaubert was acquitted. The tribunal's stipulation as to the correct function of art in its assignation of blame in Flaubert's case, however, was designed to advertise that this defense would not encounter much success in the future, at least not in France under the Second Empire. We shall see that the defense on grounds of depicting vice in the service of virtue had not yet run its course in the general scheme of things, but Flaubert's verdict had sent out an implicit warning that this reasoning would no longer do the trick in the French courtroom. Maître Chaix d'Est-Ange accordingly made little use of what was in fact a much more accurate argument in the case of Baudelaire than it had been in Flaubert's, and confined himself for the most part to reiterating salient points from the articles written in Baudelaire's defense. As Senard had also done for *Madame Bovary*, he emphasized the place of virtue in the volume as well as the importance of its being read as a whole rather than in fragments—not so easy in the case of a collection of poems—and cited numerous passages from well-known works that he claimed were much more immoral than his client's.[40]

The argument of having depicted immorality in order to warn of its pernicious effects—"inspire disgust for vice [imprimer le dégoût du vice]," as the tribunal put it—was somewhat spurious in the case of *Madame Bovary*, which although it does not, as Pinard maintains, glorify adultery, certainly does denigrate marriage, and offers no redeeming alternative. Unlike Flaubert, however, and even if he often insists that art is its own justification, Baudelaire is deeply concerned with matters of morality. The poet himself remarks that the title *Les Fleurs du mal* "says it all."[41] In his discussion of the title the defense attorney was almost forced to introduce the same argument that had been deemed inadequate as a defense in Flaubert's verdict:

> the poet warns you with his title, which is there like a signpost, announcing the nature and genre of the work; he is going to show you evil, the flora of unhealthy places, the fruits of poisonous plants, his title says this—like the title of Dante's *Inferno*—but he will show you all this in order to wither it, to horrify you with it, to inspire hatred and disgust for it.

[le poète vous prévient par son titre, qui est là, comme en vedette, pour an-noncer la nature et le genre de l'oeuvre; c'est le mal qu'il va vous montrer, la flore des lieux malsains, les fruits des végétaux vénéneux, son titre vous le dit,—comme le titre de l'*Enfer*, lorsqu'il s'agit de l'oeuvre du Dante—mais il va vous montrer tout cela, pour le flétrir, pour vous en donner l'horreur, pour vous en inspirer la haine et le dégoût.] (*Œuvres complètes*, 1:1211)

The reference to Dante, inspired by Thierry's and Barbey d'Aurevilly's ar-ticles, not only places Baudelaire among the giants of poetry but also es-tablishes his moral credentials in the context of the great bard of Heaven and, more pertinently, Hell. In the justificatory essays [*articles justificatifs*] and in the defense speech that draws on them, Baudelaire is placed in the lineage not only of Dante but of Pascal, Shakespeare, Goethe, Molière, and the more recent examples of Hugo and Gautier. Flaubert too is cited, on the strength of his recent acquittal. As for the title, Barbey even goes so far as to insist that it does not sufficiently capture the potency of the salu-brious poison within:

Only believe the title halfway! M. Baudelaire's book is not *The Flowers of Evil*. It's the most violent essence that has ever been extracted from these ac-cursed flowers. But the torture produced by this kind of poison saves us from the dangers of its intoxication.

[N'en croyez le titre qu'à moitié! Ce ne sont pas *Les Fleurs du mal* que le livre de M. Baudelaire. C'est le plus violent extrait qu'on ait jamais fait de ces fleurs maudites. Or, la torture que doit produire un tel poison sauve des dangers de son ivresse!] (*Œuvres complètes*, 1:1191–92)

In Baudelaire's case the argument of representing vice in the service of virtue was not merely the obvious line of defense for any writer accused of immorality. Here it cannot be avoided, especially because it is not all that far from being accurate. Much more than *Madame Bovary*, *Les Fleurs du mal* depict vice as repellent, as truly vicious rather than merely unsatisfy-ing. Baudelaire is no amoralist à la Flaubert, and to the extent that his po-etry is immoral, in the sense of flouting traditional Christian morality, he is not far from the characterization of immoralism à la Sade that Pinard had inaccurately ascribed to the author of *Madame Bovary*. He can legiti-mately be compared to Sade, as Flaubert cannot, in that he likes to take conventional Christian moral dicta and turn them inside out: both au-thors would be lost without the moral order they rebel against. The essen-tial (moral) difference, though, is that Baudelaire's work is melancholy, and expresses great torment about his transgressions, rather than, or in addition to, wallowing in them. In the conclusion of his prosecution speech against Baudelaire, Pinard prudently refrains from depicting the poet as a monster, and changes tone, begging for leniency on the grounds of his instability: "Don't be too hard on Baudelaire, who is disturbed and unbalanced [Soyez indulgent pour Baudelaire, qui est une nature inquiète et sans équilibre]" (*Œuvres complètes*, 1:1209). The poet is a sort of carrier: only his poems are monstrous, according to Pinard, because of their flowery insistence on evil.

As the title of his volume suggests, like Dante, Baudelaire was out to describe both Paradise and the Inferno; as it also demonstrates, however, for Baudelaire unlike Dante, they could not be dissociated. In a sense, the volume recapitulates all the contemporary debates about the function of art being to represent, alternatively, the Ideal or the Real. The first section of the book is called "Spleen and Ideal [Spleen et Idéal]," and the work as a whole vacillates, often within individual poems, between these two states. In a much-quoted fragment from *Mon coeur mis à nu* Baudelaire describes the "double postulate" that informs the vision of the world which comes across in almost every poem in *Les Fleurs du mal*, as well as its title:

> There exist in each man, at all times, two simultaneous postulations, one toward God, the other toward Satan. The invocation to God, or spirituality, is a desire to rise in rank; that of Satan, or animality, is a joy in falling.

> [Il y a dans tout homme, à toute heure, deux postulations simultanées, l'une vers Dieu, l'autre vers Satan. L'invocation à Dieu, ou spiritualité, est un désir de monter en grade; celle de Satan, ou animalité, est une joie de descendre.] (*Œuvres complètes*, 1:683)

So far so good: what is expressed here hardly departs from orthodox Christian dogma. The problems start with his application of this double postulate. For one thing, Baudelaire is quite clearly more interested in the joy of descent into Satanism than in ascending into God's spiritual ranks. What is more, aside from the blasphemous poems that led to his being accused of offenses against religious morality (*outrage à la morale religieuse*) as well as offenses against public morality and decency (*outrage à la morale publique et aux bonnes moeurs*)—only the latter charges were upheld—and even aside from the six poems that were suppressed, the aesthetic theory that comes across in the volume is informed by the double postulate, so that art itself is depicted as not just morally neutral, but morally ambivalent.

The investment of art with moral ambiguity or ambivalence becomes if anything more explicit after Baudelaire's conviction. *Les Fleurs du mal* is unlike all the other books dealt with in this study in that its trial ended up radically affecting the shape of the work itself. The book was altered not

just by the suppression of six poems—Baudelaire referred to his publisher's physical removal of the poems from unsold copies as "your ridiculous surgical operation [*votre ridicule opération chirurgicale*]"[42]—but because
their suppression gave rise to a proliferation of new material that then appeared in new editions. The poet immediately responded to the verdict by
announcing that he would write six more to replace the condemned
poems, writing to his publisher on December 30, 1857: "I have resolved to
submit myself completely to the verdict, and to write six new poems much
more beautiful than the suppressed ones [j'ai résolu de me soumettre
complètement au jugement, et de refaire six poèmes nouveaux beaucoup
plus beaux que ceux supprimés]" (Correspondance, 1:441). The idea that
he intended to outdo the suppressed poems is a strange one. On the one
hand it suggests he wanted to demonstrate that he was undaunted by the
ordeal. On the other hand, the gesture implies that the government's verdict might have been correct on some level: that the offending poems
could be replaced and the volume improved for their suppression. The
number of new poems did not stop at six. Where the first edition had contained exactly one hundred poems, excluding "Au lecteur," in the posthumous and therefore relatively definitive third edition—which still lacked,
of course, the six *pièces condamnées*—there were 151. The removal of six
poems had in the end caused the volume to increase by half.

The poems added in the second and third editions unsurprisingly lack
the redolent eroticism of the six that had been suppressed. Baudelaire's
moral vision was far from edulcorated, though, and the later pieces tend
to be increasingly morbid. They are also even more concerned with the
theme of the moral ambivalence of art. The original edition, for instance,
includes the famous sonnet "La Beauté" (XVII), in which the allegorical
figure of Beauty speaks, announcing her complete impassive indifference
to the effects she provokes. When "Les Bijoux," which had been number
XX, was suppressed in 1857, it was replaced by two poems, "Le Masque"
(XXI), and "Hymne à la Beauté" (XXII). "Les Bijoux" was doomed from
the outset, opening as it does "La très chère était nue . . . [The beloved
was nude . . .]," an incipit which could hardly have failed to attract disapproving attention. It consists mainly of a description of the complicit and
complacent naked woman, an enumeration of her erotic qualifications
containing elements of Renaissance *blason* as well as a paraphrase of the
Song of Solomon, and concludes with an appreciation of the woman's androgynous qualities. The two poems that replace it, while less erotically
charged, are much darker in implication. Both feature impassive, disturbingly ambivalent female figures: "Le Masque" describes a statue that
appears to represent a perfectly beautiful woman who turns out on closer
inspection to be a "monstre bicéphale [two-headed monster]," the face of

beauty hiding that of terrible pain. "Hymne à la Beauté" takes up the same figure as "La Beauté," except that this version apostrophizes Beauty rather than letting her speak for herself and paints a much more violent picture of the nature of Beauty and her effects. The poem repeatedly interrogates Beauty as to whether she comes from Heaven or Hell, God or Satan, concluding first that the answer is both, although the description seems to favor the latter (e.g., "De tes bijoux l'Horreur n'est pas le moins charmant [Of your jewels Horror is not the least charming]"), then finally that it does not matter. All that matters is that beauty takes the edge off the hideousness of the real. In this way "Hymne à la Beauté," unlike "La Beauté," can easily be read as an argument for art for art's sake. As this example among many others that could be cited (if we had space enough, and time) shows, Baudelaire's trial, far from cleansing his work of an unhealthy "realism," instead propelled him further into a vision of things in which the debate between realism and idealism was played out in a new and sinister, and more subversive, form. "Hymne à la Beauté" is placed in the "Spleen et Idéal" section of the volume, and it illustrates the degree to which the Ideal, for Baudelaire, is, especially following his trial, itself a function of the satanic tendency his prosecution was intended to suppress.

In other words, in the long run the trial had precisely the opposite effect to the one desired. The prosecution and subsequent excision of six poems caused Baudelaire to become more Baudelairean than ever: his aesthetic and moral vision was ever more focused on the idea that the Ideal is itself essentially demonic. The scent of corruption increasingly overwhelmed not just the roses but the musk as well. This is hardly surprising, since the suppressed poems were suppressed because of explicit eroticism, with strangely little regard to their actual "moral" implications. "Une Charogne," for instance, which as we have seen was identified as the most memorably shocking and disgusting item in the collection by a number of commentators, was left out of Pinard's indictment. Even more remarkable is the omission of "Une Martyre," which consists of the detailed, erotically charged description of a decapitated corpse of a woman in a sultry bedroom, the pillow drenched with blood and the detached head reposing on the night table. After enumerating the voluptuous charms of decor, body, and head, the poet (or poetic persona) apostrophizes the cadaver, asking it in particular whether her husband had his way with her inert form after doing her in. Here the connection between death and sexuality is no longer a figurative one, and it remains extremely difficult to explain how this apparent celebration of necrophilia managed to escape the notice of the imperial prosecutor.

Let us then take a look at the poems that were incriminated. Bourdin's *Figaro* article names four offensive poems, all of which figured among the fourteen cited by Pinard. Of these, two—"Le Reniement de Saint Pierre" and "Lesbos"—had appeared unmolested in journals long before publication of *Les Fleurs du mal,* which did not stop the tribunal from suppressing the second. The four poems identified by Pinard as presenting "an attack against religious morality [une atteinte à la morale religieuse]"—"Le Reniement de Saint Pierre," "Abel et Caïn," "Les Litanies de Satan," and "Le Vin de l'assassin"—are all evidently blasphemous. The government seemed reluctant, however, to uphold this charge, since it was dismissed in the cases of both Flaubert and Baudelaire. (As mentioned in the prologue, the category was dropped altogether in 1881, leaving only "outrage aux moeurs," or obscenity.) Under the charge of "atteinte à la morale publique et aux bonnes moeurs," four poems are cited by the prosecution that were not in the end suppressed: "Sed non satiata," "Le Beau Navire," "À une mendiante rousse," and one of the two "Femmes damnées" ("Comme un bétail pensif... [Like pensive livestock...]"). It is clear why these poems were not retained in the final verdict: while erotic, in each case they are less explicitly so than those that were ultimately removed from the volume. Also evident is that almost all of the ten poems earmarked by Pinard as violating public morals overtly foreground sexuality. "Les Bijoux" and "Le Léthé" have already been described; "Sed non satiata" celebrates the charms of a demonic, insatiable black woman; "Le Beau Navire" describes those of an "enfant majestueuse [majestic child]." "À une mendiante rousse" is an ode to a young beggar woman the holes in whose clothing reveal both her poverty and her body: her poverty itself is eroticized, but it seems to have been the enumeration of body parts that offended the government. Two more of the prosecuted poems, both suppressed, display disturbingly violent sexual imagery. In "À celle qui est trop gaie" the poet proposes to punish its subject for her excessive gaiety by opening up a new set of lips (*lèvres* refers to both lips and labia) in her flesh and infusing his "venom" through them. Baudelaire appended an "editor's note" to this poem in *Les Épaves,* insisting that its closing image was to be taken metaphorically, and that the "syphilitic" interpretation accorded the piece was a reflection of obscenity on the part of the readers alone. This suggestion anticipates the 1949 rehabilitation, which states that the judges in 1857 had taken the poems too literally and failed to uncover their symbolic meaning. "Les métamorphoses du vampire" is an allegory of the disgust that follows sex, and although the second stanza remains especially memorable for its revolting description of the woman turned pustulant monster, it is the first that Pinard cites, in which the woman herself vaunts her sexual prowess (e.g. "Moi, j'ai la lèvre humide [My lips are wet]"; "Les anges impuissants se damneraient pour moi [The impotent angels would be damned for me]").

The exception to the heavily sexual content of the poems cited by

Pinard is "Femmes damnées" ("Comme un bétail pensif"), which is not discussed separately in the prosecution. This poem seems to have suffered from association with the other "Femmes damnées," "Delphine et Hippolyte." "Comme un bétail pensif," with its contemplative bovine opening analogy, paints a sympathetic portrait of lesbians as frustrated "chercheuses d'infini, dévotes et satyres [seekers of the infinite, devout and lubricious]." The women in this poem come across not as sexually voracious sapphists so much as versions of the poet himself, with elements as well of the allegory of Beauty as presented in "Hymne à la Beauté": "Ô vierges, ô démons, ô monstres, ô martyres, / De la réalité grands esprits contempteurs [O virgins, o demons, o monsters, o martyrs, / Great spirits contemptuous of reality]." In contrast, "Delphine et Hippolyte," the longest poem in the original edition, presents a voluptuously voyeuristic post-lovemaking scene between two women, the predatory Delphine and the newly initiated Hippolyte. One of the reasons the poem is so long (104 lines) is that, suspecting this lascivious scenario might get him into trouble, Baudelaire added five stanzas to it just before publication of the volume. This concluding section, which provides a sternly moralistic condemnation of the scene presented in the rest of the poem (it begins: "Descendez, descendez, lamentables victimes, / Descendez le chemin de l'enfer eternal [Descend, descend, lamentable victims, / Descend the road to eternal hell]"), was not enough to ward off prosecution, and the poem was suppressed. "Delphine et Hippolyte" and "Lesbos," which is a long (75 lines) hymn to Sappho and her Lesbian cohorts, and which escapes the need for a moralizing coda because of its pre-Christian context, evidently represent a different sort of threat to public morality from the other poems Pinard discusses in his prosecution. The four poems cited on religious grounds are merely referred to by title and then collectively dispatched in a brief paragraph. Whether this was one of the reasons the charge was not upheld, or rather the result of knowledge that this particular cause was lost in advance, or both, is not clear. In any case the prosecution speech is perfunctory on the religious aspect. "Les Bijoux," "Le Léthé," "À celle qui est trop gaie," and "Les Métamorphoses du Vampire" are each referred to twice: once to read out the offending lines or stanzas, and then again to resume the character of the offense in the context of the accusation as a whole. When he is quoting particular sections of the poems, the three lesbian pieces receive special treatment: "Femmes damnées: Comme un bétail pensif" is not mentioned at all, while "Lesbos" and "Delphine et Hippolyte" are not excerpted. Pinard declares them to be "to be read in full [à lire tout entières]," adding: "You will find they describe in detail the most intimate practices of tribades (lesbians) [Vous y trouverez dans leurs détails les plus intimes moeurs des tribades]" (*Œuvres complètes*, 1:1207).

This is not simply a strategy designed to suggest that these poems are filled with such a quantity of lascivious material that mere quotation of a few lines or even stanzas would not suffice to demonstrate their unacceptability, although it is that as well. Pinard states that they must be read in their entirety because, unlike the other poems, which were morally suspect in the form of passages offering specifically anatomical or generally lewd references, here the subject itself is inadmissible, contaminating everything in the poems. The omission of "Une Martyre" demonstrates that even murder and necrophilia were viewed as less offensive subjects than lesbianism in 1857. The other "Femmes damnées" poem seems to have been cited primarily on the basis of its title, by association, as it cannot be said to appeal to prurient interest. In fact it has to be read carefully in order to discern exactly why the women in question are damned.

Although "Lesbos" and "Delphine et Hippolyte" were inculpated because of their voyeuristic eroticism, which fits the bill of "vulgar realism offensive to decency [réalisme grossier et offensant pour la pudeur]," lesbianism was not just a recreational voyeuristic interest for Baudelaire. It had already become a familiar theme in French literature, represented most visibly in Diderot's *The Nun* [*La Religieuse*] (first published in 1796, it contains one notable scene of female homoeroticism); Balzac's *The Girl with Golden Eyes* [*La Fille aux yeux d'or*] (1834); and Gautier's *Mademoiselle de Maupin* (1835) (the last two are cited in the defense speech). Gautier is the dedicatee of *Les Fleurs du mal*, and *Mademoiselle de Maupin*, especially its preface in which the theory of art for art's sake is laid out, was an important influence on Baudelaire's aesthetics. None of these works had originally been censored, even if Gautier's novel was deemed not to be left "in the hands of women [entre les mains des femmes]."[43] (*Mademoiselle de Maupin* was, though, as previously mentioned, prosecuted in the United States in translation in 1922.) The Second Empire regime proved to be as intolerant on the subject of female homosexuality as on others, and one Xavier de Montépin had been fined 500F and sentenced to three months in prison for his now forgotten 1855 novel *Plaster Girls* [*Les Filles de plâtre*], which prominently features lesbian scenes. Baudelaire's fascination with lesbianism went beyond the sort of titillating voyeurism in such popular novels as Montépin's. The latter is not all that far removed from Diderot's story of the hapless nun in her entertaining failure to understand the nature of her Mother Superior's passionate attentions, or Balzac's homicidal sapphist, or Gautier's Rosette in love with the eponymous heroine dressed as a man.

Baudelaire's lesbianism is of a different sort. The first title he had proposed for his volume of poems was *Les Lesbiennes*, a title designed to provoke, certainly, but which also suggests that he had intended to make this a dominant theme in his work. The word did not have the standard mean-

ing it has since acquired, at the time referring to female homosexuality
only by extension. The title *Les Lesbiennes* would have conjured up visions
of Sappho and company first, their sexual adventures only secondarily.
This is why Pinard stresses the word *tribades*, going so far as to rebaptize
"Delphine et Hippolyte" "Les Tribades" (*Œuvres complètes*, 1:1208). Even if
everyone knew what *lesbienne* meant, *tribade*, which derives from the Greek
verb "to rub" and carried unavoidably explicit sexual connotations, was
more apt to convey the "crude and offensive realism" that Pinard wished
to emphasize. Chaix d'Est-Ange waxed predictably indignant over
Pinard's title innovation, observing that he and his client would never
have used such terms. In fact in a list of titles for never-written future novels Baudelaire includes *Les Tribades*, under the rubric *Les Monstres* (*Œuvres
complètes*, 1:589). Baudelaire's attitude toward such matters is never entirely unequivocal.

It has often been supposed that his interest in lesbianism had its roots
in personal concerns, specifically the bisexuality of Jeanne Duval and
other women he was involved with. There may well be truth to this hypothesis, but as Walter Benjamin observes, the main characteristic of
Baudelaire's lesbians is that they are *not real*.[44] In a famous fragment from
"My Heart Laid Bare [Mon coeur mis à nu]" the poet writes, "La femme
est *naturelle*, c'est-à-dire abominable [Woman is *natural*, that is to say
abominable]." In the same text he also notes that "La femme est le contraire du Dandy [Woman is the opposite of the Dandy]" (*Œuvres complètes*,
1:677). The lesbian is an irresistible figure for Baudelaire because she is
the female dandy, the woman minus her abomination because *unnatural*.
We recognize here the terms of his accolade of Emma Bovary, lauded on
exactly the same terms: as a dandy, and a "bizarre androgyne." Baudelaire
is fascinated by the idea of lesbianism not so much, or at least not only, for
the lubricious voyeuristic reasons for which "Lesbos" and "Delphine et
Hippolyte" were suppressed, but because of what they represent in terms
of a fantasy of the female dandy, an androgynous ideal of pure artifice that
is the very opposite of a pruriently "realistic" portrayal of illicit sexuality.
Baudelaire's fantasy of lesbianism is in some sense his own version of
Flaubert's fantasy of a book about nothing: his *femmes damnées* represent
pure style, liberated from the shackles of mundane referentiality.

In a famous commentary Benjamin maintains that through Baudelaire
the lesbian became "the heroine of modernity."[45] Baudelaire's lesbian
poems did not go away as a result of the verdict; on the contrary, they
played a central role in the explosion of treatments of this theme in
French literature in the late nineteenth and early twentieth century. Male
homosexuality remained a taboo subject for some time: Proust's *Sodom
and Gomorrah* [*Sodome et Gomorrhe*] (1921–22) is generally viewed as the

first "serious" novel to treat the subject overtly.[46] Lesbianism, though, while retaining its power to scandalize, became increasingly visible as a theme in high-, middle-, and lowbrow literature during this period, and Baudelaire was crucial to this tendency. In the visual arts as well as in literature the influence of his lesbian poems is evident. Auguste Rodin, who was a great admirer of Baudelaire and had been drawing and sculpting "Femmes damnées" for years, was commissioned in 1887 by Paul Gallimard (father of Gaston, who founded the eminent publishing firm) to illustrate a copy of the 1857 edition of *Les Fleurs du mal*. Rodin did so, with particular attention to the suppressed poems (oddly, his illustration of "Les Bijoux" is a sketch of "The Thinker").[47] "Delphine et Hippolyte" also inspired, among other paintings, Courbet's notorious *The Sleepers* [*Les Dormeuses*], which in turn helped launch a thousand Penthouse spreads. Courbet's 1866 painting, alternatively called *Sleep* [*Le Sommeil*] or *Sloth and Lust* [*Paresse et luxure*], has for years adorned the cover of the Livre de Poche edition of *Les Fleurs du mal*. It was one of several inspired by "Delphine et Hippolyte," the first of which, titled *Femmes damnées*, was refused by the Salon de Paris in 1864, after which it was prudently heterosexualized, and classicized, as *Venus Pursuing Psyche out of Jealousy* [*Vénus poursuivant Psyché de sa jalousie*]."[48] The presence of Courbet's painting on the cover of one of the most widely available, cheap paperback editions of the poems, like Pompidou's inclusion of two of the *pièces condamnées* in his influential anthology, is testimony that the 1949 rehabilitation had not been a mere gesture toward effacing an embarrassing blot on Baudelaire's reputation. It was a necessary move, since the suppressed poems had proved not incidental but central to the poet's legacy, which had itself become a cornerstone of the French cultural patrimony.

I earlier suggested that Baudelaire's trial had effects that were the precise opposite of what it was intended to accomplish because of the ways in which *Les Fleurs du mal* evolved as an indirect result of the suppression of six poems. This is also true, as the above examples demonstrate, in a variety of other ways. Not only did Baudelaire become more Baudelairean as a result of his prosecution, the culture became Baudelairean as well. In 1861, writing in *La Revue des deux mondes*, the critic Armand de Pontmartin asked the following question: "What would be a society, what would be a literature, that would accept M. Charles Baudelaire as their poet? [Que serait une société, que serait une littérature qui accepteraient M. Charles Baudelaire pour leur poète?]"[49] Although his question was presumably a rhetorical one, meant to suggest that such a society and such a literature were unthinkable, the 1949 rehabilitation imposes an answer: France, and French literature, from the mid twentieth century on. Not only did the original verdict unintentionally produce a new text, it also ended up creating a new sort of reader. The long-term effects of the trial are visible in the 1949 rehabilitation, especially in its remarks about the failure of the judges in 1857 to read symbolically, because of their excessively "realist" approach.

Les Fleurs du mal itself contains a blueprint of its projected reader, in the form of the verse preface "Au lecteur," with its famous apostrophe of the "Hypocrite lecteur, mon semblable, mon frère [Hypocrite reader, my double, my brother]." This often-cited line, with its assumption that the reader will necessarily at once identify with the vision of the world put forth in the poems and disavow that identification, is not in fact all that much of an innovation on Baudelaire's part. The same sentiment can be found in the preface to *Les Contemplations*, published the previous year, in which Hugo similarly interpellates the reader as "insensé, qui crois que je ne suis pas toi [senseless reader, who think I am not you]," concluding hortatorily: "Prenez donc ce miroir et regardez-vous-y [Take then this mirror and look at yourself in it]."[50] Baudelaire's address to the hypocritical reader is a somewhat ruder form of the same warning that the book cannot be read with impunity: the reader should be prepared to be implicated in what he reads. Since the contents and tone of the two works are very different, however—their respective titles indicate as much—the effect of the prefatory harangue is necessarily different as well. Hugo's reader is engaged for the most part in meditations on death, *Les Contemplations* being haunted by various losses, especially the drowning death of the poet's daughter. The first stanza alone of "Au lecteur" provides a fair sampling of the themes the reader of *Les Fleurs du mal* can expect to grapple with:

> La sottise, l'erreur, le péché, la lésine,
> Occupent nos esprits et travaillent nos corps,
> Et nous alimentons nos aimables remords,
> Comme les mendiants nourissent leur vermine.

[Stupidity, error, sin, cheapness, / Occupy our spirits and work on our bodies, / And we feed our amiable remorse, / Like beggars nourish their vermin.]

Nine stanzas before being formally charged with hypocrisy, then, the reader is implicated (grammatically, by use of the first person plural) in stupidity, error, sin, and avarice, with bad faith already in the offing in the form of the pleasant remorse we nourish as beggars nourish their parasites. Among other things this poem anticipates many of the central themes of French existentialism, in its insistence on bad faith and especially in terms of the ennui the reader is accused in the last stanza of knowing all about even if he won't admit it. *Ennui* in *Madame Bovary* is boredom of the garden variety, but so pervasive and destructive as to become first a plot and then a fatality.[51] Something resembling existential *ennui* had been a pervasive theme in romantic literature starting with Chateaubriand. But Baudelaire takes this notion and puts a new spin on it, starting with the capital letter that elevates it into a philosophy and the stanzas in "Au lecteur" that characterize it as not only a vice but the most annihilating of forces. It is no accident that Jean-Paul Sartre, the major proponent of French existentialism, devoted books to both Flaubert and Baudelaire.

Baudelaire's hypocritical reader can be construed as an anticipatory portrait of Ernest Pinard, whose main point in the prosecutions of both Flaubert and Baudelaire was not that they were making things up, or even exaggerating them, but rather that they were describing things best left unmentioned. During Flaubert's trial he reads out a description of Emma waltzing at la Vaubyessard, and comments: "I am well aware that people waltz in this way, but that does not make it more moral [Je sais bien qu'on valse un peu de cette manière, mais cela n'en est pas plus moral]" (*Madame Bovary* [Pléiade], 620). In the same vein, he accuses Baudelaire of setting out to "depict everything, lay everything bare [tout peindre, tout mettre à nu]." This "realism" that so incenses Pinard, and provides the basis for the condemning verdict, is then turned back on the 1857 tribunal by the 1949 rehabilitation, which taxes the judges with too "realistic" an interpretation: in other words, with having taken the poet at his word. What had happened in the interim was both that the society had become Baudelaireanized—existentialism was in full swing in 1949, and art for art's sake had passed into the realm of platitude—and that Baudelaire had become domesticated. He could now be read "symbolically," the more disturbing implications that his poetry retained assimilated into the cult of self-destructive genius, along with the symbolist poet Nerval's suicide (the symbolist movement having been inaugurated by Baudelaire himself) and Van Gogh's self-mutilation. In "Épigraphe pour un livre condamné [Epigraph for a censored book]," a poem first published in 1861 and incorporated into the posthumous third edition of *Les Fleurs du mal* as number CXXXIII, Baudelaire takes another crack at simultaneously addressing and characterizing his reader, this time, as the title insists and its place in the volume requires, a reader fully apprised of what is at stake. The sonnet splits the hypocritical reader in two: one, "paisible et bucolique, / Sobre et naïf homme de bien [peaceful and bucolic, / Sober and naïve do-gooder]," is asked to throw the book away, as he will either understand nothing or think the author insane. The other reader is described as acquainted with the void and is implored to read the poet, "pour apprendre à m'aimer [to learn to love me]." The last line reads: "Plains-moi! . . . Sinon, je te maudis! [Feel sorry for me! . . . Or else I curse you!]" The rehabilitation can be read as a response to this ultimatum. In any case, we no longer have a choice: Baudelaire has already sent us to Hell.

∞

CHAPTER THREE

James Joyce

Leopold Bloom's Trip to the Outhouse

> He compared the barmaids with Homer's Sirens, pointing out that the
> barmaids, with careful hair-do, make-up, and smart blouses, looked well
> only to the waist, and that below the waist they wore old stained skirts,
> broken and comfortable shoes, and mended stockings. Again, when I
> once admired the phrase *'Thalatta! Thalatta!* She is our great sweet
> mother', he looked across at me and said 'Read what I have written
> above: "The snotgreen sea. The scrotumtightening sea.' "

ARTHUR POWER, *Conversations with James Joyce*

The first thing that must be said of the special place held by *Ulysses* in
the history of censorship is that Joyce's novel is now known not
only as a literary masterpiece and one of the key texts of modernism, but also—ask any English major—as perhaps the most difficult of
centrally canonical modernist works. No other required reading, not even
A la recherche du temps perdu, with its grotesque length and notoriously long
and complicated sentences, quite compares to *Ulysses* in terms of difficulty. Proust's magnum opus is rarely approached in its entirety, either in
the classroom (where even the graduate seminar format proves unequal
to its sheer bulk and intricacy) or in what is often referred to in academia
as the real world. It is also less challenging as prose than *Ulysses*; its sentences may be dauntingly labyrinthine, but Proust never engages in the
sort of formal experimentation to which Joyce was increasingly given. The
latter's final work, *Finnegans Wake*, is actually much less readable than
Ulysses: so extravagantly obscure that it has aptly been called "the ultimately reader-hostile, reader nuking immolation."[1] But as a result,
Finnegans Wake—the very title of which separates the masses from the initiated few (those who know to leave off the apostrophe)—is regarded as a
crucial text only among committed students of literary obscurity. *Ulysses* is
different: while long, it can be read by the dedicated amateur in a week or

so,[2] or included among other works on an upper-level syllabus; it is viewed as a modern masterpiece with which the educated person should be able to demonstrate some familiarity; and it is very difficult to read.

John Quinn, the attorney who first defended the novel against obscenity charges in the United States in 1920, declared, however disingenuously, that he himself did not understand parts of *Ulysses*, adding that he felt Joyce had carried his innovative narrative method too far.[3] (Unsurprisingly, the defense lost its case.) Judge John M. Woolsey's 1933 decision allowing the work into the United States, which serves as a preface to both American and British editions, stresses the fact that it "is not an easy book to read or understand." He adds that "in order properly to approach the consideration of it it is advisable to read a number of other books which have now become its satellites. The study of *Ulysses* is, therefore, a heavy task" (x). This in turn makes it difficult to understand how the book could have been deemed dangerous to the general populace in the first place, if the attorney who first defended it, and the judge appointed to decide whether the American public should be shielded from it on the basis of its corrupting potential, themselves found it to be a daunting intellectual challenge.

And yet the novel, first published in its entirety in 1922, was immediately termed by an irate journalist "the most infamously obscene book in ancient or modern literature."[4] Even among established literary figures a certain amount of moral indignation was expressed. Edmund Gosse offered the opinion that Joyce "is a sort of Marquis de Sade, but does not write so well," and George Moore called him "a sort of Zola gone to seed"; both these comparisons attest, among other things, to the enduring place held in the anglophone imagination by French writers as the *nec plus ultra* of obscene literature.[5] Virginia Woolf, who in 1918 had declined to consider *Ulysses* for publication by the Hogarth Press in Britain, and who in 1925 was to publish *Mrs. Dalloway*, her own much more decorous experimental novel detailing the events of a single relatively eventless day, appreciated Joyce's earlier efforts, but found *Ulysses* vulgar and incoherent.[6] She wrote to a correspondent that "the directness of the language and the choice of incidents, if indeed there *is* any choice, have raised a blush even upon such a cheek as mine."[7] In her diary she noted that parts of the novel made her "puzzled, bored, irritated & disillusioned as by a queasy undergraduate scratching his pimples," adding: "an illiterate, underbred book it seems to me."[8]

Margaret Anderson, founder and editor of *The Little Review*, in which the book was first published in serial form (through the thirteenth episode, that is, when it was banned by order of the court), quotes a letter written by an offended subscriber, "typical of hundreds we received," which begins "I think this is the most damnable slush and filth that ever polluted paper in print," and goes on at some length along the same lines.[9] In the words of Anthony Burgess, *Ulysses* "was one of the great dirty books, too dirty to be easily accessible, one of the trilogy of literary dirt completed by *Lady Chatterley's Lover* and *The Well of Loneliness*."[10] "Too dirty to be easily accessible": here we have the conundrum of Joyce's case in a characteristically confusing nutshell. Burgess's remark is ambiguous; presumably he means that all three works were deemed too dirty to be made available to the general public. In terms of *Ulysses*, though, the formula takes on another meaning, since Joyce's novel, unlike the other two, provides its own inaccessibility. In England the novel was formally banned by order of the Home Office (under the stewardship of the notorious William Joynson-Hicks, whom we shall meet again in the following chapters) until 1937. The British ban was instigated by the critic Shane Leslie, who deemed the book "unreadable, unquotable, and unreviewable," proceeding to read, quote, and review it in order to drive home his point.[11]

We have seen in the previous chapters that the problem of literary obscenity turns on the issue of accessibility. A work has the potential to corrupt to the extent that it is comprehensible to large groups of potentially corruptible people. This was the basis for prosecution of *Madame Bovary* and even *Les Fleurs du mal,* and this is why film and other popular media such as video games have been seen as particularly dangerous. In the case of *Ulysses*, at least from the vantage point of posterity, the charge itself seems incomprehensible, since the novel requires a great deal of work to decipher. *Ulysses*, in other words, is the most unlikely of dirty books.

Why, then, was Joyce's second novel deemed so dangerous as to remain banned in both the United States and England for thirteen years? It was not because of its plot. While it deals with extramarital intrigue, unlike *Madame Bovary* or *Lady Chatterley's Lover* it cannot be read as a glorification of adultery. To the contrary: Molly Bloom's famous soliloquy, which contains some of its most scandalously obscene passages, closes the book with a reverberating "yes" that indicates her return to the conjugal fold. What is more, the action takes place on June 16, 1904, a date that commemorates the author's first meeting with Nora Barnacle, his lifelong companion and, eventually, wife. Far from being a hymn to adultery, therefore, it is implicitly presented as a celebration of coupledom. In its way it is the most uxorious of books, which is entirely logical. The *Odyssey*, on which it is based, is the most marriage-friendly of epics, recording both Penelope's and even Odysseus's attempts to avoid infidelity in the face of the greatest of odds. In Homer's epic, Penelope at least is successful; in Joyce's neither spouse quite manages to preserve conjugal fidelity, and yet the novel reads neither as a celebration of adultery nor as a denigration of marriage. Furthermore, while it deals with various "perversions" along the way, unlike

The Well of Loneliness or *Lolita*, it cannot be read as a plea for acceptance of illicit sexual minorities.

In short, the plot is not at fault, especially because *Ulysses* does not really have a plot. It depicts the wanderings and musings of various people in Dublin during the course of that single day. Nothing much happens: the same nothing much—daily life in all its banality—which would come to characterize the plot of modernism in general. (Even when modernist works deal with war, as in Céline's *Voyage au bout de la nuit*, it is the banal details of war and its aftermath that are in question, rather than the grand picture of world events in, say, *War and Peace*.) At the time *Ulysses* was published, this emphasis on the previously unmentionable mundane led to Joyce's being viewed as an inheritor of naturalism—thus Moore's reference to a "Zola gone to seed"—much as Flaubert had earlier been taxed with the mantle of realism. The category of modernism was not invoked until later, of course, because modernism did not exist at the time: it was in the process of being invented by Joyce, among others. The author himself defined his revolutionary approach as "the new realism." "As for the romantic classicism you admire so much," he told his young friend Arthur Power, with all the prescient arrogance of Flaubert asserting that with *Madame Bovary* modern literature itself was being put on trial,

> *Ulysses* has changed all that; for in it I have opened the new way, and you will find that it will be followed more and more. In fact, from it you may date a new orientation in literature—the new realism; for though you criticize *Ulysses*, yet the one thing you must admit that I have done is to liberate literature from its age-old shackles.[12]

Like Flaubert's grandiose self-assessments, this unlikely proclamation has proved accurate. However genuinely new the orientation, though, Flaubert had shown him the way, and Joyce's novel owes a great deal to the author of *Madame Bovary*. As Ezra Pound put it, "His true Penelope was Flaubert."[13] *Ulysses*, the quintessential modernist novel, is at heart a realization, even *the* realization, of Flaubert's dream of a novel about nothing, sustained by style alone.

Style is what makes *Ulysses* difficult; "nothing" is what made it unacceptable. If the novel lacks plot, it does have structure: loosely, the structure of the *Odyssey*. *Ulysses* is modern epic, which means, as Martin Amis puts it, "degraded epic."[14] What the degradation of modernity entails in this context becomes clear on the third page, when, after a parody of the Mass ceremony performed over a mirror and razor crossed on a shaving bowl, we encounter the first hint of what it means to situate Homeric epic in the early twentieth century. Instead of the famous "winedark sea" of the

Odyssey, we find the "snotgreen sea," followed by "the scrotumtightening sea" (5). Joyce offers us both versions: the Greek ("*Epi oinopa ponton*": "upon the winedark sea") and the degraded modern (snotgreen, scrotumtightening). But the original Homeric epithet is transliterated rather than translated, as is the triumphant exclamation "*Thalatta! Thalatta!*" ("The sea! The sea!") from Xenophon's *Anabasis*. As a result, what "snotgreen" and "scrotumtightening" replace is comprehensible only to the select few, whereas these unseemly adjectives are available to all readers, in a presumably deliberate reversal of eighteenth- and nineteenth-century methods of internal censorship by recourse to Greek or Latin. The first basely physical references in *Ulysses* are therefore also the first references to its classical model, and they are at once disgusting (snotgreen) and sexual (scrotumtightening)—although emphatically not erotic. Rather, the epithet "scrotumtightening" would seem if anything to be as anti-erotic as references to snot. The degradation cannot be missed, and the heights from which we have fallen are always dimly visible in the background, in the form of the title if nothing else. *Ulysses* was bound for suppression for this if for no other reason: its modern recasting of the *Odyssey* cannot help but indict the world it contrasts with its epic antecedent, as poetic metaphors have been supplanted by the disgustingly mundane. The modified characterizations of the sea represent only the first and most obviously off-putting enactments of a degradation that is then showcased on all levels. Homer's canny warrior is replaced by a masochistic advertisement canvasser; his home island of Ithaca by middle-class housing; his heroically faithful wife by a latter-day Emma Bovary; the Sirens by barmaids; Circe's palace by a brothel; and so on. Still, it is the insistence on base bodily functions that earned Joyce's modern epic its place in the pantheon of obscene classics.

The presence of nasal secretions in the novel is not, for example, confined to the vehicle of a willfully unpleasant simile. The phrase "snotgreen sea" is suggested to Buck Mulligan because he wants to borrow Stephen Dedalus's "noserag." The snot is literal in this opening scene as well as providing the arresting neo-Homeric epithet, and it comes to form something of a leitmotif in the book, which surely features more dripping noses than does any other canonical work. One character in the novel, the duly nicknamed Nosey Flynn, is characterized chiefly by his nasal "dewdrop," about the fate of which Leopold Bloom frets as they have lunch together (173–74). Mucus may put in token appearances in other modern novels—generally a side-product of tears, and usually adorning the faces of children—and for sheer revolting detail of bodily excretions it is hard to beat Flaubert's meticulous descriptions of Hippolyte's gangrenous leg, the blind beggar's suppurating sores, and Emma Bovary's death by arsenic poisoning. We have also seen that Baudelaire's poems offer a remarkable catalogue of physical disgust and putrefaction. In the naturalist mode, moreover, descriptions such as Zola's of the eponymous courtesan's rotting visage in *Nana* (1880), the result of smallpox, had greatly upped the literary ante in terms of graphic depiction of the human body in its most unappealing moments, at the time mainly the province of French writers, as the successful prosecution of Henry Vizetelly in England in 1887 for publishing French works in translation, including novels by Flaubert and Zola, attests.[15] But the physicality of *Ulysses* has none of the dramatic, and potentially moralistic, impact of violence, horror, and death. Instead, Joyce gives us bodily functions in all their mundane unpleasantness. Like *Madame Bovary*, *Ulysses* caused a stir not only because of its sexual content—it is of course much more sexually explicit than Flaubert's novel, written as it was in a post-Flaubertian, post-Baudelairean, and post-Zolean world—but because of its insistence on the banality of the everyday. Joyce takes this further than anyone before him, to the extent of featuring the first noncomical defecation in literature.

Joyce's novel responds to Barbey d'Aurevilly's darkly contemptuous prediction in his review of Zola's *Ventre de Paris*: "There is lower than the belly. There is what goes into it and what comes out" (see chapter 3). Leopold Bloom's trip to the outhouse in the fourth chapter of *Ulysses* was hardly the first mention of shit in literature: the burlesque comic tradition is full, as it were, of shit. It is also to be found in nonburlesque contexts. Swift's horrified realization that "Celia shits" is probably the most famous use of that word in the English tradition before Lawrence, and Sade's works even contain lengthy appreciations of the role of feces in sodomy. The outhouse scene in *Ulysses*, though, does not contain the word *shit*, and its comical and transgressive aspects derive not from the description itself but simply from the fact of its inclusion. Leopold Bloom chooses reading material, makes his way to the facilities, and reads while doing his business; the scene is described in a manner neither comical nor vulgar, and represents an activity whose universality is as unquestionable as its unmentionability. In *Mrs. Dalloway*, Woolf's character Peter Walsh returns to London in 1923 from five years in India to notice a number of cultural differences, notably the fact that women wore more makeup, and the following:

> Newspapers seemed different. Now for instance there was a man writing quite openly in one of the respected weeklies about water-closets. That you couldn't have done ten years ago—written quite openly about water-closets in a respectable weekly. (71)

This passage may or may not be an oblique reference to *Ulysses*; at any rate it suggests that such matters were becoming less unmentionable, while Woolf's other writings make it clear that she did not appreciate such representations in literary texts. *Mrs. Dalloway*, which in many ways resembles *Ulysses*, would be a very different book if it contained a scene of defecation. As it is, the novel includes a remarkable number of variations on themes from *Ulysses*, from its single-day format (Clarissa Dalloway's day even takes place in June, like Leopold Bloom's, although hers is in June 1923), to the inescapable lure of modern advertising techniques, as well as details such as one character inciting others to place an earnest letter to the editor of a newspaper, the chance encounters of implicitly linked characters, to a husband's ruminations on his wife's assignation with an admirer; the full list would be far too long to include here. Woolf's version of each event and theme in question is much less ludic and more serious and directly expressed: the overall effect is to make *Mrs. Dalloway* read as anticipatory parody, anti- or ante-parody, as though Woolf had set out to provide Joyce after the fact with a straight-faced original for his anticipatorily outlandish takeoff.[16] The most likely explanation for this strange impression is, of course, what Woolf's private assessments of Joyce's work suggest: that she liked Joyce's innovative ideas, but was horrified by his treatment of them. In her diary she spoke of the novel's "filth," and more specifically noted to Roger Fry that "after all the p——ing of a dog isn't very different from the p——ing of a man."[17] *Mrs. Dalloway* would seem to be Woolf's corrective to Joyce, a version of *Ulysses* purged of the "illiterate, underbred" elements that made her queasy.

In any case, the particular taboo on defecation, unlike those forbidding the use of profanity and explicit representation of *sexuality*, remained in place for quite some time in fiction. The theme features in movies of the late twentieth century from *The Discreet Charm of the Bourgeoisie* (1972) to *La Grande Bouffe* (1973), to *Dumb and Dumber* (1994), to *Trainspotting* (1996), that take up—always in keeping with the farcical tradition—the transgressive theme of bodily elimination that had provided fodder for comical literature and theater for centuries. But while the 1967 film of Joyce's novel made by Joseph Strick reproduces both vulgar language and sex scenes, with Bloom seen fornicating and being spanked in a brothel, his visit to the outhouse is omitted.

In serious literature before Joyce, food had, when necessary, gone in, but it tended almost never to come out.[18] The most obvious exception, Rabelais, was until well into the twentieth century regarded with a certain amount of suspicion, and defecation is always comical in his works. The very mention of his name as a term of comparison for some time functioned as an index of condemnability, with Joyce among others compared by critics to Rabelais in a manner often not meant as a literary compliment, at least not in an anglophone context. (Variously, William Butler Yeats pronounced *Ulysses* on the one hand "as obscene as Rabelais" and on the other "indubitably a work of genius"; Valéry Larbaud, the French writer who translated Joyce, lauded the novel as being "as great and comprehensive and human as Rabelais";[19] and for Shane Leslie, Joyce "touch[es] the lowest depth of Rabelaisian realism.")[20] As we saw in previous chapters, the mere description of everyday foodstuffs, whether in the form of the roast veal which was the first suppression the editors of the *Revue de Paris* imposed on *Madame Bovary*, or in that of the food that formed the central subject of *Le Ventre de Paris*, was still enough to provoke scandal and outrage in the second half of the nineteenth century in France. Food had already featured in literature for centuries, but almost always marginally, in the form of either sumptuous feasts or awful famine, as an index of decadent prosperity or, conversely, miserable penury. By 1920, with naturalism an established school, routine descriptions of food as sustenance were no longer viewed as literary heresy. When Woolf observes in *A Room of One's Own* (1929) that "it is part of the novelist's convention not to mention soup and salmon and ducklings, as if soup and salmon and ducklings were of no importance whatsoever, as if nobody ever smoked a cigar or drank a glass of wine," it is of course a prelude to her announcement that she is about to "take the liberty to defy that convention" and describe a meal, something she had already done at greater and more lyrical length in *To the Lighthouse* (1927).[21] Woolf's defiance of convention stops at the bounds of conversational propriety; and while soup may have formed an integral part of everyday meals among various classes, salmon and ducklings situate Woolf's call for the iconoclastic depiction of the everyday in a more rarified culinary atmosphere. More pertinently than these fancy foodstuffs, ordinary middle-class eating habits had never before been described in a literary work. And certainly, the depiction of what happens at the other end of the digestive tract had never been attempted in noncomical literature before *Ulysses* (with the notable exception of Sade, that is, but the status of his works in terms of comedy remains ambiguous). Nor, for that matter, did anyone rush to follow this particular example.

Joyce stresses the idea that what goes in must come out. Leopold Bloom, the first fictional character to defecate as a routine matter rather than as the stuff of farce (and here it should be remembered that the word *farce* actually means "stuffing"), is also, uncoincidentally, preoccupied with what has come in our post-Freudian age to be termed anality. If his trip to the "jakes" was itself viewed from the outset as unprintable, the linkage of excretory themes with eroticism throughout the novel was, as we shall see, an aspect of the book that proved especially difficult for even the most broad-minded of readers to accept. What is more, like a number of the other books treated here (most flagrantly *Madame Bovary*, *Tropic of Cancer*, and *Lolita*), *Ulysses* contains an internal meditation on its own transgressive nature. The novel does not just represent defecation; it also, separately, ruminates on the traditional nonrepresentability of that function. In a sporadically recurring line of inquiry that begins in the eighth episode, Bloom considers whether Greek statues are provided with organs of excretion. While eating his lunch he pictures the statues of "naked goddesses" in the museum, calling their curves "aids to digestion," which prompts a further contemplation of what the gods reportedly ate, which in turn leads to the following train of thought:

> Lovely forms of women sculpted Junonian. Immortal lovely. And we stuffing food in one hole and out behind: food, chyle, blood, dung, earth, food: have to feed it like stoking an engine. They have no. Never looked. I'll look today. (176)

At the end of the day, though, the penultimate episode's catalogue of accomplishments and missed opportunities notes "a provisional failure . . . to certify the presence or absence of posterior rectal orifice in the case of Hellenic female divinities" (729). Nonetheless, however inconclusive his investigations may be, he has somehow been caught in the act of scrutiny, and Buck Mulligan draws pederastic conclusions from Bloom's examination of the statues' backsides. "O, I fear me, he is Greeker than the Greeks. His pale Galilean eyes were upon her mesial groove," Mulligan orates warningly to Stephen, providing an indictment within the novel itself of what was to trouble readers for decades to come (201). Bloom need not have taken the trouble: as we know, and as Bloom himself knows as well, even without looking, Greek statues have no posterior rectal orifices. Characters in the *Odyssey* eat too, but they do not excrete. It took Joyce to reinvent a classical model along these lines, putting the rectum (back) into serious art.

As the truncated but nonetheless comprehensible sentence "They have no" demonstrates, the part of the body in question still cannot be named, even if Joyce is here caught in the act of making it marginally representable. Bloom vacillates, as does the novel, between the ellipsis of "They have no" and absurdly ponderous circumlocutions such as "posterior rectal orifice" and "mesial groove." This is, moreover, a difficulty that never goes away—we shall see Lawrence handling it exclusively in robust dialect several years later—and the problem of vocabulary presented by the nether regions perfectly exemplifies in linguistic terms the ongoing question of representability of both excretion and sex as well. Bloom's initial sentence about the Greek statues enacts what it observes, is tautological in its incompleteness: there is no readily available word for what the statues lack, for the very same reason for which they lack it. Of course, there is also the simple anatomical explanation that the human rectum is not readily visible in the standing form and therefore literally has no place in classical statuary, but this is beside the point, which only reinforces the symbolic nature of the question. As it is, the delicately elliptical sentence itself necessarily commits the typographical obscenity of making its concluding punctuation mark into an anus.

The linked themes of eating and excretion are present from the moment we meet Bloom. The fourth episode (or "Calypso," to use the Homeric nomenclature that is absent from the text itself but became standard usage in Joyce circles as a result of Stuart Gilbert's guidebook, about which more later) begins with Bloom's gastronomic liking for the inner organs of animals before it moves on to a privileged glimpse of the workings of Leopold Bloom's own. The first thing we are told about Bloom is his liking for offal: "Mr Leopold Bloom ate with relish the inner organs of beasts and fowls." "Most of all," the first paragraph concludes, "he liked grilled mutton kidneys which gave to his palate a fine tang of faintly scented urine" (55). Not only, therefore, do we arbitrarily learn of Mr. Bloom's culinary preferences, but this form of sensual pleasure too is intimately linked with the processes of excretion, from the beginning, and in ways that are not usually foregrounded in epicurean description. He also, we learn later, likes gorgonzola, which he has for lunch on a sandwich with blobs of mustard while contemplating the mysteries of classical statuary. Bloom is not exactly a gourmet, and if his penchant for organ meat is our first glimpse of him, this is because of the emphasis Joyce places on the mundanely physical—the organic—in his presentation of the main character. The novel does not just set out perversely to include even the most sordid aspects of everyday life in its depiction of Bloom's day. To boot, it resolutely refuses any sort of idealization, going out of its way to emphasize routine disgustingness, as when the gorgonzola itself (with its "feety savor" [173], a phrase that all by itself calls into question the opposition between tastiness and disgustingness, *goût* and *dégoût*) is elsewhere characterized as the less alluring "corpse of milk" (114): a Baudelairean view of cheese. (A view absent, of course, from Baudelaire's own writings, because cheese, unlike more spectacular and classically sanctioned forms of putrefaction, was in the nineteenth century a subject radically unfit for lyric poetry.)

The technical justification for such lingering on physical functions is stream-of-consciousness narrative, a device owing its original inspiration to Flaubertian narrative technique. Flaubert had made extensive use of what came to be called free indirect style, in which the thoughts of various different characters are conveyed at different moments, not, as had previously been the case, by an omniscient narrator's direct presentation (e.g., "Emma found Charles's conversation to be as flat as the sidewalk"), but by a free-floating citation of the thought itself, which left the reader to figure out whose point of view it conveyed (e.g., "Charles's conversation was as flat as the sidewalk"). The ubiquity of this approach in *Madame Bovary* undoubtedly contributed to its being viewed as morally suspect. The technique requires work on the reader's part, therefore leaving meaning up for grabs, and, by doing away with the clarity of an identifiable omniscient narrator—point of view floats among characters rather than being firmly anchored—it furthers the sense that the novel lacks a moral center of gravity.[22] Several decades later, free indirect style gave rise to stream of consciousness, the modernist technique par excellence, which attempts to render not only specific thoughts of characters but the very processes of thought itself, in all its illogical and disjointed incoherence. (The phrase "stream of consciousness" was first used by William James as a scientific term in 1890 in his *Principles of Psychology*.) As a literary trend, stream of consciousness was not so much an innovation in itself—traces of interior monologue can be seen at least as far back as *Tristram Shandy* in the 1760s—as an innovative exploitation of existing form.

In the early twentieth century the use of interior monologue in literature was also, of course, parallel and to some extent indebted to the development of psychoanalysis, with its emphasis on free association, which was going on at the same time. Although Joyce is generally credited with having pioneered stream of consciousness narrative, it was clearly in the air in the early years of the century, as something of the sort can be seen not only in psychoanalytic theory and case studies but in the fiction of the Austrian writer Arthur Schnitzler (for example the 1901 story *Leutnant Gustl*) and in the works of Marcel Proust (the first section of whose multivolume novel was published in 1913). This technique, which came to be a central characteristic of modernism, was also later used by such writers as Woolf (*Mrs. Dalloway* [1925]; *To the Lighthouse* [1927]; and *The Waves* [1931]) and Faulkner (for example, *The Sound and the Fury* [1931]). By his own admission Joyce had borrowed the idea from Edouard Dujardin, an obscure French writer who had tried out what was later dubbed *monologue intérieur* in a novel published to little fanfare in the 1880s and subsequently rescued from complete obscurity only because of Joyce's announcement that it was Dujardin who had invented stream of consciousness.[23]

The 1887 novel *Les Lauriers sont coupés* (translated into English as *We'll to the Woods No More*; the title comes from a popular song) is a pure experiment in technique. It might reasonably be called a novel about nothing, but unlike *Ulysses* it is not sustained by its style because its style is almost as mundane as its subject. While it lacks a plot in the traditional sense, *Les Lauriers* is a classic tale of boy meets, awkwardly pursues, and eventually renounces girl. To this extent it resembles "Swann in Love," Proust's novel-within-a-novel (the novel being *Swann's Way*, the first volume of *A la recherche du temps perdu*) featuring another inept courtship of a *demi-*

mondaine by a sensitive and self-deluded playboy, except that the only larger narrative in which *Les Lauriers* takes on meaning is that of *Ulysses* as it gave rise to the modernist emphasis on banality. Dujardin himself characterized his work in terms that both recall Flaubert and anticipate Joyce: "six hours, during which *nothing*, no adventure happens . . . the most *banal* life possible, *analyzed* as completely and originally as possible."[24]

If Dujardin's novel was slated for neither censorship nor fame in France in the late 1880s, this was because his groundbreaking representation of banality was just that: banal. The six hours in the life of his protagonist contain a great deal of run-of-the-mill (and even erotic) soul-searching, but none of the unmentionable detail (the crotch-searching, as it were) that would get Joyce into trouble as he represented a day in the life of Leopold Bloom and company. Joyce's novel, in contrast, managed at once to embrace banality as subject and to escape accusations of banality as literature by taking the *Odyssey* as its explicit model, by employing a variety of different and difficult styles, and also by dealing with aspects of everyday life that may be mundane in reality but—by the same token—had never before been taken on in serious literature. As we have seen, routine bodily functions such as nose-blowing and defecation assumed an unprecedented importance in *Ulysses*. But if that book became the quintessential "dirty novel," taking first place in the triumvirate of literary dirt shortly to be formed by Joyce's work, *The Well of Loneliness*, and *Lady Chatterley's Lover*, the "dirt" in question was not just snot and shit. When Judge Woolsey announced in his 1933 decision allowing *Ulysses* to be admitted into the United States that he had not found anything in the novel that he considered to be "dirt for dirt's sake" (xvi), he was not primarily referring to the altered color of the sea, nor to Leopold Bloom's outhouse excursion, even if these aspects of the novel had already, as we shall see, been the object of censorship decisions. What Woolsey meant by "dirt," and what is almost always meant by "dirt" in such discussions, was sex. It was, above all, the relatively explicit representation of sexuality that got *Ulysses* banned in the United States and England for more than a decade after its initial publication.

Not just sexuality, that is, but also the vocabulary of sexuality. Literary "dirt" is in fact a twofold category, referring alternatively—and often simultaneously—to the "four-letter words" that took on great importance in the trials of *Lady Chatterley's Lover* and *Tropic of Cancer*, for instance, and to the depictions of sexuality that were no less at issue in those same trials. The persistent metaphors of "dirt" and "filth" as well as related terms such as "sewage" to refer to sex in literature and art, all of which were deployed unsparingly when *Ulysses* was first published, are, moreover, ample testimony to the degree to which eroticism and excretion are conflated not just for the Leopold Blooms of fiction but for their would-be censors as well. In works such as Lawrence's and Miller's, as in *Ulysses*, the use of vulgar terms is for the most part inseparable from the representations of sexual situations they accompany. But it is also true that *Fanny Hill*, an overtly pornographic work every page of which describes in detail sexual encounters, is famously free from four-letter words; its vocabulary is purely metaphoric, even if its narrative leaves nothing to the imagination. *The Well of Loneliness*, suppressed in England in 1928, was also described as filth, and also prosecuted on the basis of its sexual content—in this case, homosexual content—even though Hall's novel contains no obscene words, nor any description of sexual encounters. Its most salacious passage is the observation "and that night they were not divided."

Ulysses offers increasing doses of overt sexuality as the narrative progresses. But in the opening sections, sexuality and vulgar language, while both present, are dissociated from each other. For instance, the first arrestingly vulgar term besides "snot" (which recurs at the end of the third episode in the form of "the dry snot picked from his nostril" which Stephen Dedalus places "on a ledge of rock, carefully" [51]) is "cunt." This word is not used in a sexual context; like "scrotumtightening," the sexual reference is if anything anti-erotic. (Of course, these terms are also very different, belonging to different vocabularies, and while "scrotum" is a genital reference it belongs to a technical lexicon which would never be found in pornography; even without the "-tightening" the word is anaphrodisiac.) The use of the word *cunt* in the fourth episode ("Calypso") is an exemplary instance of stream-of-consciousness narrative, and it illustrates the ways in which that technique both produced and implicitly justified the presence of unacceptable material. Leopold Bloom is walking in the street, thinking about the Promised Land and the fate of the Jews because of an advertisement he has seen. "A dead sea in a dead land," he is in the process of musing, when an old woman clutching a bottle crosses the street, entering his field of vision and coloring his thoughts: "Now it could bear no more. Dead: an old woman's: the grey sunken cunt of the world" (61).

This passage is particularly remarkable because no sexual reverie prompts the appearance of the word *cunt*. Nor is it used as a vulgar insult. Rather, it forms a metaphor of desolation which is both anatomically referential and anti-erotic. As was true in the case of Baudelaire and would continue to surface in Joyce's legal troubles and beyond, the central criterion of obscenity turned on the issue of a work's potential to excite lustful thoughts in the reader. This was in fact the main point of the "Hicklin Rule," based on *Regina v. Hicklin*, the 1868 case that had refined the rough definition of obscenity established in the first British obscenity law, the 1857 "Obscene Publications Act," and which continued to inform both American and British obscenity law several decades after Judge Woolsey's

1933 decision on *Ulysses*. As Woolsey notes in his verdict, "The meaning of the word 'obscene' as legally defined by the courts is: tending to stir the sex impulses or to lead to sexually impure or lustful thoughts" (xvii). No one could possibly argue that the phrase "the grey sunken cunt of the world" has much potential to prompt lustful thoughts in even the most eclectic of sexual excitement-seekers. It was as though Joyce were attempting to flout the very definition of obscenity, employing obscene language toward non-sexual, even antisexual ends, thus defying the censors to take issue with a use of these terms that seemed to run counter to the way obscenity had been delimited. (Of course, it is also true that this and similar terms are later used in *Ulysses* in overtly sexual contexts.) In any case, the technique of stream-of-consciousness, at least in principle, and under the increasingly acceptable rubric of "realism," justified such usage. Ordinary people employed such terms in thought and conversation, in various different ways, the boundaries of acceptable literary usage notwithstanding.

The phrase "grey sunken cunt of the world" was removed from the first published version of this passage from *Ulysses*. It was, in fact, suppressed at the behest of Ezra Pound. The censorship history of Joyce's novel is especially strange in that it began with expurgation at the hands of Pound, another exemplary figure of modernist literary innovation. *Ulysses* first began appearing in the United States, in Margaret Anderson's avant-garde *Little Review* in 1917. Serial publication of the work was stopped in 1920 after the thirteenth episode ("Nausicaa": in which Bloom masturbates at the sight of the complicit Gerty McDowell's undergarments, to the accompaniment of municipal fireworks) by a prosecution on grounds of obscenity brought by the New York Society for the Suppression of Vice (headed by John Sumner, who had taken over from the infamous Anthony Comstock). Anderson and her coeditor, Jane Heap, lost their case, and publication of the novel ceased. This was why Joyce had so much trouble finding a publisher for his completed novel in any English-speaking country, and why he therefore enthusiastically accepted Sylvia Beach's offer to publish it in unexpurgated form through Shakespeare and Company, her Paris bookshop, in 1922. Even so, the version of the first parts of the book that had come out in *The Little Review* had already been expurgated by Pound, who was both a friend of Joyce and the foreign editor of Anderson's journal. Pound went over the opening sections of the novel and removed what he considered offensive, with the result that the text as initially published contained neither Leopold Bloom's trip to the outhouse nor, for instance, the phrase "the grey sunken cunt of the world." The former passage was selectively edited so as to preserve most of the text while carefully omitting all mention of what exactly Bloom was doing as he read *Titbits*, while in the latter "cunt" was changed to "belly."[25] It is likely that had Pound not acted as he did, *Ulysses* would have been suppressed, and its editors dragged into court, long before publication of the "Nausicaa" episode. Even as it was, four issues of the *Little Review* had already been burned by the United States Post Office.

As had been the case in 1857 when the editors of the *Revue de Paris* removed and modified passages from *Madame Bovary*—although with somewhat different results—Pound in his correspondence with Joyce insists that his motivations in expurgating *Ulysses* were aesthetic more than strategic. That is, he was not suggesting cuts and changes primarily in order to avoid censorship, but because he felt they would improve the work. "I think certain things simply bad writing, in this section" he wrote to Joyce about the fourth chapter of the novel ("Calypso," the episode containing the outhouse passage). "Bad because you waste the violence," he specifies, "violence" referring in this case to the representation of bodily functions. "The contrast between Bloom['s] inner poetry and his outward surroundings is excellent," he adds, "but it will come up without such detailed treatment of the dropping feces." After ironically suggesting that the unexpurgated text could later be published in Greek or Bulgarian translation, Pound concludes by remarking that "in the thing as it stands you will lose effectiveness. The excrements will prevent people from noticing the quality of things contrasted."[26]

In other words, Pound feared that readers would be blinded by the shit. And he was probably right. Woolf, for instance, in an essay originally published in 1919 under the title "Modern Novels" (later revised as "Modern Fiction"), lauds modern novelists, exemplified by Joyce, as attempting "to come closer to life" than their predecessors, and notes that *Ulysses* "promises to be a far more interesting work" than *A Portrait of the Artist as a Young Man*, while reserving judgment because only fragments had been published. Even so, she asserts, "whatever the intention of the whole there can be no question that it is of the utmost sincerity and that the result, difficult or unpleasant as we may judge it, is undeniably important."[27] When she had read the unexpurgated text once the volume had come out, however, the sincerity had become excessively sincere and the unpleasantness a bit too unpleasant. Woolf's diary in 1922 records not only astonishment that T. S. Eliot ("Tom, great Tom," she repeats in disbelief) thought the book "on a par with War & Peace!" but also characterizations in which terms such as "queasy," "nauseating," "illiterate and underbred" recur in a two-page spasm of uneasy disgust.[28] Since she also talks about "filth" and the slight difference between canine and human excretion (see earlier quotations), it seems likely that the restitution of previously suppressed material played no small part in Woolf's distaste for the final product.

Beyond the mere depiction of excremental functions, and beyond mere sexual representation as well, what has bothered readers from Pound to Vladimir Nabokov, even leaving aside such punitive voices as the

Vice Society, is Joyce's failure to draw a clear line of demarcation between these two categories of shameful corporeality, between the sexual and the excremental. Instead, the two are consistently conflated in *Ulysses*, from Bloom's reading of the suggestively titled "Matcham's Masterstroke" on the toilet (which title can be read as foreshadowing the later masturbation scene in the "Nausicaa" episode) to his scrutiny of the backsides of Greek statues, to his appreciative kissing of his wife's bottom in the concluding sections, which also contain much satisfying urination. Nor is the conflation of genital and anal themes confined to what might reasonably be construed as incidental detail. Even the novel's structural parallel to the *Odyssey* gets into the act, as the ten years Odysseus spends away from Ithaca are echoed in the novel by the ten years (since the death of their infant son) during which Bloom has refrained from vaginal intercourse with his wife, preferring various forms of homage to her posterior. When Nabokov taught Joyce's novel, which he loudly considered a masterpiece, in his Masters of European Fiction course at Cornell, he warned his students about this aspect of the work: "I shall not bore you with a list of his curious desires, but this I will say: in Bloom's mind and in Joyce's book the theme of sex is continually mixed and intertwined with the theme of the latrine" (*Lectures*, 287).

Nabokov, who was himself shortly to encounter charges of obscenity with his portrait of a pedophile in *Lolita* (whose *succès de scandale* allowed him to give up teaching entirely), takes pains to note that his objection is not to the emphasis on sex per se, but rather to this aberrant mingling of sexuality with "the theme of the latrine." In terms that recall Pound's protestation that some of the details would divert readers' attention from what was truly important, he continues:

> God knows I have no objection whatsoever to so-called frankness in literature. On the contrary, we have too little of it. . . . But I do object to the following: Bloom is supposed to be a rather ordinary citizen. Now it is not true that the mind of an ordinary citizen continuously dwells on physiological things. I object to the continuously, not to the disgusting. All this very special pathological stuff seems artificial and unnecessary in this particular context.

In light of the scandal of *Lolita*, these criticisms might seem like the pot calling the kettle pathological (in Nabokov's defense, though, we should remember that his Humbert is never described, even by himself, as an ordinary citizen; see chapter 7). He concludes by suggesting to his students that "the squeamish among you regard the special preoccupation of Joyce with perfect detachment."[29] Nabokov then resumes his discussion of *Ulysses* with a dig at "the kind of critic who is more interested in ideas and generalities and human aspects than in the work of art itself," and a warning to those who would try to read the novel chiefly as a reworking of the *Odyssey* (287–88).

Ironically, in light of his own disapproval of Bloom's "pathology," the sort of reading Nabokov warns against, which foregrounds classical allusions and highlights "great ideas," is precisely the approach that has allowed *Ulysses* to become a sanctified "great classic," with its more unseemly aspects accordingly glossed over, and emphasis placed on "universal" themes and values. A similar phenomenon has occurred with Proust's *A la recherche du temps perdu*, the first volume of which also figures on Nabokov's Masters of European Fiction syllabus. While it was never censored, Proust's novel created an ongoing scandal as its seven volumes were published between 1913 and 1927, because of its increasing attention to homosexuality and sadomasochism. Despite the centrality of these themes, and in part because of its daunting length, it was not long before Proust's *Recherche* came to be read for its opening and concluding passages dealing with the nature of time and memory, especially the famous "petite madeleine" scene in which the narrator recounts his experience of recalling the lost world of childhood by eating a small cake dipped in tea. *Ulysses* contains no such set-piece passage which can be excerpted and read as exemplifying the work's "universal values" to the detriment of its more unpalatable aspects. Nonetheless, Joyce's novel has been domesticated as much as Proust's, both books incorporated into the sort of narrative of "timeless greatness" which Nabokov's lectures on literature recount even as they explicitly eschew the "great ideas" approach.

In the case of *Ulysses*, perhaps the most flamboyant example of domestication—by which I mean the glossing over of unseemly preoccupations such as the lack of demarcation between sexuality and "latrine" themes—is, unsurprisingly, to be found in Judge Woolsey's decision allowing the novel into the United States in 1933. As we have seen, John Quinn, the attorney who first took on the defense of *Ulysses* in 1920, grounded his defense in the idea that he himself did not understand the book and felt that Joyce had gone too far in his literary innovations, an argument meant both to disarm the judges and to provide empirical evidence of its lack of potential to harm. The novel was, he suggested, a provocative aberration but an incomprehensible one, and therefore posed no conceivable danger to the general public. ("I argued . . . that nobody could understand what Ulysses was about and therefore it could not corrupt anyone," he wrote.)[30] And these assumptions might have been proven correct had his defense strategy succeeded. But because the judges were unmoved by his arguments, the case was lost, and the novel banned, with the usual result: fame, if not fortune, at least not for the author or editors. In other words, it was only because the novel was deemed a danger to the public that it had the opportunity to become one. Instead of an obscure reworking of the *Odyssey*, of interest only to connoisseurs of avant-garde art and accessible only at the cost of a great deal of work and intellectual energy, *Ulysses* became a sought-after "dirty book," the object of a thriving illegal import trade once it was published abroad, and doubtless read, or at least thumbed, by sections of the reading public that would never have dreamed of attempting it under less challenging circumstances. On the other hand, efforts to import Joyce's novel into England for academic purposes failed: in 1926, the eminent critic F. R. Leavis was thwarted by the British Home Office in his attempts to secure a copy of *Ulysses* for his course on Modern Problems in Criticism at Cambridge University. One of the points of contention in this dispute was that the class was mixed, and, despite arguments that the novel was already in circulation even in the women's colleges at Cambridge, Leavis was denied permission to import a copy of the book. He continued, nonetheless, to include a passage from the novel in his lectures throughout the ban.[31] The story of illegal importation and bootleg editions would become, with variations, an increasingly familiar one in the following decades, as "serious" literature from *Lady Chatterley* and *Tropic of Cancer* to *Lolita* was published in Europe sometimes decades before becoming legally available in English-speaking countries.

In New York in 1920, Margaret Anderson and Jane Heap paid fines in lieu of a jail sentence, and serial publication of *Ulysses* was curtailed after the "Nausicaa" episode, which featured the masturbation scene that had in the end been found too comprehensible to escape accusations of obscenity. The New York State Court of Special Sessions Magistrate Joseph E. Corrigan found that "there was one episode in the book that anyone could understand," specifically "the episode where the man went off in his pants, which no one could misunderstand, and that I think is smutty, filthy within the meaning of the statute."[32] To this extent, then, Joyce was found guilty of excessive comprehensibility. But the version of the novel that was on trial in this case was already an expurgated one, as we have seen, and therefore omitted those details that Nabokov later objected to. It was not until 1933 that the "latrine"-related aspects of the novel were scrutinized in a legal context. In an example of the sort of historical irony that abounds in literary censorship cases, it may have been just these elements that allowed Woolsey to pronounce his historic decision that the novel was not obscene.

When *Ulysses* was, thanks to Woolsey, at last published in the United States in 1934, it contained—like most present editions—the decision, as well as a letter from Joyce to Bennett Cerf of Random House, and a foreword by Morris L. Ernst, the attorney who successfully represented the case before the United States New York District Court in 1933. Unlike cur-

rent editions, the 1934 edition presents Ernst's foreword, a celebration of
the 1933 *Ulysses* decision as changing censorship policy forever, as the first
bit of prose the reader encounters. It begins: "The New Deal in the law of
letters is here," and continues, two paragraphs later, to say the following:

> The *Ulysses* case marks a turning point. It is a body-blow for the censors. The
> necessity for hypocrisy and circumlocution in literature has been elimi-
> nated. Writers need no longer seek refuge in euphemisms. They may now
> describe basic human functions without fear of the law. (vii)

If this had actually proved to be the case, the present study would end with
this chapter. As it was, Ernst's prediction was a bit optimistic, but as he
points out, those were heady times: "The first week of December 1933 will
go down in history for two repeals, that of Prohibition and that of the legal
compulsion for squeamishness in literature" (ibid., vii). The legalization
of *Ulysses* is like that of liquor: both are intoxicating brews, to be served
only to those able to handle them: for adults only. It is also no accident
that Ernst uses the word *squeamishness* in relation to the precedent set (in
principle at least) by this case, just as Nabokov had invited the "squeamish" among his students to "regard the special preoccupation of Joyce with
perfect detachment." Regard this special preoccupation with perfect detachment is precisely what Woolsey had taken it upon himself to do, as he
too had proclaimed himself repelled by certain aspects—evidently the
same aspects—of the novel.

One of the major ways in which the 1933 decision departed from its
precedents, and one of the major reasons Ernst felt confident that it would
do away with literary obscenity prosecutions in as definitive a manner as
the repeal of Prohibition was to do away with enforced temperance, was
that for the first time in the history of such rulings, Woolsey had taken
artistic merit into account as a positive category. But artistic merit was not,
in fact, the basis for his decision. Relatedly, and more importantly in terms
of judicial precedent—his decision went on to be cited in virtually all literary obscenity cases in the United States for the next thirty years—he had
departed from the "Hicklin" rule in two ways. First, he insisted that the potential for obscenity be judged on the basis of the work as a whole, rather
than on excerpted passages—as we have seen, this had been a bone of
contention in such trials at least since 1857, and a practice that had always
benefited the prosecution. (In Flaubert's trial, for instance, Pinard began
by the rhetorical move of lamenting that the novel could not be read out
in its entirety, but then proceeded to exploit the excerpting of specific
passages.) Woolsey also replaced the traditional "young person" criterion
by testing the novel on two examples of the "normal person" or "person
with average sex instincts." "What the French would call *l'homme moyen sen-*

suel," he adds, although the very use of this phrase would surely seem to discredit the democratic premises of his method, since anyone capable of deciphering this reference would necessarily belong to the category of highly educated men: as we have seen, traditionally the group least in need of protection. The judge bears out his implicit reframing of the question of corruptible readership by noting that his control group consisted of two friends of his who had already read *Ulysses*. Presumably these were people who used, or at least understood, the phrase *homme moyen sensuel*, more than they incarnated it in this context. Unsurprisingly, in any case, both men agreed with Woolsey's assessment of the novel:

> that reading "Ulysses" in its entirety, as a book must be read on such a test as this, did not tend to excite sexual impulses or lustful thoughts but that its net effect on them was only that of a somewhat tragic and very powerful commentary on the inner lives of men and women. (xiii)

Woolsey had previously noted that "the meaning of the word 'obscene' as defined by the Court was: tending to stir the sex impulses or to lead to sexually impure and lustful thoughts" (ibid., xiii). The original "Hicklin Rule," on which American as well as British obscenity law was still based, was more specific, the criterion being "whether the tendency of the matter charged as obscenity is to deprave and corrupt those whose minds are open to such immoral influences, and into whose hands a publication of this sort may fall."[33] This had always been taken to mean that a work was to be judged obscene which might corrupt a hypothetical "young person." But *Ulysses* was evidently not meant for the young and impressionable (any more, at least in principle, than liquor). John Quinn had in 1920 made the same argument as the one implicit in Woolsey's decision: *Ulysses* was "neither written for nor read by schoolgirls," and therefore the test should be its effect on the average person.[34] Along the same lines, Quinn's first witness, the writer John Cowper Powys, declared Joyce's novel "a beautiful piece of work in no way capable of corrupting the minds of young girls"; furthermore, it was "too obscure and philosophical a work to be in any sense corrupting."[35]

Even though his decision emphasizes the artistic merit of the work, often veering off into the language of literary criticism, the chief innovation in the decision, and the reason Ernst sees in it the end of all obscenity proceedings, is the displacement of the burden of corruptibility from young girls onto the "normal person." Woolsey concludes his discussion by noting the following:

> I am quite aware that owing to some of its scenes "Ulysses" is a rather strong draught to ask some sensitive, though normal, persons to take. But my con-

sidered opinion, after long reflection, is that whilst in many places the effect
of 'Ulysses' on the reader undoubtedly is somewhat emetic, nowhere does it
tend to be an aphrodisiac. (xiv)

There follows the historic judgment: "'Ulysses' may, therefore, be admitted into the United States" (ibid., xiv). The verdict, it is clear, turned not
on the category of artistic merit, but on the idea that even though the
novel is salacious in parts, its cumulative effect is "emetic" rather than
"aphrodisiac." *Ulysses* was allowed into the United States because its "new
realism" might make readers vomit (apparently a morally acceptable form
of reader response), but it would certainly not, at least taken as a whole,
excite them. In other words, the very passages Pound had removed from
the opening sections of the work when it was first published in *The Little
Review*, on the grounds that they caused the novel to "lose effectiveness"
because "the excrements will prevent people from noticing the quality of
things contrasted," were the same elements that provided the basis for
Woolsey's ground-breaking decision to allow the novel into the United
States in unexpurgated form.

James Douglas, the journalist who wrote that *Ulysses* was "the most infamously obscene work in ancient or modern literature," went on to say the
following: "The obscenity of Rabelais is innocent compared with its leprous and scabrous horrors. All the secret sewers of vice are canalized in its
flood of unimaginable thoughts, images and pornographic words."[36] As I
have suggested, rhetoric such as the phrases Douglas deploys to indict
Ulysses bears witness to the conflation of excremental and sexual themes
in the minds of its censors and would-be censors as well as in the novel itself. Douglas is talking about the unexpurgated version of the novel published by Sylvia Beach in 1922. Before that text was made legally available
to the American public in 1934 by Judge Woolsey's decision, the book was
known in the United States through illegally imported copies, through
hearsay, and also through a work that continues even now to introduce
readers to Joyce's novel. When Woolsey wrote of *Ulysses* in his decision that
"in order properly to approach the consideration of it it is advisable to
read a number of other books which have now become its satellites" (x),
he was referring primarily to a book first published in the United States in
1930, Stuart Gilbert's *James Joyce's Ulysses*. Gilbert, an Englishman, was a
member of Joyce's circle of admirers in Paris, and one of the team of translators which, headed by the French writer Valery Larbaud, produced the
French translation of *Ulysses*. His work remains the standard guidebook to
Joyce's novel, which has spawned a great many reader's guides. *James Joyce's
Ulysses* has gone through numerous printings and is still widely available
today in a relatively inexpensive paperback edition (less expensive, in fact,
than any extant edition of *Ulysses* itself).[37]

Gilbert's book is important in terms of the censorship history of *Ulysses* because it was available in the United States before Joyce's actual text, and thus, during the interval between its publication in 1930 and the free circulation of the novel in 1934, provided not only the helpful introductory material that it continues to offer, but also the only version of *Ulysses* to which the American public had legitimate access. It is largely thanks to this book, which was written with the authorization and even collaboration of Joyce himself, that *Ulysses* is read as it has been for seventy years and more: that is, with Homeric titles for each of the episodes, as well as with a complicated schematic breakdown of the specific scene, hour, organ, art, color, symbol and "technic" for each episode. Thus, for instance, the third chapter is labeled "Calypso," its scene is the House, its hour 8:00 a.m., its organ the Kidney, its art Economics, its color Orange, its symbol the Nymph, and its technic Narrative (mature). None of this is evident in the novel itself, not even the chapter titles. One might therefore imagine that this intricate chart is a product of the well-known scholarly emphasis on rendering everything as obscure and difficult as possible. Nabokov, for one, cautioned against the sort of approach taken by most commentators on *Ulysses*, announcing to his class that "I must especially warn against seeing in Leopold Bloom's humdrum wanderings and minor adventures on a summer day in Dublin a close parody of the *Odyssey*." Nabokov then adds a specific dig at the man most singularly responsible for propounding the reading in question: "One bore, a man called Stuart Gilbert, misled by a tongue-in-cheek list compiled by Joyce himself, found in every chapter the domination of one particular organ—the ear, the eye, the stomach, etc.— but we shall ignore that dull nonsense too" (*Lectures*, 288). As Nabokov notes, it was Joyce who had fed Gilbert the material for his chart. If it was indeed a joke, it must be counted as one of the most (or, alternatively, least) successful practical jokes in literary history.

Even with its Homeric titles in place, *Ulysses* does not in fact closely parallel the *Odyssey*. The latter comprises twenty-four "books," whereas *Ulysses* has eighteen chapters or episodes, unnumbered and untitled. Still, Joyce's novel roughly follows the structure of its epic antecedent, even if, for instance, the tenth section, "Wandering Rocks," does not have a counterpart in the *Odyssey*. In any case it is worth asking why Joyce provided his novel with a Homeric structure to match its title, then removed all internal evidence of that structure, only to allow it to resurface in the form of a commentary written by someone else. One obvious answer is that, as Joyce himself reportedly proclaimed, he wanted to give scholars centuries of material to work on. And his strategy has worked: academic exegesis of Joyce's writings shows no signs of flagging. Hundreds of books and thousand of articles have been published on *Ulysses* alone, he is one of the few authors to have annual conferences devoted solely to their work, and there even exists an *Introducing Joyce* comic book. Stuart Gilbert's guidebook has been immeasurably influential in this flood of commentary, as all scholarly work on Joyce uses his chart of references, most visibly in the form of the Homeric titles Joyce provided him with, and which quickly became the standard chapter-titles in the novel, even though they are nowhere present in the work itself. What is especially noteworthy about Gilbert's book in this context, though, is the degree to which it presanitizes Joyce's work.[38]

James Joyce's Ulysses precedes *Ulysses* itself, in two ways. As I have mentioned, Gilbert's guide was first published in 1930, some four years before *Ulysses* became available in the United States, and it therefore served as a crucial introduction to the novel. Because it became available several years before the book it was designed to present, Gilbert filled it not just with interpretation but with plot summary, and also lengthy quotations from the novel. The book consists of two parts: an introductory commentary, emphasizing "universal themes" and parallels with the *Odyssey*, and an explanatory breakdown of the individual chapters. Since it was meant at least provisionally to replace Joyce's book, it reads for the most part as a sort of highbrow Cliff's Notes version of *Ulysses*. After the novel itself was allowed to be published in the United States following Judge Woolsey's decision, Gilbert's guidebook continued to be a popular introduction to the novel, and in 1952 a new, expanded edition was published (the same edition still available today). In his preface to the second edition Gilbert cites his earlier preface, in which he stated that he had " 'quoted freely from the text' " so that those who were unable to " 'acquire the original, may, despite the censorial ban, become acquainted with Mr Joyce's epic work' " (v). Since that work was now available to all, Gilbert was faced in 1952 with the problem of what to do with these extensive quotations from the text. He decided to retain them:

> I have been told by a surprisingly large number of people that they attempted to read *Ulysses* and gave it up, as making too great demands on their attention, memory and endurance. When, however, they returned to it, after reading this commentary and understanding the thematic structure, the relation of the episodes each to each and the concatenation of the events narrated, they found it relatively easy and unusually exhilarating reading. (v–vi)

In other words, Gilbert's commentary, by design, preceded Joyce's novel because it was designed to be used, and according to its author, was in fact used, as a vast preface to the work itself, a predigested foretaste, as it were, a pre-*Ulysses* version of *Ulysses*, the literary equivalent of a practice run before a marathon. Its continuing availability in a paperback edition cheaper than the novel itself, moreover, suggests that Gilbert's 1952 remark was no idle boast. What this means is that Joyce's great dirty book, "too dirty to be easily accessible," in Burgess's words, continues to be approached as it was before it became legally accessible on these shores: through Gilbert's guidebook. And because the latter preceded Joyce's novel in English-speaking countries, it was necessarily—and less necessarily remains—a very sanitized version of *Ulysses.*

Gilbert serves up great chunks of Joycean prose in his book, and they almost always stop precisely short of the sort of passages that have been at issue in this chapter. This is no coincidence, because these passages are crucial to the aesthetic revolution that *Ulysses* represents, and that got it into trouble in the first place (1920) and especially in the second place (1933). Gilbert had a difficult balancing act to perform, at least in 1930: he had to convey and celebrate the iconoclastic aspects of the novel while remaining within the bounds of propriety so as to avoid a replay of "the censorial ban." He therefore tries hard to avoid reproduction of its more provocative elements even as he suggests both that the work represents an epoch-making break with the past and that censorship of it is an absurdity. The task is both impossible and familiar. The same sort of domestication of the unacceptable is at work in every case treated in this book: this is how "obscene" works make the transition to "classic" status, or at least how the transition is marked. We have already seen the equivalent of Gilbert's job performed by Minnelli in his film of *Madame Bovary,* for instance, and by the French court that rehabilitated the six poems removed from *The Flowers of Evil.* The salient difference in the case of *Ulysses* is that Gilbert's clean-up job effectively precedes the novel itself, rather than following it after a lapse of almost a century.

Unlike Minnelli in his treatment of Flaubert's novel, Gilbert was able to remain entirely faithful to the plot (such as it is) and structure of Joyce's work. The breakdown of each episode is impeccable: it is in the details that Gilbert sins by omission. But the devil, as always, is in the details. In his discussion of the first section, for instance, Gilbert cites Buck Mulligan's "*Thalatta! Thalatta!* She is our great sweet mother," but omits his previous references to "The snotgreen sea. The scrotumtightening sea" (Gilbert, 99). As the passage from Arthur Power's memoir cited at the beginning of this chapter suggests ("Read what I have written above: 'The snotgreen sea. The scrotumtightening sea"), Joyce was intent on refusing the tempting reading of his book which would retain the classical reference and the Swinburnean "She is our great sweet mother" while ignoring "snotgreen" and "scrotumtightening."[39] Gilbert does not, though, remove all traces of snot from the work. He quotes Mulligan's request for a loan of Stephen's "snotrag," and further cites his coinage of "snotgreen" as a "new art colour for our Irish poets" (98–99). But he appends a prudent footnote:

> The Oxford Dictionary proscribes the word "snot" and its adjective as "not
> in decent use"; but the latter, anyhow, has been canonized by the pious
> George Herbert in *Jacula Prudentum*: "Better a snotty child than his nose
> wiped off." (98 n. 3)

The canonized adjective is not "snotgreen," of course, but "snotty," and its
presence in a work by the seventeenth-century British moralist Herbert
justifies both Joyce's use of variants and Gilbert's citation of them, even
against the disapproval of as lofty an authority as the *OED*. (The much-
reprinted 1971 edition of that dictionary takes a different approach:
under the definition "the mucus of the nose," the still-current *OED* notes:
"Now *dial.* or *vulgar.* Common in the 17th cent.," and goes on to quote a
number of examples, not including Herbert.)

Later passages do not fare so well. Gilbert would have been hard put,
for instance, to find a precedent in Herbert or any equivalent moral authority for use of the word *cunt* in the fourth episode. Although that term
has been around for a very long time, the contemporary *OED* did not
even, as in the case of "snot," dignify it with disapproval—nor, for that
matter, does the word figure in the 1971 edition. Any early precedents
Gilbert might have cited would necessarily have come from literature of a
sort that would not have helped his case; even Chaucer's Wife of Bath, or
Hamlet's punning on "country matters" would not have gone far to excuse Joyce's use of the term. As a result, in Gilbert's version the passage in
which the word occurs is extensively cited, Bloom's reverie on the Dead
Sea and the Chosen People is present, and the same "bent hag" crosses
the road, but the scene ends with "Now it could bear no more. Dead . . . ,"
where Joyce's text reads: "Dead: an old woman's: the grey sunken cunt of
the world" (Gilbert, 136; *Ulysses*, 61), and the *Little Review* text retains the
rest of the sentence while substituting "belly" for the offending term.
Later in the same episode, Bloom's trip to the "jakes" is included, but in a
manner so perfunctory as to erase its importance, and even its meaning,
altogether: "Mr Bloom now visits the earth-closet at the end of his garden,
where he reads the prize story in *Tit-Bits*, "*Matcham's Masterstroke*" by
Philip Beaufoy, Playgoers' Club, London, and considers the possibility of
himself composing a 'prize titbit' " (139). The four full paragraphs devoted to Bloom's revolutionary excretion are thus elided. Gilbert's summary serves the same purpose as Pound's expurgated version: while pre-
serving the basic lines of the narrative, both make it sound as though
Bloom's visit to the "earth-closet" (a term not used by Joyce) were for
purely literary purposes.

Bloom's lunchtime rumination on the backsides of Greek statues meets
a similar fate: a great deal of the passage is excerpted, including the part
about "stuffing food in one hole and out behind: food, chyle, blood, dung,

earth, food." So far, so acceptable, since "chyle" (a Greek word for digestive fluid) has a nicely obscure classical ring to it, and "dung" conveys the
animal import of the passage while at the same time remaining within the
OED-sanctioned limits of earthy vocabulary.[40] The sentences which follow,
however, are gone, in which Bloom muses "they have no. Never looked.
I'll look today" (Gilbert, 205; Joyce, 176). In the "Nausicaa" masturbation
episode, Gilbert's account of what happens is also at once detailed and in-
complete, filled with extensive quotation, yet missing key elements, and
while Gilbert does not entirely omit Bloom's solitary voyeuristic orgasm,
he represents it in unrecognizably euphemistic terms, with recourse to the
French: "Leopold Bloom is *aux anges*," an expression meaning very happy
(284). Finally, in his commentary on the concluding "Penelope" passage,
Molly Bloom's famous soliloquy in which she goes into a great deal of detail regarding, among other unmentionable topics, the sexual performances of various men, Gilbert paves the way for generations of critics
who have seen in this extended, almost punctuation-free monologue the
voice of "an ancient wisdom, the warmblooded yet unsentimental exi-
gence of the life-force" (403).

This sort of universalizing interpretation is reductive, and even misleading. Molly Bloom's monologue is in fact quite sentimental, ending as
it does on the tender memory of her first encounter with Bloom; "warmblooded yet unsentimental" in this context is a euphemism for sexually explicit. The passage is certainly no vague celebration of the life-force. Instead it recapitulates many of the more problematic themes foregrounded
in the rest of the book, this time from Molly's point of view. It includes
such thoughts as the following, which takes up her husband's musings on
classical statuary, in a more anatomically explicit manner, as she contem-
plates the form of male genitalia:

> what are all those veins and things curious the way its made 2 the same in
> case of twins theyre supposed to represent beauty placed up there like those
> statues in the museum one of them pretending to hide it with her hand are
> they so beautiful of course compared with what a man looks like with his two
> bags full and his other thing hanging down out of him or sticking up at you
> like a hatrack no wonder they hide it with a cabbageleaf. (753)

Or this, from a passage in which the juxtaposition of sexuality and anality
is presented from a feminine perspective, with erotic fantasy meeting flat-
ulence and other unpleasant realities in Molly's semiconscious reverie:

> my hole is itching me always when I think of him I feel I want to I feel some
> wind in me better go easy not wake him have him at it again slobbering after
> washing every bit of myself back belly and sides if we had even a bath itself or

my own room anyway I wish hed sleep in some room by himself with his cold
feet on me give us room even to let a fart God or do the least thing better yes
hold them like that a bit on my side piano quietly sweeeee theres that train
far away pianissimo eeeeeee one more song. (763)

Molly Bloom too—especially, even—is concerned with the fouler points of
human anatomy, and her concluding monologue is in fact remarkably
free not only of punctuation but of the interior-monologue discretion—
the automatic self-censorship—which had earlier prompted her husband
to leave his sentences dangling, as in "They have no." Her own sentences
go on seemingly forever (the forty-five page monologue contains only one
punctuation mark, a period). The candidly fluid and unprecedentedly
streaming stream of consciousness, or semiconsciousness—she is after all
half asleep, which in part explains her candor—has led some feminist critics to claim this section of *Ulysses* as prefiguring *écriture féminine*, the specifically feminine brand of writing proposed by French feminist theorists as a
free-form alternative to phallocentric models of expression.[41] But it has
most often been construed, following Gilbert, as being some sort of
vaguely universal affirmation of "the life-force." To be sure, Gilbert can
hardly be held responsible for what amounts to a traditional critical move,
in which great works are reduced to grand, "universal" themes. This approach to literature in general is nicely parodied by James Hynes in his
novel *The Lecturer's Tale*, in which a writing instructor gives his students the
assignment "to summarize great works of literature as bumper stickers:
Moby Dick as 'Man vs. Nature: The Final Conflict' or *The Sun Also Rises* as
'Isn't it Pretty to Think So?' or the collected works of the Brontë sisters as
'Love Hurts.' "[42] The closing monologue in *Ulysses* might thus be summa-
rized as "The Earth-Mother Speaks." Gilbert was only, in this case, the first
on the scene. To reduce the anatomically specific, fart-rich account of a
woman's experience in the closing chapter of Joyce's novel to the general-
izations of a "Gaia-Tellos" life-affirmation is still, though, to suck the life
out of its affirmation.[43]

    After all, in the end the Bloom ménage is not all that different from
Flaubert's scandalous couple. Molly Bloom is a direct descendant of Emma
Bovary. Both are the bored wives of decent but unexciting men they married because it seemed like the best option at the time, and both engage
vividly in adulterous liaisons that ultimately prove to be as unsatisfying as
their married lives. If Emma's expressions of desire for something more
have never been characterized as the liberatory outpourings of the human
spirit, the difference lies in both content and style. Things had also
changed, certainly, between 1857 and 1922. But while *Ulysses* was never inculpated primarily on grounds of the unpunished female infidelity that

forms the center of what little plot the novel has, it was not because the ostensible celebration of adultery had ceased to be grounds for prosecution: this much became abundantly clear with the publication of *Lady Chatterley's Lover* in 1928. Instead, it was because Molly Bloom's 4:00 p.m. encounter with Blazes Boylan was, in the grand scheme of *Ulysses*, the least of Joyce's worries. Too many other "obscene" elements had pushed female adultery out of the forefront of unacceptability. In any case, though, Molly Bloom became a spokeswoman for "ancient wisdom" and "the life-force," despite her basic resemblance to Emma Bovary, and this for a number of reasons. For one thing, certainly, she does not allow adultery to destroy her. Instead, she frames her monologue with the reverberating "yes" that has often been read as life-affirmation, but which in fact, taken in context, more clearly indicates the provisional acceptance of a less-than-perfect marital arrangement: realism, as it happens, in yet another usage of the term. If we were to engage with *Ulysses* in the literary game of guessing what happens afterward (which Flaubert, following nineteenth-century practice, spares us), we could hardly imagine a happily-ever-after scenario for anyone involved. To some degree the "Penelope" monologue reads as though *Madame Bovary* had concluded with one of Emma's periodic unsuccessful attempts to find solace in her legitimate situation. But this, of course, would have been absurd, unacceptable within the confines of both Flaubert's novel itself and nineteenth-century fictional convention in general: Madame Bovary must die, either by her own hand or in the gutter (that is, as a prostitute, of syphilis, preferably with graphic descriptions of her face disintegrating). The rules of fiction had changed in the interim, in part because of Flaubert himself and his followers, and in part, as a consequence, because Joyce and company were still busy changing them. This shift was not just in what was acceptable in moral terms; again, D. H. Lawrence among others was to prove that adultery continued, well into the twentieth century, not to be taken lightly. It was a matter of style, too. The same radical stream-of-consciousness approach that made Joyce's novel all but unreadable was also what made Molly Bloom's soliloquy ripe for interpretation as an affirmation of the life-force, rather than merely the free-floating reminiscences of an unfaithful wife. The "Penelope" section of *Ulysses* is above all a stylistic tour-de-force. In terms of content it is an inconclusive conclusion: an appropriate ending to a novel about nothing, sustained by style alone.

In his preface to the 1952 edition of *James Joyces's Ulysses* Gilbert notes that he has "not tried to alleviate the rather pedantic tone of much of the writing in this Study. For one thing," he says,

> Joyce approved of it; and for another, we who admired *Ulysses* for its structural, enduring qualities and not for the occasional presence in it of words

and descriptive passages which shocked our elders, were on the defensive, and the pedant's cloak is often a convenient protection against the cold blasts of propriety. (ix)

Gilbert hedges his bets in such characterizations, minimizing the presence in *Ulysses* of shocking elements as though they were incidental to the novel's overall importance, and lauding those who like himself saw beyond those problematic aspects of the work. It is only in the preliminary, sanitized versions, though—his own and Pound's—and not as it was finally allowed to be published in English-speaking countries, that the novel reads this way. In *Ulysses* as Joyce wrote it these unacceptable elements are crucial, as he himself emphasized. He nonetheless approved of the "rather pedantic tone" of Gilbert's study, and of the study in general, because he wanted it both ways. Joyce wanted to stress the snotgreen, scrotumtightening aspects of his work—no "occasional presence," but central to the revolutionary import of the work—while at the same time hiding from "the cold blasts of propriety" behind the pedant's cloak. In *Ulysses*, therefore, we find not merely the most unlikely of dirty books but also, by the same token, a work that contains and anticipates its own disingenuous commentary: modern epic in all its self-referential degradation.

CHAPTER FOUR

Radclyffe Hall

The Well of Prussic Acid

As for being poisoned by a book, there is no such thing as that. Art has
no influence upon action. It annihilates the desire to act. It is superbly
sterile. The books that the world calls immoral are books that show the
world its own shame. That is all.

OSCAR WILDE, *The Picture of Dorian Gray*

A t first glance it might seem difficult to imagine a work less like
Ulysses than *The Well of Loneliness*. Where Joyce's epic offers a spectacular series of variations on the theme of nothing at all—and by
the same token everything—elaborated on the unpromising basis of an
eventless day, Hall's novel is thematic to the point of didacticism. Resolutely eschewing innovation of form, it advances an argument through
the highly conventional narrative of an involuntarily unconventional life.
Where *Ulysses* is all style, *The Well* is all subject matter. Despite—and in part
because of—the vast amount of controversy it provoked in its time, Joyce's
novel now comes to us preapproved as a cornerstone of the canon, the
very epitome of modernist aesthetics. *The Well* too generated strident
polemics, but it has not entered the general canon. Instead, it has become
a classic in the specific domain of gay literature, and as such it continues
to give rise to opprobrium and discord.

In spite of the immense aesthetic and cultural gulf between them,
though, *The Well of Loneliness* necessarily has a great deal in common with
Ulysses because of their common fate as books famously suppressed during the same period in Great Britain. They represent two parts of the "trilogy of literary dirt" alluded to by Anthony Burgess and completed by *Lady
Chatterley's Lover*.[1] Hall's novel first appeared in 1928, during the period
between the initial publication of Joyce's book and Judge Woolsey's decision allowing it into the United States. One further point of resemblance
between the two works is that unlike *Lady Chatterley*, both *Ulysses* and *The*

Well of Loneliness pose a challenge to the reader seeking prurient excitement, although in wildly divergent ways. Where Joyce's novel requires time, patience, and erudition to decipher, Hall's is an easy read, pitched to the "average reader" and demanding no special skill or knowledge; on the contrary, it is designed to please, to introduce its subject even to those readers least likely to accept its argument in advance. If it too thwarts the expectations of all but the most dedicated of thrill-seekers it is because Hall set out not to titillate the curious but to make a point about "sexual inversion." Both books, in any case, were publicly denounced during the same period, most spectacularly by James Douglas, the editor of the *Sunday Express* in London. Having perhaps prematurely attacked *Ulysses* as "the most infamously obscene book in ancient or modern literature" in 1922, Douglas found himself obliged to raise the already high moral pitch of his prose when Hall's novel was published in 1928.

The *Well of Loneliness* attracted Douglas's attention because it was the first novel in English to treat the theme of homosexuality seriously as its central subject. Unlike other discussions of the topic, it is neither prurient nor disapproving. As Hall put it in a letter to her publisher,

> Hitherto the subject [lesbianism] has been either treated as pornography, or introduced as an episode, or veiled. I have treated it as a fact of nature— a simple, though at present tragic fact.[2]

To Hall's intense disgust, as it happened, another sort of treatment of the subject was published without legal reprisal closely following the appearance of *The Well:* Compton Mackenzie's *Extraordinary Women*, a satirical novel about a colony of rich lesbians frolicking on the island of Capri, which offered recognizable portraits of a number of high-profile women including Hall herself. Mackenzie's novel sold well, especially because it was able to ride the wave of scandal produced by Hall's work, and it encountered no legal troubles or even journalistic disapproval from the likes of Douglas. It was light and breezy, contained no overt sexuality, and above all, far from pleading their cause as a beleaguered minority, treated its characters as overprivileged grotesques. *The Well*, in contrast, is both a thinly disguised, if greatly romanticized, autobiography, and above all a thinly disguised tract calling for social acceptance of same-sex couples. As such it not only attracted the ire of moralists like Douglas, but also—despite the favorable reviews greeting its publication—gave rise to a certain amount of hesitation even among readers sympathetic to its cause. Between publication of the novel in late July 1928 and the loud denunciation in the *Sunday Express* on August 19, fourteen reviews appeared. Almost all were positive, although to varying degrees, ranging in tone from tepidly supportive to emphatically laudatory. With very few exceptions critics praised Hall for her courage and sincerity in addressing what they felt to be an important topic, many deploring the bigotry described in the novel. The words *tragic* and *tragedy* recur in almost all the articles, and not a single critic writing before Douglas's call to arms objected to Hall's choice of subject. Some reviewers, though, lamented the novel's wooden style and lack of humor. Here is Cyril Connolly's view, for example:

> It is a long, tedious and absolutely humorless book. . . . 'The Well of Loneliness' may be a brave book to have written, but let us hope it will pave the way for someone to write a better one. Homosexuality is, after all, as rich in comedy as in tragedy, and it is time it was emancipated from the aura of distinguished damnation and religious martyrdom which surrounds its so fiercely aggressive apologists.[3]

One of the salient historical ironies of this story is that the sort of book Connolly hoped might follow was a very long time coming (assuming the comedy he had in mind was something more nuanced than the broadly satirical *Extraordinary Women* variety), for the very reason that Hall's novel provoked legal reprisals which for decades prevented anyone else from attempting anything of the kind. The fate of the book helped ensure that no one would dare approach homosexuality as a central topic in English fiction, at least not in anything other than a heavily condemnatory vein, for decades to come.

As one may infer from its title alone, *The Well of Loneliness* does not make its case by depicting well-adjusted homosexuals going about their unthreatening existence. Instead, somewhat analogously to the unpleasant fate Virginia Woolf invented for Shakespeare's fictional sister to illustrate the point of gender inequity in *A Room of One's Own* (published in 1929, and perhaps uncoincidentally based on lectures delivered in October 1928, while the scandal of *The Well* was in full swing), Hall offers the story of a talented, attractive, well-meaning person doomed to frustration and unhappiness by sole virtue of having been born the wrong sex.[4] The book was pathbreaking because written from the perspective of the "invert": this was unprecedented. Homosexuality was at the time a subject legitimately discussed, when discussed at all, only by "scientific experts," or else with satirical disdain in light novels such as *Extraordinary Women*. Inverts, by definition—as deviants—did not speak for themselves; they were spoken of, either derisively or in terms of sin, crime, or pathology.

The plot of the novel is roughly as follows: the heroine is born to a rich, childless couple who desire and expect a boy. Undeterred by the fact that the infant is a girl, they name her Stephen. Incoherently veering between nature and nurture as deciding factors in the development of what is now called gender identity, Hall offers the parents' keen desire for a male child as instrumental in Stephen's signal boyishness. The latter is also, however, improbably enough described from birth as being a "narrow-hipped, wide-shouldered little tadpole of a baby"(13). Her broad shoulders and narrow hips are repeatedly emphasized in the descriptions of her as a child, which would seem to suggest that her condition is innate (it also suggests the degree to which Hall likes to stack her narrative deck, against all verisimilitude, since even the most virile of small boys do not differ greatly in this regard from girls). As Stephen grows up she is close to her father, who tragically dies early on, and reviled by her cold and disapproving mother. She becomes enamored of female servants, is horrified to find them embracing male servants; later on she sets about seducing a local married woman, with mixed results. She rides, hunts, is fond of horses, makes a metaphor of the hounded fox (it is in keeping with a certain basic ambivalence in the novel that Stephen both hunts with vigor and identifies with the prey). She is courted by a young man and rebuffs his advances. Eventually she goes out into the world and becomes an ambulance driver during the war. She falls in love with Mary, a "normal" young woman, fears being rebuffed if Mary learns her true nature and desires, discovers that Mary has already figured things out and desires Stephen as ardently as Stephen desires Mary. They go to Paris, experience decadent life among the inverts. Stephen becomes an accomplished writer. The rebuffed young man reappears and courts Mary; Stephen selflessly delivers Mary into his embrace by fictitiously maintaining that she has been having an affair with one of the (female) Paris decadents. Mary goes off with the man and Stephen is left alone to lament her lot and that of her kind. The book ends with an imprecation: "Acknowledge us, oh God, before the whole world. Give us also the right to our existence!"

It should be clear even from this highly reductive summary that Hall, who semiadvertently became the spokeswoman for homosexual rights in the early twentieth century in English-speaking countries, was the most unlikely of activists. An ardent upholder of the status quo, she clearly demonstrates her support of the extant class system. What is more, her writings, including *The Well*, are larded not only with passages redolent of the racism and anti-Semitism that were routine at the time, but also, perhaps more surprisingly, with what we now call misogyny and homophobia. The world of *The Well*, strangely enough (at least to the eyes of twenty-first century posterity), is one where men should be men and women women: the former are ideally strong, taciturn, and virile; the latter fragile, emotional, and feminine. Unfortunately there are those who, like the protagonist, do not fit neatly into either category, or rather are born into the wrong one (Stephen is strong, taciturn, and virile). It is in defense of these, who cannot help themselves, that the novel is written. In accordance with the novel's essentially reactionary bent, the descriptions of life among the "inverts" in Paris are riddled with traces of the author's contempt for such individuals, especially effeminate men—there is a remarkably ambivalent portrait of a character recognizably based on Noël Coward—whom Stephen nonetheless, with great reluctance, accepts as "her kind." *The Well of Loneliness* is, in almost every way, an extremely conservative book. Add to the mix the strong religiosity that pervades all her work—Hall was a fervent convert to Catholicism—and the result is something that even a James Douglas could, under other circumstances, appreciate. And in fact he did: several years later, much to Hall's irritation Douglas published a laudatory review of her novel *The Carpenter's Son*, a Christic allegory she wrote, she said, to atone for the awful blasphemy represented by the Aubrey Beardsley-style Beresford Egan cartoon illustrating the satirical verse pamphlet *The Sink of Solitude* and featuring Hall on the cross at the time of her trial.

Radclyffe Hall presents a strange paradox in literary history. She inaugurated overtly gay literature in England, but she did so in a manner that led to a series of uneasy reversals. She was alternately vilified on the grounds that her portrayal of homosexuality was too positive and celebrated as having dared to portray such matters at all; finally, she was further vilified because her portrayal of homosexuals was insufficiently positive. *The Well of Loneliness* cannot be ignored given the attention devoted in recent years to gay works from the past, and especially because of its status as the first openly gay novel to be published in English. The first biography of Hall appeared in 1968, written by her lover Una Troubridge. This was followed in 1975 by Lovat Dickson's *Radclyffe Hall at the Well of Loneliness*, and then in 1985 by Michael Baker's *Our Three Selves*. In the late 1990s and first years of the twenty-first century three more biographies were published, as well as an anthology of essays on *The Well* and several critical studies of Hall. This resurgence of critical attention has nothing to do, certainly, with any suggestion that she was a great writer; she was not. By most accounts she was not even a good writer, and without exception recent studies are filled with agonized comings-to-terms with Hall's mediocrity as a writer and her political failings. It has even repeatedly been suggested that she may have done more harm than good to the generations of lesbians who turned to her novel to learn about themselves, because of its rigid definitions and pessimistic outlook.

Two salient points emerge from this highly ambivalent posterity: one is the astonishing efficacy of the trial and conviction of Hall's British publisher and distributor, which succeeded in putting a stop to all further publication of works treating homosexuality in anything resembling a positive light, and this for decades. Douglas characterized the novel not only as "an intolerable outrage," but also as "the first outrage of its kind in the annals of English fiction," which suggests that he expected others to follow. He went on to say that "in order to prevent the contamination and corruption of English fiction it is the duty of the critic to make it impossible for any other novelist to repeat this outrage" (Doan and Prosser, 36). In this, remarkably enough, his article came close to having the desired effect. *The Well* was not republished in England until 1949, nor were any other outrages of the sort forthcoming in such an atmosphere. Even in the United States, where the novel's publisher was brought to trial, convicted, and then acquitted on appeal, and where, as a result, the novel enjoyed a great *succès de scandale* while banned in other English-speaking countries, imitators were not forthcoming. The admonitory effect of the trials of *The Well of Loneliness* is one of the main reasons Hall's novel remained *the* lesbian "classic" for many decades; it was quite some time before anyone dared attempt another such work. To a great extent Hall has James Douglas to thank for her central place in the gay canon, and also for remaining in the public eye for years after publication, despite and above all because of the ban. Nor is hers, of course, an isolated case. We have already seen the kick-start the Second Empire gave Flaubert's career in France in 1857, and this trend only picked up pace in the English-speaking world in the 1920s and 1930s. As Burgess (born in 1917) puts it about the lure of *The Well*, *Ulysses*, and *Lady Chatterley's Lover*, among his set in the 1930s and after, "We were inflamed with a desire to get hold of these books not merely because they were outlawed, like Robin Hood, but because the reactionary press hammered at them so relentlessly." Douglas in particular, he adds, "led many of my generation to the pleasures of modern literature through the sheer bloody vehemence of his attacks."[5]

It is also surely the case that Douglas is the main reason Hall can now be cited in the same sentence as Joyce, Flaubert, or Lawrence. Like the French imperial prosecutor before him, Douglas was, in his own unlikely way, an extraordinarily effective leveler, inveighing against masterpieces and literary mediocrities alike, with predictably incoherent results. Authors denounced by Douglas and company naturally attracted not only prurient interest from Burgess's schoolboy set but also sympathetic attention from a wide audience, including the Bloomsbury group. However, the intense ambivalence toward the novel that can be seen in recent studies had its equivalent at the time of its publication as well, as it turns out, and not only among reviewers. From the outset arguments about the book centered on the topic of literary merit, in ways that are a bit different from the precedents of Flaubert, Baudelaire, and Joyce. In those cases, as we have seen, artistic merit was implicitly the argument of both sides, in that the defense cited illustrious precedents from canonical literature, while the prosecution maintained that the better written the work, the more persuasive its nefarious influence, and the stronger the case for its suppression. *The Well* was no exception in this sense: in his article Douglas ad-

dresses the topic of literary merit, insisting that "the adroitness and clev-
erness of the book intensifies its moral danger" (Doan and Prosser, 38).
Sir Chartres Biron, the presiding magistrate in the British trial, dotted any
possible remaining i's on this subject when he wrote in his judgment that
"it is quite obvious to anybody of intelligence that the better an obscene
book is written the greater the public to whom the book is likely to appeal."[6] Hall's novel differs from the previous cases we have studied, however, in the extent to which controversy raged as to the artistic merit of the
book among its defenders themselves.

   When *The Well* was published Hall was already the author of four novels,
one of which, *Adam's Breed*, had won the two most prestigious literary
awards in England at the time: the British Femina Prize and the James Tait
Black award, a feat that had only been achieved once before, by E. M.
Forster's *Passage to India* in 1924. Having established herself as a successful
author of books both popular and critically acclaimed, she had decided to
take her chances with a novel pleading the case of "the invert." Her publisher, Jonathan Cape, was well aware of the danger involved in such a
project, and took various precautions to demonstrate the seriousness of
the book, including austere presentation, elevated price, a limited first
run, and advertisements avoiding all suggestion of scandal. He also prudently refrained from sending review copies to either the *Sunday* or the
Daily Express. James Douglas nonetheless procured himself a copy of the
novel and devoted an assiduous publicity campaign to his editorial screed
against Hall's novel. On August 19, 1928, a few weeks after *The Well of Loneliness* had been published, and following the fourteen relatively positive
reviews, in five columns of well-advertised print under the banner head-
line "A Book that Must Be Suppressed," Douglas vituperated against the
novel using rhetoric that recalls Ernest Pinard's prosecution speech in the
Madame Bovary trial, although in comparison the imperial prosecutor's arguments look like discreet understatement. The editorialist had, as we
have seen, already discussed *Ulysses* in terms of "leprous and scabrous horrors" and "secret sewers of vice," indulging a taste for assonance while employing a familiar, even if unusually concentrated, vocabulary of pustu-
lence and filth. This was his stock in trade, and his modus operandi did
not vary much from one moral fury to the next. In 1927, for instance, taking on "modern sex novelists" in general, Douglas calls them "vermin" for
which there is unfortunately no known pesticide; "the deadliest bacteria in
our blood; but we have discovered no antitoxin"; he refers to "abysmal
horrors," "esoteric abominations and fetid mysteries"; and in a final spasm
of apostrophic disgust, tells these authors that they are "the lice of deca-
dence."[7] Douglas made a career out of such ventings of moral indignation:
he was the contemporary British equivalent of William Bennett and Rush
Limbaugh rolled into one influential moralist. As a result, it is hardly sur-

prising that Jonathan Cape did not send review copies to the *Express*, nor that Douglas, undaunted, lavished newsprint on *The Well of Loneliness*.

James Douglas is not now remembered for his novel *The Unpardonable Sin*, and his various polemical articles denouncing *Ulysses* and other works serve only as footnotes to the history of literary obscenity proceedings, although he was instrumental in the banning of D. H. Lawrence's novel *The Rainbow* in 1915 (see chapter 5). He is known above all for his editorial calling for the suppression of *The Well of Loneliness*, and even so what is invariably cited is one paragraph consisting of two memorable sentences which appeared in boldface toward the end of the article: "I would rather give a healthy boy or a healthy girl a phial of prussic acid than this novel. Poison kills the body, but moral poison kills the soul."[8] As can be gauged from the excerpts cited above, to the extent that this pronouncement differs from Douglas's routine characterizations of any number of other works that violated his moral precepts, it is in intensity rather than tone. His was a tough act to follow, even by himself. What is especially striking about his piece on Hall's novel, though, is its aura of ultimatum. Having previously worn out the vocabulary of sewage, filth, disease, and various toxic substances, Douglas finally put his rhetorical money where his metaphorical mouth was and suggested that this book was not just figuratively poisonous, it was *so* metaphorically lethal that it was somehow literally worse than actual poison.

This is one reason Douglas could never be the object of a sympathetic rehabilitation on the order of Ernest Pinard: he will never retroactively become a "good reader," because he protests too much: so much as to enter the realm of the absurd. (The other reason, of course, is that the object of his noisiest ire has not aged well, even as it has continued to find readers.) In the words of one recent critic, Douglas's "famous diatribe" now seems "merely risible and quaint."[9] In 1928 as well, the pitch of moral righteousness Douglas reached over Hall's novel raised eyebrows and attracted a certain amount of mockery in addition to counterindignation. Part of the problem was that he himself had previously set the rhetorical stakes so high that he was obliged to resort to an extravagant logical impasse in order to emphasize the danger posed by this particular work. Because of its over-the-top rhetoric the "prussic acid" passage has propelled Douglas, however quaintly and risibly, into posterity, but by the same token the pronouncement makes little sense. It is when the force of his objection reaches its referential apogee—I would rather give real children real poison, so terrible is this book—that it is most readily discernible as hyperbole. In other words, when Douglas insists on literal danger his argument collapses if taken literally. This conundrum was not lost on Aldous Huxley, for one, who responded by calling Douglas's rhetorical bluff:

I offered to provide Mr. Douglas with a child, a bottle of prussic acid, a copy of *The Well of Loneliness*, and (if he kept his word and chose to administer the acid) a handsome memorial in marble to be erected wherever he might appoint, after his execution. The offer, I regret to say, was not accepted.[10]

Huxley's proposal mocked by extension a long tradition of literature as metaphoric poison. Prussic acid, a form of cyanide, is an especially effective toxin, "proverbial in the nineteenth century as the ultimate poison, because of its ready availability and nearly instantaneous effect," according to Walter Kendrick, who also notes that "early combatants of obscenity put prussic acid to wide use, particularly against metaphoric children."[11] The idea of being poisoned by books had a venerable history: in *Madame Bovary*, as we have seen, the heroine's mother-in-law asserts that this is Emma's problem, that booklenders should be prosecuted as poisoners, and that all trouble in the household could be solved by cutting off her daughter-in-law's fiction supply. Her suggestion is borne out by the novel's conclusion: Emma *is* poisoned by her reading, as witness the awful taste of ink in her mouth during her death-throes. Prussic acid seems to have been more readily available in England than in France (in Zola's *Thérèse Raquin* [1867], however, the miserable adulterers kill each other with *acide prussique*). Had Emma Bovary taken it rather than the arsenic on hand in Homais's pharmacy, Flaubert's novel would presumably have been seen as even more blameworthy, as she would have been spared her extended agony; but then prussic acid seems to have been deployed for the most part, at least rhetorically, as an alternative to dangerous reading rather than an antidote to its effects. In a poignant twist of literary history, Eleanor Marx, Karl Marx's daughter and one of the first translators of *Madame Bovary* into English, committed suicide in 1898, in London, by taking prussic acid.

Despite its inherent absurdities, Douglas's apocalyptic "prussic acid" formulation, coupled with his demand that the publisher withdraw the work, and if he refused then a call to the home secretary to suppress it by law, proved remarkably effective. Jonathan Cape replied to Douglas in print, voluntarily—and without consulting the author—submitting the book to the scrutiny of the Home Office, even as it sold thousands of copies, in large part thanks to the *Sunday Express*. When it became clear that the Home Office would take action, Cape had the book reissued in Paris, with the result that the home secretary, William Joynson-Hicks (popularly known by the derisive nickname "Jix," sometimes amended to "The Preposterous Jix"), an energetic campaigner against immorality in all its possible forms—even the bishop of Durham called him a "dour fanatic" who went after causes with "dervish-like fervour"—had both Cape and the London bookseller who distributed the imported edition prose-cuted for "obscene libel."[12] The government won its case and Hall's novel was banned in Great Britain for twenty years.

The Well differs from most of the other books famously suppressed on grounds of obscenity in the nineteenth and twentieth centuries—the other exception is *Lolita*—in that what made it dangerous was not any par-ticular scene, or even an accumulation of offensive passages, but the sub-ject itself. Books like *Madame Bovary* and *Lady Chatterley's Lover* were not deemed dangerous simply because they dealt with adultery; remove adul-tery as a central preoccupation and the library of World Classics is re-duced to a few dusty shelves. Even the Hays Code recognized that adultery was "sometimes necessary plot material." Flaubert and Lawrence got into trouble, as did the filmmakers who took on their works, for refusing to give the requisite nod to conventional morality and make sure that adul-tery was sufficiently condemned and the sanctity of marriage upheld. Writers such as Baudelaire, Joyce, and later on Henry Miller ran up against the censors on the basis of graphic passages and vulgar terms, not because of general subject matter. (Lawrence, as we shall see in the next chapter, managed to offend both because of his flouting of conventional morality and because of the vocabulary with which the characters flout it.) Hall and Nabokov, in contrast to all the above—and despite having ab-solutely nothing else in common—both set out to write novels dealing with subjects that were considered taboo as a rule, and both were well aware of the dangers they faced. *The Well of Loneliness* contains no graphic depiction of sexuality. Its most explicit passage is the observation that "she kissed her full on the lips"; its most suggestive scene reaches a demure cli-max with the formula "and that night they were not divided."

Although both Douglas and Sir Chartres Biron managed to character-ize the novel in terms that make it sound like *Debbie Does Lesbos*, it is evident from both their accounts that the real problem was not explicit descrip-tion but the subject itself, and more specifically the fact that Hall deals with female homosexuality in a relatively positive light. In this sense the point of the *Well* controversy is squarely in the tradition of the *Madame Bo-vary* proceedings: the suggestion is that if Hall had treated the same situa-tions while loudly condemned the behavior of her characters the work might not have been immoral. Douglas's article takes up Pinard's central argument that *Madame Bovary* posed a danger because of its genre and therefore its readership:

> Its theme is utterly inadmissible in the novel, because the novel is read by
> people of all ages, by young women and young men as well as by older
> women and older men. Therefore, many things that are discussed in scien-

tific textbooks cannot decently be discussed in a work of fiction offered to the general reader. (Doan and Prosser, 37)

One of the many historical ironies offered by the censorship history of Hall's novel is that, precisely to give it the sort of scientific prestige Douglas refuses to accord the genre as a whole, the book was published with a prefatory note by the famous sexologist Havelock Ellis attesting to its seriousness and importance. Almost all early reviewers commented on Ellis's preface, some noting that its inclusion was what had inspired their interest in the work in the first place, while others questioned the need for such an imprimatur. Ellis's short commentary was itself modified by Cape so as to be as vague and euphemistic as possible: for instance the phrase "various aspects of sexual inversion" was changed to "one particular aspect of sexual life."[13] It is therefore all the more poignant to note that thirty years earlier Ellis's own *Sexual Inversion*, the first volume of his monumental *Studies in the Psychology of Sex*—the very sort of scientific textbook Douglas cites as the appropriate place for discussions of such matters—had been suppressed by the British courts on grounds of obscenity.[14]

Douglas's insistence that the discussion of such matters belongs rightfully to the pages of scientific textbooks rather than those of the novel, which is available to all, closely recalls Ernest Pinard's argument that *Madame Bovary* was dangerous above all because it was not a treatise on political economy and was therefore more likely to fall into the hands of girls and married women than into those of educated men. There is one point, however, on which Douglas departs sharply from Pinard in this regard, and that is his repeated emphasis on the novel's readership being equally divided among girls and boys, women and men. The hypothetical victims of his metaphorical poison are "a healthy boy or a healthy girl"; the theme of inversion "is inadmissible in the novel because the novel is read by people of all ages, by young women and young men as well as by older women and older men." This insistence on the dangers posed not only to girls and women but to men and boys may seem strange, given that the book treats lesbianism and only by extension and in passing male "inversion," and given also that it was girls and young women who had long been seen as the standard target of presumed corruption. In fact Douglas's portrayal of the novel as an equal-opportunity agent of corruption was cannily designed as a further incitement to the Home Office to prosecute, because male homosexuality was at the time a crime in Great Britain, whereas lesbianism was not. It was implicit that if the novel depicted homosexuality in general in a favorable light it could be characterized as an incitement to crime. The tenor of the presiding magistrate's judgment suggests that he needed no such argument to find Hall's publisher guilty of "obscene libel"; the failure to condemn female inversion was enough. Nonetheless, he noted in passing that "these unnatural offenses between women which are the subject of this book involve acts which between men would be a criminal offense, and involve acts of the most horrible, unnatural and disgusting obscenity."[15]

The salient fact that male homosexuality was criminalized in England at the time not only elucidates Douglas's otherwise peculiar harping on young boys and men, it also goes a long way toward explaining why *The Well of Loneliness* occupies the place it does as the first serious fictional exploration of homosexuality in English. It was not merely that the titillating depiction of lesbianism had become standard fare in French literature during the nineteenth century, and as such had become familiar and much less problematic than that of male homosexuality. (Neither male nor female homosexuality had been a crime under French law since the Napoleonic Code had taken effect, in any case.) It was also true that the trials of Oscar Wilde in the 1890s were still fresh in the public memory. Douglas's article concludes with an admonitory reference to Wilde: "Literature has not yet recovered from the harm done to it by the Oscar Wilde scandal. It should keep its house in order," he darkly warns (Doan and Prosser, 38). Although Wilde had never actually been accused of obscenity, *The Picture of Dorian Gray* was repeatedly evoked by the Marquess of Queensberry's lawyer during the first trial. Wilde was convicted under an 1885 law, the Labouchere Amendment, that criminalized "gross indecency" between men no longer just in public, as had previously been the case, but in private as well. (Male homosexuality was not decriminalized in England until 1967). As a result, anyone attempting to depict same-sex relations among men in a work of fiction was liable to prosecution not only on grounds of obscenity but, at least in principle, for incitement to crime. And even beyond this, the publication of such narrative would of course have brought the writer himself under suspicion of criminal activity.

When Radclyffe Hall's publisher was taken to trial most of the leading literary lights in England at the time were mobilized in protest, first by means of an open letter, and then to offer testimony during the trial. The main organizer of this protest was E. M. Forster, acting in tandem with Leonard Woolf. Both Forster and Woolf had reservations as to the artistic quality of the novel; Woolf had written one of the first reviews, praising its "understanding and frankness," but asserting that "the book fails completely as a work of art."[16] Forster did not review the novel, and despite his own reservations as to its artistic qualities he sprang to the defense of its author and publisher, convincing a great many prominent writers of the time—including most of the Bloomsbury group, many of whom were themselves homosexual or bisexual—to stand behind Radclyffe Hall and her publisher.

Because the subject was so volatile for so long, the history of literary censorship on grounds of homosexual content is a relatively short one, since writers are not notably given to producing works they know they cannot publish. In 1900 the Belgian author Georges Eeckhoud was brought to trial in Brussels for his novel *Escal-Vigor*, another barely veiled apologia for same-sex love; he was acquitted, and the novel promptly forgotten. Also in 1900, in France, Colette published, under her husband's name, the homoerotic *Claudine à l'école* followed by the even more risqué *Claudine en ménage* (the plot of the latter, the third Claudine novel, hinges on lesbian adultery), without legal repercussions. This was doubtless because of their light tone, and perhaps as well because of the very fact that these novels appeared under a masculine byline, which contributed to their being read as light salacious fiction rather than a declaration of female sexual independence; and finally, Claudine's sapphic adventures are sidelines to her marriage, and thus a titillating diversion more than anything else. In 1902 André Gide came out with the more ponderous *L'Immoraliste*, a work that clearly reads today as a coming-out story, but at the time was greeted as fictionalized philosophy, or philosophical fiction, much like Thomas Mann's *Death in Venice* in Germany in 1912; neither work addressed its homosexual theme overtly. In the 1920s Proust and Gide both began to tackle the subject directly, always, it was clear, looking over their shoulders for possible legal reprisals. ("I know that the battle has been lost in France and Germany," wrote Douglas, alluding to just such works, "but it has not yet been lost in England" [Doan and Prosser, 37].) Early-twentieth-century literature in Western Europe is rife with stories of same-sex love and desire, but no one had attempted the sort of manifesto that Radclyffe Hall undertook when she wrote *The Well of Loneliness*.

Except, that is, E. M. Forster. His own place in the canon has now been assured in part by opulent film productions, starting with David Lean's 1984 blockbuster version of *A Passage to India*, which was followed by a series of Merchant-Ivory adaptations of his novels. Some fifteen years before Hall published *The Well*, Forster, already an established author, had committed an unusual act for a professional writer: he had labored over a book he knew could not be published. *Maurice*, a novel that like Hall's reads as a fictional argument for tolerance of homosexuality, was duly made into a Merchant-Ivory film in 1987. Begun in 1913 and finished the following year, it was not published until 1971, after the author's death (1970), according to a proviso in his will. *Maurice* is dedicated "to a happier year," which given the chronology of its genesis could well refer to the end of the war, but in fact what Forster had in mind, as he made clear in an afterword written in the 1960s, was a time in which such stories could be told openly without fear of legal reprisal. Forster's novel of homosexuality resembles *The Well* in that it tells an exemplary story of a life marred by innate sexual orientation. Maurice is a homosexual rather than an invert: that is to say, he is "normal" in all other respects than that his sexual inclination is toward men rather than women, whereas Hall's Stephen Gordon is essentially masculine. (The word *inversion* designated a view of same-sex relations in which a man preferring men was "really" a woman, and vice versa; the term and conception come from nineteenth-century sexology and were controversial during this period. There was, for instance, an ongoing conflict between Proust and Gide in France, with the latter objecting to the former's feminizing portrayal of "inverts," preferring a Greek-based model of virile "pederasty" as depicted in Plato's *Symposium*.)

Forster did not even attempt to publish *Maurice* when he wrote it, nor would he allow the novel to be published during his lifetime. This was not only because it took on the subject of male homosexuality, and as such could have been prosecuted as an incitement to crime as well as on grounds of obscenity, but more particularly because he had insisted on giving it a happy ending. The story concludes with the protagonist, whose early love (played by the young Hugh Grant in the film) has repudiated their relations and chosen the path of marriage and normality, establishing an enduring relationship with a young man who is, moreover, a member of the working class. (During Wilde's first trial the prosecution made much of the fact that he frequented working-class youths: it was assumed—with some justice, apparently—that he would not have done so in the absence of sexual interests.) Suicide was the proper fate of such characters at the time; living happily ever after, which is essentially what Forster has them do, was out of the question. It was this above all that doomed the novel, according to Forster himself, to unpublishability during his lifetime, before the advent of "a happier year."

The example of *Maurice* is pertinent in a number of ways to the case of *The Well*. For one thing, it becomes clear, in the context of Forster's quixotic insistence on providing his protagonist with a happy ending, that the unhappy fate of Stephen and her kind, foregrounded by Hall on every page of her book and especially in its title, represents, among other things, an unsuccessful attempt to conform to societal and literary expectations and ward off censorship even as the work pleads the case of inverts. Stephen's unpleasant destiny resembles that of the *femmes damnées* consigned by Baudelaire to wander lonely and wolflike through Hell in the concluding section of "Delphine et Hippolyte," a passage also meant to discourage the censors. It is true that Stephen does not commit suicide, but she does selflessly sacrifice her love to a man, which is not all that far off according to the book's own logic: she throws herself, albeit metaphorically, into the eponymous well. No wonder generations of lesbians have been traumatized by reading Hall's novel; faced with what it presents as the noble solution to an insoluble problem, anyone might reasonably choose prussic acid instead.

In 1952 the American writer Patricia Highsmith, who had won fame with her first novel, *Strangers on a Train* (1950), made into the celebrated film by Alfred Hitchcock, sought to publish her second book, *The Price of Salt*, a sexually inexplicit novel about lesbianism. She was rebuffed by her previous editor but was able to bring the book out pseudonymously with a different publisher. *The Price of Salt* (which also appeared in one of its reprintings under the title *Carol*) sold well as a hardcover in 1952, became a paperback bestseller the following year, and was much later reissued with a postscript by the author. Until 1991, however, when Highsmith finally agreed to allow the book to appear under her name, the author was still "Claire Morgan." The 1950s saw an explosion of paperback pulp novels with homosexual themes and memorable cover art, all of which obligatorily ended with marriage, insanity, or suicide. When Marijane Meaker, who later had an affair with Highsmith, published the highly successful lesbian pulp novel *Spring Fire* in 1952 under the pseudonym Vin Packer, her editor instructed her to make sure the story ended unhappily: "otherwise the post office might seize the books as obscene."[17] *The Price of Salt* was a "serious" rather than a pulp novel—the latter were never brought out in hardcover editions—which is why it was not held to the same formula. It seems to have been the first gay novel with a (relatively) happy ending, and its unimpeded publication in 1952 testifies to the degree to which things had changed, whereas the fact that Highsmith refused for forty years to claim authorship of her book suggests the degree to which change was gradual. In her 1983 afterword, "Claire Morgan" struck a note that echoes Forster's afterword to *Maurice*:

> The homosexual novel then had to have a tragic ending. Usually it was about men. One of the main characters, if not both, had to cut his wrists, or drown himself in the swimming pool of some lovely estate, or one had to say goodbye to his partner, having decided to go straight.[18]

Unlike Forster, though, Highsmith presents herself as unconcerned with her place in literary history: "*The Price of Salt* in 1952 was said to be the first gay book with a happy ending. I am not sure this is absolutely true, as I never checked."[19] She goes on to relate that following publication of the hugely successful paperback edition of 1953 she received hundreds of letters from readers of both sexes and all ages, thanking her "for writing about two people of the same sex in love, who actually come out alive at the end and with a fair amount of hope for a happy future."[20]

The Price of Salt, with its concluding note of cautious optimism, is an anomaly in Highsmith's oeuvre; the rest of her writings, which she published under her own name, are almost uniformly concerned with horrific goings-on among dysfunctional, self-deluded characters. It is her only work to feature a happy ending for a sympathetic character, and it is also remarkably at odds with the author's own biography, a story filled with unhappy endings: although she achieved great literary fame and fortune and had many lovers, Highsmith ended up an embittered alcoholic, unable to sustain the sort of relationship she lends to the main characters in *The Price of Salt*.[21] In this sense among others Highsmith's novel presents an interesting counterpoint to *The Well of Loneliness*. Even though the latter is to some extent autobiographical, Hall's own life resembles the Capri-vacationing scenario of cavorting sapphic extravagance portrayed in Compton Mackenzie's *Extraordinary Women* more closely than it does the lachrymose plot of her novel. Forster, apparently, wrote *Maurice* not out of autobiographical reminiscence—at the time he wrote the novel, he reportedly had no sexual experience at all—but because its optimistic plot was what he wanted to envision for homosexuals. Highsmith seems to have written her lesbian book for similar reasons. *The Well*, in contrast, is neither a positive model nor a reflection of the author's experience, but rather a sort of negative model, a worst-case scenario, or rather second-worst case, absent suicide, insanity, or prison. Like Stephen Gordon, Hall went by a masculine name: for most of her adult life she was known as "John," although unlike Stephen's case this was of her own choice; she started out life as Marguerite Radclyffe-Hall.[22] Like Stephen Gordon she was born into privilege and never wanted for money or social connections, but unlike Stephen Gordon she was never lonely; she was certainly never alone. Not only did she never sacrifice any of her various lovers to male suitors, she enjoyed a succession of overlapping live-in relationships with adoring women until her death (attended by the last two). Her longest relationship, with Una, Lady Troubridge, not only lasted until her death but began with Una's leaving her husband, an admiral reputed to be the handsomest man in the British Navy, for Hall. By the latter's death in 1943 she was living with both Troubridge and Evguenia Souline, a Russian woman originally hired in Paris to nurse Troubridge through an illness and with whom Hall had been carrying on an open affair for several years.

The pessimistic tone of *The Well* can therefore hardly be construed as reflecting its author's adult experience. Homophobia was undeniably rife in England at the time, as the book's suppression clearly demonstrates. But as the many reviews hailing Hall's courage also suggest, there was, at least among the literati, a great deal of support for more open views of homosexuality. In any case homophobia did not prevent Hall from enjoying great professional and social success, nor does it seem to have hampered her private life. Social pressure certainly took its toll on her, especially in terms of conflicts with her mother (almost all her novels foreground re-pressively manipulative maternal figures; most memorably, the working title of her novel *The Unlit Lamp* was *Octopi*, with the heroine's mother as the eponymous cephalopod). Mother-daughter strife, though, is a staple of both life and literature even in the absence of conflict over sexual orientation, and while Hall's psychological trauma may well have been linked to her masculinity and homosexuality, her adult life was relatively free of the lacerating stigma she describes in *The Well*. British society of the time, at least in the circles Hall frequented, and especially in terms of relations between women, seems to have operated under a sort of tacit "don't ask, don't tell" policy which she infringed by bringing out her polemical work.

In one of the twists of historical irony that characterize the history of literary censorship, she became an evident victim of institutionalized homophobia only as a result of the novel's publication. The book's fore-grounding of the sort of crippling bigotry from which its author had not previously suffered much can be attributed to Hall's desire to dramatize the fate of the invert under contemporary societal conditions. At the same time, the unhappy ending was what allowed the novel to be published, and doubtless led Jonathan Cape to imagine he might avoid the very sort of censure the book ended up nonetheless attracting. In any case it sold like hotcakes, both before the court-ordered banning and after. Not only was *The Well* a big seller in America after the British ban, it was also sold in kiosks at the Gare du Nord in Paris, to tourists embarking on the boat-train. The British literati, however—the very people who lined up to sign petitions and appear in court in favor of the work—expressed great reservations as to its literary qualities.

Virginia Woolf was especially hard on *The Well*. Since Woolf has since become a modernist, feminist, and even a gay icon, and Hall a marginal figure, it is difficult to avoid simply concluding that Woolf was correct, even if a bit brutal in her assessments, but it is also important to remember that the two were in competition at the time (one should also recall Woolf's harsh commentaries on *Ulysses*, bearing in mind that Woolf and Joyce were exact contemporaries, vying for the same audience).[23] Two years older than Woolf, Hall came out with her lesbian work just as Woolf was publishing *Orlando*, the sexually ambiguous novel dedicated to her sometime lover Vita Sackville-West. While posterity has crowned *Orlando*, *The Well* stole much of its fire in 1928. Scholars have labored over why Hall's novel was banned while *Orlando* never caused much of a stir, but it would seem fairly clear that this was chiefly because *The Well* makes a dogmatic case for the acceptance of same-sex love, whereas Woolf's novel is a chronologically picaresque work featuring a character who changes sex over the centuries. If the idea was to stamp out subversive ideas, Hall's book, not Woolf's, was the obvious place to begin. It is another noteworthy irony that the relatively inoffensive *Orlando* is now lauded precisely for its "subversive" shiftiness, while *The Well*, with its insistent social message, is redolent of outmoded self-hatred.

While Woolf did not much appreciate *The Well of Loneliness*, she found herself at the very center of efforts to combat its suppression. She was friends with Forster, who along with her husband started the campaign to defend the book. She did not, however, like it. In her diary she termed it Hall's "dull, meritorious book." She wrote to Ottoline Morrell that "the dulness of the book is such that any indecency may lurk there—one simply can't keep one's eyes on the page" (Souhami, 186). The idea, put forth with evident malice by Woolf in terms of Hall's novel, that dullness might obviate obscenity—what might be called the boredom defense—had been articulated quite seriously in the case of *Ulysses* in a *New York Times* editorial entitled "Taste, Not Morals," about the 1921 conviction of the *Little Review* editors: "That most people would find the story incomprehensible and therefore dull is, perhaps, its complete vindication from the charge of immorality."[24] Sackville-West, in terms that surely express the thoughts of many of her contemporaries, echoed the charge leveled against Hall of dullness, but insisted on the importance of the subject undertaken in the novel. She wrote to her husband Harold Nicholson (who was later to get in trouble for publishing *Lolita* in England) that *The Well* was

> not in the least interesting apart from the candour with which it treats its subject. Of course I simply *itch* to try the same thing myself. You see if one may write about b.s.ness [backstairs business; a code term for homosexuality] the field of fiction is immediately doubled. (Souhami, 185)

To Woolf, who had written to her disparagingly about Hall ("So our ardour in the cause of freedom of speech gradually cools, and instead of offering to reprint the masterpiece, we are already beginning to wish it unwritten" [ibid., 185]), Sackville-West replied that she felt strongly about the case, "not on account of what you call my proclivities; not because I think it is a good book; but really on principle" (ibid., 185).

Despite her reservations, Woolf, along with a great many other prominent writers of the time, agreed to appear in court in defense of *The Well*. (She had already written to Sackville-West, who was off on a family holiday, that the latter's testimony would not be required, because of her well-known "proclivities.") Defense of the novel had begun with Forster and Leonard Woolf drafting a letter protesting its withdrawal from publication. They had lined up various luminaries of the time, ranging from bisexual and homosexual Bloomsbury notables such as Lytton Strachey to more conventional literary figures such as Arnold Bennett, who had already written a laudatory review. Hall objected to the terms of their letter, however, because it argued on purely legal terms and offered "no opinion on either the merits or the decency of the book."[25] Their aim was to defend free speech in general, whereas Hall felt that the literary excellence of her book should be a cornerstone of any defense. Hall drafted her own version of how such a letter should read, and Forster went to see her. According to his biographer, during this meeting Forster "incautiously hinted a mild criticism of her novel, and at this she grew violent, refusing all support from him and his friends unless her book were proclaimed not only pure but a masterpiece" (Furbank, 154). He abandoned the original protest and had a letter published anonymously in *The Nation and Atheneum* instead. Entitled "The New Censorship," the letter proclaimed that suppression of Hall's novel represented "an insidious blow at the liberties of the public" (ibid., 154). The following issue of the journal carried another letter, this time signed by Forster and Virginia Woolf, asserting that the book had been suppressed not because of any indecency but because of its subject alone.

A great number of prominent figures were mobilized to speak in Hall's defense at her publisher's trial. Some, including the archbishop of York, Sir Arthur Conan Doyle, and John Galsworthy, refused on various pretexts. George Bernard Shaw insisted that he was known as too immoral to lend credence to the defense, and Havelock Ellis, who was still annoyed at having involuntarily prefaced the book, offered a similar excuse. Nonetheless, many literary and scientific luminaries of the day turned out—about forty, according to Virginia Woolf's diary—ready to be called as witnesses to the literary merit and lack of indecency of *The Well of Loneliness* at the Bow Street Police Court on November 9, 1928. The case, *The Director of Public Prosecutions v. Jonathan Cape and Leopold Hill* (Hill being the bookseller of the imported edition Cape had had printed in Paris), was tried on the basis of the Obscene Publications Act of 1857, which "prohibited the sale of books, pictures and 'other articles' that 'depraved and corrupted' the morals of young people and shocked 'the common feelings of decency in any well regulated mind.' "[26] The specific test for obscenity, as we have already seen, was the 1868 Hicklin Rule, which stated that an obscene work is one that would tend to "deprave and corrupt those whose minds are open to such immoral influences and into whose hands a publication of this sort may fall." The magistrate, Sir Chartres Biron, announced that the "substantial question" he was to decide was "does this book as a whole defend unnatural practices between women?"

Clearly, it did. The case for the defense was doomed from the start, in part because of the criterion of obscenity enunciated by the presiding magistrate: no one could possibly argue otherwise than that the book as a whole defended "unnatural" practices between women, once it was a given that the practices alluded to, however inexplicitly, were in fact unnatural.

It was also true that the book itself defended such practices as being "natural," in the roundabout sense of being the product of a mistake of nature; but that was entirely beside the point according to the terms laid out by the court. Even beyond this logical impasse, the defense was doomed by another impasse, this time judicial. Norman Birkett, Cape's attorney, valiantly argued that the term *obscene* did not obtain in this case, and that the 1857 Obscene Publications Act had never been intended to "touch a book of this character"; he further maintained that its prosecution struck "a great blow, not only against literature, but against the public good" (Souhami, 204). He then attempted to call his first witness, the eminent literary critic Desmond McCarthy, editor of *Life and Letters*. Biron allowed Birkett to call the witness, but with the following caveat: expert witness as to whether the book was "a piece of literature" was irrelevant. "That is not the point," he explained:

> The book may be a very fine piece of literature and yet be obscene. Art and obscenity are not disassociated. This may be a work of art. I agree that it has considerable merits, but that does not prevent it from being obscene and I shall therefore not admit this expert evidence. (Ibid., 205)

Birkett protested, on the grounds that his witnesses had "knowledge of the reading public and in their view this book is not obscene." He called McCarthy to the stand and asked him whether, having read the book, he thought it obscene. Biron interrupted: the evidence was inadmissible, being only an expression of opinion. Birkett proposed to call witnesses from various professions: booksellers, biologists, a magistrate. "Oh no," objected Sir Chartres, "I don't think people are entitled to express an opinion upon a matter which is the decision of the court" (ibid., 206). As Virginia Woolf put in her diary on November 10: "We could not be called as experts in obscenity, only in art."

And art was evidently not the point. Art would not, in fact, become the point until thirty years later, when the Obscene Publications Act was revised a century after its conception to take artistic merit explicitly into consideration in such cases and allow for expert witness of the sort disallowed in the trial of *The Well*. This revision led directly to the infamous *Lady Chatterley* trial, subject of the next chapter. In 1928, though, the fact that literary merit was in principle irrelevant, and certainly not an exonerating element, sealed the already strong case against Hall's publisher. Sir Chartres Biron found against Cape, and his judgment was upheld on appeal. *The Well of Loneliness* was not published again in England for twenty years.

Its fate in the United States was somewhat different. Hall had already contracted with Knopf for American publication of the novel. Once it became clear that Cape was to be hauled into court in London, however, Knopf, which had already set the book in type, understandably began to hesitate, and after the Biron decision pulled out of the contract; as Alfred A. Knopf later put it, "We didn't see anything heroic about publishing it here after what happened in England" (cited in Boyer, 131). (Hall, who had been dealing with Blanche Knopf, expressed irritation at having to deal with the publisher's wife, writing to her American agent that "it is better for women to keep out of business negotiations," and that she found it "both difficult and tedious to deal with a woman" [Souhami, 170]). American rights to the publication were then taken over by the new firm of Covici, Friede, which had already had run-ins with the censors and which took on the project with gusto. The first thing they did was to hire the attorney Morris L. Ernst, who went on, as we have seen, to defend *Ulysses* in 1933. In 1928 he had just published *To the Pure*, a book criticizing literary obscenity law. Ernst immediately suggested that Covici and Friede invite a test case by informing John Sumner, Anthony Comstock's successor as head of the New York Vice Society, of their plans to publish Hall's novel. Sumner, who was not only horrified by the open depiction of sexual deviance but had a particular axe to grind against young upstart Jews in the publishing business, rose immediately to the bait, terming *The Well* "literary refuse," and noting that it was especially "vicious" because the sympathetic depiction of characters suggested they should be "accepted on the same plane as persons normally constituted" (Vice Society records; cited in Souhami, 133).

The Covici-Friede edition was published in December 1928. Sumner bought a copy from Friede, which led to the latter's arrest by Manhattan police, who also seized more than eight hundred copies of the book. The case went to trial in February 1929: Judge Hyman Bushel found Friede guilty and the book obscene, on grounds that it "idealized and extolled" perversion, would tend to "debauch public morals," and "deprave and corrupt minds," especially those of "the weaker members of society" (ibid., 133). Ernst appealed. An enormous amount of publicity was generated by the case; letters and telegrams were solicited and written, and there was a great deal of newspaper coverage. All the while publication continued: printing operations were transferred to Massachusetts, since the proceedings were going on in New York, and distribution now took place in New Jersey. Friede, like Ernst, felt that any publicity was good publicity, "if they spelled your name right," as Friede later put it (ibid., 133). He even tried to get the Watch and Ward Society, a Boston-based organization devoted to upholding the moral order, to prosecute as well, but to no avail, as they saw nothing wrong with the book, to Friede's regret.

Ernst's brief argued, in time-honored fashion, that the story told by Hall's book thwarted rather than inviting imitation; to suppress it, he insisted, would "prevent the proper enlightment of the public on an important social problem" (ibid., 225). He further referred to similarly themed books that were freely available, including Proust's *Swann's Way*, Mann's *Death in Venice*, and works by Voltaire, Whitman, and Swinburne. He also quoted at length from *Mademoiselle de Maupin*, Théophile Gautier's 1835 novel that had been the object of an unsuccessful Vice Society prosecution in 1922, noting that Hall's novel contained no such suggestive scenes. The defense was bolstered—as in England, but this time successfully—by laudatory reviews, the *New York Herald Tribune*, for instance, insisting that it was "as much a novel of problem and purpose as *Uncle Tom's Cabin*, as sentimental and moralistic as the deepest dyed of Victorian novels" (ibid., 228). A "strenuous letter of protest" was signed by American literary luminaries, among them Sherwood Anderson, Theodore Dreiser, F. Scott Fitzgerald, Ernest Hemingway, and Upton Sinclair. Edna Ferber too weighed in, wondering what would happen when the Vice Society discovered the indecencies of the Old Testament. If *The Well* encountered less resistance from the American literati on the basis of artistic merit than in England, it was probably because of the moral opprobrium that had already been heaped on it on both sides of the Atlantic.

In April 1929 a special three-judge special sessions court reversed the lower court decision and exonerated Covici, Friede, and *The Well* was free to be published in the United States. The publishers placed a full-page ad in *Publishers' Weekly* celebrating the fact. They also announced publication of a special twenty-five-dollar Victory Edition with Hall's autograph and Ernst's summary of the American legal proceedings. Over 100,000 copies of the novel sold in the United States in 1929, with royalties of more than sixty thousand dollars going to Hall. Gallimard published a French translation in 1929; Hall was the first female author to figure on the prestigious publisher's list. By the time the novel was reissued in England twenty years later it was still selling some 100,000 copies a year worldwide. In 1974 *The Well of Loneliness* was featured in seventeen episodes on the BBC's "Books at Bedtime" series.

Despite her taste for martyrdom, Radclyffe Hall makes a strange martyr to literary censorship history. It is a tribute to the effectiveness of efforts to repress positive representations of homosexuality that *The Well of Loneliness*, with its reactionary politics and lugubrious take on gay life, should have been the first—and for a long time only—mainstream English novel centrally concerned with same-sex love. Wilde and Forster would seem to be likelier candidates, and yet it was Hall who claimed the distinction of being the first to defend homosexuality in an anglophone novel. Forster was at once too quixotically invested in flouting the rules of conventional depiction of such matters to engage in the sort of pessimistic narrative Hall undertook, and too mindful of the consequences, to be willing to become a martyr to this cause. He wrote *Maurice*, but relied on his certainty of the eventual advent of "a happier year," posthumous though he knew it would be, to publish it. As for Wilde, he has gone down in history as doubtless the most ostentatious sacrifice on the altar of same-sex love, and yet he too makes an unlikely martyr, for reasons opposite to Hall's. He insisted, both in writing and in court, that literature has no capacity to affect public or private mores. *De Profundis*, which Troubridge read aloud to Hall during the scandal of *The Well*, is his only published work directly to address the issue of homosexuality. It was written—as a letter to Lord Alfred Douglas—after he had been sent to prison for his crime, and was not published in full for decades. His incarceration, which led to his death, resulted not from his writings, at least not directly, but *The Picture of Dorian Gray* furnished a large part of the argument against Wilde in his first trial, when he ill-advisedly brought charges of libel against the Marquess of Queensberry, Douglas's father, who had accused him of "posing as a Somdomite [*sic*]."

The Picture of Dorian Gray is pertinent here, as it was in Wilde's trial, not only for its homoerotic subtext, but also because of the theory of art that emerges from the novel. Its famous "preface" states the author's aesthetic position—the doctrine of art for art's sake pushed to the limit—in its most concise form: "There is no such thing as a moral or an immoral book. Books are well written, or badly written. That is all."[27] Much was made of this in the courtroom, of course; it was taken as evidence that the novel itself, and therefore its author as well, were immoral. It helped land Wilde in prison at the end of the nineteenth century, but this stance can be found, in watered-down form, at the center of what has been called the "aesthetic defense" effectively informing much of later-twentieth-century obscenity proceedings: the idea that art obviates obscenity; that where there is art there cannot be indecency.

Wilde specifically addresses the theme of literature as poison in *Dorian Gray*. (This did not prevent critics from making the predictable accusations: the *Daily* Chronicle, for one, termed the novel "a poisonous book, the atmosphere of which is heavy with the mephitic odours of moral and spiritual putrefaction.")[28] The amorous Lord Henry Wotton gives the title character a book, a French novel recognizably modeled on Huysmans's decadent novel *A Rebours*.[29] Dorian becomes obsessed with the volume, and ends up attributing to it all his problems. He tells his friend that he has poisoned him with a book, and enjoins him never to lend the book to anyone else, as "it does harm." Lord Henry responds:

> My dear boy, you are really beginning to moralize. . . . You and I are what we are, and will be what we will be. As for being poisoned by a book, there is no such thing as that. Art has no influence upon action. It annihilates the de-

sire to act. It is superbly sterile. The books that the world calls immoral are books that show the world its own shame. That is all. (218)

Wilde reiterated this theory of the sterile harmlessness of art, to no avail, or rather to anti-avail, during his first trial. James Douglas's insistence that *The Well of Loneliness* was more dangerous than prussic acid is the precise negative counterpart to Wilde's idea that art has no influence on action, that one cannot be poisoned by a book. Wilde's sole stated moral criterion, that of a well written or a badly written book, was paradoxically taken up by the prosecution in the trial of Hall's novel. Despite the fact that even its proponents agreed it was badly written, it was touted as artful by the prosecution and the condemning magistrate, because this made it all the more likely to corrupt its readership.

Wilde died in miserable exile in 1900 after his prison sentence had ruined his health. Hall lived on prosperously in England, publishing increasingly pious novels, until her death in 1943. Wilde is now a cultural and literary hero, in both gay studies and the culture at large, and Hall a marginal figure, known solely for *The Well of Loneliness*, the legacy of which remains an object of uncomfortable ambivalence in the history of literary censorship and especially for a gay audience. The trials of Oscar Wilde hold the painful lesson that harmlessness is in the eye of the beholder. What Hall has still to teach us is perhaps above all, ironically enough, the consequences of being earnest.

∞

CHAPTER FIVE

D. H. Lawrence

Sexual Intercourse Begins

Man is a changeable beast, and words change their meanings with him,
and things are not what they seemed, and what's what becomes what
isn't, and if we think we know where we are it's only because we are so
rapidly being translated to somewhere else.

D. H. LAWRENCE, "Pornography and Obscenity"

ady Chatterley's Lover occasioned without a doubt the most notorious
literary obscenity battle of the twentieth century. In 1960, more
than thirty years after Lawrence's novel was originally published in
Italy after being rejected out of hand by publishers in England and America, *Regina v. Penguin Books* finally ended the ban alluded to in Larkin's
poem "Annus Mirabilis." The previous year another, less publicized but
equally momentous trial, pitting Grove Press against the U.S. Post Office,
had ended the American ban on the novel. Moreover, both these epoch-
marking events had been preceded by three-part legal proceedings in
Japan against the publisher of the first Japanese translation of Lawrence's
work, which left it unavailable in that country for some years.

The third work in Anthony Burgess's triptych of obscenity would seem
to bear little resemblance to either of the others, aside from "obscenity" itself, which takes very different forms in the three novels. *Lady Chatterley's
Lover* shares with *Ulysses* the explicit—although very differently explicit—
depiction of sexual situations and the—again very different—use of four-
letter vernacular terms. It has in common with *The Well of Loneliness* not
just chronology—both were published in 1928—but also the fact that
Lawrence and Hall are true moralists, as opposed to (like Flaubert, Joyce
or, later, Nabokov) amoralists, or (like Sade or Baudelaire) immoralists.
They do not revel in the reversal of conventional morality, nor do they
paint damning portraits of their culture without offering redemptive solu-
tions. Instead, their criticism of prevailing mores is accompanied by the

advancement of a morality of their own, a new social program: both *The Well* and *Chatterley* were written, essentially, as manifestoes in fictional form. (Judge Frederick vanPelt Bryan, in his 1959 decision allowing Grove Press to distribute Lawrence's novel, calls it "almost as much a polemic as a novel.")[1] Both books are arguments for what later came to be called sexual liberation, although in very different ways, and it is likely that both authors would have been appalled at some of the social changes in favor of which their names have been invoked. Lawrence's idiosyncratically reactionary bent was such that his wife termed *Lady Chatterley* "the last word in Puritanism."[2] This puritan tendency, writes Burgess, "would have made Lawrence shudder at his realization in the 1960s that he had become a prophet of the so-called sexual revolution" (*Flame*, 266). Hall's argument against the status quo, as we have seen, is almost entirely confined to one relatively circumscribed, if controversial, point about tolerance of same-sex relations. Lawrence's quarrel with the existing moral order is a great deal more comprehensive—Aldous Huxley called him "a militant, crusading moralist"—but the two share a strong evangelical bent, if nothing else.[3] Despite their fundamental differences, Lawrence and Hall have one other important point in common as well: as a direct result of their trials, and unlike Joyce, both remain to this day best known for works that almost all critics agree were far from being their best.

Hall's reputedly best works, however, have long been relegated to literary history's scrapheap, including *Adam's Breed*, which won both major literary awards in England, and she is now known solely for *The Well of Loneliness*; not even those critics who continue to write about her works bother to mention her other novels, or her mawkish poetry, except in passing. Lawrence, in contrast, a central figure in his own time, and despite the vagaries of literary politics and aesthetics which have, at least for the moment, propelled him out of fashion in academic circles, remains nonetheless a major presence in twentieth-century English literature. To say that *The Well of Loneliness* is not Radclyffe Hall's best novel is not the same as to say that *Lady Chatterley's Lover* is not Lawrence's; the two are comparable chiefly in the context of a cultural climate that deemed them both unacceptable. Burgess goes so far as to maintain that the most immediately salutary effect of the British trial stemmed not so much from the legal change it represented as from the fact that the relative mediocrity of *Lady Chatterley* could finally be acknowledged:

> Relief among those of us who had always denounced censorship, and not only of Lawrence, derived more from our now being able to say openly that *Lady Chatterley's Lover* was not a great book, rather than from the new liberalism of the law. For it had always been necessary previously to assert that an

outstanding work of literature had been put in chains; now we could at least be honest. (*Flame*, 242)

As this illustrates, and as has already begun to emerge from the preceding chapters, one of the odd vagaries of the history of literary obscenity trials is that during the same period in which artistic merit was emerging as a salient category in these debates, both publicly and judicially, its value was being compromised by an unforeseen by-product. The attacks on such works produced a backlash that was just as ideological as the original denunciations, but tended to be expressed in aesthetic terms: mediocre works that had been condemned as obscene were defended on grounds of their artistic as well as social merit. This was then complicated by what we have seen happening most evidently in the *Well of Loneliness* trial: attempts by the defense to claim that because of its literary merit the novel did not represent a danger were successfully countered by the prosecution, on the assumption—already familiar from the *Madame Bovary* case—that aesthetic quality only exacerbated the novel's persuasiveness to a susceptible public. In other words, art for art's sake (aesthetic value as its own justification) was not yet accepted as a legitimate defense, but art for dirt's sake (the employment of aesthetically legitimate means toward a socially unacceptable end [e.g. *The Well*]), and dirt for art's sake (the employment of socially unacceptable terms toward aesthetically meritorious ends [e.g *Ulysses*]) were still grounds for condemnation. The result is resumed in Burgess's trilogy of "literary dirt": works as wildly divergent in aesthetic value, as well as in ideological content, as *Ulysses*, *The Well of Loneliness*, and *Lady Chatterley's Lover* were for some time placed in the same category and defended on the same grounds, because they had been attacked on the same grounds.[4]

In terms of ideological content, as we saw in chapter 2, the basic argument of the prosecution in Flaubert's trial was that *Madame Bovary* denigrated marriage and glorified adultery, despite the abundant evidence visible even in the passages cited by the prosecutor that the heroine's problems stemmed from the failure of marriage and adultery alike to satisfy her desires. Lawrence too was read as denigrating marriage and glorifying adultery, and the charges are just as false in his case, although they are false in a very different way. Adultery does satisfy Constance Chatterley's desires, as marriage did not; nonetheless, it is clear both from the novel itself and from Lawrence's statements about it that his intention was to write a defense of marriage, on his own idiosyncratic terms. "Marriage is no marriage that is not a correspondence of blood," as he puts it; his intention is to defend what he considers to be "real" marriage—what he likes to call "phallic" (his favorite adjective) marriage—rather than mere convention.[5] Constance Chatterley's allegorical first name is not meant to provide ironic counterpoint: to the contrary, in the end she embodies commitment. She does so, however, in a way unfamiliar to the nineteenth-century literary tradition which held that wives may not with impunity betray or leave even the most repellently inappropriate or abusive husbands, but must suffer either definitively or until the latter conveniently die and their widows are therefore free to make more satisfying arrangements.[6] One explanation for both Lawrence's innovation in this matter and the outcry against it may be found in the changing valences of marriage over the course of the nineteenth century and into the twentieth, during which time that institution mutated from an evidently social and economic contract (*mariage de raison*) to one at least in principle based primarily on love, a shift that had formed much of the unspoken material for nineteenth-century novels and which was now, to the horror of conservative critics, being addressed directly. The literature of the nineteenth century is, of course, filled with adulterous women, but they tend either to remain in secondary roles, like many of the adulterous women in Balzac's novels, or to commit suicide, like Emma Bovary or Anna Karenina.

Connie Chatterley thus represents a departure in terms of adulterous heroines. In a certain sense, even Molly Bloom is less blameworthy in that, while her tryst with Blazes Boylan is central to *Ulysses*, she renounces it at the end of the novel in favor of some sort of at least provisional acceptance of her marital lot. Connie Chatterley, though, who exhibits at least as much equanimity as Molly Bloom or Emma Bovary in the face of adulterous temptations, is nonetheless, in the end, unlike the others, last seen attempting to make a new life and family with her lover. For her, adultery pays off, but it does so by producing a new and more fulfilling marital order. This is at once what set the story off from its scandalous precedents and what caused it to be scandalous in itself. The deck is heavily stacked against the Chatterley couple from the beginning of the book. Like Emma before her, Connie comes to her marriage innocent, if not, like her predecessor, virginal. One of the main points of the novel, and one that has predictably tended to be overlooked in the wake of its scandal, is a grand-scale attack against modern—that is, industrial-age—social mores, including sexual promiscuity. The first sentence alone should have been enough to ward off prurient readers: "Ours is essentially a tragic age, so we refuse to take it tragically." It is difficult to imagine a less auspicious opening for a supposedly pornographic work than this sweepingly pessimistic sociopolitical indictment of both the age and its self-image.

By the same token it is almost as difficult, from the point of view of a posterity shaped in part by the very fact of *Lady Chatterley*'s having entered the canon, to imagine how such an earnestly preachy novel could ever have been viewed as tending essentially to deprave and corrupt those into whose hands it might have been likely to fall. For one thing, sex does not take place between the eponymous lovers before the tenth chapter. Lawrence's novel, like *Madame Bovary* now available in various "classic" editions, nonetheless retains much more of its original shock value than either Flaubert's or *The Well of Loneliness*, but almost exclusively because of its vocabulary. It centrally features language and situations—language above all—that are still, especially in the United States, viewed as problematic. Hall's work, like Flaubert's, now seems absurd as an example of dangerous literature because of its complete absence of explicit sexual content. As a result the purely ideological nature of the objection is all the more evident, and since dominant ideology has shifted considerably as far as the acceptance of homosexuality is concerned, the desire to suppress *The Well* now appears much more shocking than anything in the tediously melodramatic work itself.

The *Chatterley* case is at once similar and different. It is similar to that of Hall's novel because here too the purely political objections seem absurdly outdated; Lawrence's virulent criticism of industrial and postindustrial capitalist values having long since been assimilated into popular culture ("late" capitalism being, as many commentators have noted, characterized by a seemingly limitless capacity to assimilate and market even the most violent attacks against it). Risible too is the shock value of defending a certain narrowly defined form of sexual experimentation, especially when the main idea is that "marriage is no marriage that is not basically and permanently phallic."[7] Sentiments such as this last are highly unwelcome in our current cultural climate, and have been roughly since Kate Millett published her feminist excoriation of Lawrence, among others, in *Sexual Politics* in 1969, although for very different reasons than when the novel was first published. Few people today, of course, would advocate censoring *Lady Chatterley* on those grounds. But if Lawrence had confined his complaints about modern life to abstract pronouncements his place in posterity—and with it, posterity itself—would have looked very different. What got him into such trouble in 1928, and Penguin Books thirty-two years later, was not his criticism of social mores per se, but the language in which he couched them, and the detail he felt necessary to a full exposition of his views on sexuality.

Somewhat surprisingly, given Lawrence's moralistic bent, the plot hinges on a note of moral ambiguity. Connie marries Clifford, Lord Chatterley, who without further ado goes off to fight in World War I and is shipped back, paralyzed below the waist. The extent to which this condition is meant to be taken primarily as a metaphorical index of the socio-sexual impotence of the British ruling classes after the war is left to the reader. Lawrence himself announced that he didn't know the answer to this question. It was only when he had reread the first version of the novel, he recounts, that:

> I recognized that the lameness of Clifford was symbolic of the paralysis, the
> deeper emotional or passional paralysis, of most men of his sort and class
> today. I realized that it was perhaps taking an unfair advantage of Connie, to
> paralyse him technically. It made it so much more vulgar of her to leave
> him. Yet the story came as it did, by itself, so I left it alone. ("A Propos," in
> *Sex, Literature, and Censorship,* 110)

It was bad enough to have Emma Bovary betray a loving and faithful husband who is also a good provider and father, but at least Charles is in-
escapably dull and uncomprehending. Clifford, however—who is also
dull, but in a self-conscious, modern way—attempts to compensate by ar-
ranging bohemian house parties for his young wife, and actually encourages her to stray (within prescribed boundaries, of course: he wants both
to curtail his young wife's frustrations and to have an heir, at almost any
cost). It is difficult to sympathize fully with a heroine who leaves a husband not merely crippled but also aware of his wife's needs, as Charles Bovary is not.[8] Lawrence knew this, but wrote the novel he wrote anyway, or
at least this is how he recounts the genesis of the novel, in accordance with
the Romantic idea of the story coming unbidden and intact to the storyteller. In any case, *Lady Chatterley's Lover* is among other things testimony
to its author's quixotic and almost incomprehensible integrity, his need to
tell a story in the way he felt it needed to be told, against all odds and despite his awareness of the many ways in which it would not only offend but
also necessarily be misread. Constance Chatterley has a number of lovers
in the course of the novel, but the main one, featured in the title, with
whom she runs off in the end, pregnant with his child and intending to
marry him, is her husband's gamekeeper.

There was, it seems, something about a gamekeeper in England in the
early twentieth century. In Forster's *Maurice* as well—which was not to be
published until forty years after Lawrence's death—the protagonist finds
unlikely love with a gamekeeper. Forster himself testified for the defense
in the 1960 trial of *Lady Chatterley,* saying during his testimony that he still
considered Lawrence to be "the greatest imaginative novelist" of their
common generation, and further asserted that the work in question had
"very high literary merit," even if it was not the author's work he most admired (*Sons and Lovers* taking that honor).[9] He seems, though, to have
been irritated by the coincidence, as Lawrence's gamekeeper inevitably
eclipsed his own, if for no other reason than that his own gamekeeper
story was still eleven years away from posthumous publication. In his epilogue to *Maurice,* written in 1960, the year of *Penguin v. Regina,* he points
out that Alec Scudder, the gamekeeper with whom Maurice is last seen trying to establish an ongoing relationship, "is senior in date to the prickly
gamekeepers of D. H. Lawrence, and had not the advantage of their dis-

quisitions, nor . . . would they have more in common than a mug of beer" (252). Despite this repudiation, bolstered by the plural which makes it appear as though Lawrence's oeuvre were brimming with randy, pontificating gamekeepers—which it is, to a certain extent, as both his first (*The White Peacock* [1911]) and last novels centrally feature them—it seems clear that the lure of this particular figure was roughly the same for the two authors. And not only for them: Virginia Woolf, presumably in a spirit of Lawrence-baiting, provides Orlando with her own gamekeeper fantasy, placing the following toward the end of *Orlando* (published not long after *Chatterley* in 1928), once her hero has turned into a heroine: "Surely, since she is a woman, and a beautiful woman, and a woman in the prime of her life, she will soon give over this pretense of writing and thinking and begin at least to think of a gamekeeper."[10] Vita Sackville-West, for whom Woolf wrote *Orlando*, read Lawrence's novel when it was first published, but since this reference is already present in Woolf's original manuscript it seems likely that the insertion of this gamekeeper reference was made on the basis of hearsay alone, which gives some indication of what a scandal *Chatterley* had created even before it saw the light.

If two such dissimilar writers as Forster and Lawrence provided their lonely protagonists with understanding gamekeepers during roughly the same period, in any case, it is no mere accident but rather the convergent product of very different takes on approximately the same class issue, and class difference plays a central role in both novels. Forster was writing from the point of view of the moneyed middle class and Lawrence from that of the rural proletariat. *Maurice*, as its title announces, centrally features the perspective of its Oxbridge-educated hero, and however much the reader may be encouraged to have contempt for his essential mediocrity, we are at the same time forced to identify with him. *Lady Chatterley's Lover*, as its ambivalent title too suggests, takes a more ambiguous approach: the center of narrative gravity is the eponymous heroine, but the moral center, the real point, resides in the lover. (This bifocal approach led Kate Millett to pronounce Lawrence not only "the most talented and fervid of sexual politicians," but "the most subtle as well, for it is through a feminine consciousness that his masculine message is conveyed.")[11] It is clear that in both cases, though, the mythology of the gamekeeper is roughly the same: he is not just an employee but one in signal touch with nature, while the employers, the ruling classes (the protagonists in both cases), are relatively alienated from it. In Forster's novel, Scudder is not the protagonist's gamekeeper—Maurice comes from a less exalted background—but that of his former boyfriend who has renounced his old ways. Similarly, Mellors is not after all Connie's gamekeeper, but her husband's. In both novels the gamekeepers provide the satisfaction their employers either cannot or will not.

One important difference between the two characters is that while Scudder conforms to the stereotypical image of the alluringly virile and robust rustic (his only deviation from this norm would seem to be in terms of sexual preference, but this too can be understood according to a familiar theme of polymorphous perversity among the working class), Mellors is, contrary to cliché, physically frail and sickly, weakened by pneumonia, indeed possibly tubercular: much like the author himself. From one version of the novel to the next, the lover becomes less unequivocally class-bound and more of a mercurial autodidact—again, like Lawrence himself. Because he remains a gamekeeper, however, it is tempting to assume that the novel confirms the mythology with which it undoubtedly flirts: the back jacket copy on one recent American paperback edition, for instance, reads in part: "Filled with scenes of intimate beauty, the moving story of Constance Chatterley tenderly explores the emotions of a lonely woman trapped in a sterile marriage and her growing love for the robust gamekeeper of her husband's estate."[12] The gamekeeper's function would seem legendarily to involve robustness; the syllogism thus has it that since Lady Chatterley runs off with a gamekeeper, the latter must therefore be robust. The fact that Lawrence's novel flouts this particular cliché is no obstacle to the novel's assimilation into the mythology that it nonetheless both reproduces and helps to articulate. (Its current U.S. Library of Congress cataloguing information includes the following: "1.Married women—Fiction. 2.Gamekeepers—Fiction.") Both *Lady Chatterley* and *Maurice*, in any case, showcase unlikely happy, or at least optimistic, endings, each protagonist setting off to live happily ever after with the relevant gamekeeper. As we saw in the previous chapter, Forster did not even attempt publication of *Maurice* during his lifetime, specifically because he knew the happy ending precluded it, as homosexuals were at the time doomed to tragic endings in fiction. Lawrence too was aware that the hopeful future he insisted on giving his adulterous heroine made the story all the more difficult to publish, but he too went ahead anyway; unlike Forster, however, he was hell-bent on publishing his unpublishable work during his lifetime.

In both cases class difference added—from the point of view of the censors—to the basic problems of, respectively, homosexuality and adultery. (As mentioned in the previous chapter, class difference also played a major role in the trials of Oscar Wilde in 1895.) Within both novels, of course, and uncoincidentally, class difference was part of the solution. While Forster was entering new territory with his sympathetic portrayal of the homosexual, though, Lawrence had many now-canonical precedents for his major theme of female adultery, most obviously *Madame Bovary*, along with *Anna Karenina*. Even so, Connie Chatterley's story diverges from these others in a number of ways, chief among them the crucial matter of the optimistic ending, as well as the matter of class difference. Not only do both Emma and Anna kill themselves, neither exhibits an interest in downward mobility. (In Flaubertian terms, it is as though Emma had gone off with neither Rodolphe nor Leon, nor even Justin the adoring apothecary's assistant, but rather Lestiboudois the gravedigger; and the relative sexiness quotients between gamekeepers and gravediggers, for instance, suggests the extent to which romanticization of the rural working class had changed between the mid nineteenth and early twentieth centuries.) Nor can the fact that Lawrence's novel created such a scandal through the mid twentieth century be attributed solely to differences between French and anglophone culture, despite the fact that a French film based on the novel became the subject of American legal proceedings that went all the way to the Supreme Court in 1959, even as Grove Press was fighting the U.S. Post Office for the right to distribute the novel in the United States.

The difference between the two cases is instructive in a number of ways. For one thing, no one in England or the United States was able to attempt a film version of the novel during this period. Two Hollywood attempts had been made, in 1932 and 1950, to take on the project of a *Chatterley* film, both nipped in the bud by the Production Code Administration.[13] As for the book, a French translation of the novel had been circulating unmolested in France and other countries since 1932. The French film, however, while faithful to the plot of the novel, was completely devoid of sexually explicit content. According to Justice Felix Frankfurter it would not even have "offended Victorian moral sensibilities," but the New York State motion picture licensing board had refused to grant a license to show it on the grounds that "the theme is the presentation of adultery as a desirable, acceptable and proper pattern of behavior."[14] Justice Potter Stewart spoke for the court in finding this unconstitutional: "What New York has done is to prevent the exhibition of a motion picture because that picture advocates an idea—that adultery under certain circumstances may be proper behavior." The First Amendment, he noted, "protects advocacy of the opinion that adultery may sometimes be proper, no less than advocacy of socialism or the single tax."[15] The Supreme Court's judgment concerning the film had little bearing on the Grove Press case going on at the same time, because the two versions of the story were offensive in different ways. Because the film contained no explicit sexual images it was merely immoral, not obscene, and as such protected under the Constitution.

Accordingly, what made Lawrence's novel such an unprecedentedly problematic work was not its immorality but its obscenity: not its representation of adultery per se, but its explicit representation of the mechanics of sex, and its use of "vulgar language" in the description thereof. To put it another way, Larkin's insistence that "Sexual intercourse began / In nineteen sixty-three / . . . / Between the end of the Chatterley ban / And the Beatles' first LP" is not entirely accurate. The poem mocks the ponderous language of the prosecution: it was not sexual intercourse that had begun—nor certainly adultery—but *fucking*. It is no coincidence that Larkin's other most famous lines are "They fuck you up, your mum and dad. / They may not mean to, but they do."[16] Here the word *fuck* is not used in its sexual sense; like Joyce's "grey sunken cunt of the world," this use of an obscene term is even less aphrodisiac than "Annus Mirabilis," although no less unacceptable in a pre-*Chatterley* world. Literary fucking was what the novel began; if Joyce inaugurated various forms of excretion in serious literature, Lawrence (who hated Joyce, and especially *Ulysses*), or to be more precise Lawrence's posthumous trials, made literature safe for the vernacular description of sex acts. Burgess alludes to this elliptically when he titles his study of Lawrence *Flame into Being:* a truncated quotation from Mellors's letter to Connie that closes the novel, the original sentence reading "we fucked a flame into being." This vocabulary had certainly existed, even in print, for many centuries, in English as in other languages, and it had been abundantly disseminated—but not in legitimate (legally sanctioned) form. The language Lawrence introduced into the "serious" novel with *Lady Chatterley* in 1928 was "pornographic" language and had for centuries been confined to that genre. As a result, the work was immediately deemed pornographic, as *Ulysses* had been, in which the term also figures, although not nearly as prominently.

Another linguistic transgression is also evident in Lawrence's novel: this vernacular is not merely used incidentally among the "lower orders," nor is it used only among men. To the contrary, Mellors makes didactic use of such words when speaking to Connie and encourages her too to use them (at one point he explains to his ignorant but willing pupil the distinction between "cunt" and "fuck" [189]). Behind this vocabulary is an entire Lawrentian dogma proclaiming that nomenclature and ideology are one, and that these frank Anglo-Saxon terms go hand in hand with honest, liberatory attitudes toward sex. The use of "raw" or "crude" language is not confined to the working class in the novel, as is made clear by a frank exchange between Mellors and Connie's father; the central linguistic divide in these terms is gendered. "Decent" society—that is, middle- or upper-middle- or upper-class women—was the audience that had to be protected from this sort of language. Mellors goes out of his way to introduce Connie not only to the act of "warm-hearted fucking" (as opposed to "all this cold-hearted fucking that is death and idiocy" [220])[17] but to this way of referring to it, which represents Lawrence's program, and its perceived dangers, in a nutshell. What Pinard had observed warningly about *Madame Bovary*, that its readers were not only to be impervious men but susceptible women as well, was also true here, and as a result the main problem was that Mellors's lesson would find the audience that Connie embodies in the novel represented among its readers as well.

Lady Chatterley, then, was deemed offensive not just because it appeared to defend adultery, but also because it violated a specifically linguistic morality. And while such language has long ceased to shock in literary contexts, literary contexts are no longer where such battles are fought, and therefore a comparison with current film and television is perhaps in order. In the United States, veiled verbal and even visual references to sexual acts are commonplace in films and on television, but, unlike in other countries such as France and even England for instance, they tend to remain veiled. (Transatlantic counterexamples include the following: films of all sorts are routinely shown on mainstream French television without any cuts, and television advertising in that country has for years featured nudity; across the Channel, use of the word *fuck* was inaugurated on British television in 1965.)[18] Words and images such as those that got Lawrence into such trouble both in 1928 and thirty years later, despite their ubiquity in movies and on cable television as well as in common parlance, remain forbidden in the United States on network television and subject to strict, although tacit, ratings distinctions in commercial film, for the very same reasons that obtained in Lawrence's case in the context of a literary work: because everyone may have access to these media, and vulnerable audiences, it is felt, must be protected against such verbal or visual representations. In terms of the novel, the complexity of the compounded offense is most evident in one of its most famously obscene passages, in which Mellors praises Connie's anatomy using the rural Midlands dialect both he and Lawrence prefer to employ at such moments (Mellors, like his author, has more standard diction at his disposal, but insists on dialect in scenes like the following):

> He stroked her tail with his hand, long and subtly taking in the curves and the globefulness.
>
> "Tha's got such a nice tail on thee," he said in the throaty, caressive dialect. "Tha's got the nicest arse of anybody. It's the nicest, nicest woman's arse as is!" (237)

After Mellors has gone on a bit, explaining the precise terms of his appreciation of Connie's posterior charms, we encounter the following:

> All the while he spoke he exquisitely stroked the rounded tail, till it seemed as if a slippery sort of fire came from it into his hands. And his finger-tips touched the two secret openings to her body, time after time, with a soft little brush of fire.

"An' if tha' shits an' if tha' pisses, I'm glad. I don't want a woman as couldna shit nor piss." (238)

As is clear from the fact that we are explicitly told Mellors is caressing Connie's nether regions with his diction and his hand simultaneously, Lawrence wants to highlight the intimate relation between language and what it refers to. (And again, it is instructive in this context to recall the extent to which American film and television continue to draw entailment-rich distinctions between bodily expression and the language around it.) Words like *piss* and *shit*, *arse* and, elsewhere, the ubiquitous *fuck* and *cunt*, have much the same effect in the text in general as what Mellors is saying in this scene about his lover's body. In response to the above-cited comment, "Connie couldn't help a sudden snort of astonished laughter," and the reader may well have a similar reaction, but the gamekeeper "went on unmoved," as does the author (238). Along with Mellors, Lawrence is trying, through the use of such terms, to shock us into into an awareness and, consequently, eventual acceptance of what is inarguably an inescapable part of human existence and can be alternatively ignored, as was the acceptable stance, or celebrated, as he insisted was the only healthy approach. For this reason the "raw" language is crucial to the book, rather than, as many critics felt, unnecessary provocation. It is also true that the four-letter words and sexual descriptions can be removed from the novel without affecting the plot. Unauthorized expurgated versions were quickly produced and circulated openly throughout the duration of the ban, proving, among other things, that the ostensibly positive depiction of adultery was no longer the chief problem with this sort of narrative.

Lady Chatterley's Lover as we know it was the third version of this story, the initial title of which was "Tenderness." Another working title was "John Thomas and Lady Jane," the latter being pet names for the two main characters' genitals.[19] We can trace Lawrence's central concerns through the history of these titles. Since the novel's reputation was and still is for the raw depiction of sex, it is instructive to note the extent to which tenderness and genitals were ideally, for the author, part of the same system—as is in fact clear from the final version of the novel, in which Mellors equates tenderness with what he calls "cunt-awareness" (297). From one version to the next the vocabulary becomes more crudely "Anglo-Saxon," making the book less and less publishable and demonstrating how crucial the author felt this terminology to be. Judge Bryan recognized this in his 1959 decision, which includes the following observation:

Even if it be assumed that these passages and this language taken in isolation tend to arouse shameful, morbid and lustful sexual desires in the average reader, they are an integral, and to the author a necessary part of the development of theme, plot and character. (341)

When Lawrence himself was asked to provide an expurgated version of the novel he refused, despite the enormous financial boon it would have represented. In the essay "A Propos of *Lady Chatterley's Lover*" (cited by Bryan, and published in Lawrence's *Sex, Literature, and Censorship* and in some editions of *Lady Chatterley's Lover*, appended to the text itself), the author explains that he was approached by British publishers who urged him to try his hand at bowdlerizing his novel on the grounds that he had already lost a great deal of revenue from bootleg editions and that, even aside from the large financial rewards of such a venture, this was his chance to redeem himself, to "show the public that here is a fine novel, apart from all 'purple' and all 'words.'" Perhaps surprisingly, he reports that he was willing to try: "So I begin to be tempted and start in to expurgate. But impossible! I might as well try to clip my own nose into shape with scissors. The book bleeds" (*Sex, Literature, and Censorship*, 84).

This anatomical metaphor is less disingenuous than it may appear, as can be gauged by the fact that Lawrence, to a much greater extent than Flaubert or Hall in their own cases, was well aware of how censorable *Lady Chatterley* would be. He had already had numerous run-ins with the British and American censors. Most of his novels had been trimmed of various scenes and terms by publishers, and William Heinemann, who had published his earlier works in England, refused to touch *Sons and Lovers* in 1913; it was brought out by Duckworth. That publisher then withdrew support of the 1915 novel *The Rainbow* because Lawrence would not make the changes suggested by the editor. Methuen published *The Rainbow*, but critical outcry against the book, led by the already inevitable James Douglas—who termed it so filthy as to be "worse than Zola," the accusation that had been standard in England at least since Henry Vizetelly's conviction in the late 1880s for publishing a translation of *La Terre*—eventually led to seizure of all unsold copies, a brief hearing, and destruction of the available print run.[20]

The Rainbow, initially framed as the first section of what most critics view as his masterpiece, *Women in Love*, which itself narrowly escaped censorship in both countries, was withdrawn from publication following legal proceedings. This was in part for some of the same reasons as the later novel, although the sexual themes he explored throughout his literary career were nowhere else expressed with the sort of candor he insisted on bringing to *Lady Chatterley*, which was to be his last major work. *The Rainbow* contained a number of problematic sexual themes, including suggestions of lesbianism, but it ran into trouble largely as a result of its pacifist overtones. These were greatly compounded—especially as it was published during the middle of the war—by the fact that Lawrence's wife, Frieda von Richtofen, was not only German but also first cousin of the notorious flying ace (the "Red Baron" whose enduring fame was later assured by Charles M. Schulz's immortalization of him as the arch-nemesis of Snoopy's daydreams). Even aside from his wife's national identity, Lawrence's exceptionally collaborative and close-knit marriage added a certain amount of ambiguity to his stance as a moralist. On the one hand, and even especially because of the problems caused by Frieda's Germanness and family ties, he was known as a loyal husband. On the other, when he first met his wife she was married to his former French teacher. Like his last novel, Lawrence's life seemed to uphold the importance of marriage energetically but not categorically, and this was part of what made him suspect.

Having been through a number of run-ins with censors on both sides of the Atlantic, in any case, by the time he wrote *Lady Chatterley* Lawrence knew precisely what he was doing, and decided to do it anyway. He submitted the manuscript to his British and American publishers and does not seem to have been terribly surprised when they refused to have anything to do with it. The fact that it was not published in England did not prevent British journalists from commenting on it, however; one paper, *John Bull*, which had already weighed in censoriously on Lawrence's previous works, produced a judgment on the novel that rivaled James Douglas's diatribes in rabid indignation. Along with a photo of the author as "bearded satyr," the publication termed *Lady Chatterley* "A Landmark in Evil" and went on to call it "the most evil outpouring that has ever besmirched the literature of our country. The sewers of French pornography would be dragged in vain to find a parallel in beastliness."[21] Anticipating such treatment, aware that this novel went much further than his earlier efforts, Lawrence decided to have the novel published in Italy.

Lady Chatterley was published in Florence, by Pino Orioli, a friend of Lawrence's who was also a bookseller, with many errors—like the French printers of *Ulysses* in 1922, the Italian printers knew little or no English—in 1928. A later unauthorized, unexpurgated edition appeared in Paris. Sylvia Beach was approached, first by Aldous Huxley and then by Lawrence himself, to bring out an edition in order to stop the pirating, but she "didn't admire this work," finding it "the least interesting of its author's productions." In her 1956 memoir *Shakespeare and Company* she recounts that "it was difficult to tell him that I didn't want to get a name as a publisher of erotica, and impossible to say that I wanted to be a one-book publisher—what could anybody offer after *Ulysses*?"[22] A number of authors tried to persuade Beach to publish their works for this very reason; everyone wanted to be the next Joyce. She ended up refusing not only *Lady*

Chatterley's Lover but also Frank Harris's *My Life and Loves,* Miller's *Tropic of Cancer,* and Nabokov's *Lolita,* among other works. Many of them found a home at Jack Kahane's Obelisk Press and, later on, his son Maurice Girodias's Olympia Press. These two, as we shall see, already had names as publishers of erotica but also wanted to take up the mantle of Shakespeare and Company and were thus on perpetual lookout for the next equivalent of *Ulysses*.

Following the book's publication, Lawrence had further run-ins with British censors in 1929, first when he tried to publish a volume of poetry entitled *Pansies*—the work eventually appeared sheared of fourteen poems deemed indecent by the Home Secretary, "Jix," who had had the manuscript seized in the mail—and again when a London gallery exhibition of his watercolors, featuring nudes of both sexes and including pubic hair as well as images of men urinating, was raided by the police. What happened during the judicial hearing to decide the fate of these paintings in August 1929 closely recalls the *Well of Loneliness* trial the previous year. Dorothy Warren, the gallery owner, tried to have expert witnesses heard, notably the illustrious painter Augustus John, but the presiding magistrate would have none if it, declaring: "It is utterly immaterial whether they are works of art. That is a collateral question which I have not to decide. The most splendidly painted picture in the universe might be obscene." His final pronouncement: "I would destroy these pictures, as I would destroy wild beasts."[23] In the end the thirteen offending paintings were not destroyed, but Lawrence declined to appeal the decision, asking Warren to accept the government's offer to restore the pictures on condition that they never be shown in England again.

Lawrence was by this point tired after all his battles, and very ill; he died the following year, of tuberculosis, at forty-five. Shortly before his death he was still, though, angry enough to write a number of essays about censorship. J. M. Coetzee has observed that "the polemics of writers against censors seldom do the profession credit."[24] Lawrence provides an exceptionally ripe example of an author who does himself (if not the profession as a whole) harm with virtually every word he writes about censorship. Lawrence the essayist is remarkable especially in the extent to which he is willing to assume seemingly self-annihilating positions. Even his most ardent admirers seem appalled by his pronouncements on censorship. Henry Miller laments that "Lawrence ever wrote anything *about* obscenity, because in doing so he temporarily nullified everything he had created."[25] Geoff Dyer, English novelist, author of an idiosyncratic work on Lawrence called *Out of Sheer Rage,* and one of his most fervent current fans in a cultural climate not notably hospitable to Lawrence-worship, goes so far as to maintain—and this in the introduction to a mass-market classic edition of *Lady Chatterley*—that "Lawrence probably believed and said more stupid things than any other novelist in history."[26] What he had done to provoke such bet-hedging even among his most passionate admirers was, notably, to make bold pronouncements in favor of censorship in the very course of inveighing against that practice as it had been used against his own works. In the essay "Pornography and Obscenity" (1929), to cite the most salient example, after a number of pages expounding predictably in favor of the use of "obscene" terms and the expression of sexuality in literature and against what he called "grey Puristanism," Lawrence switches tacks in mid-rant. "But even I would censor genuine pornography, rigorously," he declares, in a passage that would end up being cited by both the Supreme Court and Judge Bryan as testimony to his moral probity. "It would not be very difficult," he continues: "In the first place, genuine pornography is almost always underground, it doesn't come into the open. In the second, you can recognize it by the insult it offers, invariably, to sex, and to the human spirit" (*Sex, Literature and Censorship,* 69).

"Pornography is the attempt to insult sex, to do dirt on it," he asserts, and goes on for many pages expanding on the harm done by "genuine pornography," in the form of both pictures and books, noting in passing about the latter that "they are either so ugly they make you ill, or so fatuous you can't imagine anybody but a cretin or a moron reading them, or writing them" (69). In the course of his extended protestation against what he considers to be truly obscence literature Lawrence casts his net remarkably wide: *Pamela, Jane Eyre, The Mill on the Floss,* and *Anna Karenina* are all placed in the capacious category of the "slightly indecent," along with "nearly all nineteenth-century literature," in which he sweepingly discovers "an element of pornography" (71). To find a really healthy candor, it turns out, one has to go back to the Renaissance, to Rabelais and Boccaccio. The great irony in his arguments against nineteenth- and twentieth-century literature and for a return to what he views as prelapsarian raunchiness is that every single accusation he levels against what he considers to be "genuine pornography" was deployed against *Lady Chatterley's Lover* as well as a number of his other works, and also that these same objections had long been made in terms of the authors he holds up as models and to which his own offenses were inevitably compared. The names of Boccaccio and especially Rabelais were bywords for obscenity among the very critics who were busy damning Lawrence's works, which they often compared to Rabelais, along with the inevitable Zola, to drive their censorious point home. And even aside from the subjective assertion that the truly obscene is that which "insults" sex, the first criterion cited in his diatribe against "genuine pornography" is that it is "almost always underground": as, of course, *The Rainbow* had been for some time, and as *Chatterley* was to remain for thirty years, even leaving aside the checkered careers of the *Decameron* and the works of Rabelais. Such books, just like the dirty postcards he dismisses in a few sentences, were necessarily "underground," for the very good reason that they had been driven there because forbidden aboveground. It is difficult to see how Lawrence could have left himself so spectacularly open to charges of hypocrisy, but the answer would seem to be some combination of his own unstoppably, self-indictingly evangelical bent and a cultural climate which strongly reinforced the idea that true obscenity existed and was to be routed out; it was just located elsewhere. (If this seems hard to understand in our current permissive culture, just think of child pornography.)

Lawrence's heaviest artillery in this essay is reserved for certain strains of contemporary literature, which he identifies, with great contempt, as "self-absorption made public" (*Sex, Literature and Censorship*, 74), the sort of "masturbatory" novels that appear "'free' in their sex, free and pure"; and yet never manage to exit what he terms the vicious circle of self-abuse: "They have mentalized sex till it is nothing at all, nothing at all but a mental quality" (76). It is clear enough from this essay and from his correspondence that Lawrence was especially appalled by such contemporary writers as Joyce and Proust, who were known for writing "freely" about sex, but not in ways Lawrence approved. He reserved particular indignation for *Ulysses*, expressing himself in terms worthy of James Douglas about the Molly Bloom soliloquy: "it is the dirtiest, most indecent, obscene thing ever written," he told his wife, adding, in case his point remained obscure: "it is filthy."[27] What especially troubled him in *Ulysses*, which he dismissively characterized as "just stewed-up fragments of quotation in the sauce of a would-be dirty mind," was that it violated the theory put forth in "Pornography and Obscenity," according to which the sexual and the excremental are opposing forces which should never be confused or conflated.[28] Coupled with "the grey disease of sex hatred," he writes, is "the yellow disease of dirt lust." By which he means that:

> The sex functions and the excrementory functions in the human body work so closely together, yet they are, so to speak, utterly different in direction. Sex is a creative flow, the excrementory flow is towards dissolution, decreation, if we may use such a word. In the really healthy human being the distinction between the two is instant, our profoundest instincts are perhaps our instincts of opposition between the two flows. (*Sex, Literature, and Censorship*, 70)

What happens when the distinction breaks down, he explains, is that "sex is dirt and dirt is sex, and sexual excitement becomes a playing with dirt, and any sign of sex in woman becomes a sign of her dirt." This, he concludes, "is the source of all pornography" (70); it is also, more specifically, the source of what horrifies him most in *Ulysses*. It has been suggested that he wrote *Lady Chatterley* in envious response to Joyce's novel; in any case what he objects to in the latter is also what Pound and Nabokov, among others, found objectionable.[29]

Lawrence's careful distinction between the sexual and excremental functions, and condemnation of those who, like Joyce, insist on confusing the two "flows" seems almost inexplicably strange given that a vivid, unmistakeable even if euphemistic description of anal intercourse between Connie and Mellors was viewed as one of the most problematic passages in the novel. (In one of the stranger turns of literary idiosyncrasy, Mellors, who is disgusted by kissing on the mouth, seems to have a marked taste for sodomy.) Moreover, even aside from this episode, the novel's love scenes are filled with references to metaphorical bowels. To take one example among many, "his bowels stirred towards her," inevitably following which, "he went in to her softly, feeling the stream of tenderness flowing in release from his bowels to hers, the bowels of compassion kindled between them" (*Lady Chatterley's Lover*, 298). While it is clear that bowels are meant in this context to stand in for the most intimate physio-emotional core of the characters' being, and evident as well that the author has recourse to the term because he wants to avoid the Romantic euphemisms of nineteenth-century novels and convey the full force of physicality he wishes to foreground, the word did however at the time also mean what it does now. As a result such scenes often contain a note of involuntary comedy, and they also appear a bit suspect coming from a writer who felt free to excoriate his contemporaries for what he considered to be their confusion of the two "flows." Nonetheless, for Lawrence, Joyce continued to represent the reviled excremental tendency.

One of his followers in this regard is Henry Miller, author of *Tropic of Cancer*, among other works banned over the course of more than three decades in various countries (and subject of the next chapter). Miller, who wrote a book about Lawrence, is the latter's ideal misreader: that is, his adulation knows no bounds, while he adamantly insists on missing the point. *The World of Lawrence: A Passionate Appreciation* (1980) was to be Miller's last work, although it had started out to be his first. In 1932 Jack Kahane, whose Obelisk Press published *Tropic of Cancer* in Paris two years later, had suggested to Miller that given the nature of the forthcoming book it might be a good idea if he began by publishing a pamphlet on Lawrence or Joyce—the two most notorious contemporary representatives of highbrow obscenity—to lend critical gravitas to his reputation. Miller was understandably offended by this proposal, but decided to take it up anyway. The project dragged on for years, first in the form of a small book on Lawrence; then a large-scale study of Lawrence, Proust, and Joyce; then back to a work primarily on Lawrence. He eventually abandoned the idea of trying to finish it; as one of Miller's biographers puts it, "he had become so involved in Lawrence's universe that he confessed he had lost all track of where Lawrence's ideas ended and his own began."[30] The study was finally published almost half a century later, put together from Miller's voluminous notes from the 1930s; it came out just after his death. *The World of Lawrence*, as its subtitle indicates, is an adulatory work. It pits Lawrence against Joyce and Proust, and the latter do not come off well. Lawrence represents the life-force, while the other two exemplify the deadened, intellectualized current of twentieth-century literature against which Lawrence himself had already begun to inveigh in the late 1920s. "It is against the moribund flux in which we are now drifting that Lawrence appears brilliantly alive," writes Miller. "Proust and Joyce, needless to say, appear more representative: they reflect the times. We see in them no revolt: it is surrender, suicide, and the more poignant since it springs from creative sources."[31] Revolt, clearly, is a term of highest praise, but Miller has narrow criteria for his definition of salutory revolt. In a letter to his literary agent in 1933, he ruminates about the Lawrence project and vividly characterizes the terms of the Joyce-Lawrence divide in the following terms:

> I think it would be a relief to have a *genuine* stench, a putrescent stench and not just the stench of *SHIT*. I think, if you will permit me the delicacy, that Joyce is such a stench. As much as I have championed Lawrence so much and more will I attack Joyce.[32]

For Miller, clearly, as for Lawrence himself, Joyce stinks. Like Lawrence, though, and for the same reason, he hesitates to employ such conventional terms of opprobrium, as both writers are well aware that this sort of invective is based on metaphors of corporeal abjection that belong to the censorious tradition they have worked to overturn (as we saw in the second chapter, Baudelaire was accused on similar grounds in 1857, and for similar reasons: "the reader holds his nose; the page stinks"). Miller thus finds himself in the position of defending one sort of stench against another, the "*genuine* stench" of honest Lawrentian putrescence as opposed to the truly offensive Joycean odor of shit. Since both Lawrence and Miller defend the right to write about everything, including, and especially, all bodily functions, and particularly given Mellors's speech to Connie about the importance of shitting and pissing, it is difficult to understand precisely on what grounds Joyce is to be condemned in this context; but such are the contradictions of twentieth-century discussions of obscenity.

The term *obscenity* itself also, predictably, gets caught up in this sort of inevitable self-contradiction mill. For Miller, as for Lawrence, it is sometimes laudatory, sometimes a term of opprobrium, depending on the context. On the one hand, for both writers "true" obscenity is political, to be located in the violence of war and nationalism and in a culture that values material goods and the like, as opposed to the healthy expression of sexuality and the raw terms in which honest individuals couch their appreciations of same. In this context "obscenity" is a blanket term of rejection, with no specific meaning. On the other hand, sometimes the word is used by such writers as Lawrence and Miller in much the same way as their detractors wield it, to designate four-letter vernacular terms and the sexual situations they refer to, except that in this case the valence of the word is overturned, and it becomes high praise. One striking example of this latter use of the term occurs when Miller, who states his view of Lawrence as "the tragic picture of that last man of genius, that last individual rebel, that lone spirit" (*Lawrence*, 174), expresses his ambivalence about the latter's last novel: "If *Lady Chatterley's Lover* represents another of Lawrence's failures it does so only because of its impurity, its compromise. And by that I mean, only wherein it is obscene is it magnificent; in its obscenity lies its great purity, its miraculous, its sacred quality." He contrasts this pure, magnificent, sacred obscenity with what he views as the novel's detritus quotient: "the rest, that padding, that cotton wool in which his visions are often wrapped" (*Lawrence*, 176). So far so good; presumably Miller means the tedious diatribes in which Lawrence's lengthy objections to the social order are couched. But then he adds, incoherently, that despite what even he (who had also by this point come under feminist attack by Kate Millet among others) acknowledges to be Lawrence's misogynistic portraits of women in this and other novels, "his obscenity is not expressed so much in his antagonistic reaction as in a ripe, earthy acceptance and enjoyment of the female, *as pure female*." This characterization, which resembles nothing so much as the standard reading of Molly Bloom's soliloquy, is followed by a celebration that makes little sense in terms of Lawrence: "His obscenity becomes positively delicious and quite unique, the more repulsive to the world, however, because it is so free of purpose, free of satire, mockery. It is nakedly, frankly *amoral*," he concludes (*Lawrence*, 177).

The freedom from purpose, the delicious, unique, repulsive obscenity Miller finds here in Lawrence, and especially the naked, frank *amorality*, could not be more absent from *Lady Chatterley* and for that matter the rest of Lawrence's writings. Miller is clearly talking about himself. (In this he follows the lead of Baudelaire characterizing Madame Bovary in terms more appropriate to his own creations; writers can often be found sketching their most grandiose self-portraits in the third person.) We will defer a full discussion of Miller's need to imbue Lawrence with deliciously purposeless amorality to the next chapter; the point I wish to make here is that Lawrence had to be made into a sexual and aesthetic anarchist— which he so emphatically was not—in order to fulfill his historically determined function as liberator: the inaugurator, as Larkin put it, of sexual intercourse in literature. For the purposes of his posthumous trial, for one thing, Lawrence was anything but. Not only for Aldous Huxley but for the thirty-five experts in literature, education, and religion who turned out to testify in London in 1960 in the case of *Regina v. Penguin Books*, Lawrence was squarely a moralist. In sharp contrast to the cases of Flaubert and Baudelaire, and despite the fact that it took place long after his death, Lawrence's trial was conducted along lines that he might well have approved: his defense accurately depicted him as a moral crusader. Not, that is to say, the crusader for sexual liberation that he has since become, nor the amoral libertine that Miller depicts him as being, but as he was: a staunch, albeit paradoxical, defender of marriage.

Before going into the details of the *Chatterley* trials in the United States and England, though, it is worth taking a look at the fate of the novel in Japan. In that country, the first unexpurgated translation had given rise to three much-discussed trials, in respectively, Tokyo District Court, Tokyo High Court, and Japan's Supreme Court, from 1950 to 1957. The result was suppression of the book—in translation at least—for decades to come. In fact it had been widely available in Japan since 1932 in both the original and in French, as well as in an expurgated Japanese translation. The publisher, Oyama, had set out to publish the complete works of Lawrence in unexpurgated translation, and one of the exacerbating factors in the case was that *Lady Chatterley's Lover* featured as the first in the series, a counter-chronological decision the Japanese courts took to be sufficient evidence of the publisher's intent to titillate. Further complicating the defense was the fact that the novel included a reader's survey, including such provocative questions as "Were you sexually aroused by reading the novel?" and "Do you think Lady Chatterley should divorce her husband?" Among the thirty-three witnesses called in the first trial, which lasted eight months, were a nun, a high-school student, a farmer, and a gynecologist. During the trial the publisher quoted at length from the offending passages in English; his testimony was then published in a literary journal, with the result that even after it became available only in expurgated editions the entire text could be reconstituted by the enterprising reader. No unexpurgated translation was published until 1973, when Kodansha quietly brought out a version that escaped the notice of censors. A new full translation was published in 1996. The *Chatterley* trials, though, continued to reverberate in Japan as recently as 2003, with the high court precedent cited in the first *manga* (adult comic book) censorship case.[33]

As for what happened in the United States and England not long after the Japanese trials, a bit of legal history is in order. Jonathan Cape's *Well of Loneliness* case, as we saw in the last chapter, had been lost in England for two major reasons. First, the many literary figures who had turned up willing to testify on behalf of Hall's publisher had been turned away on the basis that artistic merit was not a legitimate defense according to the law. Second, the law stated that the work was liable to be judged obscene on the basis of any passage that might tend to deprave or corrupt those into whose hands it might fall and whose minds were open to such immoral influences. Therefore, and even in the absence of sexually explicit passages, *The Well* had been judged obscene because of the presence of scenes clearly dramatizing homosexual relations. In 1959, a revision of the Obscene Publications Act had gone into effect in England that changed a number of provisions in the law, two of which in particular prompted Penguin Books to publish *Lady Chatterley* in unexpurgated form as a test case case. First, under the new Obscene Publications Act of 1959, artistic, historical, and educational merit were admitted as extenuating factors, and expert witnesses were accordingly allowed to testify as to such merit. A work was not to be suppressed "if it is proved that publication of the article in question is justified as being for the public good on the ground that it is in the interests of science, literature, art or learning, or other objects of general concern."[34] Second, the new criterion was that of the effect of the work as a whole, rather than specific passages. Penguin Books chose *Lady Chatterley's Lover* as its test because it was anglophone literature's most famous banned book, and because it seemed exonerable on these grounds.

In the United States a similar legal precedent led Barney Rosset of Grove Press to bring out an unexpurgated edition of the book. Rosset, who went on to play a major role in other important American censorship cases from *Tropic of Cancer* to the works of Sade in translation, later explained:

> Grove's first important censorship battle was *Lady Chatterley's Lover*. The reason I started with it was that it seemed to me impossible that people would say Lawrence wasn't a great writer. And I had this urge to test the obscenity laws. . . . My publication of it was a very cold, deliberate attack on censorship.[35]

Until 1957, despite Judge Woolsey's much-cited 1933 decision to allow *Ulysses* to circulate freely, American obscenity law still closely followed the Hicklin rule—which, as Charles Rembar, who represented the publishers in the cases of *Lady Chatterley*, *Tropic of Cancer*, and *Fanny Hill*, puts it, had "undone the American Revolution, successfully colonizing our law of obscenity."[36] In 1957 a case known as *Roth* changed the way obscenity cases were regarded under American law. Samuel Roth's name reappears at regular intervals in the history of literary censorship in the United States in the twentieth century. He started out being prosecuted for bootleg editions of parts of *Ulysses* in the early 1920s and continued provoking the

Postal Service in particular for decades. (Not only many of Roth's cases but the American *Chatterley* trial as well, among others, originated in the U.S. Postmaster General's declaration that the works in question were obscene and therefore "unmailable.") Roth finally achieved legal immortality as the object of a prosecution brought in the federal courts of New York under the Comstock Act, a case that was heard by the Supreme Court and yielded what went down in history as the *Roth* opinions.[37] The central question in this case was, in the words of Justice William Brennan's majority opinion, "whether obscenity is utterance within the area of protected speech and press." The Supreme Court ultimately decided against Roth. Brennan's famous opinion delineated the court's finding in the following highly influential and long-debated terms:

> All ideas having even the slightest redeeming social importance—unorthodox ideas, controversial ideas, even ideas hateful to the prevailing climate of opinion—have the full protection of the guaranties, unless excludable because they encroach upon the limited area of more important interests. But implicit in the history of the First Amendment is the rejection of obscenity as utterly without redeeming social importance.[38]

In other words, the notion upheld by Brennan's opinion was essentially the same as what Napoleon I meant when he declared in the beginning of the nineteenth century that there was to be complete freedom of speech in France and Italy, except for speech deemed offensive or dangerous (see prologue). However, and despite the fact that the *Roth* outcome appeared to be a victory for the forces of censorship, it paradoxically paved the way for ending the *Chatterley* ban in the United States, as well as allowing publication of *Tropic of Cancer*, *Fanny Hill*, and many other works. Largely because of the phrase "even the slightest redeeming social importance," Brennan ended up a hero to anticensorship forces, whereas Justices Hugo Black and William O. Douglas, in *Roth* and every other obscenity case heard by the Supreme Court during this period, expressed the view that freedom of expression should not be contingent but absolute.[39] The idea that the presence of even slight social importance precluded obscenity was much more valuable to the case for publication of *Chatterley* and subsequent works than a quixotically absolute adherence to the ideal of free speech, because Brennan's formulation introduced the notion that literary merit, among other sorts of value, obviated obscenity. The 1933 *Ulysses* decision, although it was cited regularly in such cases for decades, took literary merit into account, but not as an independantly exonerating factor: as we have seen, it was ultimately because he found Joyce's novel to be emetic more than aphrodisiac that Judge Woolsey deemed it safe for consumption by the American populace. The *Roth* decision finally introduced artistic merit, under the guise of "redeeming social importance," as a legally meaningful category.

Roth also departed from the Hicklin rule in a number of other ways, roughly equivalent to the innovations in British law brought about by the revised Obscene Publications Act in 1959. The book was to be considered as a whole; it was to be judged according to its effect on the "average person" rather than the "particularly susceptible"; and the criteria brought to bear were to be those of "current mores and reading habits" as opposed to those of mid-nineteenth-century Britain.[40] Charles Rembar, who represented Grove Press in the *Chatterley* case, seized on these modified criteria, as well as the nuances of the word *prurient*, arguing that interest in sexual matters need not necessarily be prurient, and further that prurient interest was at the time offered everywhere in the culture at large: "Our advertising, our motion pictures, our television, and our journalism are in large measure calculated to produce sexual thoughts and reactions," he declared. "We live," he concluded, "in a sea of sexual provocation" (124). Not only the *Roth* precedent but the *Ulysses* decision was also brought to bear, as it allowed Rembar to call literary experts Malcolm Cowley and Alfred Kazin to the stand to testify as to the aesthetic importance as well as moral seriousness of Lawrence in general and *Lady Chatterley's Lover* in particular.

Rembar's argument was successful, the decision upheld on appeal in March 1960, and Lawrence's novel was accordingly allowed free publication in the United States. In England in August 1960 Penguin Books published its edition of *Lady Chatterley* as a test case for the revised Obscene Publications Act, hiring Rubinstein, Nash, and Company, the same firm of solicitors who had defended Jonathan Cape in the *Well of Loneliness* trial, and thus began the most talked-about literary obscenity trial of the twentieth century. It was a landmark event in any number of ways. As Geoffrey Robertson points out in his introduction to the thirtieth-anniversary edition of C. H. Rolph's annotated trial transcript, first published by Penguin following the successful outcome, at the time not only were homosexuality and abortion criminal offenses, but divorced men were not allowed to read the news on the BBC.[41] Divorce itself, moreover, was allowed only on proof of "matrimonial crime" (xiii). The trial seems to have turned on the extent to which custom and the law were already out of synch with popular sentiment. Nine of twelve jurors were sympathetic to the defense from the outset. The defense had prudently waived its right to insist on an all-male jury, as had been habitual with cases involving sexually charged matter, and had also invoked its right to challenge jurors so as to gain an additional female presence on the jury, on the theory that women were more likely to be sympathetic to Constance Chatterley's situation and that men might tend to be overly protective of women in their absence. Unanimity was required, but it was not long in coming, and the prosecutor seems to have lost his case from the outset by insisting on the idea that the main question to be considered was: "Is it a book that you would have lying around in your own house? Is it a book that you would even wish your wife or your servants to read?" (17). This did not turn out to be a successful line of inquiry among people lacking servants, and even, in some cases, wives. Mr. Mervyn Griffith-Jones, the government prosecutor, seems to have grasped almost from the outset that his cause was lost, as he called no witnesses for the prosecution and offered little in the way of cross-questioning of those called by the defense. The latter was, under the terms of the revised act, able to call thirty-five expert witnesses from various walks of life, including professors of literature, clergymen, and school-teachers, carefully concluding by asking each about their own children and those under their care.

While artistic merit was a major component of the defense, it was Lawrence's place in twentieth-century literature in general that provided the main justification in aesthetic terms. The novel itself was characterized on the basis of its moral value. This was, certainly, in strict keeping with all other such arguments over the course of at least a century, perfectly reasonable and accurate in terms of the author's evident intent, and at the same time somewhat disconcerting when one considers that it had originally been not merely banned as immoral but described as, for instance, "the most evil outpouring that has ever besmirched the literature of our country." The witnesses all testified to the moral seriousness of the book and its social and even educational merit, insisting on Lawrence's great importance as an author, while also observing that *Lady Chatterley* was not his best effort. It was an impressive lineup, including, as mentioned earlier, not only E. M. Forster but Dame Rebecca West, among other literary figures. One noteworthy absence was that of F. R. Leavis, the most influential critic of the time and author of one of the first and most widely read books on Lawrence; Leavis had refused to testify for the defense. In any case the jury found Penguin Books not guilty, and the most talked-about censorship case in the twentieth century thus came to a close. This was not, however, the end of the *Chatterley* controversy. The publisher, which had been denied court costs, amply made up for its trouble by selling three million copies of the novel in the three months following the verdict.

The trial itself continued to fascinate, with television and radio reenactments finding a wide audience in Britain in subsequent years. Parliamentary debate also followed the verdict, giving rise to a statement by Lord Hailsham that conveys the remarkable extent to which literature was still being judged on purely moral grounds, and fictional characters as though they were themselves on trial:

Before I accepted as valid or valuable, or even excusable, the relationship between Lady Chatterley and Mellors, I should like to know what sort of parents they become to the child. . . . I should have liked to see the kind of house they proposed to set up together; I should have liked to know how Mellors would have survived living on Connie's rentier income of £600 . . . and I should have liked to know whether they acquired a circle of friends, or, if not, how their relationship survived social isolation.[42]

In other words, even after Penguin Books won its case, Lady Chatterley—if not *Lady Chatterley's Lover*—was still on trial. Lord Hailsham's questioning of the choices made by Lawrence's characters recalls the imperial prosecutor's suggestion that Emma Bovary might have met a different fate had either her husband or Flaubert taken the trouble to keep her in line. It also anticipates Vice President Dan Quayle's memorable vituperation against the sitcom character Murphy Brown in the early 1990s for setting a bad moral example by having a child out of wedlock. However revolutionary Justice Brennan's *Roth* pronouncement about "even the slightest redeeming social importance" may have been, what comes across from all these cases is the extent to which we continue to judge fictional characters as though they were real people and read stories for their illustrative moral value. The subject of the next chapter, Henry Miller's *Tropic of Cancer*, published in Paris six years after *Lady Chatterley* first appeared, represents, among other things, an attempt to challenge this view of the function of art.

CHAPTER SIX

Henry Miller

A Gob of Spit in the Face of Art

This then? This is not a book. This is libel, slander, defamation of
character. This is not a book, in the ordinary sense of the word. No, this
is a prolonged insult, a gob of spit in the face of Art, a kick in the pants
to God, Man, Destiny, Time, Love, Beauty . . . what you will. I am going
to sing for you, a little off key perhaps, but I will sing. I will sing while you
croak. I will dance over your dirty corpse.

Tropic of Cancer

In *Tropic of Cancer,* his first published work, Henry Miller takes up the
challenge first laid down by Flaubert and Baudelaire in the mid nineteenth century. Where Flaubert gives the reader no character with
whom comfortably to identify, and Baudelaire accuses his *hypocrite lecteur*
of various sins capped off by a refusal to recognize the abjection he has in
common with the poet, Miller bypasses such niceties and goes straight for
the jugular. He gets right to the point in the opening pages (the passage
cited above is the sixth paragraph), declaring that his work is not a book
but rather an act of desecration and that its reader is a corpse, about to be
defiled by Miller's prose. Having neatly dispatched not only God, Man,
Destiny, Time, Love, and Beauty but also Art itself, thus ostentatiously rejecting even aesthetic value along with all moral and sentimental order,
and as a result replacing art for art's sake with a gob of spit for its own sake,
the author then sets himself up to defile not only the reader but the classical tradition in which he implicitly places himself by announcing his intention to sing. Here we have the equivalent of Joyce's "snotgreen, scrotumtightening sea" where Homer's was winedark, as Miller reproduces in
degraded form the famous *arma virumque cano* that opens the *Aeneid.* What
Miller will sing of in place of Virgil's "arms and the man" becomes quite
clear in the following paragraphs, when, after repeating "This then is a
song. I am singing," to drive the point home, he specifies: "It is to you,

Tania, that I am singing," and then, after a post-Lawrentian, title-justifying
"The world is a cancer eating itself away," he moves on to sing of genitalia:
Tania's, his own, a veritable catalogue of genital organs.

Not exactly, though: what Miller sings of is not precisely genitals, any
more than what began following the end of the *Chatterley* ban was sexual
intercourse. He sings, most ostentatiously, of cunts: cunts and pricks, or, as
he alternatively characterizes them, cocks (a previous book, which he
abandoned in favor of *Tropic of Cancer*, was straightforwardly titled *Crazy
Cock*). *Tropic of Cancer* is far from being pornographic in the aphrodisiac
sense (to take up, once again, Judge Woolsey's 1933 distinction): rather it
is at least as emetic as anything Joyce managed to come up with in *Ulysses*.
Miller himself characterized *Tropic of Cancer* as "a sort of human document, written in blood, recording the struggle in the womb of death. The
strong sexual odor," he added, "is, if anything, the aroma of birth, dis-
agreeable, repulsive even, when dissociated from its significance" (*The
World of Sex*, quoted in *Henry Miller on Writing*, 119). Accordingly, and to a
much greater extent than in *Ulysses*, the aphrodisiac and the emetic are
often found welded together indissolubly in *Tropic of Cancer*. Here, for
instance, is Miller (or his narrator, who happens to be called "Henry
Miller" and to share many characteristics with the author) apostrophizing
the adulterous Tania:

> Your Sylvester! Yes, he knows how to build a fire, but I know how to inflame
> a cunt. I shoot hot bolts into you, Tania, I make your ovaries incandescent.
> Your Sylvester is a little jealous now? He feels the remnants of my big prick.
> I have set the shores a little wider, I have ironed out the wrinkles.

So far this reads like a fairly standard male pornographic fantasy of sexual
omnipotence, a sort of corrective to the negative fantasy Baudelaire bor-
rows from Juvenal for his poem "Sed non satiata," in which the woman's
sexual appetite always exceeds the man's capacity to satisfy her. But Miller
then characteristically veers off into an elaboration on this scenario that
takes it into another realm entirely:

> After me you can take on stallions, bulls, rams, drakes, St. Bernards. You can
> stuff toads, bats, lizards up your rectum. You can shit arpeggios if you like, or
> string a zither across your navel. I am fucking you, Tania, so that you'll stay
> fucked. And if you are afraid of being fucked publicly I will fuck you pri-
> vately. I will tear off a few hairs from your cunt and paste them on Boris' chin.
> I will bite into your clitoris and spit out two franc pieces. (*Tropic of Cancer*, 27)

From this passage alone it is not difficult to see why it took a U.S.
Supreme Court decision in the mid 1960s to lift the thirty-year ban on

Tropic of Cancer, which was originally published in Paris in 1934. Nor should it come as a surprise that Miller was, along with Lawrence, among the authors vilified for misogyny by Kate Millett in *Sexual Politics* in 1969; in fact Millett begins her antiphallocentric manifesto with an extended discussion of a passage from Miller.[1] And yet his vulgarity is so extremely vulgar, and his catalogue of cunts so extravagantly over the top, so grotesquely excessive in its reduction of women to their genitalia, and their genitalia as holes to be filled, that Miller places himself entirely off the map as an ideologue. Millet in fact acknowledges a certain value in Miller's work: "There *is* a kind of culturally cathartic release in Miller's writing," she concedes, "but it is really a result of the fact that he first gave voice to the unutterable," by which she means "the disgust, the contempt, the hostility, the violence, and the sense of filth with which our culture, or more specifically, its masculine sensibility, surrounds sexuality" (388). In the end, though, it might be argued that Miller's evident phallocentrism is mitigated by the sheer idiosyncratic exuberance of his prose. It requires effort, really, to maintain a stance of dogmatic disapproval in the face of such authentically offensive and yet disarming pronouncements as the following: "One cunt out of a million Llona! All cunt and a glass ass in which you can read the history of the Middle Ages" (28). Miller can and has been read alternatively as the very voice of phallocentrism and as that of a generalized sociosexual aesthetic revolution. Erica Jong, for instance, author of the emblematic feminist sexual liberation novel of the 1970s, *Fear of Flying*, with its celebration of the equal-opportunity "zipless fuck" for women, is one of Miller's biggest fans.[2] Her book about him, admiringly titled *The Devil at Large* (1993), is in fact much like Miller's own *World of Lawrence: A Passionate Appreciation*. In both works the authors celebrate themselves in the course of celebrating their ostensible subjects, and in both cases the mythology is the same. Lawrence is to Miller as Miller is to Jong, and both Miller and Jong have recourse to a mythology of the idealized writer as the last genuine prophet of liberation, misunderstood in his time and posthumously poised to enlighten the world in the face of the inauthenticity of the present, which both managed presciently to anticipate (the short-lived Lawrence, however, more presciently than Miller, who continued dispensing wisdom in California until 1980, where he died at eighty-nine.)

Although Miller remains best known for singing of cunts and pricks, his real song and celebration is always of himself. He disclaims Virgil, whom he was reluctantly made to study in Latin classes in high school, as a model; Miller displays a ripe, if ambivalent, contempt for the classical canon. "The Classics!" he wrote much later, once he had reached full guruhood, in *The Books in My Life* (1952): "Slowly, slowly I am coming to them—not by reading them, but by making them."[3] Nor does he ultimately cite as predecessor Lawrence, whom he read in Paris in the early 1930s at the urging of Anaïs Nin, herself the author of a book on Lawrence. Despite and doubtless also because of the hatred he reserved for his native country, his model is American, his greatest adulation directed at Walt Whitman:

> That one lone figure which America has produced in the course of her brief life. In Whitman the whole American scene comes to life, her past and her future, her birth and her death. Whatever there is of value in America Whitman has expressed, and there is nothing more to be said. The future belongs to the machine, to the robots. He was the Poet of the Body and the Soul, Whitman. The first and the last poet. He is almost indecipherable today, a monument covered with rude hieroglyphs for which there is no key. (221–22)

In Whitman, Miller chose a hero who was at once acknowledged as an authentic cornerstone of the American canon—he had read him in school, along with Virgil—and at the same time still viewed with a certain amount of suspicion. Only certain carefully chosen passages had been taught in school; the rest he had to find on his own at the public library. (Although it was never actually censored, Whitman's magnum opus *Leaves of Grass* was initially published without its author's, publisher's, or printer's name, and its subsequent history includes threats from the New England Society for the Suppression of Vice.[4] What is especially striking from the point of view of posterity, though, is that the homoerotic work saw publication at all in the nineteenth century, and that once published it managed to become a classic.) Allen Ginzberg would also claim Whitman as his antecedent, and Miller has much in common with the Beats who followed him, as also with the surrealists, whose works he discovered in Paris. He places himself squarely in a tradition that features not just Whitman but the inevitable Rabelais and goes on to include, especially, Rimbaud and Dostoevsky, idealizing above all a vision of the artist as visionary outcast. This lineage began in early-nineteenth-century romanticism, went on retrospectively to create a genealogy for itself starting with late-classical, late-medieval, and Renaissance figures—Petronius, Villon, Rabelais, and Boccaccio are most frequently cited in Miller's version of this canon—and continued apace throughout the nineteenth and twentieth centuries. It found renewed strength not just in Rimbaud but also, among others, Lautréamont, the surrealists, Miller himself, Jean Genet, William S. Burroughs, and the Beats, before finally migrating into music—suicide and early death in general playing an increasing role—with such martyrs as Janis Joplin, Jimi Hendrix, Jim Morrison, and, most recently, Kurt Cobain.

This is why Miller insists, when writing of Lawrence, that the latter's "obscenity becomes positively delicious and quite unique, the more repulsive to the world . . . because it is so free of purpose, free of satire, mockery . . . nakedly, frankly *amoral*" (as mentioned in chapter 5). He wants to inscribe both Lawrence and himself in the same category of iconoclastic amoralists, each of them necessarily quite unique. The model depends on uniqueness and refuses to admit much variation. Miller's misreading of Lawrence as an amoralist is to this extent reminiscent of Pinard's misreading of Flaubert as an immoralist: in both cases the work is forced, all evidence to the contrary notwithstanding, into the shape that fits the reader's ideological needs; in the same way Jong manages to see the author of *Tropic of Cancer* as a protofeminist. Miller offers the emblematic twentieth-century American version of the Romantic myth of the artist. In the 1950s the Beats took up this theme with a vengeance, Kerouac's *On the Road* (1957) offering a model of the literary genre. Ginzberg and Burroughs, both of whom also encountered censorship problems later on, represent homosexual variants of this myth. Even as he bases himself firmly in the Villon-Rabelais-Whitman tradition, the Miller version of the rebel artist truly did create a new phenomenon. Edmund Wilson was to term the figure of "the Great American Hobo Artist" "the Henry Miller type."[5]

In his emphasis on breaking previous rules not only of morality but of art itself, he escapes the classifications I have tried to establish among the writers dealt with thus far in this study: he is neither an amoralist along the lines of Flaubert (or, later, Nabokov), nor an immoralist on the order of Baudelaire or Sade, nor certainly, a moralist like Lawrence or Hall. And again, despite his ultimate belief in the redemptive powers of art, he is no proponent of art for art's sake. "Art is only a means to life, to the life more abundant," he later wrote. "In becoming an end it defeats itself."[6] Looking beyond the obviously provocative nature of the formula, therefore, we must take his "gob of spit in the face of Art" for what it is. In a 1939 essay on the genesis of *Tropic of Cancer*, published in America twenty years before the book itself was available, Miller recounts how he arrived at his method:

> At a certain point in my life I decided that henceforth I would write about myself, my friends, my experiences, what I knew and what I had seen with my own eyes. Anything else, in my opinion, is literature, and *I am not interested in literature*. (*The Cosmological Eye*, cited in *Henry Miller on Writing*, 102)

Before beginning the work that would make him famous, Miller had already written, or tried to write, several books (some, like *Crazy Cock*, eventually found posthumous publication). What had been wrong with them, what had impeded Miller from becoming a writer, was, as he tells it, his artistic ambition itself: he had tried to be literary. An important moment for Miller had been a friend's observation, after reading *Crazy Cock*, that he should try to write as he talked, as he lived, felt, and thought.[7] *Tropic of Cancer*, like all his subsequent writings, is full of rantings both for and against literature, and art in general. Miller is singularly unafraid of self-contradiction, but these pronouncements are not exactly contradictory. What he objects to is a certain consecrated conception of High Art: "We have no need for genius—genius is dead," he proclaims at one point (*Tropic*, 44). In *Black Spring*, his second published work, he repeatedly declares: "What is not in the open street is false, derived, that is to say, *literature*" (1; also 3). Miller's stated ambition was to create a literature without literariness.

There is, certainly, a long tradition of this sort of literary denunciation of literature, going back centuries and finding its aesthetic justification in the Romantic appreciation of originality and spontaneity in art, as exemplified for instance in some of Wordsworth's poems that are carefully designed to appear as though they had been composed on the spot in a sudden fit of inspiration as the poet wandered around contemplating the landscape. But the composition of a volume of prose is a different matter from that of a poem, and while Miller's emphasis on spontaneity comes from romanticism, mostly via Whitman and Rimbaud, another aspect of his antiliterary tendency can be seen as a distant product of nineteenth-century realism. In his theoretical writings of the early 1880s Zola locates the origins of the naturalist novel in *Madame Bovary*, specifically because of the ways in which Flaubert, in that novel and others, eschews the rules of literariness: he cites in particular the absence of both hero and plot in the traditional sense.[8] In this way—although not in most other ways—*Tropic of Cancer* joins *Ulysses* in the Flaubertian lineage. Miller's deep distrust of classical models and conventional literature comes, however remotely, from these nineteenth-century precedents but is also more explicitly linked in his writings to an identification with his working-class origins: his father and immigrant grandfather were tailors, and his own aspirations toward higher education were cut short in 1909 after he was made to read Spenser's *Faerie Queen* during his first semester at City College. In part because of his alienation from the canon, Miller goes further than his predecessors in propounding an ideal of art as the explosion of norms. His entire collected works present themselves as a vast, ambivalent diatribe against the classics and in favor of the idea of art explosively aligned against art itself: art *against* art's sake; art to the detriment of art.

In *Tropic of Cancer* this antiart bent becomes especially clear in a scene in which he goes to a concert—having, of course, found the concert ticket in a public toilet, the only condition under which one can imagine the narrator of this work attending such a function. After analyzing the bourgeois audience's shortcomings ("Even before the music begins there is that bored look on people's faces," he observes: "A polite form of self-torture, the concert" [84]), he finds the composer wanting as well. Ravel too falls short of the ideal, presumably because he has catered to public expectations rather than following his own creative logic to its conclusions: "Art consists in going the full length. If you start with the drums you have to end with dynamite, or TNT" (86). For Miller true art is explosive: its function is to wake the audience up, not to lull it into a familiar nap. In another passage he contrasts the relative literary perfections of Turgenev (too mannered) and Dostoevsky (admirably poised in a permanent attitude of rebellion), preferring the latter, of course, but then finding a further perfection more perfect than both. It is in Van Gogh's letters—unco-incidentally not written for publication—that resides ultimate artistic perfection, because in them he finds exemplified the true ideal: "the triumph of the individual over art" (31).

What, exactly, does Miller mean by this? His choice of Van Gogh is hardly random, of course, since that figure had already begun to take on the emblematic status he has since come fully to incarnate: the cliché of the ultimate renegade artist who ignored prevailing aesthetics, followed the dictates of his heart, and as a result ended up in an asylum and died penniless, his genius unrecognized in his time and fully appreciated only by canny posterity. (The eventual result being that his sunflowers, along with the waterlilies painted by the less fascinatingly-troubled but equally reviled-by-his-conformist-contemporaries Monet, have adorned the walls of every dentist's waiting room in North America for decades.) Miller's choice of Van Gogh's letters as representing artistic perfection is barely worthy of scrutiny, overdetermined as it is by both the painter's exemplary status and, paradoxically, the marginal nature of the work in question. The terms of his appreciation, however, are more obscure: "the triumph of the individual," certainly, but—*over art?* Thus far, especially starting with the prosecutions of Flaubert and Baudelaire under the Second Empire, art had tended to figure as the triumph of the individual against the oppressive forces of bourgeois officialdom. The notion of "the triumph of the individual over art" may therefore seem odd, but in fact it makes perfect sense according to an aesthetic trend that Miller exemplifies and that uncoincidentally, as it were, coincides with the eventual acceptance of the notion of art for art's sake as state policy.

When *Lady Chatterley's Lover* came to trial in the United States and England in 1959 and 1960 it was given the benefit of the doubt because legal precedents and revised laws allowed for consideration both of artistic merit (along with social, educational, and historical importance), and of the work as a whole. In the case of Lawrence's novel this second element was very important, as the specific words and scenes cited by the prosecution would otherwise certainly have condemned the novel even in the ab-

sence of other factors. As to the first, though, it was the *ethical* importance
of the work that was emphasized by almost all the witnesses for the defense. The aesthetic value of the novel was given short shrift, despite the
great importance of Lawrence as a writer (which clearly played its part:
the same novel written by an unknown would have encountered a very
different fate). *Lady Chatterley* was—accurately enough, as we have seen—
presented as a didactic work with a moral lesson attached, however much
that lesson, as well as its individual demonstrations, might have offended
the sensibilities of some of those present in the courtroom. Therefore, the
first novel to be tried under the new rules, although it may have taxed the
broad-mindedness of both witnesses and jury members on a number of
levels, did not really push those rules to their fullest extent. It took *Tropic
of Cancer*—which its author liked to refer to as his "fuck everything"
book—with its "prolonged insult," its "kick in the pants" to all extant values, not only those of the oppressive bourgeoisie but those of the formerly
oppressed as well, to demonstrate that the old rules really had been overturned.[9] Miller rejects the very notion of artistic perfection in the traditional sense; for this reason he dislikes Mozart. The perfection he aspires
to, and that he finds in Van Gogh's letters, is an antiperfection, the triumphant willingness to forego an ideal of aesthetic integrity in the pursuit
of a means to express a truly idiosyncratic vision of the world.

There are many remarkable aspects to the history of *Tropic of Cancer*,
but in terms of the history of literary obscenity, and even of modern literature in general, the most important is this one. At the precise moment
when the aesthetic integrity of the artistic work was officially made an exculpating factor in obscenity trials, the work that genuinely tested the limits of this legal innovation rejected the very doctrine that had given rise to
it. In other words, it took a book that spat on the notion of art for art's sake
to show that this ideal had become not merely a cliché but state policy.
Miller is the anti-Flaubert, in two related ways. First, Flaubert represents
the ideal of artistic integrity for artistic integrity's sake, always in pursuit of
the perfect word, phrase, sentence, work. For Miller, the ostensible goal is
no longer the work of art but rather the *act of writing*. (Similarly, when, like
Lawrence, he takes up watercolors, what is important is not the product,
which he admits is often mediocre, but the process of painting.)[10] And
second, Flaubert's great formal innovation, the generalized use of free indirect style, was the direct result of his doctrine of artistic impersonality.
The ideal, he wrote in a much-cited formula, was for the author to be in
his work like God in the universe: present everywhere but visible nowhere.
Thus, as we saw in chapter 2, *Madame Bovary* was regarded as dangerous
among other reasons because it offered the first literary representation of
a godless universe, God having been replaced by the author (who, in

Flaubert's case, is an implacable creator, along the lines of the Old Testament God in a particularly vengeful mood).

Miller's universe, on the other hand, is not merely godless but entirely haphazard: despite the occasional vague religiosity of his later writings, there is no longer any guiding force at all. The author is everywhere—the book *is* the author—but he no longer controls anything, even his own prose. His description of the genesis of *Tropic of Cancer* dramatizes this effect, already plain from the book itself: "Where the writing is concerned, I did nothing consciously. I followed my nose. I blew with every wind. I accepted every influence, good or bad. My intention was . . . merely to write. Or, *to be a writer,* more justly" (*Henry Miller on Writing,* 141). This is, to a great extent, pure myth-making; what Miller neglects to mention is that he rewrote *Tropic of Cancer* at least three times. It is in fact the same sort of myth-making that authors such as Wordsworth had engaged in at the beginning of the nineteenth century. But the Romantic poets were still caught up in the ideal of artistic perfection. The very way in which Miller insists on the artless spontaneity of his method, and not for small poems but for whole volumes of autobiographical prose, points to the emergence of a new ideal, an eminently twentieth-century one: the desired outcome is no longer the perfect work of art but the pursuit of Truth in the act of self-expression itself. Miller's goal is not to be an author—certainly not in the Flaubertian sense—but a *writer.*[11] None of his works is a self-contained entity; instead they represent an ongoing project of a "huge 'book of my life,' " as he later put it (*Henry Miller on Writing,* 192).

In the meantime, a notably navel-gazing strain of literary aestheticism—writing for writing's sake, the sort of tendency both Lawrence and Miller criticize in Joyce and Proust—had become a major fashion during the 1920s. (Miller's scrutiny, while fixed on himself, is directed below the navel.) As George Orwell irritably notes, this was a period when "in 'cultured' circles art-for-art's-saking extended practically to a worship of the meaningless."[12] To drive home his point, Orwell, whose 1940 essay "Inside the Whale" sets out to situate Miller in the context of contemporary English literature, cites a *Punch* cartoon, circa 1928, in which "an intolerable youth is pictured informing his aunt that he intends to 'write.' 'And what are you going to write about, dear?' asks the aunt. 'My dear aunt,' says the youth crushingly, 'one doesn't write *about* anything, one just *writes.*' "[13] Miller's brand of self-expression, which might be called autography, resembles this fashion enough for Orwell to evoke it, but *Tropic of Cancer* and his other early works distinguish themselves from it by virtue of their anarchic antiaestheticism. Miller, Orwell concludes, has little in common with this depressingly self-referential and, as he optimistically sees it, ephemeral trend. What is truly new about Miller's work, he suggests, is this:

> The *Booster*, a short-lived periodical of which he was a part-editor, used to de-
> scribe itself in its advertisements as "non-political, non-educational, non-
> progressive, non co-operative, non-ethical, non-literary, non-consistent,
> non-contemporary," and Miller's own work could be described in nearly the
> same terms.

Much of this innovation has to do with class: "It is a voice from the crowd,
from the underling, from the third-class carriage, from the ordinary, non-
political, non-moral, passive man" (19). Miller is thus remarkable, according to Orwell, for two main reasons. He represesents a previously unheard
literary voice, a new sort of "realism," on both the sociological level ("The
ordinary man, the 'average sensual man', has been given the power of
speech, like Balaam's ass" [19]); and the linguistic ("The callous course-
ness with which the characters in *Tropic of Cancer* talk is very rare in fiction,
but it is extremely common in real life" [14]). *Ulysses* has both these elements as well—the "average sensual man" played his part, in his original
guise of *homme moyen sensuel*, in Woolsey's exoneration of the novel—but
its literary pyrotechnics prevent them from coming to the forefront as
they do in Miller's work. Joyce is squarely Flaubertian, and his work is
above all *literary*, the category most noisily eschewed by Miller.

Tropic of Cancer, like everything else he wrote, defies generic expectations. In this too it is part of a certain artistic lineage, one that goes back
not just to Joyce but especially to Proust, another writer whose work is all
about the lifelong and self-referential effort to become a writer. Miller at
once point announced that his goal was to become "the Proust of Brook-
lyn," "a working-class Proust."[14] Since Proust is the most self-consciously
"literary" of writers, and since we have already seen Miller disparaging
him, along with Joyce, as representatives of the more "sterile" tendencies
of twentieth-century literature, this may seem strange. Miller's attitude
toward Proust changes with the context, but he spent a great deal of time
in Paris plunged in obsessive reading of *A la recherche du temps perdu*, and
he has a number of important points in common with Proust. Most obviously, the French writer provided a model of seemingly endless autography, and both the *Recherche* and *Tropic of Cancer* recount the stories of their
own genesis. More precisely, each recounts the story of how it came to be
written out of a failed attempt to write something else: in Proust's case an
essay on Sainte-Beuve; in Miller's, *Crazy Cock*. Another reason for Miller's
fascination with Proust was that the narrator of the *Recherche* is lengthily
obsessed with the mysteriously lesbian or bisexual Albertine, and Miller
was haunted by his relations with his maddeningly elusive, bisexual second wife. A great deal of his writing, from the abortive *Crazy Cock*—originally titled *Lovely Lesbians*—to *Tropic of Capricorn* and the later *Rosy Crucifixion*, concerns this theme, which makes brief appearances in *Tropic of*

Cancer as well. Also like the French author before him, he was unable to find his "true voice" until he gave up the traditional novelistic format of third-person narrative and adopted a free-wheeling, semiautobiographical, first-person approach, in which the narrator is to some extent indistinguishable from the author. Miller parts company, however, with Proust in the sense that he insists his works are in no way fictional, whereas the latter always carefully hedged his bets. In a later essay Miller goes so far as to complain that:

> The naive English critics, in their polite, asinine way, talk about the "hero" of my book [*Tropic of Cancer*] as though he were a character I had invented. I made it as plain as could be that I was talking in that book about myself. I used my own name throughout. I didn't write a piece of fiction: I wrote an autobiographical document, a *human* book. (*Cosmological; Henry Miller on Writing*, 102)

Elsewhere he states: "I don't care who the artist is, if you study him deeply, sincerely, detachedly, you will find that he and his work are one" (137). Proust, in sharp contrast, lamented the fact that critics tended to read his novel as autobiography and to conflate his hero with himself. He also elaborated a theory, in fact the basis for his quarrel with Sainte-Beuve, according to which the work of art is a product of a different self from the social being of the person who creates it. (At one point, though, Miller was forced by Proust himself to adopt the French writer's viewpoint: on being told that the author he so identified with was homosexual, the disconcerted Miller declared that Proust's sexuality had no ultimate bearing on his work: "It's the phenomenon and not the creature who provokes it," he wrote in a letter to Anaïs Nin.)[15] Both Proust and Miller, whatever their disagreements in this regard, belong to a lineage going back to Montaigne, who opens his *Essais* with the observation that "I myself am the material of my book [Je suis moi-même la matière de mon livre]," a claim later echoed by Rousseau in his *Confessions* (although the latter seems to believe he has invented this idea). Miller not only follows Proust's lead in the semiautobiographical genre that would come to be a dominant one in twentieth-century literature, he also takes up the specific technique that, despite his protestations to the contrary, distinguishes both *Tropic of Cancer* and *A la recherche du temps perdu* from straightforward autobiographical narrative: all names are changed except for the narrator's. "Henry Miller" may well be Henry Miller, or some half-idealized, half-degraded version thereof, but his wife's name was not Mona, nor do the other characters who veer in and out of the pages of his work correspond exactly to the author's cronies of the time, any more than Proust's Baron de Charlus (whom Miller refers to repeatedly) is anything other, finally, than a fic-

tional character, however much he may have been based on Robert de
Montesquiou.

In spite of all this it must be said that *A la recherche du temps perdu* and
Tropic of Cancer are deeply dissimilar books, and the experiences of reading them are so different that to list their generic similarities may well
seem like a perverse exercise in literary calisthenics. One further point of
comparison, though, bears mentioning. Miller's work has in common
with Proust's—and also with *Ulysses*—a certain encyclopedic bent, in the
sense that these authors appear to want to put *everything* into their works.
There is nothing, in principle, that is not grist for their mills: every
thought, event, encounter, relation, finds its place. Proust is much more
polite than the other two, of course, but in his book as in theirs the whole
of human experience, within the given bounds of the work, is offered up.
In each case the book is a baggy monster, defying the previously set limits
of literary decorum. As Orwell remarks, "What Miller has in common with
Joyce is a willingness to mention the inane, squalid facts of everyday life"
(15). Proust too was interested in the inane, the squalid, and the everyday,
even if he approached them from a more socially lofty perspective. Miller
goes beyond both Joyce and Proust, however, in that he explicitly states his
purpose as being to include what had not previously been possible. "There
is only one thing which interests me vitally now," he writes in *Tropic*, "and
that is the recording of all that which is omitted in books" (31).

To this extent Miller may be thought of as a consummate "realist"—in
the sense in which the term had been used as an accusation in the nineteenth century—hellbent as he was on making literature out of what is by
definition nonliterary. His project not only anticipates and even courts
censorship; it is also by its very nature apocalyptically antiliterary. Miller's
fantasy, again, is to explode literature itself:

> We have evolved a new cosmogony of literature, Boris and I. It is to be a new
> Bible—*The Last Book*. All those who have anything to say will say it here—
> *anonymously*. We will exhaust the age. After us not another book—for a gen-
> eration, at least. Heretofore we have been digging in the dark, with nothing
> but instinct to guide us. Now we shall have a vessel into which to pour the
> vital fluid, a bomb which, when we throw it, will set off the world. (43)

Tropic of Cancer is not precisely this book; it is neither collaborative nor
anonymous. But it is, like the rest of his works, haunted by the image of
writing that sets the very world on fire, effects a general conflagration; the
recurring metaphor is one of *explosion*.

Miller's repeated proclamations of intent to set fire to the universe with
his writing may well seem ridiculous, or at least quaint, from the perspec-

tive of a posterity that now retains the relatively decorous Proust, who would never have dreamed of making such incendiary claims, as a pillar of the canon, and relegates Miller to the margins of twentieth-century provocation. In 1984 Salman Rushdie published "Outside the Whale," a response to Orwell's 1940 essay, in which he states that "Miller's reputation has more or less evaporated, and he now looks to be very little more than the happy pornographer beneath whose scatalogical surface Orwell saw such improbable depths."[16] Miller certainly has not weathered post-1960s fashions well. On the one hand his anarchic innovations were long ago absorbed into the ambient literary culture, with the result that his writing no longer seems innovative; and on the other his evident misogyny, as well as his tendency to call a spade a spade, for instance, have for some time made him ideologically suspect. Nor did he help matters later in life by fully embracing the myth that was already in the process of becoming problematically passé. In the 1960s he remained an object of active controversy because of the many censorship controversies that led to the Supreme Court decision in 1964, after which interest in the now readily available works kept his reputation as a serious provocateur alive. The 1970s, though, saw him allowing himself to be photographed by *Playboy* in his dotage playing ping-pong with naked girls; publishing increasingly vapid screeds; and marrying a succession of women whose age decreased as his own advanced (the fifth and last was forty-eight years his junior). And yet most of his books are still in print all over the world, and his first published work truly did cause an explosion, or rather an extended series of detonations that in the end changed the way literature was viewed in the twentieth century.

Tropic of Cancer is the story, although "story" is perhaps a misleading term, of Miller's stay in Paris in the early 1930s. It is as plotless as *Ulysses*, although much more readable: unlike Joyce, Miller was not interested in providing fodder for literary scholars, for whom, as a category, he reserved special disdain. The plotlessness of *Tropic* is also, in sharp contrast to that of *Ulysses*, designed to give the appearance of artlessness. The autobiographical protagonist drifts around seeking shelter, handouts, and sex, all the while angrily railing against the "deadness" of contemporary life. To the extent that much of it is occupied with general indictments of postindustrial civilization his work resembles Lawrence's, but the fact that the book is not a novel and does not contain anything resembling a plot is not its only departure from Lawrentian indignation. Unlike Lawrence, Miller has not much in the way of suggestions to offer, beyond a vaguely Rabelaisian ideal ("fay ce que vouldras") and explosive literary ambition. The problem with Lawrence, according to Miller, is in fact precisely this: "The sin of Lawrence is his own idealism," Miller wrote in 1933. "He hated man in favor of some unknown and abstract being who will never be born."[17] Miller sees himself, in contrast, as depicting people as they are. His writing is filled with explicit sexuality and ripely obscene terminology, but the offending material is not, as in *Lady Chatterley*, couched with ideological didacticism in mind. His intent is not to provide the reader with a healthfully direct approach to sex with a view toward general amelioration of sexual relations; nor is his program to change the world, but rather to set it on fire by describing it as he sees it. His sexism is simply, in these terms, another form of realism. Miller does often refer to women as "cunts," but in *Tropic of Cancer* at least, men do not fare much better. In his subsequent works, with their obsessive insistence on his second wife's lesbian infidelity, the misogyny increases, reaching fever pitch in *Sexus* (1949). But in the earlier *Tropic* men too are defined by their genitals, and they tend, the narrator included, to be in perpetual search of a satisfaction that manifestly cannot be found on anything more than the most ephemeral of terms. The book's only real sexual encomia are devoted to prostitutes: since the true nature of every character boils down to the perpetual search for the next meal and the next fuck, the only "authentic" people are the whores, who frankly conflate the two driving needs.

Miller later insisted that when he wrote *Tropic of Cancer* he never imagined it would find a publisher, and certainly did not ever expect it to see print in his native country. In 1932, though, thanks to a perspicacious literary agent, he met his match in Jack Kahane. Kahane, father of Maurice Girodias (about whom more later), was an English Jew who had settled in France, married a Frenchwoman, and established the Obelisk Press, which catered mostly to English-speaking tourists and military men. Like his son after him (Girodias assumed his mother's name during the war to escape persecution as a Jew), Kahane made his living by publishing English-language pornography, but he also harbored literary ambitions. He was struck by the example of Sylvia Beach and desired above all both to publish Joyce himself, and, since he could no longer publish *Ulysses*, to find an equivalent. Approached by Lawrence about *Lady Chatterley*, he hesitated but in the end decided not to publish it (although he did eventually bring out the third French edition, in 1936). He begged Beach to introduce him to Joyce and bought the rights to a portion of what was later to become *Finnegans Wake*, titled *Haveth Childers Everywhere*, which he published in a sumptuous edition that would have lost him a great deal of money—Kahane's business partner was appalled by this extravagance, especially after Kahane admitted he too found the work incomprehensible—had he not found a profligate, Joyce-admiring American publisher to buy up almost the entire expensive print run. He also brought out an edition of some of Joyce's poems, *Pomes Penyeach*. In 1933, after Jonathan Cape's associate Pegasus Press went out of business, Kahane bought the rights to *The Well of Loneliness*, which continued selling briskly under the Obelisk imprint. In the meantime, though, he had found his own Joyce in Henry Miller.

On first reading the manuscript of *Tropic of Cancer*, Kahane later wrote, he felt "exalted by the triumphant sensation of all explorers who have at last fallen upon the object of their years of search." He had discovered "the most terrible, the most sordid, the most magnificent manuscript"; nothing equalled it "for the splendour of its writing, the fathomless depth of its despair, the savour of its portraiture, the boisterousness of its humour."[18] Despite his enthusiasm, for financial reasons the book was not actually published for two years—during which Miller anxiously reworked his manuscript—and even then only because Anaïs Nin put up the money for its printing. (She told Miller the funding came from her banker husband, but it was actually donated by Otto Rank, who at the time served Nin simultaneously as psychoanalyst and lover). Kahane's adolescent son Maurice drew the cover illustration: a large crab bearing a naked woman in its claws.

Tropic of Cancer was published in 1934 and garnered two reviews in the French press—one was by Miller's French-Swiss literary idol Blaise Cendrars, the other by Raymond Queneau (later a major figure in France, founder of the experimental group Oulipo and author of, among other works, *Zazie dans le métro* and *Exercices de style*)—which was more than could reasonably have been hoped given the circumstances. Miller had taken publicity into his own hands, writing letters, accompanied by copies of the book, to French writers he admired, such as Céline and Cendrars, and also to a number of the major literary figures of the day in the United States and England, including T.S. Eliot, Ezra Pound, Aldous Huxley, Theodore Dreiser, Sherwood Anderson, H.L. Mencken, Emma Goldman, Havelock Ellis, John Dos Passos, Gertrude Stein. This strategy worked, to a certain extent, and not only in France. His name, and the title of his book, at least, became known among the literati. Most of the people from whom Miller solicited praise were also targets of his expansive scorn, and what is especially remarkable is that in one instance that scorn was inscribed in the book itself. Eliot, despite the fact that his poetry had been characterized in *Tropic* as "sterile, hybrid, dry," responded by calling the book "a rather magnificent piece of work," and added that it was greatly superior to *Lady Chatterley's Lover*.[19] Miller had also characterized Pound—although not in print—as "full of shit," specifying, "the Cantos are the worst crap I ever read."[20] Pound wrote Miller a letter saying that *Tropic of Cancer* surpassed Joyce on his own terms and was much more worthy than the work of "the weak-minded Woolf female."[21] He also, writing to Olga Rudge, called *Tropic* "a dirty book worth reading," and "a bawdy which will be very useful to put Wyndham [Lewis] and J.J. [Joyce] into their proper cubbyholes; cause Miller is sane and without kinks"—this last presumably in contradistinction to Joyce's taste for the excremental (see chapter 4). (Miller too, as we shall see, likes to talk about excrement, but unlike Joyce he keeps it strictly separate from sexuality.) Huxley, another target of Miller's literary disdain, called Miller's work "a bit terrifying, but well done"; Havelock Ellis praised its psychological acumen; and Cyril Connolly went so far as to term *Tropic* "the most important thing that has come out of American Paris in the ten years since Hemingway."[22]

By the time these literary figures read *Tropic of Cancer*, they already knew *Ulysses* and *Lady Chatterley's Lover*, and therefore found neither its explicit sexuality nor its use of frank Anglo-Saxon vocabulary exciting in themselves. This sort of transgression had quickly become old hat: Joyce and Lawrence had prepared the terrain a bit too well. Orwell goes so far as to note that "when I first opened *Tropic of Cancer* and saw that it was full of unprintable words, my immediate reaction was a refusal to be impressed" (11). Clearly, it was not just because of the more obviously inflammatory aspects of the book that it was greeted as new and exciting by the likes of Eliot, Pound, Huxley, and Orwell, an audience by now jaded in the face of graphic sexuality and four-letter words. What was it, then, that made *Tropic of Cancer* more than just another dirty book in 1934? As Orwell observes, it had a great deal to do with the fact that Miller gives voice to the "underling." Joyce may already have tried this with his ad-selling Dublin Jew, but he did so both in the third person and with such literary ostentation that the proletarian thrust was lost in the artistic smokescreen. By contrast *Tropic of Cancer* was written from the point of view of the literate *untermensch*, the great unwashed autodidact: this was a first in English. The French equivalent was Céline's *Voyage au bout de la nuit*, a favorite of Miller's, another semiautobiographical narrative written in a deliberately unliterary style, and which had provoked a scandal—but not censorship— in 1932. In spite of Miller's fondness for obscure polysyllabic terms to offset his four-letter vocabulary, anyone who could read could read the book. If, that is, he could lay hands on it; which was why it was impossible legally to lay hands on it in the United States and England for some thirty years.

The "dirt" in Miller's book is fourfold. It is first of all literal: an atmosphere of grime pervades *Tropic of Cancer* (as in Orwell's *Down and Out in Paris and London*, published the previous year). This all by itself was relatively new in anglophone literature, and it was one of the reasons French writers, especially Zola, had been viewed for some time as so dangerous in English-speaking countries: because French "realism," and even more so "naturalism," undertook to describe the griminess of working-class life. But in Miller's book the grime is at once less didactic and much grimier. Squalor is everywhere, transcending class. Cleanliness and order are associated with death in the first sentences, following which, the second paragraph depicts the (male) characters shaving each others' armpits, because even in the midst of apparent order and cleanliness life prevails, specifically in the form of body-lice. The second level of "dirt" in Miller's writing is of course sex. Obviously, sex was not a new topic in literature written in any language; Zola's novels were also viewed as "dirty" because they contained sex, as of course were Lawrence's, among others.[23] But Miller's approach to sex was far more anarchic and amoral, or immoral, than anything that could be found in his predecessors. The third form of "dirt" in *Tropic of Cancer* is the dirty language, which is much more ubiquitous than in either *Ulysses* or even *Lady Chatterley's Lover*, because Miller aims to represent the frank language of characters living in squalor, and who express themselves, the narrator foremost, accordingly. Finally, there is shit: not just the word but the thing itself. Miller, like Joyce and Lawrence among others, in their very different ways, could not resist writing about shit. Barbey d'Aurevilly's dark predictions of the 1870s about what would happen if Zola's nefarious trend were allowed to continue had truly come to pass. Unlike Joyce, Miller does not eroticize the excretory functions; however, unlike Lawrence, nor does he draw strict lines of demarcation between excretion and everything else. Instead, he philosophizes the functions of the lower digestive tract. Shitting is for Miller all at once a routine function, a pretext for sophomoric humor, and also dragged into the very center of the grand scheme of things, including literary aesthetics.

Tropic of Cancer contains an extensive scene in which Miller is asked to entertain a young Indian visitor, a follower of Mahatma Gandhi, who is both earnestly idealistic—"I have the illusion of being in the presence of one of the twelve disciples," Miller mordantly observes at one point (100)—and eager to explore the realm of hedonism: "he was like a dog with his tongue hanging out" (98). They go to a whorehouse, according to plan, but while there the visitor is so overwhelmed by the circumstances that he panics. He has trouble choosing a woman, and when he finally does so—Miller is in the next room with his own choice—the young man nervously asks to use the lavatory. Not realizing the nature of the situation Miller directs him to the bidet, following which all hell breaks loose: "The five of us"—they have by now been joined by the enraged proprietress—"are standing there looking at the *bidet*. There are two enormous turds floating in the water" (99). What makes this scene something other than an act of purely gratuitous scatalogical provocation is that Miller then draws grandiose conclusions from the event, establishing a familiar juxtaposition between fertilizer and flowers, but in less familiar terms: "the monstrous thing is not that men have created roses out of this dung-heap, but that, for some reason or other, they should *want* roses" (103). We are back in the realm of antiart. The passage culminates in spectacularly Millerian fashion, with the meaning of the universe itself exultantly reduced to cosmic feces:

> And so I think what a miracle it would be if this miracle which man attends
> eternally should turn out to be nothing more than these two enormous

turds which the faithful disciple dropped in the *bidet*. What if at the last moment, when the banquet table is set and the cymbals clash, there should appear suddenly, and wholly without warning, a silver platter on which even
the blind could see that there is nothing more, and nothing less, than two
enormous lumps of shit. (103)

Nor, certainly, is this Miller's sole expansion on the theme of excretion,
which recurs, among other places, in the "Saturday Afternoon" section of
Black Spring. Here he explicitly takes up the question of literature and
defecation, arguing that reading on the toilet separates the great books
from their inferior counterparts.[24] Great books, he claims, benefit from
being read on the toilet: "only the little books suffer thereby." Only "the
little books," that is, "make ass wipers." The latter category includes works
by many of the authors from whom he had tried to elicit praise for *Tropic
of Cancer*: Huxley, Gertrude Stein, Sinclair Lewis, Hemingway, Dos Passos,
Dreiser.[25] He also uses this idiosyncratic distinction between good and bad
bathroom reading to take a special potshot at Joyce. In the course of insisting that "all my good reading, you might say, was done in the toilet,"
and noting that he owes to this activity his knowledge of Boccaccio and Rabelais among others, he goes on to specify: "At the worst, *Ulysses*, or a de-
tective story. There are passages in *Ulysses*," he continues, "which can be
read only in the toilet—if one wants to extract from them the full flavor of
their content." In this unfortunately vivid metaphor we see the force of his
ambivalent gripe against Joyce, as well as the strange position in which
Miller, demolisher of traditional hierarchies as well as promoter of such
traditionally ignoble activities as reading on the toilet, finds himself when
he wants to disparage Joyce's work as readable only on the toilet.

Presumably the passages in *Ulysses* alluded to here include the infamous
scene (censored by Pound, as we saw in chapter 4) in which Leopold
Bloom reads a story in the outhouse and then literally wipes himself with
it; in any case it is impossible to ignore the parallel. As in the various contradictory uses to which writers such as he and Lawrence put the term *obscene*, Miller seems to want both to reclaim reading on the toilet as noble
and also use it as a gauge of abjection when it suits his purposes. Here,
though, we find both valences in operation at once. He goes on in this
same passage to note about *Ulysses*'s toilet-readability that "this is not to
denigrate the talent of the author. This is simply to move him a little closer
to the good company of Abelard, Petrarch, Rabelais, Villon, Boccaccio—
all the fine, lusty, genuine spirits who recognized dung for dung and angels for angels. Fine company," he concludes, "and no *rari nantes in gurgite
vasto*" (*Black Spring*, 48). This last phrase is a reference to Virgil, who appears in "A Saturday Afternoon" as a sort of canonical fall-guy: the epigraph of the piece is "This is better than reading Vergil," and the question

"What is better than reading Vergil?" reappears throughout the chapter as a refrain, which finds its answer as, in sum: life. Life, it seems, is better than reading Virgil:

> For, whenever I think of Vergil, I think automatically—*what time is it?* Vergil to me is a bald-headed guy with spectacles tilting back in his chair and leaving a grease mark on the blackboard; a bald-headed guy opening wide his mouth in a delirium which he simulated five days a week for four successive years; a big mouth with false teeth producing this strange oracular nonsense: *rari nantes in gurgite vasto.* Vividly I recall the unholy joy with which he pronounced this phrase. A *great* phrase, according to this bald-pated, goggle-eyed son of a bitch. (*Black Spring,* 47)

It is difficult to know what to make of this passage, the immediate meaning of which is nonetheless very clear: Virgil is boring, obligatory school reading, and therefore of no interest. But for one thing, the Latin poet also appears elsewhere in this section in the company of "Dante and Montaigne and all the others who spoke only of the moment, the expanding moment that is heard forever," aligned, therefore, with the writers of life rather than death (39–40). Along with this evident contradiction one also notes that when he wrote this Miller himself sported a bald pate and spectacles, the very marks of dusty irrelevance according to his representation of school life that contrasts the dullness of Latin class with the liveliness of "recess in the toilet."

And finally, there is the matter of the obsessively retierated quotation itself. Later in the same passage he announces: "I am one individual who is going to be honest about Vergil and his fucking *rari nantes in gurgite vasto.*" The unsurprising conclusion: "recess in the toilet was worth a thousand Vergils" (47). His honesty, though, stops notably short of translating the fragment from the *Aeneid* which he cites in full four times in two pages. *Rari nantes in gurgite vasto* (*Aeneid* I.118), which means, roughly, "a few shipwrecked men floating on the vast abyss," remains untranslated because once its meaning is revealed it loses its irrelevance: it could serve as epigraph for this passage—especially with its latrine motif—and indeed for Miller's entire literary output. "A few shipwrecked men floating on the vast abyss" can also be read as the very definition of literature that stands the toilet test. It is what *Tropic of Cancer,* certainly, is about: a few hardy souls trying to escape the general deadness of the present and to imagine a brighter future in art.

Virgil, and with him the rest of the Western canon, exists alternatively or even simultaneously on both sides of the great divide for Miller, who cannot stop quoting the work he wants to discard. In his later books too the *Aeneid* resurfaces from time to time. In *Nexus* (1960), for instance, his final take on the New York years, at one point he reproduces "ET HAEC OLIM MEMINISSE IUVABIT," all in capital letters, in the middle of the page, noting, "I was sufficiently clairvoyant at this time to inscribe this unforgettable line from the *Aeneid* in the toilet box which was suspended over Stasia's cot" (43). Stasia is his wife's lover, and her "toilet box" is presumably a container for her toiletry articles, but it is surely no coincidence that once again when Miller cites Virgil the toilet motif is not far behind. Three pages later, at the end of the chapter, Miller provides a gloss, in italics but with no direct indication that it is the line in question: "*One day it will be pleasant to remember these things*" (46). A full translation of the line "forsan et haec olim meminisse iuvabit" (*Aeneid* I.203) reads: "perhaps it may one day be pleasant to remember even these things." The speaker is Aeneus, suggesting to his men that even the most awful adventures (encounters with Scylla and the Cyclops are the examples furnished) may one day form the basis for fruitful recollection: precisely what Miller was up to in the many books recounting his sordid experiences in New York and Paris.

Miller's attitude toward Virgil, clearly, is ambivalent in the extreme. In the end it is not surprising that he showers contempt on the Latin poet in *Black Spring* after echoing in scatalogical form the beginning of the *Aeneid* in the opening paragraphs of *Tropic of Cancer*. Nor is it a coincidence, surely, that his most explicit rejection of the classical model is to be found in the same piece in which he alludes to the outhouse scene in *Ulysses* in the very course of relegating that novel to the status of toilet paper. Miller was all too aware that Kahane seized on *Tropic of Cancer* as his answer to Joyce's novel, in his attempt to emulate and rival Sylvia Beach. In heaping scorn on the untranslated classical model he was trying to ensure that no one would imagine him to be a mere Joyce-imitator; especially since the *Aeneid* is itself modeled on the *Illiad* and the *Odyssey*, rolled into one. Virgil's epic, which invents a myth of the founding of Rome, recapitulates Homer's sequence in inverted form. It contains twelve books, the first six of which describe Aeneus's travels after the fall of Troy, the second half depicting war. *Tropic of Cancer* is the story of Miller's wanderings in Paris; *Tropic of Capricorn*, its sequel, concerns what had driven him to Europe: his battles over his wife's affair with a woman in New York. It is even possible to see in Miller's embrace of the first person an echo of the Virgillian "I sing," not just as it is reproduced in the opening pages of his first book, but also as it replaces the Homeric "sing to me, o Muse," and thus a repudiation of, among other things, Joyce's third-person epic. Whatever one may think about the ultimate importance of these classical allusions to an author who constantly disavowed this sort of literary gamesmanship even while engaging in his own version of it, it is clear that Miller went to great lengths to avoid playing Virgil to Joyce's Homer. Nonetheless he could not manage to escape this fate, nor, as much as he may have tried, the classical tradition from which Joyce drew his inspiration.[26]

Tropic of Cancer was much talked about after its initial publication by the Obelisk Press in 1934, and Miller's private publicity campaign had had its effect, but still the book was unimportable into English-speaking countries, and as a result it took its place alongside *Lady Chatterley's Lover* as freely available in continental Europe but firmly banned in its author's homeland. *Ulysses* was by this time newly available in the United States and was shortly to become so in England, and *The Well of Loneliness* now circulated openly in the United States if not in the United Kingdom. (Miller had read Hall's novel when it came out, and it fortified his ambition to write about his wife's same-sex adventures.) With *Tropic of Cancer* an Obelisk bestseller, further volumes were forthcoming: Kahane quickly published *Black Spring* (1936), which had initially been referred to as "Self-Portrait" (a title which might well have done service for all Miller's works, including his study of Lawrence), and then *Tropic of Capricorn* in 1939. The second *Tropic* was no less graphic than the first, and it also addresses the question of the bounds of permissibility in an extended meditation on what Miller calls "The Land of Fuck": "What is unmentionable is pure fuck and pure cunt; it must be mentioned only in *de luxe* editions, otherwise the world will fall apart."[27] Miller also, though, produced some relatively scatology-free prose, in the form of short pieces, which were published in the United States in literary journals. In 1939 New Directions, under editor James Laughlin, brought out *The Cosmological Eye*, a collection of essays, mostly drawn from works already published abroad or in progress, in places lightly expurgated. For some time, though, his books became if anything increasingly censor-defying, reaching an apex of unpublishability in *Sexus*, the first volume of a trilogy, including also *Plexus* and *Nexus*, and bearing the overall provocative title *The Rosy Crucifixion*.

Attempts to publish his obviously unacceptable works in America began not long after publication of the early works. In 1939, one K. S. Giniger of the Signet Press consulted a lawyer about setting up a test case for bringing Miller's *Tropic*s into the United States; this attempt led nowhere (Martin, 450). In 1940 the "Medusa" edition of *Tropic of Cancer* was published by Jacob R. Brussells. Printed in New York, this edition carried the spurious claim "Imprenta de Mexico," which failed to convince the authorities, and Brussells served a two-year jail sentence for his pains. (Miller apparently knew about this edition, which was sold under the counter by Frances Steloff at the Gotham Book Mart in New York, as well as in Chicago, at $10 a copy, an astronomical price at the time.)[28] In 1944 Miller discussed with Laughlin the possibility of a special New Directions edition of *Tropic of Cancer*, which was to have blanks in the place of offensive words and carry instructions for contacting Miller (who was by this time living in California) for lists of the missing words, to be pasted into the book. This too came to nought, presumably at least in part because of the cripplingly vast number of blanks to be filled. Four years later Penguin Books made what Miller termed an "unacceptable" offer to print an expurgated edition of *Tropic of Cancer*. The offer was unacceptable because Miller refused on general grounds to consider the possibility of expurgating the work; but again it is difficult to imagine how this operation might have proceeded, given the sheer ubiquity of objectionable material.[29] The first American legal case involving distribution of the book occurred in 1953, with the San Francisco ACLU losing an obscenity case over the banning of Miller's first published work. And in 1958 Stanley Kubrick and James B. Harris—who were at the same time negotiating with Nabokov for the rights to *Lolita*—approached Miller about a screen adaptation of *Tropic of Cancer*. His response was categorical: "No," he replied, explaining: "I am going to hold out to the day when we really have freedom of expression," and added: "probably not in my lifetime, if ever."[30]

The indomitable Joseph Strick, who had already made a film version of *Ulysses*, eventually, with Miller's approval, filmed the equally unfilmable *Tropic of Cancer* in 1970, after the ban on the book had been lifted by the Supreme Court, and therefore presumably in the era of true free expression. Made on location in Paris, Strick's movie stars Rip Torn as Miller and features the author himself in a cameo role. It was promptly banned in Britain (although somehow allowed a restricted run in London) and rated X in the United States, which meant that it was shown in few theaters; U.S. newspapers refused even to carry ads for the film. Twenty years later, Philip Kaufman's "Henry and June" (1990), with Fred Ward as Miller and a very young Uma Thurman as his wife, also ran into trouble because of the inevitable sex scenes. This film version recounts essentially the same story as *Tropic of Cancer*, but from the point of view of Anaïs Nin's *Diary*. (Nin, who had affairs with both Miller and his wife, does not appear in *Tropic*, no doubt at least in part because the central role she played in getting the book published allowed her unique right of refusal to be besmirched in it.) Kaufman's film too was rated X, but in response to public pressure the MPAA changed the rating to NC-17, essentially a euphemism for the X rating it supplanted. It was the first film to receive this rating, which was guaranteed to repel distributors while avoiding the obvious stigma of X. The results were approximately the same as for Strick's film twenty years earlier: "Henry and June" had a very limited run, playing in only 307 theaters in the United States.[31]

In the meantime, throughout the 1930s, 1940s, and 1950s, Miller held out: for the duration of the ban on his works in the United States and England he refused to entertain either film projects or offers to publish expurgated versions of his works. His pessimistic attitude, insisting that the books would never see publication in his native country, and certainly not in his lifetime, was influenced by the fact that even in France the moral value of his work had been legally questioned. There, an episode known as *l'affaire Miller* enlivened the year 1946. *Tropic of Cancer* and *Tropic of Capricorn* had both been published in French translation (the former by Denoël, the latter by Les Editions du Chêne, under the direction of Maurice Girodias, Jack Kahane having died in 1939) and had been prosecuted at the instigation of Daniel Parker, president of the French equivalent of the Society for the Suppression of Vice (the *Cartel d'action sociale et morale*) under a 1939 anti-obscenity law. The French goverment took action, formed a special committee to investigate the case, and the books were found in effect to be obscene and the publishers in violation of the law. A *comité de défense d'Henry Miller* was then formed, including such luminaries as André Breton, Albert Camus, Paul Eluard, André Gide, Raymond Queneau, and Jean-Paul Sartre. More than two hundred articles were published about Miller over a four-month period in France, and the *affaire Miller* was compared to the Dreyfus Affair. Girodias was delighted by the publicity, of course; even more so when the *Société des gens de lettres*, in concert with Girodias himself, brought suit against Daniel Parker, charging him with libel and slander and asking that charges be dropped against the publishers. Girodias prevailed and charges were dropped; Miller, who was by this time living in California, became a household name in France.

Sexus, writtten in the early 1940s, was published in 1949 by Girodias both in English and in French translation. The latter edition was almost immediately seized by the French police and suppressed. The *comité de défense d'Henry Miller* was suddenly silent on this score: it turned out that everyone, including Miller's disciple Lawrence Durrell, felt that *Sexus* was indeed obscene. Durrell was appalled by the book, and wrote to Miller telling him that "the moral vulgarity of so much of it is artistically painful. . . . What on earth possessed you to leave so much twaddle in?" (Martin, 432). (Miller was unmoved by this attack, writing back evenly: "Perhaps it's twaddle, perhaps not" [ibid., 432].) Even Erica Jong, writing in the 1990s, is horrified by the insistent sexual provocation of *Sexus*; clearly this is where Miller's Millerism exceeds even his most ardent fans' capacity to appreciate his work. In the end both French and English versions of the novel were suppressed by order of the French government. In 1957 *Sexus* was declared "obscene writing" by Norway's attorney general, who had all available copies of the book seized, and instituted proceedings against two booksellers who had been selling the book. The following year the booksellers were found guilty and appealed their conviction before the Norwegian Supreme Court. Miller wrote two open letters to their defense attorney, Trygve Hirsch, which were later published and which take their place among Miller's essays on obscenity and censorship, including "Obscenity and the Law of Reflection" (1945) and "Obscenity and Literature" (1949), the latter originally written to be used in court by the French attorney in the *Sexus* case.

In his essays on obscenity, Miller avoids the sort of self-indicting gestures Lawrence did not hesitate to make in his own essays on the subject; instead he cites earlier arguments against censorship, reiterating familiar themes. He emphasizes the history of literary censorship and echoes a point made by, among many others, Flaubert in his open letter defending Maupassant in 1876, to the effect that the state-sponsored suppression of artistic works tends to have a boomerang effect, bringing attention to the work in question. In his case this last observation was pertinent in the extreme, and not only in the usual sense in which attempts to censor works of art unavoidably focus public attention on them, with the result that, once the work is—as it always is in the end, even if the initial verdict goes to the censors—allowed to circulate, its notoriety is assured. This much, as we have seen, was the evident result of cases from *Madame Bovary* and *Les Fleurs du mal* in 1857 through *Lady Chatterley's Lover* a century later.

Miller's case also presents an interesting twist on this inevitable formula, in the person of Huntington Cairns. Miller wrote his first essay on the subject of censorship, "Obscenity and the Law of Reflection," published in the United States in 1945, at Cairns's behest, and including a number of references to an article the latter had written on the subject. Cairns had also been the driving force behind *The World of Sex*, a small volume elucidating Miller's views on sex, privately printed in the United States in 1940 and later reprinted by Girodias's Olympia Press in 1959. He was one of Miller's earliest and most fervent admirers, a collector of his work, and a friend. He was also Special Adviser to the U.S. Treasury Department, in charge of determining the distinction between obscene books, which were to be intercepted by Customs, and "works of art," which were in principle allowed into the country. In other words, Cairns was the very person who deemed Miller's books unsuitable for entry into the United States. Miller liked Cairns, and he was of course, in addition, delighted to find a fan in his official censor. He showed him around Paris in 1936, and at one point, while still in France, he even wrote to Cairns that he considered him to be one of only two friends he had in America.[32] It was as though Flaubert and Ernest Pinard had undertaken a walking tour together. The unexpected fellowship between Miller and Huntington Cairns demonstrates not only the remarkable hypocrisy that reigned in terms of literary censorship in the United States in the twentieth century but also the extent to which times had changed, and the hypocrisy was now taken for granted. Flaubert may have been amused to discover Pinard, later in life, as the purported author of obscene lyric poetry, but his amusement was not indulgent. Baudelaire conceived a perverse at-tachment to Pinard, imagining that the latter would invite him to dinner, and sending him copies of his books, but Pinard did not reciprocate his affection. The friendship between Miller and Cairns is testimony to the idiosyncrasies of the two men, certainly, but also to the strange moral climate of the mid twentieth century.

By the late 1950s the time finally seemed ripe for attempts to publish Miller's banned works in the United States, and Barney Rosset of Grove Press, fresh from his victory in the *Lady Chatterley* trial, was determined to make *Tropic of Cancer* his second test case. This was not merely because of its general notoriety; Rosset had personal reasons for wanting to publish the book. In 1941, twenty years before he finally managed to put his imprimatur on Miller's work, Rosset, then a freshman at Swarthmore College in Pennsylvania, had written a paper on *Tropic of Cancer*. Having heard of the book, curious to read it, and not even realizing that it was banned, Rosset made his way to the Gotham Book Mart in New York, explained that he was a college student, and bought a copy of the ostensibly "printed in Mexico" Medusa edition. His paper bore the title "Henry Miller vs. Our Way of Life," and it received a grade of B-. The grade notwithstanding, when Rosset became a publisher he was determined to bring the book out.[33] Miller was at first, and for some time, recalcitrant. Part of the reason for this was that, having founded his own legend on the basis of being a penniless artist, he had a hard time grappling with prospect of making large sums of money from the books that chronicled his contempt for such matters. He had also come to like the idea that his works were expensive and difficult to obtain. This only increased their ultimate value, especially given that, judging by his voluminous fan mail and the pilgrims who had for some time been finding their way to his California hideout, the fact that they were banned did not prevent people from obtaining and reading them.

Rosset, even seconded by Girodias, had a hard time convincing Miller to allow him the rights to publish *Tropic of Cancer* in the United States. Miller's reluctance, spelled out in a letter to Rosset, was grounded in the reasoning that he did not believe the federal and state governments would allow unexpurgated publication of the book. Furthermore, even assuming this could happen, the basic problem would still not be solved. Even if it were to appear legally in America, two undesirable effects would follow: people would erroneously believe that this meant true freedom, and the book would be read for the wrong reasons. He would forever be known as a mere purveyor of smut. This latter objection recalls Flaubert's extended regrets over becoming a famous author on the strength of a supposedly immoral work. Unlike Flaubert, though, Miller (as the *Playboy* appearances attest) eventually came to embrace—within certain limits—his own legend as King of Smut. In any case he did not have a family fortune to

sustain him, and even though his fame was assured by the late 1950s his financial situation remained somewhat precarious. Still he fretted ambiva-
lently over the notion of becoming rich. He refused to entertain the idea
of allowing the books to be published merely for the sake of the money it
would bring, but he also wrote to Rosset that the projects he had in mind
would require "a whacking sum." Miller thus simultaneously suggested
that, not being interested in money, he could not be bought; and that his
purchase would require a vast amount.[34]

It was not in the end so much the sum offered that changed his mind
but the threat of piracy. Rosset and Girodias convinced him that if did not
agree to an authorized American publication he would end up regretting
it, since in the absence of copyright protection anyone could bring out an
expurgated version of his works—there was indeed great incentive to do
so—and pass it off as the real thing. This argument got his attention: he
had not spent years of his life in poverty, refusing, Lawrence-like, to sell
out by allowing expurgated publications of his books, only to see someone
else both profit from his writing and, in the bargain, adulterate it. This
was, as Miller well knew, precisely what had happened to Lawrence: *Lady
Chatterley* had been published in many pirated editions in various countries, both intact and expurgated. Rosset agreed to separate contracts for
the two *Tropics*, and offered a substantial advance in addition to assuming
full responsibility for all costs of litigation, including a potential Supreme
Court case. James Laughlin further sweetened the deal by agreeing to renounce all claims New Directions may have had on his work. Miller finally
agreed.

What happened afterward was at once spectacular and anticlimactic.
Grove Press published *Tropic of Cancer* in 1961, with a preface by poet Karl
Shapiro calling Miller "the greatest living author." Because of the outcome
of the *Lady Chatterley* trial, there was no attempt by any branch of the federal government to intervene in distribution of the book. This did not,
however, mean that it had become acceptable. Over the course of the next
three years the book was the object of seizures and legal disputes across
the United States, in many different jurisdictions and on many different
judicial levels. From the public debates that ensued, it seems clear that a
substantial proportion of the populace did not wish to be offered access to
books such as *Tropic of Cancer*.[35] In *The End of Obscenity* Charles Rembar insists on the degree to which the eventual outcome in such cases as *Chatterley* and *Tropic* depended not on popular sentiment but on judicial interpretation: "It cannot be stressed too often that it was the United States
Constitution that saved these books, and not the will of the people" (174).
By the time the Supreme Court put a stop to these local skirmishes in 1964
there had been more than sixty lawsuits over the acceptability of *Tropic of
Cancer* in the United States. (*Tropic of Capricorn*, despite being at least as

obscene as its predecessor, was entirely eclipsed in the general brouhaha over the first volume, and its publication by Grove was never questioned legally, nor were those of *Black Spring* or even *Sexus*.)

The main problem that arose in the attempts to defend Miller's book was that the very precedent that made its publication all but immune to federal prosecution, the *Chatterley* trial with its arguments as to the moral seriousness of Lawrence's intention, as well as its nuanced legal understanding of the term *prurient*, turned out to be very difficulty to apply, when push came to shove, on the local level. *Tropic* was an entirely different matter, demanding more resouceful arguments. Rembar, who had won Grove's earlier case against the Post Office, describes his efforts to argue the case on appeal in Boston in 1962 as follows: "Here my confining 'prurient' to what was nasty, which worked very nicely for *Lady Chatterley's Lover*, worked less nicely." This was because the "judge had found *Tropic* 'filthy, disgusting, nauseating and'—showing a fine flair for anticlimax— 'offensive to good taste.' Miller's concentration on lice, turds, and the clap made it a bit difficult to put him in a category with Lawrence" (189). He nonetheless managed to win the case in Massachussetts, in what he notes was the first judicial opinion in America to give explicit recognition to the "social-value test" (193). Written by Justice R. Ammi Cutter, the Massachussetts Supreme Judicial Court's opinion went out of its way to express their lack of appreciation of the book itself:

> It is not the function of judges to serve as arbiters of taste or to say that an author must regard vugarity as unnecessary to his portrayal of particular scenes or characters or to establish particular ideas. Within broad limits each writer, attempting to be a literary artist, is entitled to determine such matters for himself, even if the result is as dull, dreary and offensive as the writer of this opinion finds almost all of *Tropic*. (Quoted in Rembar, 194)

Many further battles followed, in all sorts of jurisdictions: in New Jersey, Philadelphia, Syracuse, California, Maryland, Rhode Island, Wisconsin; all over the country, often very local cases, some of which made their way through the state judicial systems. The attorneys for Grove Press, while trying to make sure that all these local trials were won, also of course hoped that one of them would go all the way to the Supreme Court so as to put an end to the ongoing succession of small fires. The most publicized trial before 1964 occurred in Chicago. Grove Press retained Elmer Gertz, who had frequently served as a lawyer for the ACLU. Richard Ellmann, the eminent Joyce critic and biographer, was star witness for the defense, explaining the literary importance of Miller's work. Judge Samuel B. Epstein ruled that *Tropic of Cancer* was neither obscene nor pornographic, and that the citizens of the Chicago area therefore had a constitutionally protected right to read the book. He further noted in his decision the following:

> Hard-core pornography, it is agreed, has no social value whatsoever, and does not enjoy the protection of the First and Fourteenth Amendments to the Constitution of the United States, but literature which has some social merit, even if controversial, should be left to individual taste rather than to governmental edict. (Quoted in de Grazia, *Girls Lean Back Everywhere*, 379)

In the meantime, though, while this decision was being appealed in Illinois, the New York Court of Appeals, before which Rembar again argued the case, was busy finding *Tropic of Cancer* obscene and therefore worthy of suppression. Judge John F. Schileppi wrote on behalf of the court that the book

> is nothing more than a compilation of a series of sordid narrations dealing with sex in a manner designed to appeal to the prurient interests of the average person. It is a blow to sense, not merely sensibility. It is, in short, "hard-core pornography," dirt for dirt's sake, and dirt for money's sake. (quoted in de Grazia, *Girls Lean Back Everywhere*, 381)

With all the various state and local courts arriving at divergent conclusions, it was inevitable that the Supreme Court would at some point be induced to look into the matter. This finally occurred with a whimper rather than a bang, as the eventual result of a Florida judgment. The decision was announced, in a 5–4 vote, with no arguments having been heard and no opinions written. The case was linked to another censorship case decided the same day, *Jacobellis v. Ohio*, concerning the right of a Cleveland Heights movie theater manager to show Louis Malle's film *Les Amants*, which contained discreet sexuality (the nature of the offense was never referred to in the various arguments over this case, but the film, while generally decorous in its depiction of adultery, includes a scene delicately suggesting cunnilingus). The court, reversing (6–3) the Ohio conviction, made its various feelings on obscenity known. Justices Hugo Black and William O. Douglas stuck to their view that free expression was an absolute value; Justice William Brennan reiterated his *Roth* position that "a work cannot be proscribed unless it is 'utterly' without social importance," and Justice Potter Stewart took advantage of the occasion to make his famous pronouncement that although he could not define hard-core pornography he knew it when he saw it, and this was not it.[36] In the end the *Tropic of Cancer* decision got somewhat lost in the shuffle, but the result was that Miller's book was finally, thirty years after its initial publication, freely available in the United States, by order of the Supreme Court. In the meantime the book had already been published in England in 1963, by John Calder, after the latter had been told by the director of public prosecutions that no action would be taken. "On publication day, every BBC news bulletin announced that the book was now available in Britain for the first time and the line of willing buyers stretched for blocks around some bookshops" (cited in de Grazia, *Girls Lean Back Everywhere*, 432).

Miller died in 1980, having become what he had always wanted: a legend in his own time. That legend, of course, continued evolving after his death, helped along, sometimes in ways that he might not have liked, by his publisher. In 1983 Grove Press did something he had never allowed during his lifetime, even in his naked-ping-pong phase: it published a volume called *Opus Pistorum* (later reissued as *Under the Roofs of Paris*; the original title, in very approximate Latin, is meant to be something along the lines of "The Miller's Tale"), consisting of six pornographic pieces that Miller had always denied having written. They include scenes of pedophilia, bestiality, incest, orgies, and coprophilia. He is on record, along with Anaïs Nin and others, as having written pornographic stories for private collectors for a dollar per page in the late 1930s and early 1940s. Two small volumes of Nin's stories, *Delta of Venus* (1977) and *Little Birds* (1979), were published, under the rubric "erotica," immediately following her death in 1977, and became bestsellers, as Miller must have known.

Miller's biographer Robert Ferguson goes to some length to provide textual proof of Miller's authorship of the stories in *Opus Pistorum*, among which, "it would take an unusually conscientious forger to come up with the little touch of narrative curiosity about whether or not the midget has a half-size toilet in her flat."[37] This detail is indeed highly Millerian, and certainly not one that would preoccupy the average pornographer. All evidence, both textual and historical, points to Miller as author. And yet he resolutely disclaimed authorship of the stories, the titles of which include "Rue de Screw," "Sous les Toits de Paris," and "France in My Pants."[38] In response to a collector who wrote to him in 1950 seeking authentication, he wrote: "The titles of the three you mention *I* could never have invented! They are completely out of my 'line.' I abhor erotica—this sort—'smut for smut's sake'—as I suppose it to be."[39] Everyone, it seems, even its most notorious practitioners, even Henry Miller, abhors "smut for smut's sake."

Miller's ultimate place in literary history is up for grabs: his *Tropics* and other works have never gone out of print, published by Grove and also intermittently, some of them, in "classic" editions, but unlike Joyce and Lawrence he is still known, perhaps above all, as a writer of dirty books.[40] His status as a "classic" author remains uncertain: as it should be, given his own reiterated tergiversations about classic literature. It is in the end appropriate that Miller, who had set out to create a global explosion with his "fuck everything" book, his universally directed "gob of spit," should have been posthumously embarrassed to be revealed as the author of what he himself termed "smut for smut's sake," published under a spurious Latin title.

CHAPTER SEVEN

Vladimir Nabokov

Lolitigation

> The question about everything was, would it bring a blush into the cheek
> of the young person? And the inconvenience of the young person was
> that, according to Mr Podsnap, she seemed always liable to burst into
> blushes when there was no need at all. There appeared to be no line
> of demarcation between the young person's excessive innocence, and
> another person's guiltiest knowledge.
>
> CHARLES DICKENS, *Our Mutual Friend*

Lolita is an entirely different kettle of fish. All the works under discussion are necessarily very different from each other, of course. Each of the books entailed different difficulties, and the conditions in which they were—and sometimes were not—published were different as well. The case of *Lolita* differs greatly from all those we have looked at so far, both in itself and in terms of the history of its publication. Social mores and legal precedents changed during the mid twentieth century with remarkable speed, and at a certain point, around 1957 in both the United States and England—one hundred years after the trials of Flaubert and Baudelaire and the passing of England's first obscenity law—literary prosecutions became subject to a law of diminishing return. Unprecedentedly, and in a remarkably short span, each decision in favor of the publisher of an "obscene" work made it all the less likely that further obscenity prosecutions would lead to suppression of the book in question. The eventual result was, of course, that such prosecutions ceased altogether, around the same time that the Motion Picture Production Code was finally being replaced by the Ratings Code in the United States, and the inheritors of the Vice Society mantle became increasingly preoccupied with nonliterary forms of objectionable material (of course, the Legion of Decency had already been exerting immense influence in Hollywood since before the Hays Code was instituted). Before 1957, conditions had been very different: whatever the individual outcome, obscenity cases, far from contributing to a free-speech snowball effect such as occurred in the late 1950s, had tended rather to spur both governmental and social forces to renewed efforts to control artistic production. Flaubert's victory made the suppression of some of Baudelaire's poems all but inevitable; the finding against Jonathan Cape in the British *Well of Loneliness* trial made publishers even less willing to take on books like *Lady Chatterley* and also discouraged others from attempting to tackle the subject of homosexuality; and so on. But in the 1950s things began changing rapidly.

Nabokov's novel, which he finished in 1954 and was unable at first to publish in the United States and therefore brought out in Paris in 1955, came along just before these matters reached a head, with the *Roth* case in the United States in 1957, and the revised Obscene Publications Act in England shortly thereafter, each of which resulted in the successive *Chatterley* decisions in the relevant countries. *Lolita* effectively broke the by-then established rules of rule-breaking, in that it diverged radically from the twentieth-century pattern of books that violated the bounds of acceptability with four-letter words and descriptions of sex acts. It bears as little resemblance to *Tropic of Cancer*, with the latter's wild antiartistry, as it does to the humorless didacticism of *The Well of Loneliness* or *Lady Chatterley's Lover*. And, although Nabokov considered *Ulysses* the greatest novel of the twentieth century, his own linguistic extravagance and adherence to the ideal of artistic integrity have little in common with the sort of formal experimentation increasingly favored by Joyce (his admiration for the Irish writer stops short at the defiantly experimental *Finnegans Wake*). In addition to the literary ways in which it differs from its censored predecessors, *Lolita* also offers an exception to the history of literary censorship in two further particulars: first, it is the only English-language work to have been banned for obscenity in France but not in America; and second, its subject—what Humbert Humbert, its narrator, lyrically calls "nympholepsy" or, more clinically, "pederosis," now known as pedophilia—has only become more taboo in the half-century since its initial publication.

Lolita has, bizarrely enough, the most in common with *The Well of Loneliness* in terms of the censorship history of "classic" works, in that both managed to offend solely on the basis of their subject matter and in the absence of either vulgar language or explicit descriptions of sexual encounters. (It is, in fact, more sexually graphic than Hall's novel—times had changed—but not by all that much, and in any case this was not the main problem.) Among other things, it is an extremely shifty parody of the sort of work most famously represented by *The Well*: a narrative manifesto pleading for tolerance of a sexual minority. "We are not sex fiends!" Humbert insists, explaining how inoffensive nympholepts are: "We do not rape as good soldiers do. We are unhappy, mild, dog-eyed gentlemen, sufficiently well integrated to control our urge in the presence of adults, but ready to give years and years of life for one chance to touch a nymphet" (88). Later on he refers to himself as "a pentapod monster" (284) while expressing his continued tender love for the lost Lolita and lamenting all the damage he did her. The tone veers disconcertingly between poignant romanticism and ferocious comedy, sometimes in the course of a single sentence. With the exception of a "Foreword" by an equally fictional psychologist, it is all delivered in the nympholeptic first person. Nabokov's most famous novel is in this way surely the ultimate test case for Flaubert's doctrine of the impersonality of the work of art (in terms of writing) and Proust's insistence (in terms of reading) that because it emanates from a different being from the social identity of the author, the work must be kept separate from the person of the artist. With publication of *Lolita* two new words entered the English language, *lolita* and *nymphet*—some forty years after the novel's initial appearance Amy Fisher, the teenage girl who tried to murder her auto-mechanic lover's wife, was immediately dubbed "Long Island Lolita"—and the previously respectable author suddenly became known as a connoisseur of little girls.

If *Ulysses* is, as I have maintained, the least likely of "dirty books" because of its lofty artistic pedigree and reader-defying obscurity, *Lolita* presents an equally odd case, for a number of reasons. Despite its recondite prose ("You can always count on a murderer for a fancy prose style," declares Humbert on the first page of his narrative), the novel is eminently readable, which in principle makes it all the more liable to corrupt. Since it is not merely *about* pedophilia but narrated by an undeniably charming, somewhat successful, and only ambiguously repentant pedophile, we find ourselves in even murkier waters. Nonetheless *Lolita* not only immediately became a *succès de scandale* but then, not long afterward, a classic as well. Ironically enough, especially given that its author initially tried to have the book published anonymously or under an assumed name for fear that, given its subject, it would otherwise cost him his position as professor of literature at Cornell, it has for decades regularly been taught in college and even high-school English classes.

Nabokov's novel also offers a singular case in the context of literary censorship history in its self-conscious display of references to that very history. We have seen that books such as *Madame Bovary* and *Ulysses* include their own internal meditations on the theme of censorship, but Nabokov goes much farther than either Flaubert or Joyce in this direction. *Lolita*'s "Foreword," ostensibly penned by one John Ray, Jr., Ph.D., ponderously places the text in the historical context of literary censorship, alluding for instance to Judge Woolsey's 1933 decision in the *Ulysses* case. Humbert's narrative itself, which he announces as having been written in a psychiatric observation ward and then in prison, is couched as a very long defense speech. It is larded from the first page with ironic imprecations to the "ladies and gentlemen" of an imaginary jury, whom he goes on to address with provocative variations such as "winged gentlemen" and "frigid gentlewomen" of the jury. Moreover, the novel as a whole deliberately foregrounds and dramatizes the subject that had been at the center of debates on literary censorship long before the trial of *Madame Bovary*: the corruption of the "young person." And finally, *Lolita* offers a strange contradiction in terms of the tenuous alliance between the notions of "realism" and "art for art's sake," which we have seen uneasily coexisting in the history of modern "obscene" literature. The novel courted censorship by taking on a subject so volatile in itself as to presuppose a moral response, as though it were a *Well of Loneliness* for pedophiles, while at the same time being written in such a way as to preclude that very sort of reading, demanding to be taken as High Art having nothing to do with morality.

Lolita not only takes into account the vagaries of artistic censorship in the twentieth century; its history also exemplifies them, sometimes in ways that its author could never have anticipated. It was at various points subject to time-honored forms of censorship, not only in terms of the French government's repeated suppressions but also in the shape of the 1962 Kubrick film, which by necessity—the Motion Picture Production Code was by this time on its last legs, but still in effect—changed the story in ways that recall what happened to *Madame Bovary* in Hollywood. The novel also encountered a form of suppression that was certainly not new in the 1950s but has since—as the history of *Lolita* itself demonstrates—come almost entirely to replace traditional varieties of censorship. This phenomenon, which might be called economic censorship, operates not through government enforcement but through the threat of financial harm as the result of real or imagined social pressure. It is a latter-day variation on the conventional effect that the threat of governmental censorship was meant to exert, and which we find in exemplary operation in the *Well of Loneliness* trial in England, the outcome of which discouraged all further such attempts for decades. Similarly, Nabokov had recourse to Maurice Girodias's Olympia Press in Paris when he was unable to find a publisher in the United States in the mid 1950s, because American publishers were afraid of being dragged into costly legal battles.

After *Lolita* had been published, and after the battles over *Lady Chatterley* and then *Tropic of Cancer* had been won in the United States, these conditions no longer obtained, but a new form of suppression took their place, this time operating chiefly in terms of film and television. (As we saw in the previous chapter, the ratings code includes its own, subtler, and more economically driven, forms of censorship: as when the films "Tropic of Cancer" and "Henry and June" were, in 1970 and 1990 respectively, both consigned to cinematic limbo because of X or NC-17 ratings.)

Whereas Kubrick's film version was subject to the strictures of the Production Code, when Adrian Lyne made his own movie of *Lolita* more than thirty years later he was unable to find an American distributor; they were all afraid of economic reprisals from boycott groups. As a result, something very similar to the initial fate of the novel occurred in the mid 1990s: the film was shown in Europe and elsewhere for more than a year before it finally became available in the United States—unrated, which might itself have guaranteed oblivion had it not by that time gained a measure of notoriety—after being bought by the Showtime cable network.

Once again, history repeats itself. As happened in the case of the Minnelli film of *Madame Bovary*, which ended up reproducing many of the conditions of Flaubert's trial in the very act of filming it, after the novel came out *Lolita* again encountered some of the same problems in cinematic form. Twice over, in fact, since there have been two films of *Lolita*, each of which entailed its own set of era-specific difficulties. Nabokov's novel, in any case, even more than Flaubert's, was asking for it: from the start it was destined to provoke history in the latter's most extravagantly self-repetitive inclinations. "Nympholepsy" turned out to be the perfect taboo subject for the second half of the twentieth century. In "On a Book Entitled *Lolita*," an essay he wrote to introduce the novel in 1957 before its publication in the United States and later appended to the text itself, Nabokov observes that

> there are at least three themes which are utterly taboo as far as most American publishers are concerned. The two others are: a Negro-White marriage which is a complete and glorious success resulting in lots of children and grandchildren; and the total atheist who lives a happy and useful life, and dies in his sleep at the age of 106. (314)

Times have changed a great deal since then, at least as concerns interracial marriage—the last miscegenation law was overturned in 1967—and even, although perhaps less so, atheism. Nabokov's two comparison examples now seem antiquated. (It is also true, of course, that these subjects would hardly make for blockbuster fiction, since tales of unhindered satisfaction are not notable for their literary interest, and the plot-elements outlined above would have to be confined to the final three pages.) Pedophilia is quite another story. That subject, almost alone among traditional targets of moral disapproval such as interracial marriage and homosexuality, continues to attract universal opprobrium; and, of course, fascination.[1] The JonBenet Ramsay case—its victim a bit too young even to Humbert's taste, but in all other respects a sort of grotesquely magnified Lolitian nightmare scenario (a nightmare's nightmare)—dominated the American media for years, bits of breaking nonnews still resurfacing in the supermarket tabloids almost a decade after the initial crime. The battlefield of representation has mostly shifted from literature and film to the internet and the intermittently Michael Jackson–fueled media, but the battle itself continues apace, not only in the United States but in general. (To cite one relevant if minor example, in the late 1990s a novel called *Rose Bonbon* was suppressed in France because it was felt to present an apologia for pedophilia.) In the late-twentieth- and early-twenty-first-century atmosphere of pedophilophobic fervor, with beauty pageants for the under-seven set and makeup and jewelry lines marketed directly to prepubescent girls at the same time that the pedophile is public enemy Number One, Nabokov's novel seems at once remarkably prescient and almost quaint.[2]

Lolita is the story of a nympholept and the nymphet who ultimately causes his downfall. Somewhat like the proverbial shoe fetishist who falls in love with a stiletto heel and to his consternation ends up with the woman who wears it, Humbert gets much more than he bargains for when his dreams of happy nympholepsy are miraculously made (barely pubescent) flesh. Early on in the narrative he explains his preoccupation:

> Now I wish to introduce the following idea. Between the age limits of nine and fourteen there occur maidens who, to certain bewitched travelers, twice or many times older than they, reveal their true nature which is not human, but nymphic (that is, demoniac); and these chosen creatures I propose to designate as "nymphets." (16)

He goes on to discuss, in taxonomic terms, the nuances of nymphetry: not all girls between these ages are nymphets; nymphets are by no means the young girls ordinarily designated as attractive; nor are they necessarily destined to turn into beautiful women. In short, common criteria do not apply. To the contrary: "You have to be an artist and a madman, a creature of infinite melancholy, with a bubble of hot poison in your loins and a super-voluptuous flame permanently aglow in your subtle spine" to discern the nymphet among her human playfellows (17). Nabokov thus stacks the deck against his novel almost from the beginning, ostensibly placing it in the Romantic, Millerian aesthetic-iconoclast tradition, with its identification between the artist and the madman-criminal. (Henry Miller himself, predictably enough, disliked *Lolita* when Girodias proudly gave him a copy of the Olympia Press edition; he considered it too literary.) Here, certainly, any accidental resemblance to Miller ends; Nabokov is if anything more Flaubertian than Flaubert himself, and Humbert represents not an autobiographical emanation of the author, but rather a carefully distilled creation along the lines of Emma Bovary. In these terms Nabokov was if anything more impersonal than Flaubert. He compared himself to Flaubert in shedding tears over the final scene of his novel, as his predecessor describes himself doing over Emma's death scene, but he apparently wept over some combination of Lolita's fate and his own prose, not his protagonist, and spent years saying the equivalent of "Humbert, ce n'est pas moi."

Humbert's proclamations, in any case, must obligatorily be taken with many grains of salt. For one thing, there is the foreword, which not only places the narrative in the context of twentieth-century literary censorship proceedings, but also explains, among other things, why Humbert addresses his readers throughout as "ladies and gentlemen of the jury." The pseudonymous author-within-the-novel of the story we are about to read, and which is straight-facedly presented as "Lolita, or the Confession of a White Widowed Male," is dead: he "died in legal captivity, of coronary thrombosis, on November 16, 1952, a few days before his trial was to start" (3).[3] The foreword does not explain what Humbert was on trial for, although the latter's opening pronouncement about the fancy prose style one may expect of murderers gives us a clue. Since Dr. Ray provides the reader with information about Lolita's fate only in highly coded form, we might be forgiven for imagining that Humbert is on trial for having killed her, since she is the only thing we know about him at the start, along with the criminal insanity that forms the interest of his case for the psychologist. The latter concludes his "foreword" with a bouquet of socio-psychologico-moral clichés that are ultimately destined to disconcert in this context, by paradoxical virtue of the fact that they are as familiar (with a few variations of vocabulary) to the twenty-first-century reader as they were in the mid 1950s:

> As a case history, "Lolita" will become, no doubt, a classic in psychiatric circles. As a work of art, it transcends its expiatory aspects; and still more important to us than scientific significance and literary worth, is the ethical impact the book should have on the serious reader; for in this poignant personal study there lurks a general lesson; the wayward child, the egotistical mother, the panting maniac—these are not only vivid characters in a unique story: they warn us of dangerous trends; they point out potent evils.

Dr. Ray ringingly concludes: "'Lolita' should make all of us—parents, social workers, educators—apply ourselves with still greater vigilance and vision to the task of bringing up a better generation in a safer world" (5–6). This moralistic discourse passes unnoticed, so used are we to its like, but once the reader has progressed into Humbert's narrative, with its persistent playing with the very same sort of hackneyed language, the foreword becomes retrospectively as suspect in its own way as the pedophile's story that follows. That is, to those who choose to read in this manner. Nabokov was playing with fire, since, in the absence of any clear authorial indication to the contrary, he ran the risk that readers would simply agree with Dr. Ray, or skip the foreword entirely, and condemn the whole for presenting the point of view of the pedophile, its artistry—we are on familiar ground—only increasing its nefarious potential. This was in fact what many readers, and reviewers, did. *Lolita* takes Flaubert's refusal to provide clear moral guidelines for the reader to its logical conclusion.[4]

Between the "foreword," with its proliferation of comfortable clichés, and Humbert's romantic explanation of nympholepsy, Nabokov introduces an element that makes all this even less easily assimilable into any extant literary pigeonhole. From the beginning of Humbert's narrative we learn that his nympholepsy is not merely some sort of inherent erotic variation; if this were the case the text as a whole would read something like *The Well of Loneliness* with an expanded version of Havelock Ellis's prefatory note attached. Instead, Humbert provides us from the start with a genealogy of his nympholeptic tendencies. Lolita had a predecessor, and this is presented as determining everything that follows. When he was himself a "faunlet," he explains, back in prelapsarian Europe, he loved, and was loved by, a nymphet, Annabel Leigh. Their fevered adolescent or preadolescent fumblings were cut short by importunate interruptions and then by her death from typhus (13). All this happened, we are repeatedly told, "in a princedom by the sea." Lest the inattentive reader have missed the numerous allusions to the poem by Edgar Allan Poe, the girl's name should clue him in: the entire determining prenympholepsy episode is one big reference to "Annabel Lee," Poe's 1849 poem about a girl the poet loved when "*She* was a child and *I* was a child, / In this kingdom by the sea." Envied by the "winged seraphs of Heaven," the girl in the poem, like the girl in the novel, dies, and the narrator of the poem, like that of the book, never gets over her death. Later on, among numerous other references to Poe, the narrator dubs himself "Mr. Edgar H. Humbert" (75).

Lolita was originally to be titled *Kingdom by the Sea*, which gives an idea of the capital importance accorded the poem in the novel's genesis. Since Nabokov dropped the idea, it may seem pedantic to insist on this point, but the "Annabel Lee" allusion is in fact crucial, especially coming as it does between John Ray, Jr.'s, incitement to further vigilance against panting maniacs, and Humbert's apologia for those same maniacs. The Poe references ensure that neither one of these accounts of the story can be taken at face value, since the determining factor in Humbert's nympholepsy turns out to be not so much a poignant memory as a literary allusion. (In any case, even if we wanted to take his explanation seriously, it makes little sense that a thwarted reciprocal youthful love affair would give rise to a perversion predicated not merely on age-limits but on predatory age-difference.) The identification of the original nymphet as

"Annabel Lee" makes the entire text into something very different from a moral tale; it becomes instead a vast game of literary and metaliterary reference. At least in principle, it is there to prevent the reader from doing precisely what he will inevitably do: that is, either identify with Humbert, or revile him, or both. *Lolita* has much in common with *Madame Bovary*, but especially this: both novels owe their considerable, and enduring, capacity to disturb to the fact that in both cases the reader is invited to identify with a central character who is at once repellent and attractive. We can neither claim nor entirely disavow our sympathy for Emma Bovary as she betrays her boring husband, neglects her daughter, is seduced by Rodolphe and seduces Léon; our ambivalence reaches its climax, along with hers, as she commits suicide. Similarly, Humbert forces us into an attitude of simultaneous repulsion and reluctant sympathy as he marries Lolita's mother in order not to lose his (initially chaste) contact with the nymphet. Once Charlotte is out of the picture—conveniently, but through no fault of his own—we can hardly blame him, even as we fully blame him, for taking Lolita off on a road trip; but by this time we have signed on for the duration. And finally, after she has been taken from him by "Aubrey McFate" (his term for destiny, the name of one of Lolita's classmates), in the person of Clare Quilty, an even less scrupulous version of himself, we are dragged along as nauseated but faintly cheering passengers on his quest for vengeance.

The general reader could hardly, of course, have been expected to understand *Lolita* as a giant literary game on the basis of Dr. Ray's platitudinous foreword and the Poe allusions. And if Nabokov rails against the stupidity of identificatory readings of literary works, it is because he well knew, if only from reading criticism and teaching undergraduates, that this is in fact how readers tend to read.[5] As he was aware, his novel was destined to be taken as what it is, in the main: the first-person narrative of a dedicated pedophile, with whom the reader is inevitably and uncomfortably led to identify. He remained in any case as resolutely uninterested in moral interpretations of his or any other work as he was in psychoanalytic explanations. Flaubertlike, he alternately claims great moral value for his novel ("please mark that it is a highly moral affair," he writes to the dubious Edmund Wilson in 1956) and rejects such considerations entirely.[6] Also in the tradition of Flaubert, Nabokov considers that art exists in a realm entirely separate from, and superior to, ordinary morality. Humbert, like *Madame Bovary*'s Rodolphe before him, uses this very sort of argument about the limitations of ordinary morality in order to justify his nefarious designs (unlike Rodolphe, he is aware of the duplicitousness of this claim; of course he is his novel's protagonist, Rodolphe a minor player). But Nabokov insists on disavowing any relation to morality in his work, distancing himself from his character even in terms of Humbert's sense that what he is doing is immoral. In 1966 a *Paris Review* interviewer asked Nabokov how he felt about "relationships between men of forty and girls very little older than Lolita," given that his "sense of the immorality of the relationship between Humbert Humbert and Lolita is very strong." The author responded: "No, it is not *my* sense of the immorality of the Humbert Humbert-Lolita relationship that is strong; it is Humbert's sense. *He* cares, I do not. *I* do not give a damn for public morals, in America or elsewhere."[7] He goes on to point out that "anyway, cases of men in their forties marrying girls in their teens or early twenties have no bearing on Lolita whatever. Humbert was fond of 'little girls'—not simply 'young girls'" (*Strong Opinions*, 93). His insistence on this distinction, which would repeatedly be glossed over (Amy Fisher was seventeen when she tried to murder her boyfriend's wife), is testimony to Nabokov's refusal even to acknowledge the ways in which Humbert's story could be assimilated into accepted cultural practice. Social commentary was strictly the last thing he had in mind.

Accordingly, when Maurice Girodias ran into trouble with the French government not long after publication of the Olympia Press edition of the novel and urged the author to join his legal campaign, Nabokov responded by refusing to get involved with what he referred to as "lolitigation," insisting: "My moral defense of the book is the book itself." He added that: "On the ethical plane, it is of supreme indifference to me what opinion French, British or any other courts, magistrates, or philistine readers in general, may have of my book" (*Selected Letters*, 210). (His other stated motivation for refusing to sue the French government was that he did not want to embarrass Cornell University.) Nonetheless, for whatever reason, he included from the start something that at least resembles the gesture of an author wishing to present potentially volatile plot-elements while avoiding censorship problems: before his narrator says a word, the reader is informed that he has gotten his comeuppance. It is as though Flaubert had begun *Madame Bovary* by announcing Emma's suicide and then recounting the rest in flashback form. This might conceivably have changed perceptions of the plot, but beginning at the end is a characteristically twentieth-century narrative technique. In *Lolita* the foreword reveals that Humbert is not only dead, but has died "in legal captivity" while waiting to be tried; that is, his happy career in nympholepsy has been cut short by the long arm of the law. It is just possible that this eminently moral introductory conclusion contributed to official decisions in both the United States and England not to seize the novel, but of course we will never know.

It seems unlikely that Humbert's death in incarceration is announced at the beginning as a move to avert censorship; rather it is an integral part of the false verisimilitude of the parodic foreword, a parody of a moral gesture. But the fact is that when we turn to his story it is with the awareness that he has committed premeditated murder, a capital crime, and will be sentenced accordingly.[8] Of course it is also true that, once under the spell of his narrative, we may well have a tendency to forget this, but the gesture has been made. Like Flaubert, Nabokov does give something resembling a nod to the traditional demand for punitive moral closure. Nabokov also pays homage to Flaubert, though, in sparing his protagonist the full consequences of his sins; we may well choose to decide that coronary thrombosis prior to sentencing is too soft a fate for Humbert, just as many readers apparently felt that messy suicide was more than Emma Bovary deserved. In both cases, the protagonists are their own worst enemies. Despite her best efforts, Emma does not have all that much of a good time along the way, and (as did not go unnoticed) offs herself not in a spirit of moral repentance but rather because she is not enjoying herself and cannot foresee a way to do so in future. Humbert's case is a bit more complicated. He is, certainly, much more self-aware than Flaubert's heroine and knows from the start that (as Proust, another of Nabokov's fetish-authors, puts it) the only true paradise is the one that has been lost. He knows that what he is doing is wrong, and what makes *Lolita* so ultimately poignant, what led Lionel Trilling to write in 1958 that "in recent fiction no lover has thought of his beloved with so much tenderness, no woman has been so charmingly evoked, in such grace and delicacy, as Lolita," is that while he starts out enraptured by her as a specimen, he ends up falling for her as a whole.[9]

Let us not, however, fall under Humbert's spell as thoroughly as Trilling seems to have. The fact is that it is hardly an accident if "no woman has been so charmingly evoked," since Lolita is not a woman at all: this is the point. Humbert is repelled by actual women, from his first wife, Valeria, who mutates before his horrified but resigned eyes from "a pale little gutter girl" into "a large, puffy, short-legged, big-breasted and practically brainless *baba*" (26), to Charlotte Haze, Lolita's mother, charitably described in the following manner: "The poor lady was in her middle thirties, she had a shiny forehead, plucked eyebrows and quite simple but not unattractive features of a type that may be defined as a weak solution of Marlene Dietrich" (37). In other words, Humbert recognizes Charlotte to be a perfectly respectable and even attractive example of her type; the problem is that he finds her type disgusting. He marries her to get at her daughter: a perfect plan, except that nympholepsy is unlike shoe fetishism in that nymphets are in the midst of metamorphosis; this is at once their charm and their flaw. They turn, fatally, into women. Relatedly, the great lure of the nymphet is her blend of the "demoniac" and of innocence, which—*Lolita* is the story of this—is irresistible only to the extent to which it can be defiled, after which it is no longer innocence, and therefore no longer desirable. But in addition to the paradox of innocence, the novel also plays out Humbert's own transformation, from primarily a nympholept (he reports that his experience does not cure him of this [257]) into a lolitaphile. Perhaps because she seems to him to be the reincarnation of Annabel Leigh, perhaps because she too has been taken away from him, this time not by death but by Clare Quilty, who is not only another nympholept but a devil-may-care, equal-opportunity pervert and pornographer to boot, in the end Humbert throws nympholepsy to the winds and sacrifices himself for a girl who is now seventeen—well beyond nymphet range—"with her ruined looks and her adult, rope-veined narrow hands and her goose-flesh white arms" (277). What is more, she is now married to a happily oblivious young man, and pregnant.

Nonetheless: "I insist the world know how much I loved my Lolita, *this* Lolita, pale and polluted, and big with another man's child" (278). He offers her the money that is her rightful inheritance from her mother's estate and begs her to go off with him; she misunderstands, thinking he wants to take her to a motel; he is appalled, gives her the money, and sets off to kill Quilty. The latter crime is the one that lands him in prison. Humbert's own estimation of his culpability is that he merits hard time for what he did to Lolita but should be acquitted for having rid the world of Quilty: "Had I come before myself I would have given Humbert at least thirty-five years for rape, and dismissed the rest of the charges" (308). It is in these expressions of culpability for what the reader too, presumably, considers to be the "real" crime, more than in the knowledge that Humbert is dead and was in any case in the hands of the law, that the novel's moral thrust appears to lie. Lest we may still be harboring doubts, just before Humbert is taken into custody, a lyrical passage fully establishes his moral gravitas: hearing the sounds of children playing in the valley below, he insists that "the hopelessly poignant thing was not Lolita's absence from my side, but the absence of her voice from that concord" (308). Thus he comes (better late than never) to realize that the real tragedy is not that Lolita has been taken away from him but that he has taken her childhood from her. The problem, obviously, with this genuinely moving scene is that it is the conclusion to a defense speech, and therefore comes as proof of the inevitable fact that we, the reader, have been hornswoggled into sympathizing and identifying with a self-identified murderous pedophile with an admittedly very fancy prose style.

The novel's ambiguity, along with the novel itself, reaches its climax at the conclusion to part 1. It is here that Humbert finally has his way with Lolita, or rather, unexpectedly, she has her way with him, in room 342 at the Enchanted Hunters Hotel. He has laboriously prepared—indeed has spent his entire adult life preparing—for this moment, which of course takes place in a manner very different from what he had imagined:

> Frigid gentlewomen of the jury! I had thought that months, perhaps years, would elapse before I dared to reveal myself to Dolores Haze; but by six she was wide awake, and by six-fifteen we were technically lovers. I am going to tell you something very strange: it was she who seduced me. (132)

Further on he adds: "Sensitive gentlewomen of the jury, I was not even her first lover" (135). She has already, it seems, learned about kissing from another girl and about sex from her summer camp's sole boy. Lolita's demoniac innocence leads her to regard sex as a game, the exclusive reserve of youth. ("What adults did for purposes of procreation was no business of hers" [133].) She is both completely unprepared and all too prepared for what Humbert has in store for her. Throughout the novel she vacillates between utter innocence and cagey experience. This is at once: (1) to be expected in a self-consciously modern adolescent; (2) not surprising in a young girl having an affair with her stepfather; and also, finally, (3) the product of Humbert's fantasies of his perfect nymphet, since all we ever know about Lolita is what he tells us.

Charlotte Haze has by now already been killed in a highly fortuitous car accident—this is what allows Humbert to put his Enchanted Hunters plan into motion—but Lolita does not yet know it. The short, single-paragraph concluding chapter to part 1, just after he tells her of her mother's death, is the novel's ambiguous apogee. After providing a catalogue of the items he buys her (e.g., "four books of comics, a box of candy, a box of sanitary pads, two cokes, a manicure set, a travel clock with a luminous dial," etc., the sanitary pads standing out in this banal list as mute, sinister testimony either to her incipient adulthood or to the damage he has done her, or both), he concludes the first of the novel's two parts with the following: "At the hotel we had separate rooms, but in the middle of the night she came sobbing into mine, and we made it up very gently. You see, she had absolutely nowhere else to go" (142). The tone of this last is entirely undecidable: "she had absolutely nowhere else to go" is obviously a testimony to his recognition of Lolita's utter helplessness, but this recognition may be taken as triumphant (she is at last firmly in my clutches), or else as poignantly empathic (she is helpless and in my care). "We made it up very gently" suggests that Humbert imagines her grief and despair to be reducible to some minor lovers' quarrel, which stacks the deck in favor of the former interpretation, while the opening "you see" implicitly calls the reader, whether or not a member of the jury, to witness the difficulty of his custodial predicament. However one chooses to read it, this passage exemplifies the ultimate difficulty of assigning any definitive ethical valence to the story of Lolita as told by Humbert.

In terms of the taxonomy I have tried to establish among moralists (Lawrence and Hall), immoralists (Baudelaire, following Sade), and amoralists (Flaubert and Joyce), Nabokov clearly fits the category of amoralist. In many ways he represents the apogee of this trend. He greatly resembles Flaubert, and also Wilde, in his constant insistence that art and morality have nothing to do with each other. Using language that recalls Wilde's pronouncement that no one could be harmed by a book because "art has no influence upon action," Nabokov declares that "a work of art has no importance whatever to society." His explanation, however, disavows any attempt to place him in the lineage of the most famous spokesman for literary aestheticism:

> Although I do not care for the slogan "art for art's sake"—because unfortunately such promoters of it as, for instance, Oscar Wilde and various dainty poets, were in reality rank moralists and didacticists—there can be no question that what makes a work of fiction safe from larvae and rust is not its social importance but its art, only its art.[10]

Nabokov thus wholeheartedly embraced the notion of art for art's sake, but would have liked to reject the phrase itself on the grounds that its proponents themselves dragged morality into the picture by the back door. (As it were: the attack on Wilde and his "dainty" poetic cohorts lends a flavor of homophobia to his dislike of this brand of aestheticism, thus leaving him open in turn to charges of moralism in his rejection of the perceived moralism of other amoralists.) His amoralism, in any case, is rendered all the more problematic by his tendency to play with these sorts of moral stances, masquerading alternatively as a sometimes moralistic immoralist (Humbert, whose attitude toward his own perversion vacillates between celebration and opprobrium) and as an earnest moralist (Dr. Ray).

He stacks the deck against a realistic (and therefore moralistic) reading of his novel by filling it with literary allusions. He marshals Dante and Beatrice, Petrarch and Laura, as well as Poe and his child-bride, as illustrious predecessors. Most importantly, with Annabel Leigh, literature takes the place of reality: from the start, therefore, literary reference replaces memory. In this way *Lolita* reveals the inherently moralistic nature of "realism" by taking on such a loaded subject as pedophilia. To the extent that the events in the novel are read as though they were occurring in life, they can only be condemned, even by their own protagonist. At the same time that the book baits the reader with a moral quandary, it does everything to preclude a flatly referential reading, and the literary allusions collectively form one of the major ways it does this. Flaubert himself, the antirealistic father of realism, is omnipresent, although in much subtler form than Poe. For instance, the consummate amoralist Quilty becomes "Uncle Gustave," and, more directly if less explicitly, when Lolita disguises her extracurricular activities as piano lessons her piano teacher is dubbed "Miss Emperor (as we French scholars may conveniently call her)" (202). The alert reader (or reader of the annotated edition) recognizes a reference to Mlle Lempereur, Emma Bovary's neglected piano teacher under whose innocent pretext she goes to Rouen for assignations with Léon. Thus Lolita's infidelities both take the same form as Emma's and are presented under their sign. Baudelaire too comes up, as when Humbert addresses his audience as "Reader! *Bruder!*" (262), a clear, if Germanicized, reference to "Au lecteur." Humbert dubs his car "Melmoth," a nod to Mathurin's 1820 gothic novel *Melmoth the Wanderer*, which had earlier supplied Oscar Wilde with the name under which he checked in to the Paris hotel where he died in 1899, Sebastian Melmoth. And, along with references to Lewis Carroll's *Alice* books, Proust (whom Nabokov revered), and Dostoevsky (whom he disliked), among others, Mérimée's *Carmen* reappears in many guises, including an insistently repeated popular song that seems to have been invented by the author.[11] (A full catalogue of these allusions would fill volumes, and in fact has; see Alfred Appel's *Annotated Lolita*, which he notes was the first annotated edition of a living author's work in English.)

In addition to this elaborate system of literary reference, which the casual reader (however brotherly) may not always be relied on to catch, Nabokov employs other techniques to circumvent realistic readings of Humbert's tale and place it squarely in the realm of the aesthetic. Names, for instance, often call attention to themselves as ludic inventions: Humbert Humbert is, Dr. Ray tells us, a self-inflicted pseudonym; Annabel Leigh (whose mother was the former Vanessa Van Ness) comes courtesy of Poe. Others are difficult to read as anything more than products of Humbert's sometimes allegorical imagination, like Mr. Swine, the unhelpful desk clerk at the Enchanted Hunters hotel. Much of this can be put down to Humbert's inventiveness; he eventually meets his match in Quilty, who leaves a trail of resonantly false names in hotel registers to bait his pursuer. The foreword tells us the names have been changed to protect the proverbially innocent. But this game spills over into the foreword itself: for instance, not only does the text contain an allusion to "explorer and psychoanalyst Melanie Weiss" (302), the pedestrian-sounding name meaning "black white," but Dr. Ray has already cited one Dr. Blanche Schwartzmann (5), which of course yields "white blackman." The fact that name play extends beyond Humbert's narrative, where it can be explained away as obviously fictional touches added to the telling of a supposedly true story, into the frame itself adds another obstacle to realistic reading.

Lolita strains verisimilitude on every level. It is filled with the most extravagantly unlikely of chance occurrences, the most obvious example being the accident that kills Charlotte at the very moment when she has discovered Humbert's secret and is about to reveal it to the world and take Lolita from him forever. He himself calls attention to this astounding piece of luck, especially given that he had earlier contemplated killing her but found himself unable to do so; presumably as a reward Aubrey McFate intervenes on his behalf. The plot also depends on another remarkable windfall that passes unnoticed in the general mayhem: Lolita appears to have no extended family whatsoever, not a single grandparent or aunt or uncle who might object to her being taken out of school on an extended joyride by her stepfather. And finally, what Humbert calls "the long hairy arm of coincidence" is in ostentatious evidence everywhere. Since the overuse of coincidence in literature has at least since the advent of realism been viewed as a crime against verisimilitude and therefore the very hallmark of narrative vulgarity—a credulity-taxing mainstay of the newspaper *feuilleton* and later on of its inheritor, soap opera—Nabokov's open allegiance to coincidence is bound to disconcert. All the way back to Aristotle's *Poetics* the good plot is one that avoids the merely possible and sticks to the probable. But Nabokov is not aiming for classical tragedy; his book may well elicit both pity and terror, as Aristotle recommends, but in the end this is not what matters. The ultimate goal, for Nabokov, is not catharsis but "aesthetic bliss" (314).

Toward this end he tries to force his audience to forsake the habit of realistic reading. Humbert goes out of his way to draw our attention to the many coincidences that fill the text. As he takes pains to point out, for instance, 342 is at once the Haze address (342 Lawn Street), the room at the Enchanted Hunters in which he and Lolita first consummate their relationship, and the number of motels they stay in on their year-long road trip.* A full list of fortuitous accidents in *Lolita* would take up many pages; one further example should suffice to give an idea of the implications of Nabokovian coincidence. The summer camp to which Charlotte dispatches Lolita is called Camp Q in the novel; it is situated in a town with the unlikely name Climax, which is all by itself enough to raise readerly eyebrows. (In Kubrick's film, in which Quilty's role is expanded enough to dispense with such details, the institution itself is called Camp Climax, which somehow made it past the MPAA censors.)[12] "Q," sometimes spelled "Cue," is later revealed to be Quilty's nickname; the fact that it is also the name of the camp Lolita is sent to, locus of her first loss of innocence, can

---

* I feel compelled to add that when I first taught *Lolita*, my office was 342 Cabell Hall at the University of Virginia: the long hairy arm of coincidence thus reached out of the book into my office hours.

only be put down to an ostentatious system of verisimilitude-defying coincidence that the author later defined in his 1969 novel *Ada*: "Some law of logic," he writes, "should fix the number of coincidences, in a given domain, after which they cease to be coincidences, and form, instead, the living organism of a new truth."[13] Because this theory is being advanced in the context of a novel, of course, its formulation assumes coincidence to be the fruit of pure chance, whereas fictional coincidence is the work of the author, not Aubrey McFate himself but his metafictional counterpart. Too much coincidence reveals the presence of the author as puppeteer, which negates realism. The new truth of which coincidence is a living organism is evidently the work of art itself.

It is here that we see Nabokov's full debt to Flaubert: the book is the universe in which the author plays his godlike role, present everywhere; but Nabokov goes one step beyond Flaubert, in making him visible almost everywhere as well.[14] Through such elements as the omnipresence of implausible coincidence and the literary allusions without an understanding of which the text can only be read as a scabrous story of pedophilia, Nabokov makes it all but impossible to read his novel as a representation of reality and therefore with its moral implications in mind. All but impossible, that is, and yet somehow probable. Flaubert was horrified by this sort of reading, which was even more obligatory in the 1850s than a century later. As we have seen, every contemporary commentator except Baudelaire read the story of Emma Bovary for either its moral or its immoral value. A century later, reactions to *Lolita* make it clear that things had not changed all that much, in this regard at least, in the interim. Reviewers still tended to come down on either side of the moral divide, but the Baudelaire variant had gained ground. Because both realism and art for art's sake had become commonly accepted values, even if still regarded with a certain amount of suspicion in extreme cases like that of *Lolita*, reactions were nuanced, sometimes borrowing elements from all available categories.

Ironically enough, "realism," with its emphasis on the sordid details of life rather than idealistic depiction, had only solidified the tendency to read for moral value. Moral value had simply been displaced, with a new emphasis on social concerns. Zola, who took up the mantle of "realism" in the guise of "naturalism," makes it impossible to read his novels otherwise; like earlier nineteenth-century writers such as Balzac, Hugo, and Dickens, he attaches implicit moral labels to all his characters: so that we may get on with the story without any room for distracting confusion or ambiguity, and relatedly, so that the story may include its moral, whether or not we choose to read it primarily in that light. Their worlds include coincidence, but it is coincidence of the "realistic" variety, kept under control so as to avoid calling attention to the author as author and to retain the illusion of an ultimately deistic system, in which traditional moral values, with the addition of social conscience, obtain. Even more flagrantly than Flaubert, Nabokov refuses to play by these rules. He may kill off his nympholept, but he also kills off his nymphet; nor does he do so in the melodramatic manner of Dickens offing Little Nell.[15] He takes his cue from Flaubert in presenting a universe in which God has been quite evidently replaced by the author, a deity interested in dispensing aesthetic rather than moral justice. In short, Nabokov is a fundamentalist of the Flaubertian school of literary theology. At the same time, though, as he must have anticipated, the subject he chose to address in *Lolita* made it unlikely that most readers would accord the book anything other than a moralistic reading.

It is no wonder, then, that opinions were so wildly divergent from the start. Edmund Wilson wrote the following to Nabokov in November 1954: "Nasty subjects may make fine books, but I don't feel you have gotten away with this. It isn't merely that the characters and the situations are repulsive in themselves, but that, presented on this scale, they seem quite unreal." While giving a nod to art for art's sake, Wilson therefore objected to the novel on grounds of both morality and verisimilitude. (To the publisher Jason Epstein he said simply: "It's repulsive.")[16] He also included along with this letter opinions of the book written by his wife, Elena Wilson, and his ex-wife, the writer Mary McCarthy. The former liked the book a great deal (her husband put this down to her being Russian) and didn't see why it should be any more shocking than "all the new commonplace 'études of other unpleasant moeurs.' These peculiar tastes are surely as prevalent even if they haven't been written about as often." (The reference is to the Balzacian trend of *études de moeurs*, quasi-sociological novelistic studies of social mores.) After suggesting it should perhaps be published abroad and then brought back to the United States in expurgated form, she concludes: "In other words, I couldn't put the book down and think it is very important." McCarthy's judgment was neither damning nor very positive, occupying "a midway position"; she found the book "mystifying" and "enigmatic" but "thought the writing was terribly sloppy all through."[17] Thus in one envelope the author received the three basic reactions the novel would continue to elicit for some time: repulsive; important; puzzling.

Lolita was Nabokov's twelfth novel. He was already the author of a number of well-received works in both English and Russian and in various genres when he wrote the book for which he gained notoriety and enduring fame. Born in St. Petersburg in 1899, he left Russia shortly after the revolution, was educated at Cambridge in England, and then spent eighteen years based in the Russian émigré colony in Berlin, writing novels in Russian and living off private lessons in English, French, tennis, and boxing, as well as giving lectures and readings, before emigrating to the United States in 1940. He taught Russian and comparative literature for some twenty years at various colleges, notably Wellesley and Cornell, while continuing to write novels and criticism, gradually transforming himself into an American author. He began writing his first English novel, *The Real Life of Sebastian Knight*, even before reemigrating. (All this in addition to his famously keen interest in entomology in general and lepidoptery in particular; he retained for some time, while teaching literature at Wellesley and for a time at Harvard, a research fellowship at the latter institution's Museum of Comparative Zoology.) By the time he wrote *Lolita* he was also regularly publishing pieces, both fiction and nonfiction, in prominent periodicals such as *The New Yorker* and *The Atlantic*.

Nothing that he had written up to that point had prepared his friends, acquaintances, or readers for *Lolita*. Nabokov moved in circles that reviled censorship. He was of course radically opposed to the Soviet regime that had caused his family's expulsion from Russia (this was a great bone of contention between him and various interlocutors, Wilson, for one, given the American intelligentsia's wavering on the subject of the Soviet Union, especially during the McCarthy era), and therefore railed regularly against the censorship that prevented his own works from seeing the light in his native country. But there was also censorship in America, brought home with especial clarity by the fact that Doubleday had been prosecuted on obscenity charges over Wilson's *Memoirs of Hecate County*, a collection of interconnected stories, shortly following its publication in 1946. The case against the book, which contained a certain amount of explicit description of adulterous goings-on in East Coast suburban circles, made its way to the Supreme Court, where its suppression on grounds of obscenity was upheld in 1948.[18] It was in large part the example of *Memoirs of Hecate County* that made publishers wary of taking on *Lolita* when Nabokov first sought to bring it out in early 1954.

He was well aware of the dangers involved, referring to the book as "a timebomb" in a letter to James Laughlin asking him whether New Directions would be interested in publishing it.[19] Even aside from the obvious reasons for the trouble he had finding an American publisher for the novel when he first set out to do so in 1954, there was the additional complication that Nabokov initially insisted on bringing it out anonymously, or under a pseudonym.[20] Taking infinite (and vain) precautions as to who might have access to the reading copy of the manuscript, in the end he submitted it to four American publishers: Pascal Covici of Viking, Laughlin of New Directions, Wallace Brockway of Simon and Schuster, and Roger Straus of Farrar, Straus, Young. Covici predicted that all involved would "go to jail if the thing were published."[21] Laughlin had already published a number of Nabokov's books, but as with *Tropic of Cancer*, he was unwilling to drag New Directions into a messy and expensive court case. Brockway reported that his colleagues regarded the book as pornographic and suggested Nabokov try Grove Press. Straus was impressed by *Lolita* and proposed to publish it, but in the end withdrew his offer when Nabokov refused to consider signing his name to it. Assuming legal proceedings to be all but inevitable, Straus felt that anonymity would make the case hopeless: without the possibility of defending it by invoking the author's good name and reputation, he had little chance of convincing the authorities that the book was anything other than opportunistic pornography.

The New Yorker, where he had placed many pieces, also declined the opportunity to publish any part of the book. After it had been turned down by all the above, Edmund Wilson, despite his misgivings, tried to help his friend publish the book by passing it along to Jason Epstein, then a rising star at Doubleday, which had brought out *Memoirs of Hecate County*. Epstein loved the novel, as did his editor-in-chief, and they were delighted at the prospect of publishing such a brilliant and innovative work. The president of the company, however, with the memory of the large amount of money squandered on Wilson's novel still fresh, refused even to read the novel, and that was that. Epstein resigned his position at Doubleday, in part over *Lolita*.[22] Nabokov did not try Barney Rosset's fledgling Grove Press, as Brockway had suggested. He does not record his reasons for this, but presumably he found the idea of a young publisher eager to take on the censors distasteful. If he had approached Rosset, who was shortly to tie up the courts with *Lady Chatterley*, *Tropic of Cancer* and a variety of other works, the history of literary censorship proceedings might have been considerably different; but then this very prospect was doubtless part of what dissuaded him. Nabokov wanted *Lolita* to be considered exclusively as art, not a test case for censorship laws. If this was indeed his reason for not trying Grove, Aubrey McFate was having a laugh at his expense, as he ended up publishing the novel with Maurice Girodias, under the imprint of the Olympia Press.

Nabokov later claimed that he had had no idea Girodias was a purveyor of pornography; he had been misled by the Éditions du Chêne imprint, under which Girodias published fine art books. Whether or not this is true, relations between Nabokov and Girodias quickly turned sour, and conflicts dragged on nastily for years, but in the beginning their joint venture was a happy one. Nabokov was delighted to see his *Lolita* in print; Girodias was convinced—rightly as it turned out—that he had found his own Joyce in Nabokov, as his father, Jack Kahane, had discovered his in Henry Miller. (Before arriving at Olympia, Nabokov, like Lawrence and Miller before him, had tried to get Sylvia Beach to publish his magnum opus; but she was resolutely a one-masterpiece woman.) In an essay written long after his relations with the author had become acrimonious, accordingly titled "A Sad, Ungraceful History of *Lolita*," Girodias recounts that he was from the start enthralled by the novel, with "its near absolute perfection. I was struck with wonder, carried away by this unbelievable phenomenon: the apparently effortless transposition of the rich Russian literary tradition into modern English fiction," he writes. Relations between author and publisher degenerated largely as a result of predictable financial conflict over control of international rights, but what comes next in Girodias's encomium to *Lolita* gives us a clue as to the ideological differences that also played a not inconsiderable role in their battles:

> This was, in itself, an exercise in genius; but the story was a rather magical demonstration of something about which I had so often dreamed, but never found: the treatment of one of the major forbidden human passions in a manner both completely sincere and absolutely legitimate. I sensed that *Lolita* would become the one great modern work of art to demonstrate once and for all the futility of moral censorship, and the indispensable role of passion in literature.[23]

In July 1955, while relations between the two were still sunnily cordial, Nabokov wrote the following optimistic note in a letter to Girodias: "You and I know that LOLITA is a serious book with a serious purpose. I hope the public will accept it as such. A *succès de scandale* would distress me."[24] He was in a sense right: both he and Girodias took the work to be a serious book with a serious purpose; however, they diverged wildly as to what that purpose was. In his autobiography Girodias makes it even clearer that he took *Lolita* to be at once a work of artistic genius and a defense and illustration of one sexual taboo among others. He is neither shocked by its depiction of "nympholepsy" nor much inclined to take seriously its claims to be a particularly objectionable perversion in its own right. This was partly because, as a career pornographer, he was hardly inclined to take a stance of moral opprobrium toward even the most exotic of sexual inclinations. It was also, though, because he read the book not for the finer nuances of nympholepsy but rather as the story of a man who likes young girls, which he found perfectly comprehensible. He recounts that even before reading the book, on the strength of its description alone, he spent the night dreaming of young Lolitas.[25] His attitude toward the novel is double, with both aspects exemplifying the ways the author did not want his book to be read. He sees it as describing a perfectly comprehensible desire to have sex with young girls, thus glossing over the truly perverse nature of nympholepsy, which, as the author and narrator alike take pains to point out, involves not young girls but *little* girls, an entirely different category. At the same time he is happy to take on the book as the defense of a true perversion, one that does not seem to interest him personally.

Girodias was Nabokov's nightmare publisher, for both these reasons.

He read the book not morally but *immorally*. He was much too willing to understand and forgive Humbert Humbert, on two seemingly contradictory grounds at once. The author wanted his book greeted as a work of genius, and the publisher did that too, but given his excessive enthusiasm for the novel's theme Girodias's sympathetic reading must have appalled Nabokov much more than Edmund Wilson's expressions of horror. Even the idea that the novel was a repulsive, nefarious expression of a perverted mind could scarcely have been more unwelcome than the related notions that it was both fertile grounds for fantasy and a liberatory argument for acceptance of pedophilia. Girodias greeted *Lolita* as though it were a cross between *Ulysses* ("an exercise in genius") and *The Well of Loneliness* (an apologia for "a major forbidden human passion"). That is, he read it as a brilliant work of sociosexual realism. Nabokov did not recognize the existence of such a category. He wanted his novel to be taken purely as a work of art, but he found himself caught between the Scylla of American publishers' refusal to take on such an incendiary subject and the Charybdis of Olympia Press's cheerfully pornographic Traveler's Companion series, pitched to the English-speaking tourist and military market in Europe. The only publisher willing to take on the novel under Nabokov's terms— although he did manage, with the help of the author's literary agent, to convince him to sign his name to it—was, like it or not, chiefly a publisher of pornographic works.

But not only that: the mission of Girodias's Olympia Press, and his father Jack Kahane's Obelisk Press, its precedent, deserves a bit of comment. Both Kahane in the 1920s and 1930s and Girodias after him pursued an occupation that inadvertently harked back to the eighteenth century with its confusion of the pornographic and the "philosophical." Girodias himself explained his professional modus operandi, modeled on his father's, as publishing works of avant-garde literature—his eventual list included not just Miller and Nabokov but also works by Samuel Beckett, Jean Genet, Lawrence Durrell, William S. Burroughs, Georges Bataille—while financing this end of the business by publishing straightforward pornography. "I had made an absurd bet, associating the discovery and launching of avant-garde literature with a financial backing of pornography—and the relation between these two enterprises was to hold many surprises," as he puts it in his memoirs.[26] He retained an impressive stable of pornographers who churned out prose to order. His expedient method of operation involved publishing lists of forthcoming titles, taking orders for individual works, and then hiring writers to crank out works more or less corresponding to the titles in question (e.g., *The Sexual Life of Robinson Crusoe*; *Scream, My Darling, Scream*; *With Open Mouth*). In this manner he became the publisher of a great many forgettable "dirty books," but it is notable that, like his eighteenth-century forebears, he also succeeded in fostering a number of examples of the emerging hybrid genre of avant-garde "dirty books." In *Lolita*, especially—it was his great money-maker—Girodias succeeded in bringing together his two lines in a way that may well have distressed the naïve author but was fully in accord with the general trend of cutting-edge mid-twentieth-century literature.

There were in the end two basic problems between Nabokov and Girodias. The more obvious was practical and would probably have arisen even if both had not been highly difficult characters. The Olympia Press came along to rescue *Lolita* when no one else was willing to publish it, and for that Nabokov was grateful. Once the book became famous Nabokov no longer needed Girodias and indeed ardently wanted to get rid of him, as he now represented both an obstacle to full control of international rights and an unwelcome reminder of the novel's unsavory beginnings. Girodias, however, considered himself to have discovered *Lolita* and, even aside from the large financial stakes, felt that his hand in midwifing it should be centrally acknowledged. Add to this the fact that not only was Nabokov extremely irascible, meticulous, and idiosyncratic in every detail concerning his own work, but Girodias tended to take a proprietary approach to the works he published (unsurprising, given his history of commissioning prose to order), and the stage was set for apocalyptic conflict (in fact the copyright struggles between Girodias and Nabokov were to drag on for almost fifteen years).

Underlying these evident grounds for disagreement, however, there seems also to have been a more subtle battle of wills taking place. Girodias repeatedly stated—and we may perhaps believe him in this at least, although he is the most unreliable of narrators—that he had not initially expected to make money from *Lolita*. For him, at least before Nabokov's novel came along, books were divided into two categories: those that made money (pornography), and those that did not make money but brought prestige (literature). Sylvia Beach had never made money from *Ulysses*; Jack Kahane had not made a fortune publishing Miller, and there was no reason to believe that things would change. *Lolita* apparently belonged to the category of books that brought not money but prestige. Within that rubric he made little distinction between *Ulysses* and *The Well of Loneliness*; he was no literary critic. Girodias was a pornographer with social-crusader and literary ambitions, and this was what Nabokov could never quite stomach. He could not abide the fact that his novel was brought out under the same imprint as such titles as *Debby's Bidet* or *Tender Thighs* (Nabokov's contemptuous although not inaccurate version of Traveler's Companion titles, which included *White Thighs*, although no titular bidets) nor did he appreciate Girodias's celebration of his novel as a pedophilic version of *The Well of Loneliness*.[27]

Once the Olympia Press version came out, in September 1955, things changed quickly. In December, Graham Greene unexpectedly named *Lolita* one of the three best books of the year in the London *Sunday Times*.[28] This generated a great deal of publicity for a novel that was not only unknown but unpublished and unpublishable in England. One of the by-products was a scathing article by John Gordon, James Douglas's successor as editor of *The Sunday Express*, the same right-wing newspaper that had prompted the *Well of Loneliness* trial with Douglas's famous pronouncement about the relative dangers of Hall's novel and prussic acid. Gordon took the "respectable" *Times* to task for "publicising pornography." In prose reminiscent of Douglas's in vehemence but lacking his predecessor's flair for invective, Gordon wrote, "On [Greene's] recommendation I bought *Lolita*. Without doubt it is the filthiest book I have ever read. Sheer unrestrained pornography. The central character is a pervert with a passion for debauching what he calls 'nymphets.' These, he explains, are girls aged from 11 to 14." Since the actual parameters of nymphethood as described by Humbert begin at nine, not eleven, it seems that either Gordon was either blinded by indignation as he read, or else had not actually read the book, which was in fact even more perverted than his fulminations suggest. He concludes, "The entire book is devoted to an exhaustive, uninhibited, and utterly disgusting description of his pursuits and successes. It is published in France. Anyone who published or sold it here would certainly go to prison."[29]

In the spirit of Huxley offering to provide Douglas with a child, a phial of prussic acid, and a copy of *The Well of Loneliness* in order to test his rhetoric, Greene responded by founding the John Gordon Society, the purpose of which was "to examine and if necessary to condemn all offensive books, plays, paintings, sculptures and ceramics." He went so far as to hold a meeting, attended by, among others, Christopher Isherwood, Angus Wilson, and A. J. Ayer, during which resolutions were passed on such matters as the need to keep Scrabble words clean. They also proposed inviting publishers to adorn books with the label "Banned by the John Gordon Society."[30] In the meantime Nabokov learned about the Greene-Gordon skirmish through a column in the *New York Times Book Review*, which mentioned the title of the book but not the name of its author. The British government had also taken notice of Gordon's diatribe, as well as the fact that the controversy had led to many copies of *Lolita* being privately imported across the Channel. Under the auspices of an International Agreement for the Repression of Obscene Publications, the Home Office approached the French government about looking into Girodias's activities; according to him this was not the first time, but it was not until then that the French police decided to do anything about it. Nabokov's novel and some twenty-five other works were seized and banned. Thus began what became known as *l'affaire Lolita*.

It was Girodias who came up with this sonorous term, which was meant to recall both what the French press had dubbed *l'affaire Miller,* when *Tropic of Cancer* was banned a decade earlier, and also, most important, the Dreyfus Affair. Girodias's sense of publicity and personal grandeur was such that he did not hesitate to compare himself to Zola in the latter's campaign to free Captain Dreyfus, wrongly accused of treason in the 1890s.[31] He should, however, be given his due: throughout his legal troubles he took on the French government with admirable tenacity, and ultimate success. In the first instance he argued that the 1949 law under which his books had been banned was being wrongly applied, having originally been framed to suppress foreign works of a politically seditious character. In April 1957 he published a pamphlet, *L'affaire Lolita: Défense de l'écrivain,* in order to drum up support for his case. As we have seen, Nabokov was unwilling to provide much help, but he did offer an essay about the book which he had written for a special edition of *The Anchor Review* that Jason Epstein was putting together to further the cause of the novel in America: "On a Book Entitled *Lolita,*" now included in the book itself. *L'affaire Lolita* contained this essay, excerpts from the novel, an essay by Girodias comparing it to *Ulysses,* and some documents about censorship, all in French. A few months later *The Anchor Review* published Nabokov's essay, together with excerpts from the novel amounting to almost a third of the text, and a laudatory article by the literary critic F. W. Dupee. *Lolita* was well on its way to international success.

Remarkably enough, Girodias won his case against the French government. In the meantime, spurred on by Raymond Queneau (who went on to publish his own vaguely *Lolita*-like *Zazie dans le métro* in 1959), the preeminent publisher Gallimard had contracted to bring out a French version of the novel. The translator they hired was Eric Kahane, Girodias's younger brother, who translated all the texts for *L'affaire Lolita.* In May 1958, however, the Fourth Republic fell, and under General de Gaulle's new regime the minister of the interior appealed the Paris Tribunal's previous verdict in the Olympia Press case. *Lolita* was once again banned in France. Girodias now countersued, for damages, on the basis that his equal rights were being violated by the fact that Gallimard's translation was being published unmolested, while his English-language version was banned. He was eventually called to the ministry of the interior and told that the ban would be lifted if he desisted from his claim of damages. He agreed, and the book circulated in both English and French versions in France, with of course, a thriving private export trade as well.

While all this was going on, Nabokov continued to assume an attitude of regal indifference. By this time his motivations included not merely a refusal to care about what various "Philistines" thought about his novel but also his discovery of a clause in French law under which, if the publisher went out of business or was otherwise unable to distribute the book, all rights reverted to the author. Since at this point it had become clear that *Lolita* would, sooner rather than later, be published in the United States—two copies had been seized by Customs and then let go, which augured well, even if it did not constitute legal precedent—and that when it was published it was likely to become a bestseller—all this meant that Nabokov could only benefit if Girodias lost his case. As it was, while a number of publishers began expressing keen interest after the Greene-Gordon controversy in England, since reprint rights were shared between Nabokov and the Olympia Press, negotiations continued for some time. Walter Minton of Putnam's eventually won the prize, after a trip to Paris to mollify Girodias. (Minton brought with him Rosemary Ridgewell, the Copacabana showgirl who had first called the book to his attention, having read the *Anchor Review* issue, and to whom he had promised a share of the proceeds as finder's fee; she ended up going off with Girodias himself to complete her Paris tour.)

The Putnam's edition of the book came out in August 1958. Within three weeks a hundred thousand copies had been sold, a rate previously achieved only by *Gone with the Wind* in 1936. *Lolita* quickly topped the bestseller lists. (After seven weeks it was, to Nabokov's intense irritation, dethroned by *Doctor Zhivago*, for which he had great disdain.) Reviews were mixed, along the same lines as the three opinions Wilson had sent Nabokov in 1954: they were variously laudatory, damning, and perplexed. The *New York Times* came down squarely on both sides of the fence, publishing divergent opinions in successive editions. On August 17, in the Sunday *Book Review*, Elizabeth Janeway wrote:

> The first time I read *Lolita* I thought it was one of the funniest books I'd ever come on. . . . The second time I read it, uncut, I thought it was one of the saddest. . . . Humbert is every man who is driven by desire, wanting his Lolita so badly that it never occurs to him to consider her as a human being, or as anything but a dream-figment made flesh. . . . As for its pornographic content, I can think of few volumes more likely to quench the flames of lust than this exact and immediate description of its consequences. (Cited in Boyd, *Vladimir Nabokov*, 364.)

In other words, echoing Judge Woolsey's 1933 *Ulysses* decision, Janeway found the book to be not just compelling as art but also emetic rather than aphrodisiac. The next day, in the Monday edition, Orville Prescott disagreed, arguing that its emetic properties did not prevent it from being both pornographic and uninteresting:

> *Lolita*, then, is undeniably news in the world of books. Unfortunately, it is bad news. There are two equally serious reasons why it isn't worth any adult

reader's attention. The first is that it is dull, dull, dull in a pretentious, florid and archly fatuous fashion. The second is that it is repulsive. . . . Mr. Nabokov, whose English vocabulary would astound the editors of the Oxford English Dictionary, does not write cheap pornography. He writes highbrow pornography. Perhaps that is not his intention. . . . Nevertheless, *Lolita* is disgusting. (Cited in de Grazia, *Girls Lean Back Everywhere*, 253n.)

The *Times* then published a breakdown of reviews in the novel's first two weeks: of nineteen, eleven were positive, five negative, and three equivocal.[32] Among the many subsequent reviews offering divergent estimations, Dorothy Parker, writing in *Esquire*, found that *Lolita* was not pornography, "either sheer, unrestrained, or any other kind." She added that it was "a fine book, a distinguished book—alright then—a great book."[33] Several months later, a further item in the *Times Book Review*, in J. Donald Adams's column of October 26, 1958, weighed in on the negative side, suggesting that it was all at once artistic, emetic, nonpornographic, and to be recoiled from:

Here is admirable art expended on human trivia. Mr. Nabokov rightly insists that his book is not pornographic. I found it revolting, nevertheless, and was reminded of John Randolph's excoriation of Edward Livingston: "He is a man of splendid abilities but utterly corrupt. He shines and stinks like rotten mackerel by moonlight." (cited in de Grazia, *Girls Lean Back Everywhere*, 253n.)

The fact that it was generating controversy of this vehemence while avoiding censorship made the book even more of a hot item. British rights were bought early on by Weidenfeld and Nicolson, but publication was delayed as the revised Obscene Publications Act made its way through the parliamentary system before becoming law. Once again, *Lolita* came along just as things were changing—after *Roth* in the United States, after the proposal of the revised Act in the United Kingdom—but before they had definitively changed, that is, before the *Chatterley* trials in both countries. In this context there was a great deal of controversy around the publication of *Lolita*, accompanied by a great deal of uncertainty. Nigel Nicolson of Weidenfeld and Nicolson (son of Harold Nicolson and Vita Sackville-West and, later on, author of *Portrait of a Marriage*, which detailed his mother's affair with Virginia Woolf) was at the time not only a publisher but also Conservative Member of Parliament. As such he was under a great deal of pressure, and while taking part in public deliberations on the proposed law he also found himself forced to defend his firm's decision to publish the novel, which had been invoked during debate in Parliament. He wrote in the *Daily Express*, echoing at least a century of defense speeches, that "*Lolita* has a built-in condemnation of what it

describes."[34] Twenty-one prominent literary figures, including Isaiah
Berlin, Compton Mackenzie (of *Extraordinary Women* fame), Iris Murdoch,
V. S. Pritchett, Stephen Spender, and Angus Wilson, signed a letter to the
London Times objecting to the possibility that the novel might not see publication in England. The letter observes that "when to-day we read the proceedings against *Madame Bovary* or *Ulysses*—works genuinely found shocking by many of their contemporaries—it is Flaubert and Joyce whom we
admire, not the Public Prosecutors of the time."[35] When the Revised Obscene Publications Act finally became law it was still not clear that Weidenfeld and Nicolson would be able to go ahead with the novel; the attorney general had estimated chances of prosecution at 99 percent.[36] They
printed an initial run and submitted copies to the Home Office. It was not
until during a dinner to celebrate publication of the book that Nicolson
received word from a clerk in the Department of Public Prosecutions that
the Home Office would not prosecute. If the decision had been different,
twenty thousand copies of *Lolita* would have been destroyed; Weidenfeld
and Nicolson were apparently not prepared to test the new law.[37] Nicolson
climbed on a table to announce the news. He had already lost his seat in
Parliament in part because of the *Lolita* controversy, but the book sold out
on the day of publication.

Inevitably, there began to be talk of a movie. The otherwise astute Girodias, hardly imagining such a thing possible, had not bothered to argue
over film rights, so Nabokov and Walter Minton of Putnam's controlled
the rights. At first the author was reluctant to entertain the idea of a film
version; as he had earlier insisted that no image of a girl appear on the
cover of the book, he now balked at the idea of a young actress playing his
nymphet. He wrote that he would "veto the use of a real child. Let them
find a dwarfess."[38] A first proposal came from Stanley Kubrick and James
Harris, who hoped to persuade the author himself to write the screenplay.
The problem, of course, was that *Lolita* presented if anything more difficulties as a film than as a novel; without the texture of Nabokov's prose the
story is simply that of a man who likes little girls. Having consulted with
the MPAA censors, Kubrick and Harris decided that the only way to get
around the Production Code was to have Humbert and Lolita marry in the
end, with the blessing of an adult relative.

This may now seem grotesque, but at the time it must have appeared
entirely logical. Let us not forget that 1958, the year the novel appeared in
the United States, was also the year of *Gigi*, Vincente Minnelli's film version of the Lerner and Loewe musical based on Colette's story. *Gigi*, which
features Maurice Chevalier's unforgettable rendition of "Thank Heaven
for Little Girls," tells the story of Gaston Lachaille (Louis Jourdan, who
had earlier played Rodolphe in Minnelli's *Madame Bovary*), a man about
Humbert's age who falls for the eponymous little girl (Leslie Caron). In

the original she is fifteen, beyond nymphethood but still jailbait. Taken out of context the famous song, along with the scenes of girls playing in the background as Chevalier (Gaston's bachelor uncle, an elderly rake) sings it, seems to be a hymn to nympholepsy. And so it is, to a certain extent, but the refrains "They grow up in the most delightful way" and "For without them what would little boys do?" make the little girls into women. Moreover, the entire story insists on the fact that Gaston has known Gigi since she was an actual tot and until now has taken a purely avuncular interest in her; it is only when he suddenly sees her as all grown up that sparks fly. The little girls of the song turn out to be metaphorical enough to pass muster.

Minnelli ran into problems with the Production Office over the film and had to modify it repeatedly, but this was not so much because of its pedophilic overtones as because Colette's story hinges on the fact that Gigi is being raised to be a courtesan. The story was viewed as "too French," that is, too licentious in general.[39] The Production Code Administration had already refused to approve for American distribution a 1947 French film of *Gigi* on grounds that it "treated as acceptable what was essentially a form of prostitution."[40] Dore Schary of MGM initially declined to support a *Gigi* film proposal, but when the Broadway musical starring Audrey Hepburn turned out to be a hit, MGM took on the project, emphasizing the heroine's girlish innocence. Its saving grace was the conclusion: Gaston and Gigi get married, with the blessing of a number of adult relatives (all of them retired courtesans, as it happens, but this aspect was toned down somewhat). The Frenchness that made *Gigi* suspect also, in the end, saved it. While "Thank Heaven for Little Girls" became a huge hit, no one but Chevalier with his music-hall French accent ever attempted to record it. In the early 1970s Alan Jay Lerner, who had written the lyrics for not only *Gigi* but also *My Fair Lady* and *Camelot*, tried his hand at making a musical out of *Lolita*. *Lolita, My Love* was an embarrassing flop; Nabokov's story could not be stretched that far into acceptability.

Gigi was not the only story with nympholeptic overtones to have been made into a successful film in the years preceding *Lolita*. In 1947 Dore Schary, who would later hesitate over Gigi, produced *The Bachelor and the Bobby-Soxer*. This film starred Cary Grant (who was to become an obvious candidate to play Humbert, along with fellow suave Englishmen David Niven and Laurence Olivier) and Shirley Temple, formerly the world's most famous little girl. Its plot revolves around the remarkable premise of the womanizing painter Grant being forced, by order of a judge under the advice of a court psychiatrist, to pose as amorous teenager Temple's suitor (under the Hollywoodian reasoning that proximity will cure her of her crush). Grant plays along, but he is bored and repelled by having to fend off the girl's advances; at one point he says with heavy irony "that's great,

I'm recommended for children." He only has eyes for Myrna Loy, her much older sister, the spinster judge who acts in loco parentis. Viewed in the context of *Lolita, The Bachelor and the Bobby-Soxer* looks strangely like parody-by-anticipation. All the elements of Humbert's story are there (even if the seventeen-year-old girl is over the hill by his standards), in inverted form: the judge and the psychiatrist are the enforcers of pedophilia; Grant is an artist; he encourages the girl to choose a more age-appropriate partner; he has a rival in the assistant district attorney, who ineffectually taunts him; and, finally, he pretends to court the girl in order to get at her guardian. Like *Gigi, The Bachelor and the Bobby-Soxer* is a romantic comedy, and here too the faint whiff of pedophilia is allowable because subsumed in an overarching marriage narrative. At the end Grant and Loy are sent off on a plane together by the wily ministrations of Uncle Court Psychiatrist.

Kubrick and Harris's suggestion of having Humbert and Lolita marry at the end with the blessing of an adult relative thus makes perfect sense, as does Nabokov's adamant refusal to consider such a notion. The film project was shelved for the moment. The author's life had in any case changed irrevocably; he began to realize that far from putting an end to his teaching career through a scandal, as he had feared, the novel would instead put an end to his teaching career by freeing him from the financial need to teach. The situation had become clear in fall 1958: he asked for a leave of absence from Cornell as of the spring semester (it was granted, with the proviso that he find his own replacement). A year later, around the time he spurned the first Hollywood offer, he tendered his resignation. The novel's success would also, ironically enough—since in response to accusations that *Lolita* was anti-American he always indignantly protested that it represented his love affair with the English language and his most valiant effort to be an American writer (he declared himself "as American as April in Arizona")—eventually spur him to leave the United States definitively and take up residence in Switzerland, where he and his wife lived in a hotel for the rest of their lives.

Kubrick and Harris then made another offer to turn *Lolita* into a film, with Nabokov as screenwriter, and this time he accepted. The author is given sole credit for the screenplay, which was nominated for an Oscar. But resemblances between his adaptation and the final product are few and far between. The screenplay as it was eventually published is in fact a greatly reduced version of Nabokov's original effort, of which James Harris later noted, "You couldn't make it. You couldn't even *lift* it."[41] Nabokov enjoyed the result, while observing that it had little to do with his story (he seems not to have been much bothered by this because he had always maintained that he viewed the project in the light of money rather than art). Kubrick's *Lolita* is an excellent film, but it is not an excellent adaptation of the novel. Kubrick and Harris had gotten Nabokov to agree to the project (and to an actual girl playing the role of Lolita) because they agreed to drop the idea of having the characters marry at the end and try instead to produce something like a faithful version of the novel (they also offered almost twice the original fee, which played its part in changing the author's mind). But this was impossible, and so certain changes were made. The Annabel Leigh story, and with it all traces of the theory of nympholepsy, disappeared. As for Lolita herself, despite the fact that Sue Lyon was fourteen when cast, fifteen when the film was completed, she looks and acts sixteen or so; she resembles a sexier version of Shirley Temple as bobby-soxer.

In the novel she is twelve when Humbert first meets her; at fourteen she is his "aging mistress." In the film she becomes a teenager, and she has no predecessor, with the result that it tells the story of a man who quite understandably falls for a gorgeous young woman. In this sense it is Girodias's version of the story, or what *The Bachelor and the Bobby-Soxer* would have been had it remained true to the promise of its title. If he has to marry her mother, the unforgettably overbearing Shelley Winters, in order to get at her, this adds a risqué touch, certainly, but (in the words of Joe E. Brown proposing to Jack Lemmon at the end of *Some Like It Hot*) nobody's perfect. The film dispenses with the background story and includes the news of Humbert's coronary thrombosis while awaiting sentencing for the murder of Quilty, but this is the only death it announces, because its genre does not invite obituaries. Kubrick's version is a comedy, as no doubt it had to be. The casting choice of Peter Sellers as Quilty was instrumental in making it into an effective comedy. Sellers took the role and ran with it, transforming the story in the process, greatly expanding Quilty's presence, and making Humbert—James Mason, earlier seen as Gustave Flaubert—into a straight man. Screwball elements are also introduced at various points to pave over the potential danger zones, especially the Enchanted Hunters hotel room scene, in which a recalcitrant folding cot and vaudevillean bellhop intervene to thwart Humbert's evil designs and also distract the viewer from them. The film begins and ends with Quilty's death, thus establishing Humbert as a murderer. Because of Sellers's extravagantly camp performance, though, even the murder scene is comical. In the book Quilty is an unreal cipher, whereas in the Kubrick film he is a coolly manic jack-in-the-box, and his killing seems like nothing more than a grand guignol touch to round things out. The publicity campaign for the film featured the rhetorical question "How did they ever make a movie of LOLITA?"; Hollywood wags aptly responded: they didn't.

It was not until the 1990s that anyone was willing, or able, to attempt a faithful treatment of the novel. The irony of this is that by the time cinematic mores permitted an explicit treatment of the story's sexual dimension, pedophilia had become such a volatile subject that no one wanted to distribute the film. The director, Adrian Lyne, who had made *Flashdance, 9 1/2 Weeks, Fatal Attraction,* and *Indecent Proposal,* approached the story as romantic tragedy. His version of *Lolita* foregrounds precisely those elements that Kubrick left out, and vice versa. It is as if the two directors had split the very tone of the novel down the middle, taking the disconcerting mixture of satirical humor and poignant drama and wrenching these elements apart. It is not that Lyne's version lacks a sense of humor; there are some very funny moments in the film, but on the whole it is bathed in a romantic glow that precludes the sort of tension-relieving sharp satire that makes Nabokov's story bearable. Unlikely though it may seem, the comedy in the second film comes from the fact that Lyne takes pedophilia seriously. He too leaves out the theories of nympholepsy, while including the Annabel Leigh episode, bathed in an even warmer nostalgic aura than the rest. This means that the story is neither about a nympholept, as in the novel, nor about a man who understandably falls for a comely young woman, as in the first film, but rather about someone who cannot get over his past. Lacking Nabokovian style, at times it seems more Proust lite than Nabokov.

Its moments of humor depend on the fact that Dominique Swain as Lolita truly does come across as a child, so that when she swoons on Humbert's lap while reading the comics and we realize that they are having sex, the effect is disturbing; but when she noisily toys with a jawbreaker in the car we fully understand Humbert's evident desire to break her jaw. What is admirable about this film version (which received a very mixed press in both Europe and the United States) is that not only does Swain persuasively incarnate both the innocence of the early Lolita and her growing cynicism after she finds herself in Humbert's snare, Jeremy Irons's nuanced performance as Humbert also fully conveys the genuine paternal tenderness mixed in with his lubricity. (One memorable scene, absent from the book, is especially resonant on this score: Humbert looks on with a smile of great affection in which there is not a trace of sex as Lolita, who does not know she is being watched, sits on the floor in front of the open refrigerator spooning ice-cream from the container with one hand and eating raspberries off the fingertips of the other.) Lyne's movie manages to convey pedophilia from both perspectives: that of the violated child and that of the lubricious adult who finds himself suddenly in the coveted and dreaded position of full-time parent. The film's great flaw, ironically enough, is that it tries to present *Lolita* as it was written. The concluding scenes are emblematic in this regard: Humbert provides details that are both awful and resonant, such as the "big pink bubble with juvenile connotations" that forms on Quilty's lips as he is dying of multiple bullet wounds (304), which, when filmed, lose their resonance and become merely horrible to watch. Even Dmitri Nabokov, the author's son, who found Lyne's version "superb," felt that it was a bit too faithful to his father's original.[42] The cultural conditions that made a true cinematic version of *Lolita* possible also invited the filmmaker to overstep the bounds of Nabokov's vision.

Significantly, both films leave out nympholepsy; neither the word nor the idea is mentioned in either. In the early 1960s it would have been impossible to get a theory of perversion past the Production Code Administration, but this particular perversion turns out to have been just as unacceptable in the absence of formal censorship. Since the idea of nympholepsy is the very crux of the novel, *Lolita* is still, and perhaps always will be, unfilmable. One of the main reasons for this is the strange place Nabokov's story holds in relation to the history of censorship. Because it is all about the corruption of the Young Person, that figure no longer represents its hypothetical target of corruptibility. In principle the problem is not that the story will spawn potential Lolitas but potential Humberts.

In 1959 Philip Toynbee, one of the signatories of the letter to the *London Times* in support of the novel's publication, wrote an article for the *Observer* on "the *Lolita* question," in which he argued that the book should be suppressed if "a single little girl was likely to be seduced as a result of its publication," or if any could be proven to already have been seduced as a result of publication in the United States. No examples were forthcoming; Toynbee's point had been made.[43] When Kubrick's film came out, Sue Lyon was too young to attend the Los Angeles premiere of the film, which the Legion of Decency had succeeded in having recommended "for persons over 18 only"; in England, where the film was made, it was off limits to those under sixteen. Even in her older film incarnation, Lolita still represented the audience which had to be protected from films like "Lolita." But the peculiarity of the story is precisely that it nullifies the category "for adults only"; here adults are the source of the trouble. According to the logic of censorship which posits imitation as the sincerest form of corruption, the audience to be shielded from this work is the very category traditionally exempted from suspicion: highly educated men.

It is difficult to imagine twentieth-century literature, or for that matter popular culture, without *Lolita*. Even aside from the ubiquitous references to lolitas and nymphets, it has spawned, in addition to the two films, countless scholarly studies and also many literary parodies and spin-offs, from an Italian novel retelling the story from the girl's perspective (*Lolita's Diary* by Pia Pera), to Umberto Eco's pastiche "Granita," narrated by a man ("Umberto Umberto": Eco must have found the subject irresistible) fatally attracted to octogenarians.[44] The novel's publication was a life-changing event for its author in any number of ways. Not only was he was able to quit his academic job and move to a luxurious hotel in Switzerland, but many of his subsequent books became bestsellers, including his next novel, *Pale Fire* (1962), a work that does not, as its title might have led readers to hope, feature the confessions of an albino pyromaniac. Rather, it is almost as daunting as *Ulysses*: written in the form of a critical edition of a 999-line poem, its plot emerges through cross-references in the editor's annotations. There followed *Ada* (1969), less structurally challenging than *Pale Fire* but very long and complicated (a family tree is included to help the reader keep the characters straight); it makes beach reading for only the most intrepid sunbather. The tremendous success of *Lolita* allowed Nabokov to pursue both racy themes—homosexuality in *Pale Fire*, incest in *Ada*—and also literary complication, since each new novel was greeted as though it were another *Lolita*. (True to his adherence to aesthetic amoralism, Nabokov said about *Ada*, "I don't give a damn for incest one way or another. I merely like the 'bl' sound in siblings, blue, bliss, sable.")[45] The author remained known for nympholepsy rather than homosexuality or incest; nor did he harbor illusions as to what the journalists who beat a path to his door were looking for, telling a British journalist that he knew what the world wanted to find were the diaries that would reveal *Lolita* to be autobiographical.[46] No such document has ever come to light (Nabokov donated all his papers to the Library of Congress, but with the stricture that they be off limits for fifty years after his death and those of his family.) His predilections appear to have extended no farther than a special appreciation of certain of his Wellesley students: "He did like young girls. Just not *little* girls," observed a former student, interviewed by Stacy Schiff (*Véra*, 140).

This crucial distinction was to prove lost on posterity. "Lolita" and "nymphet" now refer almost invariably either to teenage girls long past Humbert's criteria or, when applied to prepubescents, designate their prematurely ostentatious sexuality, encouraged by makeup and clothing manufacturers. In both cases it is the aggressive sexuality of the girl that we see; the culture at large is nympholeptic. The fact that the novel continues to fascinate is surely a tribute both to its greatness and also to our enduring preoccupation with what we purport to revile the most: witness the ongoing Michael Jackson saga, Amy Fisher, JonBenet Ramsey. Witness also the cover of the Vintage paperback edition of the late 1990s and early years of the twenty-first century, which features the lower half of a classic schoolgirl, with feet in white socks and saddle shoes, topped by an abbreviated pleated skirt. The pose suggests a juvenile Marilyn Monroe on her subway grating, wearing a school uniform. This photograph encapsulates the erotic-innocence appeal of the nymphet, dewy childhood with an implicitly pornographic edge. In *Lolita*, novel and legend, we find the apotheosis of the Young Person, traditional object of the censors' protection, in all her dangerous corruptibility.

Epilogue

The Return of the Repressed

The greatest men, those of the first and most leading taste, will
not scruple adorning their private closets with nudities, though, in
compliance with vulgar prejudices they may not think them decent
decorations of the staircase or saloon.

John Cleland, *Fanny Hill*

I am in the habit of reading at breakfast, but I found that *Les 120 Journées*
was the only book that I could not face while eating.

Edmund Wilson, "The Documents on the Marquis de Sade"

In 1957, the year of the *Roth* decision and therefore the turning point
for the legal definition of obscenity in the United States, Jean-Jacques
Pauvert was convicted in France on approximately the same grounds
on which Flaubert and Baudelaire had been charged one hundred years
earlier. His crime was the publication of four novels by the Marquis de
Sade, three of which had originally been published in the 1790s. One of
the more unexpected turns taken by the history we have been considering
is that as that history was drawing to a close, as became all but inevitable
after the *Chatterley* trials, the last big literary obscenity trials in France and
the United States involved the publication of works dating from the eighteenth century. Both Sade's novels and John Cleland's *Memoirs of a Woman
of Pleasure*, more familiarly known as *Fanny Hill*, have now been fully canonized, easily available, for instance, in various "classic" editions in various
different languages. Much more than any of the works we have previously
dealt with, these books are pornographic according to almost anyone's
standards.

Almost anyone, that is, with the exception of those who have a professional stake in maintaining otherwise. In his preface to the Penguin Classics edition of *Fanny Hill*, for instance, Peter Wagner works hard to argue

221

that Cleland's work "deserves a place beside the novels of Richardson, Fielding, and Smollett" in the eighteenth-century canon (16). He also insists that if the novel "acquired a bad name and was relegated for more than two centuries to the realm of 'pornography', it was mainly because of the illustrations," which were added to later editions (15). (This last is a resourceful variant on the old line that one reads *Playboy* for the Nabokov interviews and not the pictures.) Similarly, many Sade scholars, taking a cue from Guillaume Apollinaire and, later on, intellectuals such as those who went to court to defend Pauvert's publication of Sade's works in 1957, argue that even the most sexually and violently explicit of his writings are not pornography but a hybrid of art and philosophy that is important in itself and also key to an understanding of the Enlightenment, human nature in general, and even some of the more horrifying events in twentieth-century history. To the casual reader, however, both *Fanny Hill* and most of Sade's works fall unmistakably under the rubric of hard-core pornography. These two cases represent, in their different ways, the final frontier of acceptable indecency. The fact that they have both been vigorously defended as nonpornographic demonstrates the extent to which even when apparently pornographic works become classic the categories of "pornography" and "classic" are still viewed as mutually exclusive.

Cleland's novel, first published in two volumes in 1748–49, was for a very long time the most famous pornographic novel in English. In mutual denunciations of their respective books as opportunistic pornography, for instance, Nabokov and Edmund Wilson each at different times accused the other of having written a new *Fanny Hill* in *Memoirs of Hecate County* and *Lolita* respectively. Cleland's work is pornographic not only in the colloquial use of the term but in the strict sense as well: "pornography" literally means "prostitute-writing"—that is, writing either about or by prostitutes—and Cleland's novel responds to both meanings suggested by this etymology.[1] Written in the form of a former prostitute's memoirs, it is an extended narrative of sexual activities of various sorts, alternatively participated in, observed by, or recounted to the eponymous narrator. It contains scenes of masturbation, lesbianism, sodomy, flagellation, fetishism, and general copulation. It contains, moreover, little else, although it is famously free of obscene language, employing throughout a charmingly (or offensively, depending on one's viewpoint) metaphorical vocabulary rich in "truncheons," "instruments," and "steeds" on the one hand, and "soft pleasure-conduits" and "genial seats of pleasure" on the other. *Fanny Hill* does not pretend to be anything other than what it is, except of course in the sense that it is a novel written by a man pretending to be the memoirs of a woman. In that sense it is part of a lineage going back at least to Defoe's *Moll Flanders* (1722), and forward to Arthur Golden's *Memoirs of a Geisha* (1997). It is also, among other things, one of the many parodies of

Pamela, Richardson's 1740 blockbuster novel of female virtue sorely tried. Henry Fielding had inaugurated the trend of anti-*Pamela*s in 1741 with *Shamela*, and then again the following year exploited the comical possi-bilites of male virtue sorely tried with the story of Pamela's brother, *Joseph Andrews*.

Cleland's novel makes a gesture toward epistolarity by taking the form of two very long letters (each of which took up a volume), recounting her beginnings as the daughter of honest but impoverished parents who die of smallpox, leaving her an orphan at fifteen. She makes her way to Lon-don with the intention of becoming a servant but is taken under the suc-cessive wings of two "bawds"; she is given thorough hands-on training by her new colleagues and embarks on a successful career as a "woman of pleasure." Fanny includes a nod to conventional morality in the form of an internal depiction-of-vice-in-the-service-of-virtue plea. "If you do me then justice," she writes at the end of her story, "you will esteem me perfectly consistent in the incense I burn to virtue: if I have painted vice in all its gayest colours, if I have decked it with flowers, it has been solely in order to make the worthier, the solemner, sacrifice of it to virtue" (224). Sade would later (however disingenuously) make a similar argument: the les-sons of virtue are lost if vice is not fully depicted.[2] By this time in her nar-rative, in any case, Fanny is in a good position to judge the relative merits of vice and virtue, since the conclusion finds her happily married to her true love, who is uncoincidentally the very man who had earlier deflow-ered her, and the mother of five legitimate children. She is also rich, hav-ing inherited the fortune of a benevolent protector. This conclusion is of course somewhat ambiguous or at least highly problematic in terms of conventional morality. Fanny firmly opts for love, sex within marriage, and bourgeois living, but while her story is perfunctorily one of virtue tri-umphant, "virtue" in this case is relative, it certainly cannot be taken as the euphemism for virginity that it most often served as in terms of female characters, and in any case an awful lot of vice is lengthily depicted along the way. It was this last that made *Fanny Hill* one of the most censored books in the history of English literature.

Cleland finished writing the novel in debtors' prison; it seems to have been his ticket out. Shortly after the two volumes were published (anony-mously: but anonymity was a different matter in the eighteenth century) under the title *Memoirs of a Woman of Pleasure*, he was arrested again as a re-sult of the book, charged with corrupting the king's subjects. He quickly produced a shorter, expurgated version; it was this book that originally bore the title *Fanny Hill*. Both sold extremely well. Cleland then followed up with a masculine version, *Memoirs of a Coxcomb* (1751), but this novel met with little success, and he turned to other forms of (hack) writing. He never again managed to capture the public's interest, and died penniless and obscure, *Fanny Hill* his only accomplishment of note. The decades following its publication saw many more editions of the book, some with illustrations that increased its already considerable pornographic aspect. It was translated into French as *La Fille de joie*. In 1821 it earned the distinction of being the first book to occasion an obscenity trial in the United States; its Boston publisher was sent to jail on the strength of a particular illustration as well as the text itself. No further attempts were made to publish the book openly in America—or anywhere else—until Walter Minton of Putnam's decided to bring out an unexpurgated edition not long after his firm had published *Lolita*.

Putnam's may have managed to avoid obscenity proceedings with Nabokov's novel, but *Fanny Hill* was a different matter. It was the subject of three trials, in New York, Massachussetts, and Hackensack, New Jersey, before the Massachussetts case made its way to the Supreme Court. The book was more difficult to defend than *Chatterley* or *Tropic*, according to Rembar, who defended all three, because of its overtly pornographic nature. One prosecution witness, a former army psychiatrist turned pediatrician who was also vice president of an organization called Citizens for Decent Literature, irately termed *Fanny Hill* "sex for sex's sake," and when asked whether in his opinion the book contained a philosophy, replied, "Yes, there is a philosophy of pleasure for pleasure's sake, hedonism" (Rembar, 350).[3] The variations on the phrase "art for art's sake" that Woolsey had started with his characterization of *Ulysses* as not representing "dirt for dirt's sake" had by this time become all but obligatory in arguments on both sides of these debates. Post *Roth*, in any case, the criteria of obscenity had changed, or rather were in the process of changing. The *Fanny Hill* case reaffirmed what was already implicit in the 1957 opinion: a philosophy of pleasure for pleasure's sake, or even a demonstration of sex for sex's sake, was not enough for a book to be found obscene and therefore censorable. Obscenity and pornography were no longer synonyms. This much became clear to the bemused spectators when, during the Supreme Court hearing, Justice Brennan raised a laugh by asking whether "well-written pornography" would, according to the defense argument, be outside the parameters of obscenity. Rembar responded by saying that "if by pornography your Honor means sexually arousing. . . . I think it has been clear for some time that material whose effect is to stimulate a sexual response in the normal person is not for that reason to be denounced" (457). Brennan could only agree; he had written the text that made this point clear.

One of the more remarkable aspects of the case was that the author of the groundbreaking opinion on which the defense's case depended, and who ended up writing the prevailing opinion in this case as well, had not actually read the book. Rembar's opening argument had noted that the very terms under which the book was previously found obscene conceded that it had some value. The lower court had not taken into account the value test set forth in *Roth*, and as a result inadvertently provided material for their own decision to be overturned even in the absence of knowledge of the work itself. Rembar therefore, with impressive audacity, suggested that the justices need not have bothered to read Cleland's novel in order to pronounce on the case, and Brennan admitted that in fact he had not read it (454). The defense gambit worked, and Brennan wrote the prevailing opinion in the *Fanny Hill* case. On March 21, 1966, the court reversed the Massachussetts decision to suppress the novel.

"Well-written pornography" was now constitutionally protected. By the same token, "well-written obscenity" became an oxymoron (436). This is what justifies Rembar's entitling his book *The End of Obscenity*: as a result of the *Roth* and *Fanny Hill* opinions, literary merit, which is what good writing is, obviates obscenity. During his Supreme Court argument he said: "Obscenity is worthless trash. That is its definition constitutionally" (467); and since none of the nine justices disagreed with him, it seems that this is what obscenity is, legally. The notion of "the end of obscenity," therefore, does not mean that worthless trash ceased being produced in 1966, but rather that actual literature, even the literature of sex for sex's sake, could no longer be put in the same category. The problem, of course, with this happy scenario, is that worthless trash is still in the eye of the beholder, just as pornography, as he puts it in one of his more memorable formulations, "is in the groin of the beholder" (492). Rembar, writing in 1967, concludes his book with the optimistic prediction that the end of literary obscenity would bring about the end of worthless trash itself, which as of the beginning of the twenty-first century has yet to come to pass (493). In any case, his complacent faith in the enduring legacy of Brennan's *Roth* opinion proved unfounded, as even Brennan himself later expressed doubts about the efficacy of his formulation.

In 1973, deciding on a pornography case known as *Miller v. California*, a Supreme Court with a somewhat different and more conservative cast of characters (among other changes, the chief justice was now Warren Burger rather than Earl Warren) replaced the "utterly without redeeming social value" test with the more restrictive idea that the First Amendment does not protect speech which "lacks *serious* literary, artistic, political, or scientific value." (Brennan dissented.) Moreover, the emphasis was now placed on local, rather than national, community standards of decency, on the theory, as expressed by Chief Justice Burger, that it was "neither realistic nor constitutionally sound to read the First Amendment as requiring that the people of Maine or Mississippi accept public depiction of conduct found tolerable in Las Vegas or New York City."[4] Despite these revised criteria, and despite vigorous congressional objection to a 1970 report by

the National Commission on Obscenity and Pornography (initiated under
the Johnson administration and unwelcome by the time Nixon was in office) which found no evidence that sexually explicit material promoted
crime or debauchery, the era of literary obscenity proceedings was over,
and pornographic material of all sorts became increasingly available.[5]

Among the consequences of the 1966 decision, Rembar notes, is that
the works of the Marquis de Sade, "openly published in unexpurgated
form for the first time, encountered no interference from the government" (488). This was not simply the result of the *Fanny Hill* case, though;
what had happened in France a few years earlier also played its part.
France's legal code had not changed much in terms of its definition of obscenity since offenses against public and religious morals had been
stricken from the books in 1881, leaving only *outrage aux bonnes moeurs*, a
vague category of moral offensiveness that could be extended to whatever
the government wished to suppress. Sade himself (1740–1814) had tested
the tolerance of successive regimes—Ancien Régime, the various stages
of the Revolution, Empire—in all spending more than a third of his life in
jail. Starting in his youth, he got into repeated trouble for his actions,
jailed, twice sentenced to death (at one point he was executed in effigy, as
he could not be found when the sentence was to be carried out), on
charges ranging from sodomy and attempted poisoning early on to *moder-
antisme* (insufficient revolutionary zeal) after he had been made a judge
during the revolution. He became a writer in prison, wrote many of his
works while incarcerated, and then once Napoleon came into power he
was again jailed for having written them.

Sade, who lent his name to the most damaging of perversions, is both
the consummate immoralist and also one of the most mythologized of authors, a Rorschach test for the zeitgeist. The translators' foreword to the
first openly published English edition of *Justine* begins, "That the marquis
de Sade *also* wrote books is a fact now known to almost everyone who
reads" (emphasis added), which suggests to what extent his books themselves are not the best-known part of his legacy. At the same time, that
legacy depends on his books. Without them he would have remained a
minor annoyance to his family, a number of unfortunate prostitutes, and
various governments. It was *Justine, ou les malheurs de la vertu*, published in
1791, that earned him both lasting notoriety and lasting imprisonment.
Justine was in fact written three times, the final *Nouvelle Justine* (1797)
much more violently explicit than the first. Sade was an exceptionally prolific author, doubtless in part because of the imposed leisure afforded him
in prison. Although he wrote both *La Nouvelle Justine* and its companion
piece, *Juliette*, while at liberty, *Les infortunes de la vertu*, which was what
started him on this trend, was a product of his stay in the Bastille. It is possible that had he been left to his own devices he would not have become

the father of sadism but rather a casual practitioner of cruelty. He also seems to have had a marked taste for what later, thanks to Leopold von Sacher-Masoch, author of *Venus in Furs*, became known as masochism. He always claimed that his monstrous imagination was given free rein in his writings only, and that in life, although he had been a great libertine, he was not, for instance, a murderer. We will never know whether this was in fact the case.

The first *Justine* (*Les infortunes de la vertu*), brought out anonymously (bearing a spurious Dutch imprint), was his first published work. The plot remains essentially the same from one version to the next, while the vocabulary, level of violence, and sexual explicitness is ratcheted up considerably, and the heroine is further victimized in *La Nouvelle Justine* by having her previously first-person narrative taken away from her, her misfortunes now recounted in the third person. All three published versions relate the story of a relentlessly virtuous girl subjected to equally relentless mistreatment; the final version describes her mistreatment at greater length and in extravagantly violent detail. It reads like an apocalyptic version of *Pollyanna*, or less anachronistically, like a pornographic female adaptation of *Candide* (Voltaire is referred to on the first page). Justine never loses her sunny outlook, but at the end of the novel she is felled by a bolt of lightning. The text concludes with an uplifting moral directive:

> O you who have wept tears upon hearing of Virtue's miseries; you who have been moved to sympathy for the woe-ridden Justine; the while forgiving the perhaps too heavy brushstrokes we have found ourselves compelled to employ, may you at least extract from this story the same moral which determined Madame de Lorsange!

Madame de Lorsange is Justine's sister, a negative (that is, in Sade's universe, positive), libertine version of our guileless heroine and the protagonist of his equally monumental *Histoire de Juliette, ou les prospérités du vice*, which was published along with *La Nouvelle Justine* in ten volumes in 1797. At the end of the first *Justine*, after her sister's immolation, Juliette is seen abjuring her ways, entering a convent, and becoming an example to her fellow Carmelite nuns (in *Juliette* the ending is different, and she does not convert). The moral concludes:

> May you be convinced, with her [Mme de Lorsange], that true happiness is to be found nowhere but in Virtue's womb, and that if, in keeping with designs it is not for us to fathom, God permits that it be persecuted on Earth, it is so that Virtue may be compensated by Heaven's most dazzling rewards.
>
> (743)

Even a work as extravagantly offensive as this carried its homage to conventional morality, although unlike the moral coda to *Fanny Hill*, this lesson is difficult to read other than ironically coming after the text of *Justine*. The edifying conclusion was obviously not enough to save the work its own author acknowledged to be immoral, and the ending of *Juliette* is emphatically anti-edifying. In 1801, both Sade and his publisher were arrested. The latter was released on condition that he turn over his stock of *Juliette*, but the writer was thrown into prison and eventually transferred to the Charenton asylum, where he spent the rest of his life.

Justine, with its catalogue of horrors inflicted on a comely, long-suffering heroine, was in its way entirely in keeping with one of the major currents in eighteenth-century fiction in both France and England. *Fanny Hill* is in fact much less typical than Sade's most famous novel, since all ends well for Cleland's heroine, who also manages to enjoy at least some of her adventures. The lightning bolt that ends Justine's travails may be a particularly Sadean touch (it is perhaps not a coincidence that this is also how Humbert's mother dies in *Lolita*), but in his general plotline the author was only taking a hackneyed formula and pushing it to its logical conclusion. From *Clarissa* to Diderot's *Religieuse* to Rousseau's *Nouvelle Héloïse* (which Sade considered one of the greatest of all novels), extended assaults on intransigently virtuous heroines were the hallmark of eighteenth-century literature, and things did not often end well for the beleaguered protagonists. (*Pamela* is an exception: she eventually marries her seducer, which is why her story is subtitled *Virtue Rewarded*.) *Justine* represents the culmination of this trend. Sade preserves the general shape of the standard assault-on-virtue novel; he departs from its conventions, however, in making the sexual violence entirely explicit, by the same token exposing the essentially pornographic underpinnings of the genre.[6]

During the nineteenth century Sade was quietly celebrated by writers such as Flaubert and Baudelaire. The latter wrote in his notebook, "One must always come back to Sade, that is, to *Natural* Man, to explain evil [Il faut toujours revenir à De Sade [*sic*], c'est-à-dire à l'*Homme Naturel*, pour expliquer le mal]" (*Œuvres complètes*, 1.595). Given the title and concerns of his magnum opus, we can only conclude that Baudelaire himself viewed Sade as a key to the understanding of his work. As for Flaubert, according to Edmond de Goncourt's *Journal* he talked endlessly about Sade, and among the books that corrupt Madame Bovary are "extravagant books containing orgiastic scenes with bloody situations [des livres extravagants où il y avait des tableaux orgiaques avec des situations sanglantes]," which is reminiscent of Sade and would appear to be a reference to the Gothic novels that took their cue from his works. (One shudders to contemplate what would have happened to Emma had the local lending library offered access to *Justine* or *Juliette*.) The influence of Sade on nineteenth-century literature was both deep and wide, but it was also mostly implicit.[7] It was not until the twentieth century that "the Divine Marquis" came into his own. In 1909 the poet Guillaume Apollinaire published *Œuvres du marquis de Sade, pages choisies*, an edited volume of necessarily expurgated selections from Sade's writings. This was the first attempt to publish Sade openly since the Revolution. In Apollinaire's much-cited preface he accurately predicts that the new century will provide Sade with the appreciation he had received neither during his lifetime nor for some hundred years subsequently: "It seems the time has come for these ideas that have ripened in the infamous atmosphere of library dungeons, and this man who appeared to count for nothing during the whole nineteenth century may well dominate the twentieth [Il semble que l'heure soit venue pour ces idées qui ont mûri dans l'atmosphère infâme des enfers des bibliothèques, et cet homme qui parut ne compter pour rien durant tout le XIXe siècle pourrait bien dominer le XXe]." The reference to "les enfers des bibliothèques" alludes to the French practice of locking up suspect works in a special section of libraries with restricted access, picturesquely called "enfer" or Hell; the "enfer" of the French National Library was where the editor had done his research.) Apollinaire then calls Sade "the freest spirit who ever existed [cet esprit le plus libre qui ait encore existé]," thus providing the terms under which he would be celebrated over the course of the next hundred years.[8]

The idea of Sade as the incarnation of liberty was to have a great deal of staying power. He was successively lauded by dadaists, surrealists, existentialists, structuralists, and poststructuralists, and as noted by Rembar, the "end of obscenity" only contributed to his status as a cultural hero by allowing his works free circulation. He thus became the emblematic free spirit shackled during his lifetime by the repressive forces of the past, and finally appreciated by a more enlightened posterity. That posterity did not, however, fully occur until the 1960s. In 1947, shortly after the *affaire Miller*, the young French publisher Jean-Jacques Pauvert began to publish Sade's complete works. This was the first time most of the books had appeared with the names of author and publisher and place of publication (Pauvert's parents' garage, as it happened) openly and accurately printed. The police quickly took an interest in his activities, although their arrival on the scene was delayed because they at first assumed the publication information given in the books was spurious. One official enquiring into what the publisher thought he was doing expressed open incredulity as to why he would want to embark on such an obviously doomed endeavor. Pauvert found himself unable to explain.[9] When he had brought out his entire collection he was prosecuted for four of the books: *La Philosophie dans le boudoir*, in which a group of libertines initiate a young girl into the theory and practice of debauchery, featuring sex scenes interrupted by philosophical disquisitions explaining such matters as why sodomy is superior to other forms of sex (mainly because it is unnatural and cannot result in procreation), and ending with a spectacularly sadistic scene involving the girl's mother; *La Nouvelle Justine*, *L'Histoire de Juliette*, and *Les Cent Vingt Journées de Sodome*, the book that is generally agreed to be his most shocking.

Les Cent Vingt journées had not seen print at all until the 1930s, published by Maurice Heine, who devoted much of his life to rehabilitating Sade. His first major work, it had been written in the 1780s in prison, on a continuous roll of something like toilet paper; then, still in prison, the author painstakingly recopied it, but lost the manuscript when he was transferred to another institution. The work is a Sadean, and highly sadistic, version of the sort of structure found in the *Arabian Nights*, *Canterbury Tales*, *Decameron*, or *Heptameron*; that is, it consists of a series of stories told to each other by a group of libertines over the course of a set period of time (although, because the work was never finished, less than the four months alluded to in the title). It is as though Boccaccio had collaborated with Krafft-Ebing, with the further innovation that the stories are recounted by women (whom he refers to as *historiennes*). This is the book that put Edmund Wilson off his breakfast in the remark cited at the beginning of this epilogue; in it Sade truly outdid himself. Addressing the reader within the text, he explains that he set out to surpass in indecency all extant literature of modern as well as classical times. This book is, he boasts, "the most impure tale that has ever been told since our world began, a book the likes of which are met with neither amongst the ancients nor amongst us moderns" (253). It reads as a catalogue of the most monstrous practices imaginable (in some instances barely imaginable), and in its taxonomic bent it has been read as anticipating the works of Krafft-Ebing, Havelock Ellis, and Freud. It has also, along with Sade's other works, been seen as a how-to manual for sadistic criminals. The notorious "moors" murder trial in England in 1966 is often cited in discussions of—and especially arguments against—Sade, because the defendants in these gruesome murders testified that they had read and been influenced by his works.[10] Of course, as Rembar aptly notes, this does not make much of an argument for the efficacy of suppression, since when the murderers were reading Sade his books were in fact banned; he also observes that the perpetrators of equally grisly crimes have variously cited Cecil B. DeMille's film *The Ten Commandments* and the Anglican High Church service as having provided inspiration for their misdeeds (393–94).

Pauvert showed up to court with a phalanx of prominent writers (Jean Cocteau, André Breton, Jean Paulhan, Georges Bataille) to testify as to the literary, philosophical, and historical importance of Sade's works, but he was convicted all the same. The following year (1958) his sentence was annulled, and the conviction partially overturned, on appeal. He published the testimony of his witnesses, along with other relevant documents, in a small book entitled *L'Affaire Sade*. (Pauvert shared with Maurice Girodias not only a flair for righteous self-promotion and a taste in titles, but also for some time an office, and a number of authors. They often brought out, respectively, French and English versions of many of the same books, such as the highly Sadean *Story of O* and works by Jean Genet among others. The still standard Grove Press translations of Sade's works were initially published under the Olympia imprint.) The complete works of Sade were not freely published in France until they were brought out in an expensive edition in fifteen volumes sold by subscription starting in 1962. By the late 1960s another, more widely available edition was published; in the meantime Sade never ceased to be a major topic of discussion in intellectual circles.

In 1952 Gilbert Lely published the first volume of his monumental Sade biography; the same year Simone de Beauvoir brought out her essay "Must We Burn Sade? [Faut-il brûler Sade?]" (The answer was no.) The mid 1960s saw Peter Weiss's play known as *Marat/Sade* (full title: *The Persecution and Assassination of Marat as Performed by the Inmates of the Asylum of Charenton under the Direction of the Marquis de Sade*; the fact that Sade had directed asylum inmates in plays has continued to interest), also made into a film by Peter Brook in 1973. Other films directly or indirectly inspired by Sade and his works followed, including Luis Buñuel's *Voie lactée*. Peripheral works by Sade were published, including plays and journals. In 1971 Roland Barthes published *Sade, Fourier, Loyola*, juxtaposing Sade with the utopian philosopher and the patron saint of Jesuits as founders of comparable discursive systems. The most spectacular cinematic adaptation of one of his works came out in 1975: Pasolini's *Salò*, which transposed the *120 Days of Sodom* to the well-suited Fascist context. This film brought out into the open what was already implicit: the heightened relevance of Sade's works in terms of twentieth-century history. Arguments come down squarely on both sides: Sade is alternatively depicted as an important figure for understanding such unimaginable horrors as the Holocaust; and all the more awful in the light of such events in that he depicts human cruelty as an inescapable fact and therefore to be cultivated and celebrated rather than futilely repressed.[11]

Moving away from such arguments, the past few years have seen a number of cinematic adaptations not of Sade's works but of episodes from his life. By representing his works only indirectly and concentrating on the man himself, these films present a very different Sade from the one defended by Pauvert's witnesses in 1957. He is still, certainly, the very incarnation of spiritual freedom, but in a much more abstract way than a read-

ing of his novels would suggest. This trend was launched by Roland
Topor's strange animated film *Marquis* (1988), which takes place in the
squalid Bastille, with all the characters played by animals. Sade himself is a
meditative dog who spends most of the film in philosophical dialogue
with his erect penis, another (smaller) dog inexplicably named Colin. Perhaps inspired by Topor's idiosyncratic take on matters, two more recent
films have also portrayed Sade in prison. Benoît Jacquot's 1999 film *Sade*,
based on a novel by Serge Bramly, is a fictional elaboration on a two-year
period of which little is known, starting in 1794, during which Sade was
imprisoned at the end of the Terror with other members of the nobility in
the Picpus asylum. The film recounts his flirtation with an adolescent girl,
daughter of aristocrats, whom he initiates into the mysteries of sex
through the intermediary of a (robust) young gardener. The film's only
salient departure from what is known of his life, and the novel on which it
was based, is that by this time enforced inertia and gourmandise had combined to make Sade by all accounts, even his own, obese. Played by Daniel
Auteuil he is slim and seductive; the real marquis seems rather to have re-
sembled Charles Laughton (or at the very least Gérard Depardieu). But
such a portrayal would not have conveyed what the filmmakers had in
mind, which was a sexily discreet and heroic Sade, incarnation, as the director emphasized in interviews, of the ideal of freedom.

The following year saw another cinematic Sade, in *Quills*, directed by
Philip Kaufman (who had also directed *Henry and June*), and based on a
play by Doug Wright. *Quills*, which stars the equally slim Geoffrey Rush as
Sade at the end of his life, when he was imprisoned in the Charenton asylum, is similar to the French film in that the author is depicted as seductive and even admirably self-controlled. In this version he demonstrates
his love for laundress Kate Winslet by not having sex with her. What is remarkable about this story is its relentless disregard for historical and biographical fact. All three films, with varying degrees of heavy-handedness,
portray Sade as the relatively innocent bystander or victim, locating the
real violence in historical events, notably the Terror. *Quills* even begins by
casting the public executioner with his guillotine—an instrument which
has gone down in popular accounts as representing the more horrifying
aspects of Revolutionary vengeance, but which was in fact invented as a
more humane alternative to hanging—as a sadist repugnant to Sade himself (who was, in fact, a lifelong opponent of capital punishment, no
doubt at least in part because he had twice been sentenced to death). The
opening scene toys with viewers' expectations by representing the leering,
hooded figure lubriciously preparing to dole out punishment to a terri-
fied attractive young woman. Before we see the guillotine and understand
that this is a scene of execution, therefore, the implication is that we are
witnessing a sadomasochistic sexual scenario from the writer's life or

books. Once this idea has been planted and then dispelled by the hero's disapproving commentary, the film's central point is made: history, not Sade, is the true source of sadism.

In this wildly inaccurate account of his last days the writer is represented as valiantly insisting on self-expression in the face of the most daunting forces of repression. Aside from the executioner, the most sadistic character is a hypocritical doctor played by Michael Caine (based on a historical figure), who takes away the eponymous writing instruments so as to deprive our hero of all means of cathartic self-expression. He goes from writing with quills in ink on paper, to writing with chicken bones in wine on his bedsheets, then—when everything has been removed from his formerly opulent quarters and his food has been deboned—with his finger in his own blood on his clothing. When he still manages to smuggle out his writings with the help of Kate Winslet, the resourceful writer is stripped naked and reduced to an early form of the game "telephone," necessarily played with inmates of the asylum. Things go fatally and predictably wrong at this point, and since no further instruments can be taken from him his tongue is cut out without benefit of anesthesia and he is chained in a dungeon, where he intrepidly resumes writing, this time on the walls with his own excrement. In the last scene, learning that he is indirectly responsible for the laundress's death at the hands of a lunatic behemoth inflamed by his prose, he deliberately chokes himself to death by swallowing a crucifix.

He did not in fact die this way. Although Sade's writing instruments were at one point taken away, Wright (who also wrote the screenplay) simply made up the more extravagant aspects of the story in accordance with the myth he was at once reproducing and embroidering. Sade expired of natural causes at the ripe age of seventy-four, at Charenton, attended by the woman who had been his companion for the last twenty-five years of his life and who had moved into the asylum to be with him. If stories like the one told in *Quills* are now being invented for him, and if he is still inspiring multiple films almost two hundred years after his death, it is surely not because of his books themselves. *Justine* plays a significant part in all these films, but it is purely a symbolic, liberatory one. In *Quills* her clandestine reading of the novel prompts the evil Michael Caine's innocent young wife to run off satisfyingly with the comely young architect he has hired to redecorate his requisitioned chateau. In the more nuanced *Sade* the hero tries to prevent the young girl from reading his prose, and when she persists she is at first horrified but then comes back hoping for practical instruction. Which he is happy to give, but not in the way she expects: in both films he talks a good game but refuses to engage in actual sex acts. This much may well be historically accurate; the real Sade seems to have a certain amount of trouble performing in canonical ways (which, in com-

bination with his erotomania, may go some way toward explaining his un-
hinged imagination). But historical accuracy does not seem to have been
the point. The point, rather, is that the Sade of these films is the Sade of
our times: a hero, a master of self-control, and a liberating force through
his writings and his teachings.

This Sade is a guru: not the guru of the moors murderers, not the Marquis de Sade who flagellated and poisoned whores, recommended giving
full expression to the most damaging impulses, and wrote detailed accounts of all the horrible things human beings could conceivably do to
one another, but a thoroughly domesticated version. He has become a
sort of libertine Dalai Lama, dispensing wisdom and preaching personal
liberation through the shedding of sexual and social inhibition. Sade—
this Sade—is the perfect figure for our time, the incarnation of an abstract
ideal of transgression, purged of content. It is significant that *Justine* plays
such a large and yet veiled role in these films; the actual text of the novel
is never alluded to. We know that it is banned, and we know that reading it
causes young girls to cast off the shackles of decorum and seek pleasurable
sex; but this is all we learn about *Justine* from these films. The plot of the
novel would certainly get in the way: since the book consists largely of horrible punishments inflicted on its heroine, any girl inspired by its example
would have to surrender to self-abnegating masochism rather than the
Fear of Flying-style self-assertion displayed by the doctor's young wife in
Quills. Nor could her sister Juliette's story be used, since she spends her
narrative savagely punishing others. None of his actual books could have
been showcased in this context, and so what is shown is the purely symbolic cover of *Justine.* The liberating effect of the novel that got Sade into
so much trouble during his lifetime becomes simply an incitement to sexual self-exploration. Between reading what is on his desk and coming to
her new mentor for practical lessons, the young girl in *Sade* tries to mas-
turbate but is interrupted by her intrusive mother, voice of moral disapproval. The films present Sade's writings as though they were *Fanny Hill,* or
(more to the point) *Lady Chatterley's Lover.*

It is also significant that in *Quills* the hero ends up writing with his own
excrement: here again we do not see what he has written, only that he has
covered the walls with coprography. This is what Baudelaire, Zola, and
Joyce were metaphorically accused of doing and what censors and would-
be censors had always predicted would happen if authors were allowed to
write about whatever they wanted. It is also what the impressionists were
excoriated as doing in paint; there seems to be a persistent fantasy among
guardians of the moral order that if left to their own devices artists of all
sorts would revert to corrupting the public by publicly playing with their
own shit.[12] In the late twentieth century, however, the valence of writing
with excrement has changed: it is no longer a metaphor deployed to in-

dict the author but rather literalized as a triumph over the exterior forces that have left him bereft of all other means of self-expression. His shit represents all the persecuted writer has left after the censors have has their way with him. His writing itself is not excremental in this account, despite the fact that the actual works are quite literally loaded with excrement. (An example selected at random: Thérèse, a character in the *120 Days*, declares that "in all her days . . . , she had never once wiped her ass, whence we have proof positive that the shit of her infancy yet clung there" [Grove, 234]; this is one instance among hundreds. *La Philosophie dans le boudoir* also contains theoretical meditations on the role of feces in sodomy.) Nonetheless, here the excremental quotient, like the sadism, is imposed on him. Unlike Zola and company, the Sade who writes in excrement on the dungeon walls has not chosen this abject means of expression; the forces of censorship have driven him to it.

In these films the violence comes from without; sadism is everywhere, except in the Marquis de Sade. Both *Sade* and *Quills* make much of the public executions that occur by official order; headless corpses are piled outside the asylum for all to see, the severed heads hoisted on pikes or tossed around by employees of the state. It is true that in *Quills* the laundress's murderer is directly inspired by listening to the story Sade tells, in a plot twist that at first resembles an illustration of traditional censorship laws' function of protecting both those who might be particularly open to such influences and their potential victims. In this instance the person influenced is particularly exemplary, a compilation of characteristics emanating from the censor's repertoire of stock dangers: he is a large, retarded, sexually frustrated inmate of an insane asylum. But this would-be example of the corrupting effects of salacious literature is precorrupted: he is the lubricious executioner from the opening guillotine scene. To drive the point home, in case the viewer has missed the fact that they are the same character, we also see him attempting to rape his victim before hearing a word of the story (she fends her attacker off with a hot iron to the face, thus providing him with a scar to remind us of his conduct). And finally, it is only because all other avenues of self-expression have been taken from him that the storyteller is forced to rely on lunatics to publish his tale. Had he been left alone, the film suggests, he would have continued scribbling away harmlessly in his comfortable cell. Therefore, even despite the horrific outcome in *Quills*, Sade himself still emerges as a hero and a victim, and certainly not a sadist. In the French film he is portrayed as a melancholy masochist, his physical participation in the sex scene mostly confined to asking the reluctant gardener to flagellate him a bit, to keep his interest up.

Sade without sadism, then, is what happens after the end of literary obscenity, when books no longer pose a conceivable threat. *Madame Bovary*,

Les Fleurs du mal, *Ulysses*, and *Lolita* have long formed the backbone of required reading lists. Lawrence's randy gamekeeper is fodder for BBC
miniseries; *The Well of Loneliness* a mainstay of Queer Studies curricula;
Henry Miller's unseemly railings now seem quaint, and *Fanny Hill* is an
"erotic classic" on the margins of the eighteenth-century canon. Sade
alone retains a whiff of danger, but it is the legend we appreciate more
than the books themselves. "To sympathize with Sade too readily is to betray him," writes Simone de Beauvoir in 1952: "For it is our misery, subjec-
tion, and death that he desires."[13] This Sade is not the one our culture has
embraced. We have conveniently forgotten about this aspect of his writings and instead made him into an abstract incarnation of the subversive.
"The supreme value of his testimony lies in his ability to disturb us," adds
Beauvoir at the end of her argument against burning Sade (64). What we
have retained is the concept of disturbance rather than its reality. The figure of Sade returns to us in edulcorated form as reassurance that ours is a
culture that has shed the pointless repressions of the past and fully embraced transgression as an absolute—and therefore empty—value. Our
age is all for subversion, as long as the ideas subverted are other than our
own.

∞

Notes

PROLOGUE

1. Sainte-Beuve, "M. de Balzac," in *Pour la critique* (Paris: Gallimard, 1992), 326.

2. Zola claimed Balzac as his inspiration, but he owes a debt to Sue as well; the fact that he never mentions Sue in his genealogy of naturalism attests to the extent to which the latter's reputation had tarnished by the 1880s.

3. Cited in Yvan Leclerc, *Crimes écrits: La littérature en procès au XIXe siècle* (Paris: Plon, 1991), 371. All translations are my own unless otherwise indicated.

4. Ibid.

5. *Les Mystères du peuple* enjoyed a brief resuscitation during the 1970s, republished by Régine Desforges with a preface by François Mitterand. Although it was reviewed by Michel Foucault, this edition encompassed only the first volume and quickly went back out of print. More recently, however, renewed interest in popular culture of the past has led to a new edition, published by Laffont Bouquins.

6. It should be noted that French laws are referred to by date of passage.

7. Dalloz, *Répertoire de la législation*, quoted in Leclerc, *Crimes écrits*, 23.

8. Flaubert, *Correspondance*, 4 vols. (Paris: Gallimard, 1973–98), 2:759; Baudelaire, "Notes pour mon avocat," in *Œuvres completes*, 2 vols. (Paris: Gallimard, 1975), 1:194–95. Hereafter, this work will be abbreviated *OC.*

9. This equivocal judgment, in which the authors were at once acquitted of the crime and at the same time held to be somewhat guilty, anticipates Flaubert's verdict in the case of *Madame Bovary*. The Goncourts describe their experience of the trial at some length in their *Journal*, 3 vols. (Paris: Laffont, 1989), 1:63–72. The verdict is reprinted in full on p. 72, n. 1.

10. The word *fille* is equivocal in French: it can mean, depending on context, anything from the relatively straightforward "girl" to "whore"; unmodified, in the nineteenth century it tends to mean the latter, which presumably was part of the reason the second printing of the poem led to trouble.

11. It has also been suggested that Flaubert was in fact Maupassant's real father, a rumor propagated in Edmond de Goncourt's *Journal* in 1893; see Jacques-Louis Douchin, *La Vie érotique de Flaubert* (Paris: Pauvert, 1984), 274–92. Maupassant was the son of Laure le Poittevin, sister of Flaubert's beloved friend Alfred.

237

12. "Procès qui m'a fait une réclame gigantesque, et à laquelle j'attribue les trois quarts de mon succès." Cited in Leclerc, *Crimes écrit*, 389.

13. In the late 1950s and early 1960s, when the obscenity cases dealt with in the last chapters of this book were being decided, two U.S. Supreme Court Justices, Hugo Black and William O. Douglas, maintained that the First Amendment decree that "Congress shall make no law . . . abridging the freedom of speech, or of the press" was to be taken literally, as an absolute. This position was never accepted by the court as a whole, and it was not the basis on which publication of such works as *Lady Chatterley's Lover, Tropic of Cancer,* or *Fanny Hill* was eventually allowed (see chapters 5 and 6 and epilogue).

14. Letter of October 1812, cited in Robert Netz, *Histoire de la censure dans l'édition* (Paris: PUF, 1998), 78–79.

15. Cited in ibid., 6.

16. Martyn Lyons, "Les nouveaux lecteurs au XIXe siècle," in *Histoire de la lecture dans le monde occidental,* ed. Guglielmo Cavallo and Roger Chartier, 393–430, esp. 395 (Paris: Seuil, 1997).

17. See Martyn Lyons, *Le Triomphe du livre* (Paris: Le Cercle de la Librairie, 1987); see also Lyons, "Les nouveaux lecteurs au XIXe siècle."

18. John Tebbel, *A History of Book Publishing in the United States,* 4 vols. (New York: Bowker, 1972–81), 2:17off, quoted in de Grazia, *Girls Lean Back Everywhere: The Law of Obscenity and the Assault on Genius* (New York: Random House, 1992), 18.

19. I do not in any way wish to suggest by this that films produced subsequent to the Production Code are better because of their more explicit content. To the contrary: as has also been the case for books, the removal of ostensible censorship, along with the related historically inflected tendency to celebrate the subversive, has in the past decades produced a cultural climate in which both authors and filmmakers feel compelled to explore ever-shifting borders of unacceptability, with sometimes unfortunate results.

20. The most visible current forms in the United States are in films and on network television, where, for instance, in the 1990s much controversy was generated by use of the word *asshole* on *NYPD Blue,* notwithstanding this raw verisimilitude, the show continued to depict police officers and criminals saying "frig" and "crap" in place of the more likely terms allowed only on cable.

21. Cited in Holbrook Jackson, *The Fear of Books* (New York: Scribner's, 1932), 55. See Noel Perrin's *Mr. Bowdler's Legacy: A History of Expurgated Books in England and America* (New York: Atheneum, 1969) for a history of expurgated books in English.

22. Burgess, *Flame into Being: The Life and Work of D. H. Lawrence* (New York: Arbor House, 1985), 2–3.

23. Sainte-Beuve, "À propos des 'Fleurs du mal,' " in *Pour la critique,* 353–54.

24. Derek Jarman did, however, make a pornographic film about Saint Sebastian with dialogue entirely in Latin (*Sebastiane,* 1976), but given its explicit visual content it seems unlikely that his aim was to protect the sensibilities of the viewing public.

25. Gerald Gardner, *The Censorship Papers: Movie Censorship Letters from the Hays Office* (New York: Dodd, Mead, 1987), 216–17.

26. It is also true that music lyrics, particularly rap, have at times come to the forefront of discussion in terms of what children should be allowed access to in the United States. Tipper Gore gained national fame in the 1980s for spearheading

the movement to require age-based ratings for album lyrics; the rap group 2 Live Crew was prosecuted during the 1990s; and there have been renewed calls for the music industry to police itself, as an alternative to government intervention: that is, a similar debate to the one that gave rise to the Hays Office in the 1930s.

1. GUSTAVE FLAUBERT

1. Larkin, *Collected Poems* (London: Faber and Faber, 1988), 146.

2. Letter to Champfleury, February 4, 1857, *Correspondance* (Paris: Gallimard), 2:678.

3. Letter of January 16, 1857; Flaubert, *Correspondance*, 2 vols. (Paris: Gallimard, 1973), 2:667. This passage contains a certain amount of pronoun confusion, as Flaubert refers to his book alternatively as grammatically masculine (because of *livre*), or feminine ("la *Bovary*": conflation of the book with its eponymous heroine).

4. Note that the Pléiade edition of *Madame Bovary* quoted extensively in this chapter is in vol. 1 of Flaubert's *Œuvres*.

5. The idea of including the trial proceedings in the 1873 edition came from the iconoclastic publisher Charpentier, who also published the ever-scandalous Zola. Flaubert hesitated before giving his consent, in his continued reluctance to see his name associated with what he saw as the facile notoriety of *Madame Bovary*; see his letter to his niece Caroline, June 18, 1873 (*Correspondance*, 4:675).

6. Doubtless the most ardent connoisseur of cliché in literary history, Flaubert appended a "Dictionary of Received Ideas" to his last, unfinished novel, *Bouvard et Pécuchet.*

7. LaCapra, *"Madame Bovary" on Trial* (Ithaca: Cornell University Press, 1982), 33.

8. Rachel Bowlby, *Shopping with Freud* (London: Routledge, 1993), 33.

9. Letter to his cousin Louis Bonenfant, December 12, 1856, *Correspondance* 2:652.

10. Letter to Edma Roger des Genettes, October 30, 1856, *Correspondance* 2:643–44.

11. Balzac, generally seen as having inaugurated the realist trend in French literature with his depictions of sordid squabbles among money-obsessed characters and project of depicting French society as a whole in the encyclopedic *Comédie humaine*, tries to get around the apparent incompatibility between realism and idealism by claiming that while fiction should depict the world in a favorable light, "the novel would be nothing if this august lie were not true in the details [le roman ne serait rien si, dans cet auguste mensonge, il n'était pas vrai dans les détails]." He also insists that his virtuous characters outnumber their immoral counterparts. See his 1842 preface to *La Comédie humaine*, 12 vols. (Paris: Gallimard, 1976–81).

12. "Le titre de réaliste m'a été imposé comme on a imposé aux hommes de 1830 le titre de romantiques," Courbet, "Manifeste de 1855," cited by Pierre Larousse in his *Grand Dictionnaire universel du XIXe siècle* (Paris: Administration du grand dictionnaire universel, 1866), under the article "Réalisme."

13. Émile Zola, *Le Roman naturaliste*, ed. Henri Mitterand (Paris: Librairie Générale française, 1999), 53.

14. Ibid., 53–57.

15. See Walter Kendrick, *The Secret Museum: Pornography in Modern Culture* (New York: Viking Penguin, 1988), 163–67.

16. For instance, in an article on the Italian writer Italo Svevo in *The New Yorker*, January 7, 2002, Joan Acocella notes that "Svevo was now a convert to French realism: Balzac, Flaubert, Daudet, Zola above all" (74–75). The label has undergone modifications over the years but the list stays for the most part the same, with Maupassant, protégé of both Flaubert and Zola, usually included as well.

17. It has been suggested that Flaubert's acquittal was for political reasons, having to do with his family's influence among other matters; it has also been asserted, by Flaubert himself among others, that the prosecution was motivated by factors having little to do with the novel, which would according to this theory have been a mere "pretext" for persecuting the *Revue de Paris* in which the work was serialized. Since these questions have never been conclusively resolved, and in the absence of new material on which to speculate, I will discuss the trial of *Madame Bovary* on its own terms, assuming that the issues explicitly raised are really the issues in question.

18. In Baudelaire, *OC*, 1:1201.

19. Ibid., 1:1209.

20. Zola, "De la moralité," in *Le Roman expérimental* (Paris: Charpentier, 1880), 272.

21. "'Ah! Death is nothing much! she thought; I shall fall asleep, and it will all be over!' She drank a sip of water and turned towards the wall. The awful taste of ink persisted. ['Ah! C'est bien peu de chose, la mort! pensait-elle; je vais m'endormir, et tout sera fini!' Elle but une gorgée d'eau et se tourna vers la muraille. Cet affreux goût d'encre continuait]" (*Madame Bovary* [Paris: Pléiade], 579).

22. *Le Moniteur universel*, founded in 1789, became the official government journal in 1799, and served successive regimes; conflicts with the Second Empire eventually led to a dissolution of its state function in 1869, although it continued publication as a conservative journal until 1901. Despite its official function, however, and as we shall see in the next chapter, articles published in *Le Moniteur universel* were not automatically in accord with government decisions during this period.

23. Cited by René Dumesnil in his introduction to *Madame Bovary* (Paris: Pléiade) 1:281.

24. Cited in Dumesnil's edition of *Madame Bovary* (Paris: Belles-Lettres, 1945), cliii (Leclerc, *Crimes écrits*, 53).

25. The letter, dated June 23, 1857, was published by Jean Bruneau, editor of Flaubert's correspondence, but is not to be found in the collected letters. Cited in Leclerc, *Crimes écrits*, 31.

26. Since the most famous legend around the novel is Flaubert's supposed exclamation "Madame Bovary, c'est moi," it is important to remember that the novelist never went on record with this pronouncement. Its origin is a 1909 work by René Descharmes, *Flaubert avant 1857*, in which Descharmes reports that someone who had known Amélie Bosquet, one of Flaubert's correspondents, told him that when Mlle Bosquet asked Flaubert how he had come up with the character he had said "Mme Bovary, c'est moi—D'après moi!" (Cited in Albert Thibaudet, *Gustave Flaubert* [Paris: Gallimard, 1935], 92). Especially since he gave various different accounts of the origin of his character in different contexts, it is hard to gauge

how much credence to lend to this fourth-hand statement, but it certainly has staying power, although, interestingly, almost never taking into account the second part.

27. Flaubert's preliminary notes for *Madame Bovary* often, in fact, read like passages from Sade, although he removed all discernable traces of such material from the final version of the novel. See Flaubert, *Plans et scenarios* (Paris: Zulma, 1995). As we shall see in the next chapter, Pinard had an easier time prosecuting Baudelaire, whose poems display an evident Sadean "immoralism," as opposed to Flaubert's "amoralism."

28. In his autobiography Minnelli records producer Pandro Berman as having said he didn't know why he wanted to make the film: "'The subject matter wasn't of any interest to the audience, nor was the period. On top of that, the movie code didn't find adultery an appropriate subject for a picture'" (*I Remember It Well* [New York: Samuel French, 1990], 201).

29. Ibid., 202.

30. Ibid., 206.

31. I am grateful to Cheryl Krueger for first pointing out to me the resemblances between Minnelli's *Madame Bovary* and *Gone with the Wind*. See her "Being Madame Bovary," *Literature/Film Quarterly* 31, no. 3 (2003): 162–68.

32. The novel itself, certainly, emphasizes Emma's masculine side: e.g., in her relations with the young and inexperienced Leon, "he became her mistress more than she was his [il devenait sa maîtresse plutôt qu'elle n'était la sienne]" (544).

33. See Minnelli, *I Remember It Well*, 203–4.

34. Minnelli notes that David Selznick "had opposed the casting of Van Heflin as Charles Bovary, for he felt Van's offbeat good looks were romantic enough to keep Emma Bovary home." He was nonetheless retained, on the basis of his strength as an actor (205).

35. *Plans et scénarios*, 1.

36. Rembar, *The End of Obscenity: The Trials of Lady Chatterley's Lover, Tropic of Cancer, and Fanny Hill* (New York: Harper and Row, 1986), 492.

37. This had not, however, prevented the makers of *Gone with the Wind* ten years earlier from representing, at least audibly, the amputation of a Civil War soldier's leg without benefit of anesthesia.

2. Charles Baudelaire

1. Cited in Leclerc, *Crimes écrits*, 339.

2. The first Pléiade edition of Baudelaire, edited by Y-G Le Dantec, has since been replaced by the Pichois edition (Paris: Gallimard, 1975), from which references are drawn here.

3. Julian Barnes, *Something to Declare* (London: Picador, 2002), 111–112.

4. Flaubert, *Correspondance* 2:758.

5. Ibid., 744–75.

6. In his desire to write "un livre sur rien" Flaubert can be considered a precursor of Jerry Seinfeld (among others). January 16, 1852, *Correspondance*, 2:31.

7. Baudelaire, "Bribes," *OC*, 1:188. The most famous formulation of this is in the final couplet of his second project for an epilogue to the second (1861) edition of *Les Fleurs du mal*: "Car, j'ai de chaque chose extrait la quintessence, / Tu

m'as donné ta boue et j'en ai fait de l'or [I have extracted the quintessence of all things, / You gave me your mud and from it I made gold]," in *OC*, 1:192.

8. Proust, *Le côté de Guermantes*, in *À la recherche du temps perdu*. 4 vols. (Paris: Gallimard, 1987–91), 2:789.

9. The author of this memorable formula was a Jesuit: R. P. Etienne Cornut, S.J., *Les Malfaiteurs littéraires* (1892), quoted in Guy Bechtel and Jean-Claude Carrière, *Dictionnaire de la bêtise et des erreurs de jugement* (Paris: Laffont, 1990), 476.

10. Henri Troyat, *Zola* (Paris: Flammarion, 1992), 180.

11. Barbey, *De Balzac à Zola: Critiques et polémiques* (Paris: les Belles Lettres, 1999), 214.

12. Flaubert took his revenge in a letter to George Sand about *Les Diaboliques*, writing that he found the book involuntarily comical and "grotesque in the extreme" (December 2, 1874). See Flaubert, *Correspondance*, 4:893.

13. Quoted in Leclerc, *Crimes écrits*, 59 n.2.

14. See ibid., 156–57.

15. It should also be noted that defecation and other disgusting bodily functions form an obsessive theme as an impediment to eroticism, to tragicomic effect, in the British tradition, especially Swift's poetry: see William Ian Miller's discussion in *Anatomy of Disgust* (Cambridge: Harvard University Press, 1997), 68–70.

16. Éd. Schérer, *Études critiques*, quoted in Bechtel and Carrière, *Dictionnaire de la bêtise*, 50.

17. *OC*, 2:57–58. Champfleury had been a close friend of Baudelaire's, although their friendship was somewhat tempestuous.

18. *OC*, 1:1206. Because Baudelaire could not afford to hire a stenographer as Flaubert had done for his trial, the trial documents were not published until 1885, and the extant text of the prosecution speech is of unclear origin, probably reconstructed by Pinard from notes. I have therefore tried not to rely too much on textual analysis of the prosecution and defense speeches.

19. Cited in Flaubert, *OC* 1:683.

20. Thierry's article in *Le Moniteur universel* defending Baudelaire before his trial is proof that despite its official status, that journal did not always toe the party line. Baudelaire excerpted this review, which was not unilaterally positive, for his *articles justificatifs*, the collection of four essays defending his work which he circulated. *OC*, 1:1187.

21. Letter of December 31, 1856. Flaubert, *Correspondance*, 2:656.

22. Benjamin, "On Some Motifs in Baudelaire," in *Illuminations*, trans. Harry Zohn (New York: Schocken, 1988), 192.

23. Charles Dickens, *Our Mutual Friend* (Harmondsworth, UK: Penguin, 1998), 175.

24. Baudelaire, *OC*, 1:181. After writing four attempts at a preface, he finally gave up, and the second edition of *Les Fleurs du mal* was published without any prefatory material. In "Fusées" he takes a slightly different tack: "This book cannot scandalize my wives, my daughters, or my sisters [Ce livre ne pourra pas scandaliser mes femmes, mes filles, ni mes sœurs]." *OC*, 1:660.

25. Letter of July 19, 1857. Baudelaire, *Correspondance*, 1:411.

26. Cited in Baudelaire, *OC*, 1:1203.

27. Flaubert, *Correspondance*, 2:652. The Prix Montyon was a prize awarded to morally uplifting literature, which Flaubert often referred to mockingly. The am-

biguous tone of this and many other letters written by Flaubert concerning the morality of his work, in which he seems to be at once ironic and serious, is analogous to that of Baudelaire in, for instance, his references to his wives, daughters, and sisters.

28. Jean Bruneau suggests Piron's play as the reference in this letter: *La Métromanie*, acte III, sc.vii; see Flaubert, *Correspondance*, 2:1331.

29. Claude Pichois notes that this comment cannot in fact apply to Baudelaire's work. See *OC*, 1:1208.

30. "Notes pour mon avocat," ibid., 1:194.

31. The lines in which the poet breakfasts, displaying Hugo's characteristic love of enjambment, read in full: "We have breakfast while reading the newspaper. All day long / Our thoughts are mixed with hope, work, love. [On déjeune en lisant le journal. Tout le jour / On mêle à sa pensée espoir, travail, amour.]" Victor Hugo, "We live, we talk, we have the sky and the clouds above [On vit, on parle, on a le ciel et les nuages]" in *Les Contemplations* (Paris: Gallimard, 1943), 222–23.

32. Cited by Frédéric Dulamon in his *article justificatif* first published in *Le Présent*; see *OC* 1:1189. The four poems identified by Bourdin as particularly offensive are: "Le Reniement de Saint Pierre," "Lesbos," and the two poems entitled "Femmes damnées." All four were mentioned by Pinard in his prosecution speech. See ibid., 1:1177.

33. Claude Pichois among others has made this point: see his commentary in Baudelaire, ibid., 1:890. Sainte-Beuve's remark can be found in *Pour la critique*, 352.

34. *OC*, 1:32.

35. In regard to the final stanza, Ronsard's "Quand vous serez bien vieille" (reworked by Yeats as "When you are old and grey") is more immediately analogous than his "Ode à Cassandre."

36. The ascetic tradition represented, for instance, by John Chrysostom's fourth-century advice to the lovelorn: "If you consider carefully what things lie hidden under the skin which seems beautiful to you, what is concealed within the nostrils and within the throat and stomach, these seemly external features (filled within with all kinds of vileness) will proclaim the beauty of this body to be nothing else but a whited sepulcher." Quoted in Miller, *Anatomy of Disgust*, 93.

37. Letter of May 14, 1859. *Correspondance*, 1:573–74.

38. "Chaque jour vers l'Enfer nous descendons d'un pas, / Sans horreur, à travers des ténèbres qui puent [Each day toward Hell we descend ever closer, / Without horror, through shadows that reek]." "Au lecteur," *OC*, 1:5. Even unerotic poems are filled with sometimes strange olfactory imagery, e.g.: "Il est des parfums frais comme des chairs d'enfants [There are perfumes as cool as baby's flesh]," "Correspondances," in *OC*, 1:11.

39. See ibid., 1:1207–8.

40. The ineptitude of Chaix d'Est-Ange's defense speech is almost always cited as a major reason for Baudelaire's failure to be acquitted. In fact the poet had probably intended to hire his lawyer's father, an eminent attorney who then became chief imperial prosecutor, in which role he approved the reduction of Baudelaire's fine from 300F to 50F in 1859. While it may be true that Chaix d'Est-Ange *fils* did not defend Baudelaire brilliantly, it should also be said in his defense that the odds against him would have required Ciceronian talents to overcome.

41. See Baudelaire, *Correspondance*, 1:410.

42. Ibid., 1:429, italics in text.

43. See Michel Crouzet, "Le 'Banquet' romantique," in Gautier, *Mademoiselle de Maupin* (Paris: Gallimard, 1973), 13. The preface to *Mademoiselle de Maupin* contains a lengthy polemic against censorship and moralism in the arts.

44. Benjamin, *Charles Baudelaire: A Lyric Poet in the Era of High Capitalism*, trans. Harry Zohn (London: Verso, 1983), 93.

45. Ibid., 90.

46. Male homosexuality is visible as a theme in nineteenth-century French literature primarily in the character of Vautrin in various Balzac novels, but does not become a central plot device until the early twentieth century. See chapter 4.

47. See Frederic V. Grunfeld, *Rodin* (New York: Da Capo, 1998), 276–77. Rodin was himself accused of an odd form of realism that might be termed plagiarism of the real: he was falsely charged with *surmoulage*, casting from live models, his sculptures seen as too lifelike to be "art." As Grunfeld pertinently observes, a century later the sculptor George Segal would make his career on just this form of hyper-realism (Ibid., 100).

48. See *OC*, 1:1127.

49. Quoted in Bechtel and Carrière, *Dictionnaire de la bêtise*, 49. The fact that Pontmartin's query—a prescient one in 1861—is cited in a dictionary of stupidity and errors of judgment a century later is itself ample answer.

50. Hugo, *Les Contemplations* (Paris: Garnier, 1969), 240. The alternation between *tu* (informal) and *vous* (formal when not plural) forms of address that marks Hugo's address to the reader is not uncommon in French literature and other forms of discourse, and marks changing emotional relations. In Racinian tragedy, for instance, moments of crisis are almost always heralded by this shift, and Baudelaire himself constantly vacillates between *vous* and *tu* when writing to his mother.

51. Flaubert was also, certainly, aware of the volatile potential that *ennui* had begun to take on as a result of romanticism, later to be reified by Baudelaire. As early as 1844 he asked a correspondent: "Are you familiar with ennui? Not that common, banal boredom that stems from laziness or illness, but the modern ennui that eats away at a man's entrails, and makes an intelligent being into a walking shadow, a sentient phantom. [Connaissez-vous l'ennui? Non pas cet ennui commun, banal, qui provient de la fainéantise ou de la maladie, mais cet ennui moderne qui ronge l'homme dans les entrailles et, d'un être intelligent, fait une ombre qui marche, un fantôme qui pense]." He further compares ennui to leprosy (June 7, 1844, *Correspondance*, 1:208–9).

3. JAMES JOYCE

1. Martin Amis, *The War against Cliché* (New York: Random House, 2002), 442.

2. At least, so Amis maintains, ibid.

3. Anderson, "*Ulysses* in Court," cited in De Grazia, *Girls Lean Back*, 12.

4. James Douglas, cited in ibid., 26.

5. Cited in Richard Ellmann, *James Joyce*, rev. ed. (New York: Oxford University Press, 1983), 529.

6. See Woolf's essay "Modern Fiction," first published in 1919, for her positive remarks about *A Portrait of the Artist as a Young Man* and hopeful attitude toward

Ulysses, which had only been published in part at the time (*The Common Reader* [London: Hogarth, 1984], 1:150–51.)

7. Woolf, *Letters*, 2:231; cited in Kendrick, *The Secret Museum*, 184.

8. Wednesday 16 August 1922, *Diary of Virginia Woolf*, 10 vols. (New York and London: Harcourt, Brace, Jovanovich), 2:188–89.

9. Anderson, *My Thirty Years' War* (Westport, Conn.: Greenwood Press, 1971), 212. This memoir was originally published in 1930, before *Ulysses* was allowed into the United States.

10. Anthony Burgess, *ReJoyce* (New York: Norton, 1968), 18.

11. See Alan Travis, *Bound and Gagged: A Secret History of Obscenity in Britain* (London: Profile Books, 2000), 21.

12. Arthur Power, *Conversations with James Joyce* (Dublin: Lilliput, 1999), 64.

13. Pound, "E.P. Ode pour l'élection de son sépulcre," *Poems and Translations* (New York: Library of America, 2003).

14. *The War against Cliché*, 442.

15. Nineteenth-century French literature is filled with disgusting descriptions of once-beautiful women ravaged by diseases with moral overtones, taking a cue from Mme de Merteuil's disfiguring bout with smallpox at the end of *Les Liaisons dangereuses* (1782). Nana's physical disintegration is essentially a repetition of the death of the equally meretricious Mme Marneffe in Balzac's 1846 *Cousine Bette*. Barbey d'Aurevilly's remarkable story "La Vengeance d'une femme," one of his *Diaboliques* (1874), features the disintegrating face of a noblewoman turned prostitute as the result of a deliberately contracted case of syphilis.

16. Similarly, the Oulipo group in France has a category of "anticipatory plagiarism."

17. Cited in Panthea Reid, *Art and Affection: A Life of Virginia Woolf* (Oxford: Oxford University Press, 1996), 207.

18. Jasper Fforde's series of comic metaliterary novels, starting with *The Eyre Affair* (New York: Penguin, 2003), has much fun with such conventions, playing with the idea of literary characters encountering "real life": they regard breakfast, much less bathrooms, as exotic rarities, etc.

19. Both quoted in Ellmann, *James Joyce*: Yeats 578n; Larbaud 514.

20. Leslie, review of *Ulysses*, in *Quarterly Review* (October 1922), 238, in *James Joyce: A Literary Reference*, ed. A. Nicholas Fargnoli (New York: Carroll and Graf, 2001), 205.

21. Woolf, *A Room of One's Own* (New York: Harcourt Brace, 1929).

22. It has been argued that *style indirect libre* was what gave rise to Flaubert's prosecution: see especially Hans Robert Jauss, "Literary History as a Challenge to Literary Theory," (1970), in *Toward an Esthetics of Reception* (Minneapolis: University of Minnesota, 1982).

23. Valéry Larbaud, the French writer and translator of *Ulysses*, coined the term *monologue intérieur*.

24. Letter from Dujardin to his parents, June 13, 1886; my translation. Cited in Dujardin, *Les Lauriers sont coupés* (Paris: Flammarion, 2001), 125.

25. Paul Vanderham, *James Joyce and Censorship: The Trials of Ulysses* (New York: New York University Press, 1998) 21. Vanderham's study is the first fully to trace the censorship history of *Ulysses*, and includes a complete catalogue of the passages deemed offensive by various censors and would-be censors, starting with Pound.

26. Ibid.

27. Woolf, "Modern Fiction," *Common Reader*, 151.

28. Woolf, *Diary*, 188–89.

29. Nabokov, *Lectures on Literature* (New York: Harcourt Brace Jovanovich, 1980), 287.

30. Quinn wrote this in a letter to Shane Leslie, the critic whose characterization of *Ulysses* as "unreadable, unquotable, and unreviewable" had prompted the British Home Office's ban on the novel. Quoted in Vanderham, *James Joyce and Censorship*, 48.

31. See Travis, *Bound and Gagged*, 26–36.

32. Quoted in Vanderham, *James Joyce and Censorship*, 46.

33. *Regina v. Hicklin.*

34. Cited in Vanderham, *James Joyce and Censorship*, 49.

35. Quoted in ibid., 48.

36. Quoted in de Grazia, *Girls Lean Back*, 26.

37. Both Joyce's *Ulysses* and Gilbert's *James Joyce's Ulysses* are published in the United States by Random House.

38. Vanderham makes this point at length; I am indebted to his analysis in *James Joyce and Censorship*.

39. Arthur Power, *Conversations with James Joyce* (Dublin: Lilliput Press, 1999), 41. The sea as "great sweet mother" is a quotation from Swinburne's "The Triumph of Time" (1866).

40. The food to food (or dung to dung, as it were) sequence alludes to Giordano Bruno's 1584 *Cause, Principle, and Unity*. See Gifford's *Ulysses Annotated* (Berkeley: University of California Press, 1989), 183.

41. Hélène Cixous, one of the foremost proponents of the French feminist *écriture féminine* movement in the 1970s and 1980s, wrote her doctoral dissertation on Joyce, with special reference to Molly Bloom's soliloquy. Marilyn French, author of the bestselling feminist novel *The Women's Room*, published *The Book as World*, a critical examination of *Ulysses* which also foregrounds the final episode.

42. James Hynes, *The Lecturer's Tale* (New York: Picador, 2001), 182.

43. Burgess too pays homage to this cliché: "There, then, is Penelope. But she is also Gea-Tellus, Cybele, our great earth-mother" (174). Gaia (or Gea) and Tellus (or Tellos) are the female and male Greek deities corresponding to the Earth.

4. Radclyffe Hall

1. Anthony Burgess, *Re/Joyce* (New York: Norton, 1968), 18.

2. Cited in Diana Souhami, *Trials of Radclyffe Hall* (New York: Doubleday, 1999), 171.

3. Published in *The New Statesman*, August 25, 1928; quoted in Laura Doan and Jay Prosser, eds., *Palatable Poison* (New York: Columbia University Press, 2001), 67–69.

4. Jane Marcus has argued that *A Room of One's Own* should in fact be read as a response to Hall's work. See "Sapphistory: The Woolf and the Well," in *Lesbian Texts and Contexts*, ed. Karla Jay and Joanne Glasgow (New York: New York University Press, 1990), 164–79.

5. Anthony Burgess, *Flame into Being: The Life and Work of D. H. Lawrence* (New York: Arbor House, 1985), 3.

6. Quoted in Doan and Prosser, eds., *Palatable Poison*, 41.

7. In *The Daily Express*, November 29, 1927; cited in Laura Doan, *Fashioning Sapphism* (New York: Columbia University Press, 2001), 15.

8. These sentences have been reprinted in a wide variety of publications, although the entire text is hard to come by. It is reprinted (pp. 36–38), in Doan and Prosser, eds., *Palatable Poison*, a useful collection of responses to Hall's novel encompassing both contemporary reviews and more recent rereadings (above citation p. 38).

9. Terry Castle, afterword, in Doan and Prosser, eds., *Palatable Poison*, 397. Castle goes on to assign something very much like the inadvertent acuity that others have seen in Pinard to Sir Chartres Biron, presiding magistrate in the 1928 British trial, asserting that his judgment "has in spite of its well-tempered stupidity the strange virtue of spotlighting precisely those passages in *The Well of Loneliness* that give the book, for me at least, its ultimate force: Sir Chartres quotes them all. And they are stirring indeed" (400).

10. Huxley, "To the Puritan All Things are Impure," in *Music at Night* (London: Chatto and Windus, 1931), reprinted in *Complete Essays* (Chicago: Ivan R. Dee, 2001), 3:240.

11. Walter Kendrick, *The Secret Museum: Pornography in Modern Culture* (New York: Viking Penguin, 1988), 259 n.53.

12. Quotations from bishop of Durham from Souhami, *Trials of Radclyffe Hall*, 179.

13. See ibid., 70.

14. Ellis, who had not written his note for publication, hesitated to give his approval, warning Hall that his name would not protect her from scandal, and was displeased to find his imprimatur included in the book. It has been retained in subsequent editions.

15. Quoted in Doan and Prosser, eds., *Palatable Poison*, 41–42.

16. In *Nation & Atheneum*, August 4, 1928; quoted in Doan and Prosser, eds., *Palatable Poison*, 53–54.

17. Quoted in Andrew Wilson, *Beautiful Shadow: A Life of Patricia Highsmith* (New York: Bloomsbury, 2003), 165.

18. Patricia Highsmith, *The Price of Salt* (Naiad Press, 1991), 277.

19. Ibid.

20. Ibid., 277–78.

21. See Andrew Wilson's *Beautiful Shadow*; see also Marijane Meaker's memoir of her affair with Highsmith, *Highsmith: A Romance of the 1950s* (San Francisco: Cleis Press, 2003).

22. The French translation of *The Well*, originally published in 1930 but out of print for many years, has recently (2005) been reprinted under the byline Marguerite Radclyffe Hall.

23. Woolf and Joyce were in fact precisely exact contemporaries: both were born in 1882 and both died in 1941.

24. In 1933 following the Woolsey decision, another *Times* editorial employed a similar formula: "incomprehensible but dull"; this variation contains the very different implication, bolstered no doubt by responses to contemporary art, that what is incomprehensible is assumed to be interesting unless, as in the case of Joyce's novel, proved otherwise. Both editorials are quoted in Rosa A. Eberly, *Citizen Critics: Literary Public Spheres* (Urbana: University of Illinois Press, 2000), 51.

25. Cited in P. N. Furbank, *E. M. Forster: A Life* (New York: Harcourt Brace Jovanovich, 1978), 2:154.

26. Trial transcript, as cited by Souhami, *Trials of Radclyffe Hall*, 202.

27. Wilde, *Picture of Dorian Gray* (Oxford: Oxford University Press, 1974), xxiii.

28. Cited in Isobel Murray's introduction to the Oxford edition of *Dorian Gray*, vii.

29. The main character of *A Rebours* (translated as *Against Nature*) was based on Robert de Montesquiou, the same extravagant dandy on whom Proust reportedly modeled the Baron de Charlus.

5. D. H. Lawrence

1. Judge Bryan's decision is appended to the Modern Library edition of the novel (New York: Random House, 2001); see p. 340. All citations of both the novel and the decision refer to this edition.

2. Cited in Anthony Burgess, *Flame into Being : The Life and Work of D. H. Lawrence* (New York: Arbor House, 1985), 235.

3. Aldous Huxley, "To the Puritan All Things Are Impure," in *Complete Essays* (Chicago : Ivan R. Dee, 2000–2002), 3:238.

4. Remarkably, therefore, James Douglas and his like may be counted among the precursors of the cultural trend they would surely most vehemently have reviled had they been around to witness it: attempts to demolish the aesthetics elitism of the canon and replace it with ideologically motivated representative multiculturalism.

5. "A Propos," in D. H. Lawrence, *Sex, Literature and Censorship: Essays*, ed. Harry T. Moore (New York: Twayne, 1953), 101. Kate Millett maintains that Lawrence "used the words 'sexual' and 'phallic' interchangeably," which is not quite true; "phallic" always carries a positive connotation, whereas "sexual" does not. Of course, Millett's aim is to point out the literal as well as figurative phallocentrism that is indisputably present in *Lady Chatterley*. See *Sexual Politics* (New York: Doubleday, 1969), 316.

6. This tradition dates back further than the 19th century, although not just classical but also medieval literature offers many relatively positive adultery stories, perhaps the most famous example in the chivalric tradition being the Arthur-Guinevere-Lancelot triangle. Seventeenth-century France provides the ultimate antiadultery narrative in the *Princess of Cleves*, in which the latter remains faithful to her dull but loving husband even after his convenient death and despite the considerable allure and repeated attentions of the suave duc de Nemours. In the nineteenth century George Eliot's *Middlemarch* provides an exemplary story of the inappropriate husband's demise allowing the heroine to rectify youthful error.

7. "A Propos," *Sex, Literature, and Censorship*.

8. It is also true, though, that contemporary reviews, the imperial prosecutor's remarks, and even the response of today's undergraduates suggest that Charles Bovary can be seen as a fine husband whose wife might well have shut up and made do with her appointed lot in life.

9. Other commentators, including Burgess, tend to identify *Women in Love* as Lawrence's masterpiece. For Forster's full testimony see the published transcript of

the British trial: C. H. Rolph, ed., *The Trial of Lady Chatterley* (Harmondsworth, UK: Penguin, 1961), 112.

10. Virginia Woolf, *Orlando* (London: Penguin, 1993), 187.

11. Millett, *Sexual Politics*, 317.

12. Bantam Classic edition, copyright 1983. The Bantam Classic edition has since been revised for the seventy-fifth anniversary of the book's publication; this blurb appeared on the back cover of an edition in print in 2002.

13. See Frank Miller, *Censored Hollywood: Sex, Sin, and Violence on Screen* (Atlanta: Turner, 1994), 170.

14. Quoted in Charles Rembar, *The End of Obscenity: The Trials of Lady Chatterley's Lover, Tropic of Cancer, and Fanny Hill* (New York: Harper and Row, 1986), 146.

15. Quoted in Edward de Grazia, *Girls Lean Back Everywhere: The Law of Obscenity and the Assault on Genius* (New York: Random House, 1992), 339.

16. Philip Larkin, "This Be the Verse," in *Collected Poems* (London: Faber and Faber, 1988), 142. Both poems were first published in 1974 in the collection *High Windows*.

17. Here we find a version of the distinction Lawrence draws between "phallic" sexuality and other varieties.

18. Geoffrey Robertson, QC, attributes this pioneering use of language on British television to the *Chatterley* trial, which he notes "was, after all, brought as a 'test case', so that a jury could 'set the public standard.' " See Robertson's foreword to the 30th anniversary edition of C. H. Rolph, ed., *The Trial of Lady Chatterley*, xv.

19. The title "John Thomas and Lady Jane" was suggested in a spirit of scandalized irony by Juliette Huxley, sister-in-law of Aldous, whose wife Maria typed part of the manuscript after the original typist gave up in protest; the title was briefly taken up by the author.

20. See Moore, "D. H. Lawrence and the 'Censor-Morons,' " in *Sex, Literature, and Censorship*, 12.

21. Quoted in de Grazia, *Girls Lean Back*, 90.

22. Sylvia Beach, *Shakespeare and Company* (Lincoln: University of Nebraska Press, 1991), 92–93.

23. De Grazia, *Girls Lean Back*, 87.

24. J. M. Coetzee, *Giving Offense: Essays on Censorship* (Chicago: University of Chicago Press, 1996), 8. Lawrence is the subject of one of the essays in this collection.

25. Henry Miller, *The World of Lawrence: A Passionate Appreciation* (Calder: London, 1985), 177.

26. Dyer, introduction to 75th Anniversary Signet Classics edition, of D. H. Lawrence, *Lady Chatterley's Lover* (New York: Signet, 2003), x.

27. Quoted in Richard Ellmann, *James Joyce* (New York: Oxford University Press, 1983), 628n.

28. D. H. Lawrence, *Collected Letters*, ed. Harry T. Moore (New York: Viking, 1962), 6:507; quoted in Dyer, introduction, 75th anniversary ed., *Lady Chatterley's Lover*, vi.

29. See chapter 4. On the hypothesis that Lawrence wrote the novel "because he thought he could do as well as Joyce, probably better," see Burgess, *Flame into Being*, 236–37.

30. Robert Ferguson, *Henry Miller: A Life* (New York: Norton, 1991), 221.

31. Miller, *World of Lawrence*, 91. Lawrence himself indicts Proust not only in his

essays but also in *Lady Chatterley's Lover* itself, by having Lord Clifford defend the French writer's "subtlety and his well-bred anarchy," which Connie points out makes him "very dead, actually" (Bantam, 209).

32. Letter quoted in full in Hinz and Teunissen, introduction in Miller, *World of Lawrence*, 19.

33. Information about the Japanese trials is based on Kirsten Cather, "The Great Censorship Trials of Literature and Film in Postwar Japan," Ph.D. diss., University of California– Berkeley, 2004.

34. Quoted in Rembar, *The End of Obscenity*, 159.

35. Interview with de Grazia; quoted in *Girls Lean Back Everywhere*, 369.

36. Rembar, *The End of Obscenity*, 121.

37. The Comstock Act, "the archetype of American antiobscenity legislation," as Rembar terms it (ibid., 21), dates from 1873 and represents the triumph of Anthony Comstock, founder of the notorious New York Society for the Suppression of Vice.

38. Quoted in ibid., 48–9.

39. Edward de Grazia's *Girls Lean Back Everywhere* is dedicated to Brennan.

40. See Rembar, *The End of Obscenity*, 125.

41. Robertson, foreword to Rolph, *The Trial of Lady Chatterley*, xiv.

42. Quoted in Robertson, ibid., xiii–xiv.

6. HENRY MILLER

1. It is perhaps worth noting that the passage Millett chooses to open her book comes not from *Tropic of Cancer* but *Sexus* (1949), which even Miller's most loyal supporters tend to find problematic (*Sexual Politics* [New York: Doubleday, 1969]).

2. Jong's admiration of Miller began when he wrote her a fan letter on reading *Fear of Flying* shortly after it first came out in 1973. He manifestly saw her as a young female version of himself, and she was delighted to participate in an ongoing festival of mutual identification; however, she had little knowledge of his work before hearing from him. She recounts the story in detail in *The Devil at Large*.

3. Henry Miller, *Henry Miller on Writing* (New York : New Directions, 1964), 131.

4. See Edward de Grazia, *Girls Lean Back Everywhere: The Law of Obscenity and the Assault on Genius* (New York: Random House, 1992), 332.

5. Cited in Jay Martin, *Always Merry and Bright: The Life of Henry Miller, An Unauthorized Biography* (Santa Barbara: Capo Press, 1978), 241.

6. *The Wisdom of the Heart* in *Henry Miller on Writing*, 110.

7. See Martin, *Always Merry and Bright*, 250.

8. See Zola, *Ecrits sur le roman* (Paris: Livre de poche, 2004). Zola's novels are themselves much more plot-heavy than Flaubert's, but in principle his works are "experimental," based on a natural science rather than a traditionally literary model. He does follow the example of Flaubert in that his protagonists are at least as unheroic as the latter's, even if differently so.

9. He referred to *Tropic* in its early versions as "the Paris book: first person, uncensored, formless—fuck everything!" Quoted in Robert Ferguson, *Henry Miller: A Life* (New York: Norton, 1991), 186.

10. See "The Angel Is My Watermark!", the fourth section of *Black Spring*, for

Miller's account of the chaotic genesis of a painting he unhesitatingly terms a "masterpiece."

11. In "The Greatest Living Author," an essay on Miller which became the foreword to the Grove Press edition of the book, the poet Karl Shapiro insists that Miller is "not a writer, but an author." "Henry James is not a writer," he explains; "Miller is a talker" (vii). However, since Miller himself says his goal was "*to be a writer*," it seems that the same point can be made using the terms interchangeably.

12. "Inside the Whale," *Collected Essays* (London: Secker and Warburg, 1961), 27.

13. Ibid., 28.

14. Cited in de Salvo, preface to Signet edition; see Ferguson, *Henry Miller*, 149.

15. Cited in Ferguson, *Henry Miller*, 197. Miller's horror is pertinent: the desire to distance himself from the representations of homosexuality in his own work had without a doubt been a determining factor in Proust's elaboration of his antibiographical theory.

16. *Granta* 11 (1984), 11; quoted in Ferguson, *Henry Miller*, xv.

17. Letter to Emil Schnellock, quoted in Ferguson, *Henry Miller*, 220.

18. Kahane, *Memoirs of a Booklegger* (London: Michael Joseph, 1939), 260; quoted in John de Saint-Jorre, *Venus Bound: The Erotic Voyage of the Olympia Press and Its Writers* (New York: Random House, 1996), 3.

19. Quoted in Martin, *Always Merry and Bright*, 304.

20. Quoted in Ferguson, *Henry Miller*, 240.

21. Quoted in Martin, *Always Merry and Bright*, 304. This gender-specific slur recalls Baudelaire's contemptuous references to the author of *Lélia* as "la femme Sand."

22. Ibid. In 1963 Connolly was to revise his opinion, now finding *Tropic of Cancer* to be "an interminable rhapsody deriving from Lautréamont, Whitman, Joyce, Lawrence and Céline" (quoted in Ferguson, *Henry Miller*, 352).

23. The sex-as-dirt metaphor does not exist in French, with the result that the notion of "dirt for dirt's sake" is untranslatable into that language.

24. This passage has been published separately in France as a small volume under the title *Lire aux cabinets* (Paris: Allia, 2000.

25. *Black Spring* (New York: Grove Press, 1963), 49.

26. Raymond Queneau observed, in an essay on Flaubert, that all novels fall into the categories of *Illiad* or *Odyssey*; Miller, like Virgil, and in his very efforts to foresake this tradition, wrote both. He insisted in 1959 that he had only recently read Homer's epics, and only then because Gallimard had asked him to preface an edition of the *Odyssey*. See "Second Letter to Trygve Hirsch," in *Henry Miller on Writing*, 211.

27. *Tropic of Capricorn* (London: Harper Perennial, 2005), 174.

28. See Ferguson, *Henry Miller*, 346.

29. See Martin, *Always Merry and Bright*, 450.

30. Quoted in ibid., 450.

31. See Frank Miller, *Censored Hollywood*, 12.

32. Ferguson, *Henry Miller*, 271.

33. See de Grazia, *Girls Lean Back Everywhere*, 367–68.

34. Quoted in Martin, *Always Merry and Bright*, 461. Miller's equivocations recall the legendary George Bernard Shaw anecdote (alternatively recounted about Winston Churchill) in which a woman, on being asked whether she would have sex

with a stranger for one million pounds, hesitates, upon which he asks her if she would do so for one hundred pounds. What do you take me for, she asks indignantly, to which the answer comes: we have established what you are; now we are trying to determine your price.

35. The *Tropic* case in Chicago in particular gave rise to lively public debate in such fora as the "letters to the editor" to newspapers. Rose A. Eberly provides an interesting account of these popular reactions to the publication of the novel in *Citizen Critics: Literary Public Spheres* (Urbana: Illinois University Press, 2000).

36. See Rembar, *The End of Obscenity*, 205–7.

37. *Henry Miller*, 277

38. Since all three of these titles seem to have been viewed as embarrassingly smutty, and since "Sous les Toits de Paris," which was the title of a famous 1929 film by René Clair, simply means "under the roofs of Paris" (the title under which the whole volume was later republished), the word *toit* was most likely meant as a laborious pun on "twat."

39. Quoted in Ferguson, *Henry Miller*, 277.

40. A 1995 Signet Classic edition of *Tropic of Cancer* has now gone out of print in the United States, for instance, leaving only the Grove edition. In the United Kingdom, as of 2005, Harper Perennial Modern Classic editions of both *Tropic*s remain available, their covers featuring erotic photographs apparently from the 1920s or 1930s.

7. VLADIMIR NABOKOV

1. As for homosexuality, Nabokov reports, one imagines facetiously, in "On a Book Entitled *Lolita*," that a reader for one of the publishing houses suggested his firm might be interested in the book if Lolita were transformed into a twelve-year-old "lad" and Humbert into a farmer (314). In a letter to Graham Greene he wrote that "if I had made her a boy, or a cow, or a bicycle, Philistines might never have flinched" (*Selected Letters, 1940–1970* [New York: Harcourt Brace Jovanovich, 1990], 197).

2. It is perhaps relevant to add that in the course of a number of years of teaching seminars on literary censorship, I have observed that while undergraduates invariably love *Lolita*, it is also the only work among those treated here which some of them assert should perhaps after all be censored.

3. Alfred Appel, Jr., painstaking annotator of *The Annotated Lolita* (New York: Random House, 1991), observes of this title that "the term 'white widowed male' occurs in the case histories of psychiatric works, while the entire subtitle parodies the titillating confessional novel, such as John Cleland's *Memoirs of a Woman of Pleasure*" (319).

4. This technique has since, in the absence of literary censorship, become a commonplace one, reaching a sordid apogee in Bret Easton Ellis's *American Psycho* (1991), recounted in great detail from the point of view of a sadistic yuppie serial killer and purporting to be an indictment of eighties materialism. Ellis's novel provided fodder for journalists for a while as cries of censorship arose after an editor for the company which had originally contracted to publish the work protested, with the eventual result that the contract was voided, despite the author's large advance; another prominent publishing house then bought and published the novel

in a paperback edition, which immediately became a bestseller as a result of the publicity; a film was also made on its basis. It is misleading to speak of censorship in such a case; on the same basis the author of any inferior work may claim that rejection by a publisher constitutes censorship.

5. For Nabokov's objections to identificatory reading, see *Lectures on Literature* (New York: Harcourt Brace Jovanovich, 1980).

6. *Dear Bunny, Dear Volodya: The Nabokov-Wilson Letters, 1940–1971*, ed. Simon Karlinsky (Berkeley: University of California Press, 2001), 331.

7. The interviewer was the novelist Herbert Gold, whom Nabokov named as his replacement when he left Cornell. Reprinted in *Strong Opinions* (New York: Random House, 1990), 93.

8. Because of Nabokov's remarkable discretion, accounts of his life and work—even the exhaustive two-volume Boyd biography—offer comparatively little in the way of genesis of his fiction, so that where it is possible to track many other authors' grapplings with strategies to avoid censorship through biography, autobiography, and letters, and despite the many pleasures of reading, especially, his autobiographical and occasional writings and correspondence, not much is to be learned from them about the specific decisions he made in the writing of *Lolita* or his other novels.

9. Trilling, "The Last Lover," quoted in Boyd, *Nabokov: The American Years* (Princeton: Princeton University Press, 1991), 227.

10. *Playboy* interview, 1964, reprinted in *Strong Opinions*, 33.

11. Appel remains uncharacteristically silent on the Carmen song, which I therefore take to be Nabokov's invention.

12. The Kubrick film contains a number of lubricious jokes, absent from the novel, which seem to have presented less of a problem than the overall story itself. Two more examples. (1) When Humbert abruptly decides to take the room in Charlotte Haze's house she wants to know why: was it the "piazza"? Or her cherry pies? Gazing at Lolita he says, "cherry pies." (2) In one of their few bedroom scenes, Charlotte tells Humbert that when he touches her she goes as limp as a noodle; Humbert replies that he knows the feeling well. Geoffrey Shurlock, then head of the Production Code Administration, at first insisted that this last exchange be removed, but eventually relented. A few other cuts were made; see Frank Miller, *Censored Hollywood*, 190–93.

13. *Ada* (New York: McGraw-Hill, 1969), 361. Balzac (whom Nabokov considered overrated) says the following in the foreword to *La Comédie humaine*: "Chance is the greatest novelist in the world: to be prolific one need only study it [Le hasard est le plus grand romancier du monde: pour être fécond, il n'y a qu'à l'étudier]."

14. Flaubert in fact came close to anticipating Nabokov and other self-consciously metaliterary writers of the twentieth century, such as Pirandello, Borges, and Queneau, in terms of the explicit inscription of the author in the text. In an "epilogue" to *Madame Bovary* that he eventually decided to abandon, Flaubert gave Homais, the complacent, pontificating pharmacist, a moment of self-doubt in which he wonders whether he is not perhaps in the end a fictional character invented specifically to prove that he does not actually exist (see *Plans et scénarios*, 61). If he had included this episode in 1857, all of modern literature might have taken a different turn, as one of the most characteristic moves of the twentieth century would have been inaugurated some fifty years in advance.

15. This pathetic scene in *The Old Curiosity Shop* prompted Oscar Wilde's fa-

mous comment that no one who had a heart could read the death of Little Nell without laughing. In Nabokov's novel not only is Lolita's death not described, but her fate is announced, in the foreword, under her married name, so as to be comprehensible only to the alert rereader.

16. See Stacy Schiff, *Véra: Mrs. Vladimir Nabokov* (New York: Random House, 1999), 205n.

17. *Dear Bunny, Dear Volodya*, 320–21.

18. The decision was affirmed without an opinion; see Marjorie Heins, *Not in Front of the Children* (New York: Hill and Wang, 2001), 48.

19. *Selected Letters*, 144.

20. At the start of his literary career Nabokov had in fact published a number of works under the pseudonym V. Sirin, to avoid confusion with his father, whose name was Vladimir Dmitrovich Nabokov. Girodias maintains that Nabokov wanted to use this same pseudonym for *Lolita*, which seems odd, as it would have been recognizable; Schiff has him intending to sign Humbert Humbert, which seems even less likely, since this would have guaranteed that the text be read as a case study rather than a novel.

21. de Grazia, *Girls Lean Back Everywhere*, 243.

22. See ibid., 247–48.

23. Girodias, "The Sad, Ungraceful Story of *Lolita*," in *The Olympia Reader*, ed. Girodias (New York: Grove Press, 1965), 535.

24. *Selected Letters*, 175.

25. Girodias, *Une Journée sur la terre* (Paris: Éditions de la différence, 1990), 295.

26. "J'avais fait un pari absurde, celui d'associer la découverte et le lancement de l'avant-garde littéraire avec une activité alimentaire de pornographie—et le rapport entre ces deux objectifs s'annonçait riche en surprises" (291).

27. See "*Lolita* and Mr. Girodias," Nabokov's 1967 response to Girodias's "Sad, Ungraceful History," first published in the *Evergreen Review* and reprinted in *Strong Opinions*, 275; see also 271 for his views of Girodias's hope that the novel "might lead to a change in social attitudes toward the kind of love described in it."

28. The two others: *Boswell on the Grand Tour* and *The State of France*.

29. Cited in de Grazia, *Girls Lean Back Everywhere*, 260.

30. Boyd, *Vladimir Nabokov*, 295.

31. See Girodias, *Une Journée sur la terre*, 344.

32. Cited in Schiff, *Véra*, 242n.

33. Cited in Norman Page, *Nabokov: The Critical Heritage* (London: Routledge Kegan Paul, 1982), 125.

34. Quoted in Boyd, *Vladimir Nabokov*, 375.

35. For the full list and the letter itself, see de Grazia, *Girls Lean Back Everywhere*, 268.

36. Schiff, *Véra*, 256–57.

37. Ibid., 257.

38. Letter to Walter Minton, March 3, 1958; see also Boyd, *Vladimir Nabokov*, 374.

39. See Minnelli, *I Remember It Well* (New York: Samuel French, 1990) (the title of this memoir is taken from another of Chevalier's songs from the musical), for his account of what had to be done to get *Gigi* past the censors, see 125.

40. Miller, *Censored Hollywood*, 169.

41. Quoted in Richard Corliss, *Lolita* (London: British Film Institute, 1994), 19.

42. Cited in Wood, "Revisiting *Lolita*," in *Vladimir Nabokov's Lolita: A Casebook*, ed. Ellen Pifer (Oxford: Oxford University Press, 2003), 184.

43. Cited in de Grazia, *Girls Lean Back Everywhere*, 268.

44. "Nonita" in the original. Eco, *Misreadings* (New York: Harcourt Brace Jovanovich, 1993).

45. *Strong Opinions*, 123.

46. Cited in Schiff, *Véra*, 259.

EPILOGUE

1. The word was for all practical purposes coined in the mid eighteenth century. In his *Secret Museum* Walter Kendrick points out that its meaning has changed greatly over the course of its lifetime, with an 1857 medical dictionary defining "pornography" as "a description of prostitutes or prostitution, as a matter of public hygiene," whereas in 1975 the *American Heritage Dictionary* gives "Written, graphic, or other forms of communication intended to incite lascivious feelings" (1). *The Secret Museum* traces the notion of pornography from the excavation of Pompeii in the 1860s through modern times.

2. See his "Essay on Novels," first published as an introduction to *The Crimes of Love (1800)*, trans. David Coward (New York: Oxford University Press, 2005).

3. Citizens for Decent Literature later filed an amicus curiae brief in the Supreme Court case. As Rembar observes, "The Citizens for Decent Literature, Inc., has a twentieth-century name, redolent with affirmation. Its members, and the members of its predecessor, the National Organization for Decent Literature, apparently want to tell us that they are not against literature, but on the contrary, for it. Anthony Comstock and John Sumner were not troubled by such nuances. It was the Society for the Suppression of Vice, and no nonsense about it" (469).

4. Cited in de Grazia, *Girls Lean Back Everywhere*, 569.

5. On both the Obscenity and Pornography Commission Report and *Miller v. California*, see ibid., chap. 28.

6. Diderot's *Religieuse* began as a sort of serious practical joke, a series of letters written by the author to his friend the marquis de Croismare in the guise of appeals for help from a young nun trapped in a convent. She recounts to Croismare the various ways she has been mistreated in order to convince him to help her escape. Diderot's motivation in writing this narrative in 1760 was in part to lure his friend back to Paris; it was posthumously published in 1796 and has been read as an argument against the system of enforced vows, but its detailed first-person account of Suzanne's persecutions at the hands of priests, mothers superior, etc. makes her one of *Justine*'s many precursors.

7. In the still-useful *Romantic Agony*, his seminal study of nineteenth-century decadent romanticism, first published as *La carne, la morte e il diavolo nella letteratura romantica* in 1933, the great Italian critic Mario Praz analyzes the many influences of Sade on writers during this period.

8. Cited in Pauvert, *La Traversée du livre* (Paris: Viviane Hamy, 2004), 144.

9. See ibid., 152.

10. A notable example from recent years is Roger Shattuck's *Forbidden Knowledge: From Prometheus to Pornography* (New York: Harcourt Brace, 1996), which devotes a seventy-five-page section to Sade, whom Shattuck terms "the most chal-

lenging test case of a forbidden author" (228). He discusses the moors murders and also Ted Bundy in terms of Sade's influence. The book contains a warning that "parents and teachers should be aware that Chapter VII [on Sade] does not make appropriate reading for children and minors."

11. Among Pauvert's intimates Raymond Queneau was particularly skeptical about the idea of Sade as incarnation of liberty in the light of recent historical events. "The charnel-houses are the logical extension of these philosophies [Les charniers complètent les philosophies]," he wrote in 1945 about the relation between Sade's works and Nazi concentration camps. Albert Camus and, later on, Michel Foucault also expressed reservations along these lines. Cited in Pauvert, *La Traversée du livre*, 144.

12. "Those people paint as though they were on the toilet, I tell you. . . . It's the end of the nation, the end of France [Ces gens-là font de la peinture sous eux, vous dis-je. . . . C'est la fin de la nation, de la France]," wrote Jean Gérôme, for instance, in *Le Journal des artistes* about impressionist technique in 1894; cited in *Le Dictionnaire de la bêtise*, 211.

13. Reprinted in Grove edition of *120 Days of Sodom*, trans. Richard Seaver and Austryn Wainhouse (New York: Grove Press, 1990), 61.

Bibliography

Amis, Martin. *The War against Cliché*. New York: Random House, 2002.

Anderson, Margaret. *My Thirty Years War*. Westport, Conn.: Greenwood Press, 1971.

Arnold, Bruce. *The Scandal of Ulysses: The Sensational Life of a Twentieth-Century Masterpiece*. New York: St. Martin's Press, 1991.

Baker, Michael. *Our Three Selves: The Life of Radclyffe Hall*. New York: Morrow, 1985.

Balzac, Honoré de. *La Comédie humaine*. 12 vols. Paris: Gallimard 1976–81.

Barbey d'Aurevilly, Jules. *De Balzac à Zola, critiques et polémiques*. Paris: Les Belles lettres, 1999.

Barnes, Julian. *Something to Declare*. London: Picador, 2002.

Baudelaire, Charles. *Œuvres complètes*. 2 vols. Paris: Gallimard, 1975.

Beach, Sylvia. *Shakespeare and Company*. Lincoln: University of Nebraska Press, 1991.

Bechtel, Guy, and Jean-Claude Carrière, eds. *Dictionnaire de la bêtise et des erreurs de jugement*. Paris: Laffont, 1990.

Benjamin, Walter. *Charles Baudelaire: A Lyric Poet in the Era of High Capitalism*. Translated by Harry Zohn. London: Verso, 1983.

——. *Illuminations*. Translated by Harry Zohn. New York: Schocken, 1988.

Black, Gregory. *Hollywood Censored: Morality Codes, Catholics, and the Movies*. New York: Cambridge University Press, 1994.

Bongie, Lawrence. *Sade: A Biographical Essay*. Chicago: University of Chicago Press, 1998.

Bourdieu, Pierre. *Les Règles de l'art*. Paris: Seuil, 1992.

Bowlby, Rachel. *Shopping with Freud*. London: Routledge, 1993.

Boyd, Brian. *Vladimir Nabokov: The American Years*. Princeton: Princeton University Press, 1991.

Boyer, Paul. *Purity in Print: The Vice Society Movement and Book Censorship in America*. New York: Scribner's, 1968.

Budgen, Frank. *James Joyce and the Making of "Ulysses."* Bloomington: Indiana University Press, 1960.

Burgess, Anthony. *Flame into Being: The Life and Work of D. H. Lawrence*. New York: Arbor House, 1985.

——. *Re/Joyce*. New York: Norton, 1968.

Cather, Kirsten. "The Great Censorship Trials of Literature and Film in Postwar Japan." Ph.D. diss., University of California, Berkeley, 2004.

Cleland, John. *Fanny Hill.* Edited by Peter Wagner. Harmondsworth, UK: Penguin, 1985.

Cline, Sally. *Radclyffe Hall: A Woman Called John.* London: J. Murray, 1997.

Coetzee, J. M. *Giving Offense: Essays on Censorship.* Chicago: University of Chicago Press, 1996.

Colum, Padraic, and Mary Colum. *Our Friend James Joyce.* New York: Doubleday, 1958.

Corliss, Richard. *Lolita.* London: British Film Institute, 1994.

Crouzet, Michel. "Le 'Banquet' romantique." Preface to Théophile Gautier, *Mademoiselle de Maupin.* Paris, Gallimard, 1973.

Darnton, Robert. *Forbidden Bestsellers of Pre-Revolutionary France.* New York: Norton, 1995.

De Grazia, Edward. *Censorship Landmarks.* New York: Bowker, 1969.

——. *Girls Lean Back Everywhere: The Law of Obscenity and the Assault on Genius.* New York: Random House, 1992.

De Salvo, Louise. Introduction to Henry Miller, *Tropic of Cancer.* New York: Signet, 1995.

Dickens, Charles. *Our Mutual Friend.* Harmondsworth, UK: Penguin, 1998.

Dickson, Lovat. *Radclyffe Hall at the Well of Loneliness: A Sapphic Chronicle.* New York: Scribner's, 1975.

Doan, Laura. *Fashioning Sapphism.* New York: Columbia University Press, 2001.

Doan, Laura, and Jay Prosser, eds. *Palatable Poison.* New York: Columbia University Press, 2001.

Douchin, Jacques-Louis. *La Vie érotique de Flaubert.* Paris: Pauvert, 1984.

Dujardin, Edouard. *Les Lauriers sont coupés.* Paris: Flammarion, 2001.

Dyer, Geoff. Introduction to D. H. Lawrence, *Lady Chatterley's Lover.* 75th Anniversary ed. New York: Signet, 2003.

Eberly, Rosa A. *Citizen Critics: Literary Public Spheres.* Urbana: University of Illinois Press, 2000.

Eco, Umberto. *Misreadings.* Translated by William Weaver. New York: Harcourt Brace Jovanovich, 1993.

Ellmann, Richard. *James Joyce.* Rev. ed. New York: Oxford University Press, 1983.

——. *Oscar Wilde.* New York: Random House, 1987.

Ernst, Morris L., and Alan Schwartz. *Censorship: The Search for the Obscene.* New York: Macmillan, 1964.

Ernst, Morris L., and William Seagle. *To the Pure . . . : A Study of Obscenity and the Censor.* New York: Viking, 1929.

Fargnoli, A. Nicholas. *James Joyce: A Literary Reference.* New York: Carroll and Graf, 2001.

Ferguson, Frances. *Pornography, the Theory: What Utilitarianism Did to Action.* Chicago: University of Chicago Press, 2004.

Ferguson, Robert. *Henry Miller: A Life.* New York: Norton, 1991.

Fforde, Jasper. *The Eyre Affair.* New York: Penguin, 2003.

Field, Andrew. *VN: The Life of Vladimir Nabokov.* New York: Crown, 1986.

Flaubert, Gustave. *Correspondance.* 4 vols. Paris: Gallimard, 1973–98.

——. *Œuvres.* 2 vols. Paris: Gallimard, 1936.

——. *Madame Bovary: Plans et scenarios.* Edited by Yvan Leclerc. Paris: Zulma, 1995.

Forster, E. M. *Maurice.* New York: Norton, 1971.

Foucault, Michel. *History of Sexuality: An Introduction.* Translated by Robert Hurley. New York: Random House, 1985.

Furbank, P. N. *E. M. Forster: A Life.* New York: Harcourt Brace Jovanovich, 1978.

Gardner, Gerald. *The Censorship Papers: Movie Censorship Letters from the Hays Office.* New York: Dodd, Mead, 1987.

Gifford, Don. *Ulysses Annotated.* Berkeley: University of California Press, 1989.

Gilbert, Stuart. *James Joyce's Ulysses.* New York: Random House, 1952.

Girodias, Maurice. *Une Journée sur la terre.* Paris: Editions de la différence, 1990.

——. "The Sad, Ungraceful Story of *Lolita*." In *The Olympia Reader,* ed. Maurice Girodias. New York: Grove Press, 1965.

Goncourt, Edmond, and Jules Goncourt. *Journal.* 3 vols. Paris: Laffont, 1989.

Grunfeld, Frederic V. *Rodin.* New York: Da Capo, 1998.

Hall, Radclyffe. *The Well of Loneliness.* New York: Doubleday, 1990.

Heins, Marjorie. *Not in Front of the Children: "Indecency," Censorship, and the Innocence of Youth.* New York: Hill and Wang, 2001.

Highsmith, Patricia. *The Price of Salt.* Talahassee, FL: Naiad Press, 1991.

Hugo, Victor. *Les Contemplations.* Paris: Gallimard, 1943.

Huxley, Aldous. *Complete Essays.* 6 vols. Chicago: Ivan R. Dee, 2000–2002.

Hynes, James. *The Lecturer's Tale.* New York: Picador, 2001.

Jackson, Holbrook. *The Fear of Books.* New York: Scribner's, 1932.

Jauss, Hans Robert. *Toward an Esthetics of Reception.* Translated by Timothy Bahti. Minneapolis: University of Minnesota Press, 1982.

Jong, Erica. *The Devil at Large: Erica Jong on Henry Miller.* New York: Turtle Bay, 1993.

Joyce, James. *Ulysses.* New York: Random House, 1961.

Julius, Anthony. *Transgressions: The Offenses of Art.* London: Thames and Hudson, 2002.

Kahane, Jack. *Memoirs of a Booklegger.* London: Michael Joseph, 1939.

Kelly, Joseph. *Our Joyce: From Outcast to Icon.* Austin: University of Texas Press, 1998.

Kendrick, Walter. *The Secret Museum: Pornography in Modern Culture.* New York: Viking Penguin, 1988.

LaCapra, Dominick. *Madame Bovary on Trial.* Ithaca: Cornell University Press, 1982.

Ladenson, Elisabeth. "The Imperial Superreader, or Semiotics of Indecency." *Romanic Review* 93, no.1–2 (January–March 2002): 81–90.

Larkin, Philip. *Collected Poems.* London: Faber and Faber, 1988.

Larousse, Pierre. *Grand Dictionnaire universel du XIXe siècle.* Paris: Administration du grand dictionnaire universel, 1866.

Lawrence, D. H. *Collected Letters.* Edited by Harry T. Moore. New York: Viking, 1962.

——. *Lady Chatterley's Lover.* New York: Random House, 2001.

——. *Sex, Literature, and Censorship: Essays.* Edited by Harry T. Moore. New York: Twayne, 1953.

Leclerc, Yvan. *Crimes écrits. La littérature en procès au XIXe siècle.* Paris: Plon, 1991.

Lever, Maurice. *Sade: A Biography.* Translated by Arthur Goldhammer. New York: Farrar, Straus, Giroux, 1993.

Lyons, Martyn. "Les nouveaux lecteurs au XIXe siècle." In *Histoire de la lecture dans le monde occidental,* ed. Guglielmo Cavallo and Roger Chartier, 393–430. Paris: Seuil, 1989.

——. *Readers and Society in Nineteenth-Century France: Workers, Women, Peasants.* New York: Palgrave, 2001.

MacKinnon, Catharine A. *Only Words.* Cambridge: Harvard University Press, 1996.

Marcus, Jane. "Sapphistory: The Woolf and the Well." In *Lesbian Texts and Contexts,* ed. Karla Jay and Joanne Glasgow, 164–79. New York: New York University Press, 1990.

Martin, Jay. *Always Merry and Bright: The Life of Henry Miller, An Unauthorized Biography.* Santa Barbara, CA: Capo Press, 1978.

Meaker, Marjorie. *Highsmith: A Romance of the 1950s.* San Francisco: Cleis Press, 2003.

Miller, Frank. *Censored Hollywood: Sex, Sin, and Violence on Screen.* Atlanta: Turner, 1994.

Miller, Henry. *Black Spring.* New York: Grove Press, 1963.

——. *Henry Miller on Writing.* New York: New Directions, 1964.

——. *Tropic of Cancer.* New York: Grove Press, 1961.

——. *Tropic of Cancer.* New York: Signet Press, 1995.

——. *Tropic of Capricorn.* London: Harper Perennial, 2005.

——. *The World of Lawrence: A Passionate Appreciation.* London: Calder, 1985.

Miller, William Ian. *Anatomy of Disgust.* Cambridge: Harvard University Press, 1997.

Millett, Kate. *Sexual Politics.* New York: Doubleday, 1969.

Milton, John. *Areopagitica.* London: Oxford University Press, 1944.

Minnelli, Vincente. *I Remember It Well.* New York: Samuel French, 1990.

Moore, Harry T. *D. H. Lawrence and His World.* New York: Viking, 1966.

Nabokov, Vladimir. *Ada.* New York: McGraw-Hill, 1969.

——. *The Annotated Lolita.* Edited by Alfred Appel, Jr. New York: Random House, 1991.

——. *Dear Bunny, Dear Volodya: The Nabokov-Wilson Letters, 1940–1971.* Edited by Simon Karlinsky. Berkeley: University of California Press, 2001.

——. *Lectures on Literature.* New York: Harcourt Brace Jovanovich, 1980.

——. *Selected Letters, 1940–1970.* New York: Harcourt Brace Jovanovich, 1990.

——. *Strong Opinions.* New York: Random House, 1990.

Netz, Robert. *Histoire de la censure dans l'édition.* Paris: PUF, 1998.

Orwell, George. *Collected Essays.* London: Secker and Warburg, 1961.

Page, Norman, ed. *Nabokov: The Critical Heritage.* London: Routledge and Kegan Paul, 1982.

Parkes, Adam. *Modernism and the Theater of Censorship.* New York: Oxford University Press, 1996.

Pauvert, Jean-Jacques. *La Traversée du livre.* Paris: Viviane Hamy, 2004.

Pease, Allison. *Modernism, Mass Culture, and the Esthetics of Obscenity.* Cambridge: Cambridge University Press, 2000.

Pera, Pia. *Lolita's Diary*. Translated by Ann Goldstein. New York: Farrar, Straus, Giroux, 1999.

Perrin, Noel. *Dr. Bowdler's Legacy: A History of Expurgated Books in England and America*. New York: Atheneum, 1969.

Pifer, Ellen, ed. *Vladimir Nabokov's Lolita: A Casebook*. Oxford: Oxford University Press, 2003.

Pound, Ezra. *Poems and Translations*. New York: Library of America, 2003.

Power, Arthur. *Conversations with James Joyce*. Dublin: Lilliput, 1999.

Praz, Mario. *The Romantic Agony*. Translated by Angus Davidson. London: Oxford University Press, 1933.

Proust, Marcel. *A la recherche du temps perdu*. 4 vols. Paris: Gallimard, 1987–89.

Queneau, Raymond. *Bâtons, chiffres et lettres*. Paris: Gallimard, 1965.

Reid, Panthea. *Art and Affection: A Life of Virginia Woolf*. Oxford: Oxford University Press, 1996.

Rembar, Charles. *The End of Obscenity: The Trials of Lady Chatterley's Lover, Tropic of Cancer, and Fanny Hill*. New York: Harper and Row, 1986.

Rolph, C. H., ed. *The Trial of Lady Chatterley*. Harmondsworth, UK: Penguin, 1961.

Sade, Marquis de. *The Crimes of Love*. Translated by David Coward. New York: Oxford University Press, 2005.

——. *Justine, Philosophy in the Bedroom, and Other Writings*. Translated by Richard Seaver and Austryn Wainhouse. New York: Grove Press, 1987.

——. *The 120 Days of Sodom*. Translated by Richard Seaver and Austryn Wainhouse. New York: Grove Press, 1990.

Saint-Jorre, John de. *Venus Bound: The Erotic Voyage of the Olympia Press and Its Writers*. New York: Random House, 1996.

Sainte-Beuve, Charles Augustin. *Pour la critique*. Paris: Gallimard, 1992.

Schauer, Frederick F. *The Law of Obscenity*. Washington, D.C.: Bureau of National Affairs, 1976.

Schiff, Stacy. *Véra: Mrs. Vladimir Nabokov*. New York: Random House, 1999.

Schumach, Murray. *The Face on the Cutting Room Floor*. New York: Morrow, 1964.

Segall, Jeffrey. *Joyce in America: Cultural Politics and the Trials of "Ulysses."* Berkeley: University of California Press, 1993.

Shattuck, Roger. *Forbidden Knowledge: From Prometheus to Pornography*. New York: Harcourt Brace, 1996.

Souhami, Diana. *The Trials of Radclyffe Hall*. New York: Doubleday, 1999.

Stora-Lamarre, Annie. *L'Enfer de la IIIe République: Censeurs et Pornographes (1881–1914)*. Paris: Imago, 1990.

Sutherland, John. *Offensive Literature: Decensorship in Britain, 1960–1982*. London: Junction Books, 1982.

Tebbel, John. *A History of Book Publishing in the United States*. 4 vols. New York: Bowker, 1972–81.

Thibaudet, Albert. *Gustave Flaubert*. Paris: Gallimard, 1935.

Thirouin, Laurent. *L'Aveuglement salutaire: le réquisitoire contre le théâtre dans la France classique*. Paris: Champion, 1997.

Travis, Alan. *Bound and Gagged: A Secret History of Obscenity in Britain*. London: Profile Books, 2000.

Troubridge, Una. *Life of Radclyffe Hall.* New York: Citadel, 1961.

Troyat, Henri. *Zola.* Paris: Flammarion, 1992.

Vanderham, Paul. *James Joyce and Censorship: The Trials of Ulysses.* New York: New York University Press, 1998.

Virgil. *Aeneid.* Translated by H. Rushton Fairclough. Cambridge: Harvard University Press, 2000.

Wilde, Oscar. *The Picture of Dorian Gray.* Oxford: Oxford University Press, 1964.

Wilson, Andrew. *Beautiful Shadow: A Life of Patricia Highsmith.* New York: Bloomsbury, 2003.

Woolf, Virginia. *The Common Reader.* 2 vols. London: The Hogarth Press, 1989.

——. *Diary of Virginia Woolf.* Edited by Ann Olivier Bell. New York: Harcourt Brace Jovanovich, 1977.

——. *Letters.* Edited by Nigel Nicolson. New York: Harcourt Brace Jovanovich, 1975–80.

——. *Mrs. Dalloway.* New York: Harcourt Brace, 1964.

——. *Orlando.* London: Penguin, 1993.

——. *A Room of One's Own.* New York: Harcourt Brace, 1929.

Zola, Emile. *Écrits sur le roman.* Paris: Livre de poche, 2004.

——. *Le Roman expérimental.* Paris: Charpentier, 1880.

——. *Les Romanciers naturalistes.* Paris: Fasquelle, 1923.

Index

Abelard, 174
Abortion, 154
Adams, J. Donald, 213
Adultery, 16, 36–45, 56, 80, 104–5, 116,
    133–40, 142, 248 n.6
Aeneid, 157, 159, 175–76
Alice in Wonderland, 201
Amants, Les (film), 184
American Civil Liberties Union, 178, 183
American Psycho, 252 n.4
Amis, Martin, 81
Anchor Review, 211–12
Anderson, Margaret, 79–80, 91, 95
Anderson, Sherwood, 128, 171
Anna Karenina, 134, 138, 146
Annotated Lolita, The, 201
Antisemitism, 110, 127
Apollinaire, Guillaume, 222, 229
Appel, Alfred, Jr., 201
Aquinas, Thomas, xvii
Ardrey, Robert, 20
Aristotle, xvi–xvii, 202
"art for art's sake," xii, xviii–xix, 8, 20, 22,
    29–30, 34, 46, 70, 73, 77, 129, 133,
    157, 161, 163–64, 190, 200, 203, 224
L'Artiste (journal), 34
Asselineau, Charles, 26–27, 58–59
Atheism, 191
Atlantic, The, 205
Augier, Émile, 56
Augustine, Saint, xvii
Auteil, Daniel, 232
Ayer, A. J., 210

Bachelor and the Bobbysoxer, The (film), 215–
    17
Baker, Michael, 111
Balmer, Jean-François, 42
Balzac, Honoré de, 1–2, 11, 25, 35, 56, 134,
    203–4, 239 n.11, 253 n.13; *La Cousine*
Bette, 245 n.15; *La Fille aux yeux d'or*,
    73; *La Vieille fille*, 11
Barbey d'Aurevilly, Jules-Amédée, 6–7,
    51–3, 67, 83, 173, 242 n.12; *Les Dia-*
    boliques, 6–7; "La Vengeance d'une
    femme," 245 n.15
Barnacle, Nora, 80
Barnes, Julian, 49
Barthes, Roland, 231
Bataille, Georges, 208, 230
Baudelaire, Charles, 1, 5–8, 14, 90, 149,
    200, 221; and art for art's sake, 29–30,
    73; anti-progress stance, 20; Barbey
    on, 67; becomes more Baudelairean as
    result of trial, 68–70; compared to
    Dante, 67–68; compared to Flaubert,
    49–51, 59–61, 66–67, 76–77; com-
    pared to Joyce, 87; compared to Sade,
    67; gender of readership, 56–58, 60–
    61; and Hugo, 61; and hypothetical fe-
    male relatives, 57–58; immoralist, 131,
    161, 200, 234; on *Madame Bovary*, 34–
    36, 38, 40, 74, 150, 203; Henry Miller
    compared to, 158; objects to being
    called Prince of Putrefaction, 63–64;
    odor in poems, 64–65, 70; putrefac-
    tion in poems, 53, 62–64, 82–83, 87;
    read by Flaubert, 49–50, 53, 55; and
    realism, 23, 47–48, 53–54, 73–74; rela-
    tionship with mother, 58; rehabilita-
    tion, 47–49, 71, 75, 77, 101; taste for
    masculine women, 35–36; turns mud
    into gold, 51
—Works:
    Les Épaves, 48, 71
    Fleurs du mal: "Abel et Caïn," 71; "A
        celle qui est trop gaie," 14, 49, 71–72;
        "Au lecteur," 64, 69, 76–77; "A une
        mendiante rousse," 71; "Le Beau
        navire," 71; "La Beauté," 69–79;

Baudelaire, Charles (*continued*)
"Bénédiction," 58; "Les Bijoux," 49,
69, 72, 75; "Épigraphe pour un livre
condamné," 77; "Femmes damnées:
Comme un bétail pensif," 71–73;
"Femmes damnées: Delphine et Hip-
polyte," 72–75, 120; "L'Héautonti-
moroumenos," 64; "Hymne à la
Beauté," 70–72; "L'Invitation au voy-
age," 58; "Lesbos," x–xi, 71–74; "Le
Léthé," 64–65, 72; "Les Litanies de
Satan," 71; "Le Masque," 69–70; "Les
Métamorphoses du vampire," 71–72;
"Le Reniement de Saint Pierre," 71;
"Sed non satiata," 71, 158; "Le Vin de
l'assassin," 71; "Une charogne," 51–52,
63, 65, 70; "Une martyre," 70, 73
  Les Fleurs du mal and trial, 26–27, 36,
  48–55, 65–76, 80, 151, 164, 180, 187–
  88
  Fusées, 52
  Mon coeur mis à nu, 68
Beach, Sylvia, 91, 98, 144–45, 170, 176,
  206, 209
Beats, the, 160–61
Beauvoir, Simone de ("Must We Burn
  Sade?"), 231, 236
Beckett, Samuel, 208
Benjamin, Walter, 56, 74
Bennett, Arnold, 124
Béranger, Pierre-Jean de, 4–6, 50
Berlin, Isaiah, 214
Berman, Pandro, 20, 241 n.28
Bestiality, 185
Birkett, Norman, 126
Biron, Sir Chartres, 113, 125–27
Black, Justice Hugo, 153, 184, 238 n.13
Bloomsbury group, 112, 118, 125–27
Boccaccio (*Decameron*), 14, 146, 160, 174,
  230
Bonaparte, Napoléon. *See* Napoleon I
Bonnetain, Paul (*Charlot s'amuse*), 24
Boredom defense, 124
Bourdin, Gustave, 62, 70
Bowdler, Rev. Thomas, 14
Bowdlerization, 14
Bowlby, Rachel, 21
Boyer d'Argens, Jean-Baptiste de (*Thérèse
  philosophe*), 9
Bramly, Serge, 232
Breakfast, 61, 63
Brennan, Justice William, 153, 156, 184,
  224–25
Breton, André, 179, 230
Brockway, Wallace, 205–6
Brook, Peter, 231
Brown, Joe E., 217

Brown, Murphy, 156
Bruno, Giordano, 246 n.40
Brussells, Jacob R., 177
Bryan, Judge Frederick Van Pelt, 132, 142–
  43, 146
Burger, Chief Justice Warren, 225
Buñuel, Luis, 231
Burgess, Anthony, xii, 14, 80, 101, 112,
  131–33, 140, 246 n.43
Burroughs, William S., 160–61, 208
Bushnel, Judge Hyman, 127

Caine, Michael, 233–34
Cairns, Huntington, 180–81
Calder, John, 185
Camus, Albert, 179, 256 n.11
Candide, 227
Cape, Jonathan, 113–15, 117, 123, 125–27,
  151, 154, 170, 188
Caron, Leslie, 214
Carroll, Lewis, 201
Castle, Terry, 247 n.9
Céline, 81; *Voyage au bout de la nuit*, 171–72
Cendrars, Blaise, 171
Cerf, Bennett, 95
Chaix d'Est-Ange, Gustave, 66, 74, 243
  n.40
Champfleury (Jules Husson), 23, 32, 43–
  44, 53
Chateaubriand, François-René de, 10, 77
Chabrol, Claude, 42
Chaucer, Geoffrey, 102
Chevalier, Maurice, 214–15
Citizens for Decent Literature, 224
Cixous, Hélène, 246 n.41
Clarissa, 228
Cleland, John, 223–24. *See also Fanny Hill*
Cobain, Kurt, 160
Coetzee, J. M., 145
Colet, Louise, 34, 50
Colette, 119, 214–15
Collier, Gertrude (Mrs. Tennant), 32–34
Comstock, Anthony, 91, 127
Comstock Act, 153, 250 n.37
Conan Doyle, Sir Arthur, 125
Connolly, Cyril, 109, 171
Constant, Benjamin, 20
Coprography, 51
Coprophilia, 185
Cornell University, 93, 189, 196, 205, 216
Cornut, Étienne, 242 n.9
Corrigan, Joseph E., 95
Courbet, Gustave, 23, 25, 51, 53, 75
Covici, Pascal, 205
Covici and Friede (publishers), 127–28
Coward, Noël, 111
Cowley, Malcolm, 154

Crawford, Joan, 41
Cunnilingus, x, 184
Cutter, Justice R. Ammi, 183

Dadaism, 229
Daily Express, 213
D'Alembert, 9
Dante, 66–68, 175, 200
Daudet, Alphonse, 25
De Grazia, Edward, xv
Declaration of the Rights of Man, 9
Debby's Bidet, 209
Defoe, Daniel, 222
De Gaulle, Charles, 211
Dickens, Charles, 203–4; *Our Mutual
    Friend*, 57; *Pickwick Papers*, 11
Dickson, Lovat, 111
Diderot, Denis, 9; *La Religieuse*, 73, 228,
    255 n.6
Dietrich, Marlene, 197
Discreet Charm of the Bourgeoisie, 84
Divorce, 154
Doctor Zhivago, 212
Dos Passos, John, 171, 174
Dostoevsky, Fyodor, 160, 201
Doubleday (publisher), 206
Douglas, Lord Alfred, 129
Douglas, James, 98, 108, 111–19, 143–44,
    210
Douglas, Justice William O., 153, 184, 238
    n.13
Dreiser, Theodore, 128, 171, 174
Dreyfus Affair, 179, 211
Duckworth (publisher), 143
Dujardin, Édouard (*Les Lauriers sont
    coupés*), 88–89
Dumas, Alexandre, 1–2
Dumb and Dumber, 84
Dupee, F. W., 211
Duranty, Louis Edmond, 23, 32
Durham, Bishop of, 115
Durrell, Lawrence, 179, 208
Duval, Jeanne, 74
Dworkin, Andrea, xvii
Dyer, Geoff, 145–46

Eco, Umberto, 219
Eeckhoud, Georges, 119
Ellis, Bret Easton, 252 n.4
Ellis, Havelock, 117, 125, 171–72, 194,
    230
Eliot, George, 248 n.6
Eliot, T. S., 92, 171–72
Ellmann, Richard, 183
Eluard, Paul, 179
Emon family, 58, 60
Encyclopédie, 9

Epstein, Jason, 206, 211
Epstein, Judge Samuel B., 183–84
Ernst, Morris L., 95–97, 127–28
Esquire, 213
Existentialism, xvii, 76–77, 229

Faulkner, William, 88
Fanny Hill, 90, 152–53, 221–28; 234–36;
    plot of, 223
Fellatio, x
Ferber, Edna, 128
Ferguson, Robert, 185
Ferry, Jules, 4
Fforde, Jasper, 245 n.18
Fielding, Henry, 222–23
Figaro, Le, 70
Fisher, Amy, 189, 196, 220
Fitzgerald, F. Scott, 128
Flaubert, Gustave, 1, 5, 7–8, 15–16, 71,
    116, 143, 161, 164–65, 180, 188–89,
    192–97, 203, 214, 217, 221, 228;
    amoralist, 131, 161, 200; anti-progress
    stance of, 20; Barbey on, 52–53, 67; on
    Baudelaire, 49–50; bourgeois lifestyle
    of, 49; claimed as predecessor by natu-
    ralists, 24–25; compared to Baude-
    laire, 49–51, 53, 55, 59–61, 66–67, 76–
    77; and cult of style, 21; free indirect
    style, 87–89, 164–65; on function of
    criticism, 34; grandiose self-assessment
    of, 17–18; Joyce and, 81; likes depict-
    ing disgusting things, 43–44, 82;
    "Madame Bovary, c'est moi," 240 n.26;
    Nabokov and, 188–89, 192–97; Pont-
    martin on, 52; project of book about
    nothing, 50–51; and realism, 22–26;
    on Sade, 228
—Works:
    Bouvard et Pécuchet, 239 n.6
    Madame Bovary: adultery in, 36–43,
        134; Baudelaire on, 34–36, 38, 40, 74,
        150; compared to *Lady Chatterley's
        Lover*, 133–35, 138–39; compared to
        Ulysses, 85, 104–5; and *feuilleton*, 55–
        56; Minnelli film version, xvi, 15–16,
        18–20, 36, 39–47, 101, 190–91;
        Nabokov and, 192–97; and realism,
        31–35; trial as part of novel, 17–18;
        Zola on, 162
    Madame Bovary and trial, xvii, 1, 9, 11–
        12, 15–16, 80, 96, 113, 115–117, 133,
        140, 151, 156, 163–65, 180–81, 187,
        191, 195–96, 200–201, 214, 235–36,
        253 n.14; defense, 26, 34, 66 (*see also*
        Senard, Jules); prosecution, 33–35
        (*see also* Pinard, Ernest); verdict, 25–
        26, 30–32, 55–56, 61, 65–66, 77

Forrest Gump, 45
Forster, E. M., 118–22, 124–25, 128–29, 136, 155; *Maurice*, 119–21, 136–38; *Passage to India*, 113
Foucault, Michel, xv, 237 n.5, 256 n.11
Frankfurter, Justice Felix, 139
French, Marilyn, 246 n.41
Frenchness, 42
Friede, Donald, 127
Freud, Sigmund, 230
Fry, Roger, 84

Gallimard (publisher), 48–49, 75, 128, 211
Galsworthy, John, 125
Gamekeepers in literature, 136–39
Gautier, Théophile, 34, 58–59, 67; *Mademoiselle de Maupin*, 20, 73, 128
Gazette des tribunaux, 31
Genet, Jean, 160, 208, 231
Gertz, Elmer, 183
Gide, André, 8, 119–20, 179
Gigi (film), 214–16
Gilbert, Stuart, 87, 98–106
Giniger, K. S., 177
Ginzberg, Allen, 160–61
Girodias, Maurice, 145, 170–71, 179–82, 190, 192, 196, 206–12, 214, 217, 231
Goethe, Johann Wolfgang von, 67
Gold, Herbert, 253 n.7
Goldman, Emma, 171
Golden, Arthur: *Memoirs of a Geisha*, 222
Goncourt, Edmond and Jules, 6–7, 23–25, 228
Gone with the Wind, 40, 212, 241 n.37
Gordon, John, 210
Gore, Tipper, 238 n.26
Gosse, Edmund, 79
Gotham Book Mart, 177
Grande Bouffe, La, 84
Grant, Cary, 215–16
Gravediggers in literature, 139
Greene, Graham, 210
Griffith-Jones, Mervyn, 155
Grove Press, 131–32, 139, 152–53, 181–85, 206, 231

Hailsham, Lord, 155–56
Hall, Radclyffe: biographies and critical studies of, 111; compared to Lawrence, 131–32, 143; conservatism of, 110–11; life of, 122–23; makes a strange martyr, 128; moralism of, 131, 161, 200; quarrels with defenders, 124–25
Work:
The Well of Loneliness, xii, 80–81, 90, 170, 177, 208–9, 236; and "Books at Bedtime," 128; commercial success of, 123, 128; compared to Baudelaire, 120; compared to *Lady Chatterley's Lover*, 131–32, 135; compared to *Maurice*, 119–21; compared to *Ulysses*, 107; compared to *Uncle Tom's Cabin*, 128; contemporary reviews of, 108–9; James Douglas's campaign against, 111–19; first serious fictional treatment of homosexuality in English literature, 118, 128; history of censorship, 118–22; plot of, 109–10; *Lolita* compared to, 188–190; V. Woolf on, 123–24
The Well of Loneliness **and trials:** UK trial, 125–26, 145, 151–52, 154, 188, 190, 210; U.S. trial, 126–28
Harris, Frank, 144
Harris, James B., 178, 214, 216–17
Hays, Will, 13
Hays Code, xvi, 13, 15–16, 36, 39–46, 116, 187. *See also* Motion Picture Production Code
Heap, Jane, 91, 95
Heflin, Van, 41–42
Heine, Maurice, 230
Heinemann, William, 143
Heins, Marjorie, xv
Hemingway, Ernest, 128, 171, 174
Hendrix, Jimi, 160
Henry and June (film). *See* Miller, Henry
Herbert, George, 102
Hicklin Rule, 90–91, 96–97, 125, 154
Highsmith, Patricia, 121–22
Hill, Leopold, 125
Hirsch, Trygve, 179
Hitchcock, Alfred, 121
Homer, 80–82, 157, 176; *Illiad*, 176
Homosexuality, 74–75, 90, 94, 108–9, 111–12, 116–25, 135, 138, 152, 154, 160–61, 167, 188, 192, 220, 244 n.46. *See also* Lesbianism
Hugo, Victor, 20, 67, 203; *Les Contemplations*, 61, 63, 76; *Les Misérables*, 2; *Notre Dame de Paris*, 51; *Ruy Blas*, 28;
Huxley, Aldous, 114–15, 132, 144, 151, 171–72, 174, 210
Huysmans, Joris-Karl, 24, 129
Hynes, James, 104

Illiad. *See* Homer
Impressionism, 163, 234, 256 n.12
Incest, 185, 220
Index librorum prohibitorum, 8
Inferno. *See* Dante
Irons, Jeremy, 218
Isherwood, Christopher, 210

Jackson, Michael, 192, 220
Jacobellis v. Ohio, 184
Jacquot, Benoît, 232
James, William, 88
Janeway, Elizabeth, 212
Jarman, Derek (*Sebastiane*), 238 n.24
John, Augustus, 145
John Bull, 144
John Gordon Society, 210
Jones, Jennifer, 39–40
Jong, Erica, 159, 161, 179; *Fear of Flying*, 159, 234
Joplin, Janis, 160
Joyce, James, 25, 53, 144, 170–71, 185, 188–89, 200, 206, 214, 234; collaborates with Gilbert, 99 compared to Flaubert, 81–83, 166; compared to Rabelais, 84–85, 98; compared to Zola, 79, 81; Lawrence on, 147–48; Miller on, 148–49, 174, 176–77; and modernism, 81
—Works:
Finnegans Wake, 78, 170, 188
Pomes Penyeach, 170
Portrait of the Artist as a Young Man, 92
Ulysses: bodily functions in, 82–87, 92–93, 101–6, 174; comic book explaining, 100; compared to *Lady Chatterley's Lover*, 134, 140, 144; compared to *Mrs Dalloway*, 83–84; compared to Proust, 78, 94; compared to *Well of Loneliness*, 133; difficulty of, 78–79; expurgated by Pound, 91–92; four-letter words in, 89–91; Stuart Gilbert's version, 98–106; Lawrence on, 147–48; and *Madame Bovary*, 81–83, 104–5; Molly Bloom soliloquy, 80, 103–5, 147, 150; Nabokov on, 92– 4; and *Odyssey*, 80–82; plotlessness, 81; and stream of consciousness technique, 87–91, 105; Strick film adaptation of, 84, 178; V.Woolf on, 79, 92, 123
Ulysses **and trials**, xviii, 55, 144–45, 152–54, 166, 168–72, 188–89, 214, 208–9, 214, 220, 224, 236; and boredom defense, 124; 1933 decision (*see* Woolsey, Judge John M.)
Jourdan, Louis, 42, 214
Joynson-Hicks, William ("Jix"), 80, 115–16, 145
Justine. See Sade, Marquis de
Juvenal, 158

Kafka, Franz, 25
Kahane, Eric, 211
Kahane, Jack, 145, 148, 170–71, 176–77, 179, 206, 208–9, 232
Kaufman, Philip, 178, 232

Kazin, Alfred, 154
Kendrick, Walter, 115, 255 n.1
Kerouac, Jack, 161
Knopf, Alfred A., 126–27
Knopf, Blanche, 127
Kodansha (publisher), 151
Krafft-Ebing, Richard von, 230
Krueger, Cheryl, 241 n.31
Kubrick, Stanley, 178, 190–91, 202, 214, 216–19

Labouchere Amendment, 118
Laclos, Pierre Choderlos de: *Liaisons dangereuses*, 7, 245 n.15
LaCapra, Dominick, 20–22, 27, 29, 31
Lady Chatterley's Lover. See Lawrence, D. H.
Larbaud, Valéry, 85, 98, 245 n.23
Larkin, Philip, 17, 131, 139–40, 150
Laughlin, James, 177–78, 182, 205
Lautréamont, 160
Lawrence, D. H., 53, 83, 85, 114–15, 170, 173–74, 180, 182, 189, 206; and class difference, 137–40; compared to Hall, 131–32; on contemporary literature, 147–48, 165; dislike of Joyce, 140; gamekeepers in novels of, 136–39; horror of "genuine" pornography, 146; life and death of, 144–45; Miller on, 148–50, 159, 169–70, 185; moralist, 131–32, 161, 200; pacifism of, 143–44; puritanism of, 132–33; quixotic integrity of, 136; as watercolorist, 145, 164; writings on censorship, 145–48
—Works:
Lady Chatterley's Lover: autobiographical elements in, 138, 144; compared to *Madame Bovary*, 133–36, 138–39; compared to *Ulysses*, 131, 133–34, 140; compared to *Well of Loneliness*, 107–8, 131–33, 135, 236; dialect in, 141; early versions of, 142; explicit sex and four-letter words in, 139–44; expurgation of, 142–43, 151; French film adaptation of, 139; French translation of, 139, 151; and gendered readership, 140–41; initial publication of, 144–45; Frieda Lawrence on, 132; not his best book, 132, 155; political aspect of, 134–35; read by Miller, 150; sodomy in, 148
Lady Chatterley's Lover and trials, 17, 21, 59–60, 80, 89–90, 105, 116, 126, 163–64, 170, 172, 180, 182, 188, 206, 224, 234; Japanese trials, 131, 151; UK trial, 131, 154–56, 163–64, 188, 221; U.S. trial, 131, 142–43, 153–54, 182–83, 190, 221

Lawrence, D. H. (*continued*)
  Pansies, 145
  Sons and Lovers, 136, 143
  The White Peacock, 137
  Women in Love, 143, 248 n.9
Lawrence, Frieda, 132, 144
Leavis, F. R., 95, 155
Leclerc, Yvan, xv
Legion of Decency, 13, 187, 219
Lely, Gilbert, 231
Lerner and Loewe, 214
Lerner, Alan Jay, 215
Leroyer de Chantepie, Mlle, 33–34
Lesbianism, 72–75, 108, 111–12, 116–25,
  143, 166–67, 169, 222. *See also* Homo-
  sexuality
Leslie, Shane, 80, 85
Lewis, Sinclair, 174
Lewis, Wyndham, 171
Library of Congress, 220
Little Review, The, 91–92, 98, 102
Lolita. See Nabokov, Vladimir
Lolita, My Love, 215
Lolita's Diary, 219
London Times, 214, 219
Loy, Myrna, 216
Lyne, Adrian, 191, 218–19
Lyon, Sue, 217, 219
Lyric poetry, 56–61, 87

Mackenzie, Compton, 108; *Extraordinary
  Women,* 122, 214
MacKinnon, Catharine, xvii
Madame Bovary. See Flaubert, Gustave
Mallarmé, Stéphane, 50
Malle, Louis, 184
Manet, Édouard, 51
Manga, 151
Mann, Thomas, 119, 128
Marquis, 232
Marvell, Andrew, 63
Marx, Eleanor, 24, 115
Marx, Karl, xvi, 24
Mason, James, 16, 19–21, 36, 42, 46, 217
Masturbation, 24, 91, 95, 103, 147, 222
Mathurin, Charles (*Melmoth the Wanderer*),
  201
Maupassant, Guy de, 7–8, 24–25, 50, 180,
  237 n.11
Maurice. See Forster, E. M.
McCarthy, Desmond, 126
McCarthy, Mary, 204
McFate, Aubrey, 195, 202–3, 206
Meaker, Marijane, 121
Melmoth the Wanderer. See Mathurin, Charles
*Memoirs of a Woman of Pleasure. See Fanny
  Hill*

Memoirs of Hecate County. See Wilson, Edmund
Mencken, H. L., 171
Mérimée, Prosper (*Carmen*), 201
Methuen (publisher), 143
Metro Goldwyn Mayer, 20, 215
Mill on the Floss, The, 146
Miller v. California, 225
Miller, Henry, xii–xiii, 206, 209; adulates
  Whitman, 160; "L'Affaire Miller," 179,
  229; as anti-Flaubert, 164–65; and art
  for art's sake, 161–62; and Beats, 160;
  and the canon, 159–60, 162, 174–77,
  185; and class, 162, 166, 172; compared to Flaubert and Baudelaire,
  157–58; compared to Joyce, 157; declares Pound "full of shit," 171; disdain
  for scholars, 169; dislikes *Lolita,* 192;
  on Eliot, 171; essays on obscenity,
  180–81; *Henry and June* (film), 178,
  190; on Lawrence, 145, 148–51, 159–
  61, 169–70; life of, 162, 185–86; misogyny of, 159, 170; in *Playboy,* 169, 181;
  on Proust and Joyce, 148–49, 165–66;
  read by Erica Jong, 159, 161; read by
  Kate Millett, 159; reads Proust, 166–
  68; on *Tropic of Cancer,* 158, 161, 165,
  167; on *Ulysses,* 174; as watercolorist,
  164
—Works:
  Black Spring, 162, 174–77, 183
  The Books in My Life, 159
  The Cosmological Eye, 177
  Crazy Cock, 158, 161–62, 166
  Nexus, 175–77
  Opus Pistorum, 185–86
  The Rosy Crucifixion, 166, 177
  Sexus, 177, 179–80, 183
  Tropic of Cancer, xii–xiii, 53, 145,148,
    156–58, 162, 166–69, 173, 176–77,
    188, 205–6, 211, 224; anti-literariness,
    162–65, 168–69, 172–73; compared to
    A la recherche du temps perdu, 166–68;
    compared to *Lady Chatterley's Lover,*
    158, 173, 177; compared to *Ulysses,*
    85, 89–90, 157–58; forms of "dirt" in,
    172–74; "fuck everything" ethos of,
    163–65, 186; Grove edition, 181–86;
    plot of, 169; initial publication of,
    170–71; reception of, 171–72, 177;
    references to Virgil in, 157, 159, 174–
    76; Strick film adaptation of, 178, 190
  Tropic of Cancer and trials, 152–53, 178,
    182–85, 190
  Tropic of Capricorn, 177, 179, 182–83
  The World of Lawrence, 148–150, 159
  The World of Sex, 180

Millet, Kate (*Sexual Politics*), 135, 137, 150, 159
Milton, John (*Areopagitica*), xvii
Minnelli, Vincente: *Gigi* (film), 214, 254 n.39; *Madame Bovary* (film), xv, 15–16, 18–20, 36, 39–47, 101, 191, 241 n.28
Minton, Walter, 212, 214, 224
Miscegenation, 191
Moll Flanders, 222
Molière, 67
Monet, Claude, 163
Moniteur universel, Le, 31–32, 55, 240 n.22
Monroe, Marilyn, 220
Montaigne, Michel de, 167, 175
Montépin, Xavier de (*Les Filles de plâtre*), 73
Montesquiou, Robert de, 168, 248 n.29
Moore, George, 79, 81
Morgan, Claire. *See* Highsmith, Patricia
Morrell, Lady Ottoline, 124
Morrison, Jim, 160
Motion Picture Production Code, 13, 15–16, 139, 187, 190, 202, 214–15, 219, 238 n.19. *See also* Hays Code
Mozart, Wolfgang Amadeus, 164
Mrs Dalloway. See Woolf, Virginia
Murdoch, Iris, 214
My Fair Lady, 215

Nabokov, Dmitri, 219
Nabokov, Vladimir, 148, 178, 222; against identificatory reading, 195; amoralist, 131, 161, 200; early attempts to publish *Lolita* in U.S., 205–6; on Stuart Gilbert, 99, 116; on incest, 220; on Joyce, 92–96, 188; and Kubrick film, 214–17; life of, 204–5, 216, 219–20, 253 n.8; more Flaubertian than Flaubert, 192–95, 200–201, 203–4; as neologist, 189, 220; and Olympia Press, 206–212
—Works:
   Ada, 203, 220
   Lolita, 81, 85, 93, 116, 145, 224, 228, 236; "L'Affaire Lolita," 210–11; ambiguity in, 198–200; antirealist devices in, 200–203; coincidence in, 202–4; compared to *Ulysses*, 188–89, 208, 211; compared to *Well of Loneliness*, 188–90, 194, 208; contemporary reactions to, 203–4, 212–14; "foreword" to, 189, 193–94, 196–97; and Jon-Benet Ramsey case, 191–92; Kubrick film adaptation, 178, 190–91, 202, 214–17, 219; literary allusions in, 200–201; Lyne film adaptation, 191, 217–19; Miller's dislike of, 192; names in, 201; published in UK, 213–14; published in U.S., 212; references to Poe in, 194–95, 200–201; Trilling on, 197
   "On a Book Entitled Lolita," 191, 211
   Pale Fire, 220
   The Real Life of Sebastian Knight, 205
Nadar, Félix, 63–65
Napoleon I, 5, 9–10, 12, 153, 226
Napoleon III, 3, 5
Napoleonic Code, 118
Nation and Atheneum, The, 125
National Commission on Obscenity and Pornography, 226
National Vigilance Association, 24
Naturalism, 23–25, 53, 81–82, 85, 162, 172, 203
Necrophilia, 70, 73
Nerval, Gérard de, 77
New Directions (publisher), 177,182, 205
New England Society for the Suppression of Vice, 160
New York Herald Tribune, 128
New York Society for the Suppression of Vice, 20, 91–93, 127–28
New York Times, The, 210, 212–13
New Yorker, The, 205–6
Nicolson, Harold, 124, 213
Nicolson, Nigel, 213–14
Nietzsche, Friedrich (*The Gay Science*), 4
Nin, Anaïs, 160, 167, 171, 178, 185
Niven, David, 215
Nixon, Richard, 226
Nouvelle Revue française, 48
NYPD Blue, 238 n.20

Obelisk Press, 145, 148, 170, 177, 208
Obscene Publications Act, 1, 90–91, 125–26, 152, 154, 188, 213–14
Observer, The, 219
Odyssey, The, 80–82, 86, 89, 93–95, 99–100, 176
Ofili, Chris, xix
O'Hara, Scarlett, 40
Olivier, Lawrence, 215
Olympia Press, 145, 180, 190, 192, 196, 206–12, 231
Orioli, Pino, 144
Orwell, George, 165–66, 168–69, 172; *Down and Out in Paris and London*, 172
Oulipo, 171, 245 n.16
Oyama (publisher), 151

Packer, Vin. *See* Meaker, Marijane
Pamela, 146, 222
Paris Review, 196
Parker, Daniel, 179
Parker, Dorothy, 213

Pascal, Blaise, 67
Pasolini, Pier Paolo, 231
Paulhan, Jean, 230
Pauvert, Jean-Jacques, 221–22, 229–31
Pedophilia, 185, 188–98, 200, 203–4, 208–9, 214–20
Penguin Books, 135, 152, 154–56, 178, 221
Pera, Pia (*Lolita's Diary*), 219
Petrarch, 62, 174, 200
Petronius, 160
Pinard, Ernest, xiv, x–xi, xvii, 11–12, 18, 21, 27, 33, 35–8, 40, 43, 46, 49, 53–57, 60–61, 65–67, 70–74, 77, 96, 113–14, 116–17, 140, 156, 161, 180–81
Piron, Alexis (*La Métromanie*), 60
Plato, xvi–xvii; *Symposium*, 119
Playboy, 169, 222
Poe, Edgar Allan, 194–95, 200–201
Pompidou, Georges, 49, 75
Pontmartin, Armand de, 52, 75
Pornography, 140, 146, 170, 183–86, 198, 205–10, 212–13, 221–28
Possessed (film), 41
Pound, Ezra, 81, 91–93, 98, 106, 148, 171–72
Pouilloux, Jean-Yves, 270
Power, Arthur, 81
Powys, John Cowper, 97
Prescott, Orville, 212–13
Princesse de Clèves, La, 26, 248 n.6
Pritchett, V. S., 214
Production Code. *See* Motion Picture Production Code
Prohibition, 96
Prostitution, 170, 173–74
Proust, Marcel, 25, 51, 74–75, 78, 88–89, 94, 119–20, 128, 147–49, 165–69, 189, 197, 201, 218, 251 n.15
Psychoanalysis, 88
Pulp fiction, 121
Putnam (publisher), 212, 214, 224

Quayle, Dan, 156
Queensbury, Marquess of, 118, 129
Queneau, Raymond, 171, 179, 211, 251 n.26, 256 n.11
Quills, 232–35
Quinn, John, 79, 94, 97

Rabelais, François, 53, 84–85, 146, 160, 169, 174
Rachilde (Marguerite Eymery), 6
Racine, Jean (*Phèdre*), 18
Ramsey, JonBenet, 191–92, 220
Random House, 95
Rank, Otto, 171
Ratings Code, 13, 187

Ravel, Maurice, 163
Realism, xiii, 20, 22–26, 31–37, 47–56, 65, 70, 73–74, 77, 81, 85, 91, 98, 105, 166, 168–70, 172, 190, 200–204, 208
Réalisme, Le, 23
Regina v. Hicklin. See Hicklin Rule
Regina v. Penguin Books, 135–36, 151, 154–56
Rembar, Charles, xv, 21, 43, 152–53, 182–84, 224–26, 229–30, 255 n.3
Renaissance, 61–63, 69, 146
Revue de Paris, Le, 11, 18, 43, 45, 52, 55–56, 85, 92
Richardson, Samuel, 222–23, 228. *See also Pamela*
Ridgewell, Rosemary, 212
Rimbaud, Arthur, 160, 162
Robertson, Geoffrey, 154, 249 n.18
Rodin, Auguste, 75, 244 n.47
Rolph, C. H., 154
Romanticism, 19–20, 30, 50, 61, 136, 148, 161–62, 165, 189, 192
Ronsard, Pierre, 61–63, 65
Rose Bonbon, 192
Rosset, Barney, 152, 181–82, 206
Roth, Samuel, 152–53
Roth decision, 152–54, 156, 188, 221, 224–25
Rousseau, Jean-Jacques, 9, 167, 228
Rudge, Olga, 171
Rush, Geoffrey, 232
Rushdie, Salman, 169
Russo, Elena, 270

Sacher-Masoch, Leopold von, 227
Sackville-West, Vita, 123–24, 137, 213
Sade, Marquis de, xvii, 9–10, 38, 53, 60, 67, 79, 83, 85, 131, 152, 161, 200, 221–23; *Cent vingt journées de Sodome*, 230–31, 235; films based on life of, 231–36; life of, 226–28, 232–36; Pauvert's publication of and subsequent trial, 22, 229–31; read in 19th century, 228–29; *Juliette*, 226–28, 230, 234; *Justine* (three versions of), 226–30, 233–34; *Philosophie dans le boudoir*, 229–30, 235
Sade, 232–35
Sadomasochism, 94
Sainte-Beuve, Charles Augustin, 1–2, 5, 7, 14, 31–35, 38, 62, 166–67
Sand, George, 1–2
Sappho, 72, 74
Sartre, Jean-Paul, 77, 179
Schary, Dore, 215
Schiff, Stacy, 220
Schileppi, Judge John F., 184
Schnitzler, Arthur, 88

Schulz, Charles M., 144
Scrabble, 210
Scream, My Darling, Scream, 208
Seinfeld, Jerry, 241 n.6
Sellers, Peter, 217
Senard, Jules, 18, 21–23, 29, 34, 36, 41, 43, 60, 66
Serrano, Andres, xix
Sexual Life of Robinson Crusoe, The, 208
Shakespeare, William, 14, 67, 102
Shakespeare and Company, 91, 144–45
Shapiro, Karl, 182, 251 n.11
Shattuck, Roger, 255 n.10
Shaw, George Bernard, 125, 251 n.34
Shit, 53, 83–87, 89, 142, 149, 173–74, 234–35
Shurlock, Geoffrey, 253 n.12
Sinclair, Upton, 128
Smollett, Tobias, 222
Snoopy, 144
Snot in literature, 82, 89–90, 101–2
Société des gens de lettres, 179
Sodomy, 148, 222
Some Like It Hot, 217
Souline, Evguenia, 122
Spender, Stephen, 214
Spenser, Edmund (*Faerie Queen*), 162
Staël, Germaine de, 10
Stein, Gertrude, 171, 174
Steloff, Frances, 177
Stendhal (*Le Rouge et le noir*), 5, 25
Stewart, Justice Potter, 139, 184
Strachey, Lytton, 124
Straus, Roger, 205–6
Strick, Joseph, 84, 178
Sue, Eugène, 1–3; *Les Mystères de Paris*, 2–3; *Les Mystères du peuple*, 10–11
Sumner, John, 91, 127
Surrealism, xvii, 160, 229
Swain, Dominique, 218
Swift, Jonathan, 83
Swinburne, Charles Algernon, 128

Tahureau, Jacques, 7
Temple, Shirley, 215–17
Tender Thighs, 209
Tennant, Gertrude Collier. *See* Collier, Gertrude
"Thank Heaven for Little Girls," 214–15
Thierry, Édouard, 55, 67
Thurman, Uma, 178
Tolstoy, Leo: *Anna Karenina*, 134; *War and Peace*, 81, 92
Topor, Roland, 231
Torn, Rip, 178
Toynbee, Philip, 219
Trainspotting, 84

Trilling, Lionel, 197
Tristram Shandy, 88
Tropic of Cancer. See Miller, Henry
Troubridge, Lady Una, 111, 122, 129>
Turgenev, Ivan, 163
Turner, Lana, 39

Uncle Tom's Cabin, 128
United States Post Office, 92, 131, 139, 152–53, 183

Van Gogh, Vincent, 77, 163–64
Venus in Furs, 227
Verlaine, Paul, 7, 50
Villon, François, 174
Virgil, 157, 159–60, 174–76
Vizetelly, Ernest, 24
Vizetelly, Henry, 24, 83, 143
Voltaire, 9, 128, 227

Wagner, Peter, 221–22
Warren, Dorothy, 145
Warren, Chief Justice Earl, 225
Watch and Word Society, 127
Weidenfeld and Nicolson (publishers), 213–14
Weiss, Peter, 231
Well of Loneliness. See Hall, Radclyffe
West, Rebecca, 155
White Thighs, 209
Whitman, Walt, 128, 160, 162
Wilde, Oscar, 118, 120, 128–30, 253 n.15; *De Profundis*, 129; *Picture of Dorian Gray*, 129–30, 138, 200–201
Wilson, Angus, 210, 214
Wilson, Edmund, 161, 195, 204, 206, 208, 222, 230; *Memoirs of Hecate County*, 205–6, 222
Wilson, Elena, 204
Winslet, Kate, 232–33
Winters, Shelley, 217
With Open Mouth, 208
Woolf, Leonard, 118, 124
Woolf, Virginia, 25, 79, 85, 88, 109, 123–26, 137, 171, 213; *Mrs Dalloway*, 79, 83–84; *Orlando*, 123–24; *Room of One's Own*, 85, 109; *To the Lighthouse*, 85
Woolsey, Judge John M., xviii, 17, 55, 79, 89–91, 94–98, 100, 152–53, 158, 166, 189, 212, 224
Wordsworth, William, 162, 165
Wright, Doug, 232–33
Xenophon (*Anabasis*), 82

Yeats, William Butler, 84–85
York, Archbishop of, 125

Zola, Émile, 2, 23–25, 27, 51–53, 79, 81,
     143, 146, 162, 172–73, 203, 234–35;
     depicted as writing while seated on
     chamber pot, 24, 51; *Nana*, 24, 83; *Pot*

Bouille, 24; *La Terre*, 24, 143; *Thérèse
Raquin*, 115; *Le Ventre de Paris*, 51,
85